AF305216

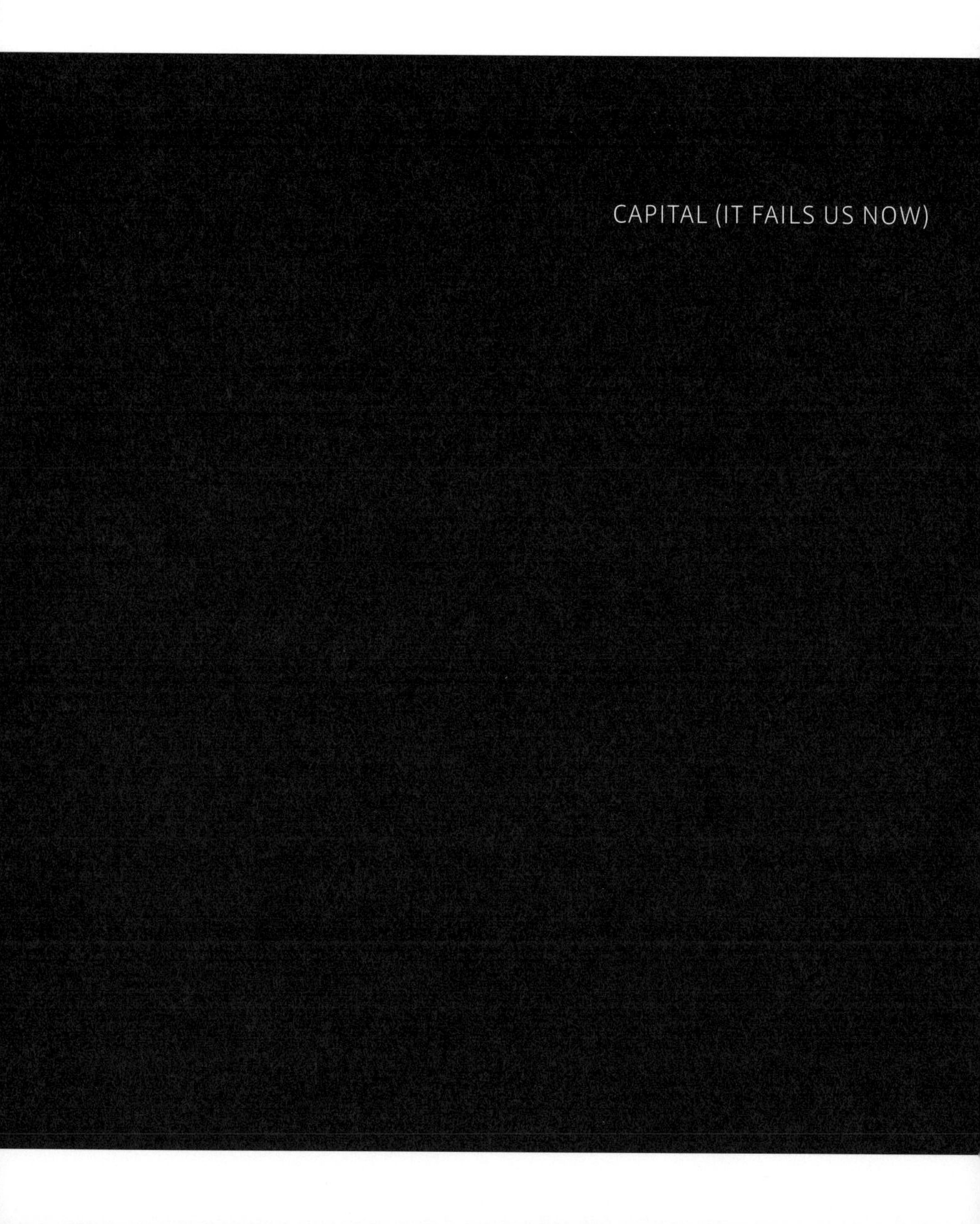
CAPITAL (IT FAILS US NOW)

oe & b_books

CRITICAL READERS IN VISUAL CULTURES #7

CAPITAL
(IT FAILS US NOW)

EDITED BY SIMON SHEIKH

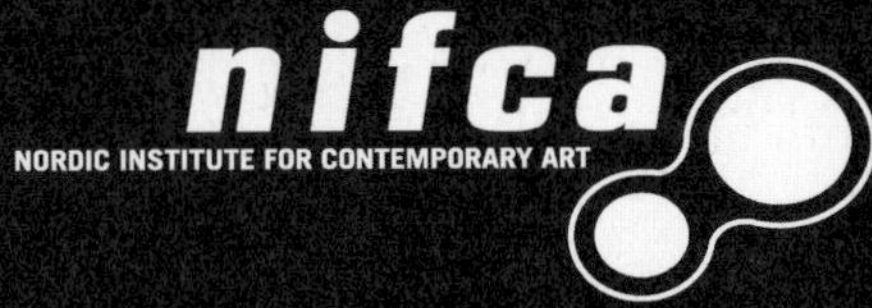

NIFCA, NORDIC INSTITUTE FOR CONTEMPORARY ART, IS THE NORDIC COUNCIL OF MINISTERS'
EXPERT ORGAN FOR VISUAL CULTURE: VISUAL ART, ARCHITECTURE AND DESIGN.

WWW.NIFCA.ORG

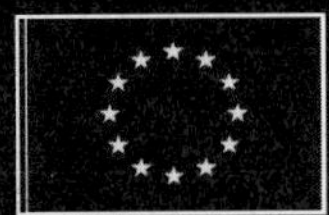

Education and Culture

Culture 2000

THE PROJECT HAS BEEN CARRIED OUT WITHIN THE FRAMEWORK OF TRANSFORM AND
WITH THE SUPPORT OF THE CULTURE 2000 PROGRAMME OF THE EUROPEAN UNION.

THIS PUBLICATION REFLECTS THE VIEWS ONLY OF THE AUTHOR, AND THE COMMISSION
CANNOT BE HELD RESPONSIBLE FOR ANY USE WHICH MAY BE MADE OF THE
INFORMATION CONTAINED THEREIN.

ACKNOWLEDGEMENTS:

THANK YOU TO ANDERS HÄRM, TRUDE IVERSEN, EIJA MÄKIVUOTI AND KJERSTI SOLBERG MONSEN. SPECIAL THANKS TO MARITA MUUKKONEN FOR YEARS OF CONVERSATIONS AND DISCUSSIONS LEADING UP TO THE REALIZATION OF THIS PROJECT.

CAPITAL (IT FAILS US NOW)

EDITED BY: SIMON SHEIKH

OE CRITICAL READERS IN VISUAL CULTURES #7
NIFCA PUBLICATION 29
BERLIN: B_BOOKS, 2006

THIS BOOK IS PUBLISHED IN RELATION TO THE EXHIBITION
CAPITAL (IT FAILS US NOW)
UKS, OSLO, NORWAY 2005 AND KUNSTIHOONE, TALLINN, ESTONIA 2006.

THIS BOOK IS ONE IN A SERIES OF OE-READERS.
SERIES EDITORS: KATYA SANDER AND SIMON SHEIKH

COPY EDITOR: ZACH FORMWALT
GRAPHIC DESIGN: KATYA SANDER

WWW.OE.DK

1st EDITION, BERLIN 2006

B_BOOKS, LÜBBENERSTRAßE 14, 10997 BERLIN
X@BBOOKSZ.DE

ISBN: 3-933557-69-0

CONTENTS

CONTENTS

Domination, Competition and Exploitation:
An Introduction to the Socialization of Capital (and How It Fails Us)

by Simon Sheikh

> Capital shows itself more and more to be a social power, with the capitalist as its functionary – a power that no longer stands in any possible kind of relationship to what the work of one particular individual can create, but an alienated social power which has gained an autonomous position and confronts society as a thing, and as the power that the capitalist has through this thing.[1]
>
> –Karl Marx

> Capital is not an abstract category, it is a semiotic operator at the service of specific social formations. Its function is to record, balance, regulate and overcode the power formations inherent to developed industrial societies, power relations and the fluxes that make up the planet's overall economic powers.[2]
>
> –Félix Guattari

In his book on Marx – slyly subtitled *Adventures and Misadventures of a Critique* – Daniel Bensaïd writes about Marxism as a critical theory rather than an ideological doctrine. It is a theory of struggle and transformation (or revolution, if you will), granted, but not a prophesy, scientific orthodoxy, or even sociology. Bensaïd instead tries to posit a postmodern Marx, a set of critical tools that can be employed to analyze and criticize contemporary forms of capital. This means, then, that Marxist terms must be seen as open to interpretation and use (value), but also as taking part in a certain history – thus the adventures and misadventures. Seen in this light, the fall of the so-called communist regimes of the Soviet Bloc is not to be viewed as the end of the critical theory of Marx, but rather as a (new) beginning hereof, freed from hardened orthodoxy and the burden of Stalinism. According to Bensaïd, Marx's project consists of three fundamental critiques: that of historical reason, economic reason and scientific positivism. Three critiques, which complement each other in turn, and that are

> directly relevant to current questions about the end of history and the representation of time; about the relationship between class struggle and other types of conflict; about the destinies of hard sciences tormented by the uncertainties of the narrative sciences.[3]

It is in this line that the current publication is to be read: as an effort to engage in a critique of dominant narratives and assumptions. A critique that takes as its point of departure the notion of capital as its central idea, and indeed as a centralizing machinery in the current world system. It is an effort to state that if there is indeed such a thing as an empire, which is highly debatable, the advent of this empire is driven by a specific mechanism, a specific organizing and socializing principle: capital. As such, we have returned, albeit by way of a *différance*, to the central and key notion of capital itself as the basis for our enquiry. But what exactly is capital?[4] As capital(ism) becomes increasingly essentialized and naturalized, it is tempting to see capital as a universal, or at least universalizing norm: To state that we all live under the conditions of capital, although that sounds both too obvious and too obtuse. Also, it seems antithetical to the theory of Capital to see it as universal, since the theory does not try to establish a universal history or theory thereof, but rather a theory of transformation, of possible change, counter-narratives and new hegemonies. Capital is, rather, what Cornelius Castoriadis would call an imaginary order, which does not mean that it does not have real effects, quite the contrary. It acts as a universalizing principle of measuring and (ac)counting, but it can, crucially, also be countered by other imaginaries. Capital is, then, a specific situation with specific histories and contingencies, but also with undeveloped potentialities, that can be directed towards its expansion as well as towards its demise.

The essays and projects presented in this book are all engaging in such critiques – of historical and economic determinism, and of scientific positivism – in establishing and challenging such dominant imaginaries. They try to analyze and visualize the contemporary conditions of capital, arguably very different from the conditions present when Marx wrote his theory of Capital. There is the evident change from industrialism to post-industrialism, although these modes of production are as much simultaneous as chronological, and as much geographical as they are temporal (as is the shift between Fordist and post-Fordist production).[5] The undeniable rise of immaterial labor does not only indicate a new relationship to the production of (surplus) value in the ways in which capital circulates through the body of the worker, but also in the ways that commodities manifest this value. In the case of immaterial labor, we should perhaps talk of capital not only going through the body as in material labor, but also through the very soul (!) of the worker, while in the case of the commodity we can speak of a dematerialization of value: in either case we are speaking of an almost ghost-like presence. This then also requires new understandings of technologies, so central to the knowledge economy of post-Fordism. In writing about technology, Marx famously described the difference between a tool and a machine, with the former being an extension of the body and the latter an exploitation of the body. If this distinction is to be upheld, we will then need to discern between mental and bodily machines (and tools), and see how technical innovation in this area influences production in other sectors. According to Marx, machines alter the relations to nature (ecology), mental relations (the way we think, imagination), social relations (the way we act) as well as the reproduction of human life, and as such the machine, with its productivity, autonomization, exchangeability and measuring devices, is an apt image of capital itself. Here we can maintain a focus on the processes of capitalization and its effects, economically as well as subjectively. It is thus not merely the economic aspects of capital that must be followed, but also capitalization as a matrix for subjectivity and interpersonal, even intimate, relations.

The logic of capital itself, rather than a broad concept of capitalism as an economic system, is of course often overlooked, forgotten, hidden or taken for granted as naturalized in the current language game of politics with its focus on democracy, liberty and human rights. Current debates seem to indicate that there is no alternative to the market, to capital. We know this from the media, academia and social situations. A couple of examples: a relative of mine recently said that he believed in capitalism as the only system, since communism and socialism had always failed; a former colleague of mine once stated that she would like to believe in socialism, but that she was afraid it was against human nature. But one could argue whether capitalism really is so successful, and if so, on what grounds? And is human existence not based as much on collaboration as on the survival of the fittest? In any case, these examples show how certain notions have become naturalized and essentialized, how deeply they have become internalized in the way we think, talk and feel. However, such ideas which regard capitalism as the only game in town can be questioned on a number of levels, since they conflate the market with capital – there were market economies before capitalism, of course – making this a highly dubious historical argument, that is not only essentialist, but that effectively presupposes an end to history, a possible equilibrium beyond conflict and indeed politics. But does our world really appear so stable and endless? Are there not conflicts between our daily lives and global capital? Are we not affected and placed in various struggles, from the upkeep of bare life to the attempts to live up to role models from advertising and popular culture? Indeed battle lines seem to exist not only between factors seen as external to capitalist/liberal democratic society, such as the increasing gap between rich and poor countries and the global ecological problems due to the endless expansion and industrialization of capital, unable to stop itself, but also internally, between who belongs to a workforce and who doesn't along with the increasing gap between images of desirability – independence, upward mobility, physical beauty, functioning family, etc. – and the ability to actually live them, both financially and psychologically.

The reproductive family, sexuality and childrearing, as well as notions of working as living, as identitarian, are among the battle lines being drawn by the commodification of everything, of all aspects of human existence from bare life itself to the (apparent) multiple choices of life style. In *Numéro Deux*, a seminal film by Jean-Luc Godard and Anne-Marie Mieville from 1975 (which is exactly the time of the shift from Fordist to post-Fordist production in Western Europe), there is a crucial line which goes, "there was a landscape, and we put a factory in it." The film describes the difficulties of living under capitalistic conditions, specifically the impossibility of maintaining a bourgeois nuclear family under industrial living conditions, and shows the family as a factory. The film therefore concludes with the altered line: "There was a factory, and we built a landscape around it." It is the factory then, the machine of capital itself that produces our environment, not vice versa. We have naturalized a specific cultural construction, and it is one of the purposes of our project to de-naturalize our present: To show how capital fails us.

In this way capital(ism) does seem universal as a common denominator which is, naturally, also part of its effect as being the great calculator; measuring, translating and pricing everything and everyone. Capital acts doubly, on the one hand it is an equalizer: everything becomes the same in the sense that it can be exchanged, but on the other hand, everything becomes different through the exchange, through its exchange value, as it were. This is capital's universalist claim, its universalizing move. However universal capitalism acts or seems though, the universal is essentially empty or void, only to be filled with a particular content making claims for the universal, such as is the case with capitalism now.[6] So in order to understand how capital works as universalizing, it is crucial to study its particularities, its local as well as global workings and effects. Hence the focus on *location*, here particularized by double, but connected sites or economic, territorial organizations: the (post)welfare state (as exemplified by Norway) and the post-communist country (as exemplified by Estonia), the two places where the exhibitionary interventions took place. But our exploration of the notion of capital must proceed along dual lines: on the one hand the aforementioned *locationality*, and on the other, *subjectivity* – how capitalism affects our daily lives, our very structure of feelings and perceptions: the machine is both mental and bodily. We shall focus on the current moment in history, with its structural changes, and, arguably, crisis, within global capital, and look at the two specific locations as models, as machinery within the production and proliferation of capital. Partly, the Western European model of the welfare state is undergoing a massive structural change, if not deconstruction. This can also be seen in the refined variation of the welfare state, the Nordic social democratic model of redistribution and equilibrium; a compromise between liberalism and socialism, but also a temporal territorial alliance between capital and labor that is now historical. In other words, capital must be localized and historicized, as suggested by Immanuel Wallerstein with his notion of 'historical capitalism'. This is also the case on the margins of the new Europe, with the rapid and massive deregulation of the post-communist countries, where the former state capitalism (as a mode of production as much as an 'official' ideological state formation: "communism equals socialism plus electricity"[7]) is being transformed into a neoliberal, transnational market system. But how do these formations, or variations, affect each other? What are the routes between them and are they tending towards merger or secession? As borders get reconfigured, new battle lines are drawn around notions of territory and alliances, no longer maintained between exploited and exploiters, but rather among the exploited themselves: those with work and those without, those with papers and those without. It's the effects of global capitalism, rather than its principle, that such a historical belief in the nation-state attests to; that the nation-state will somehow save us from globalism (as the key word replacing capitalism). Unfortunately, trade unions and left-wing parties in most of the former welfare states subscribe to this historical model of nation and production, that was part and parcel of the rise of capitalism, and has since been left behind by capital in its later, current stages: When will it be left behind by the (historical) left?

The project is, then, to discuss these specific models of capital and (cultural) production and how we can visualize the current changes. These essays and projects take their point of departure in these specific models of (re)production and (re)distribution, and look at how production is changing in the Western countries, mainly from industrial production to immaterial labor, and in the East from state capitalism to a deregulated (post)industrialism with a new commodification and codification of the labor force, and thus of all social as well as economic relations. What are 'new' economies, and what kinds of technologies of the self are they producing, and indeed, enforcing? Thus, in these pages you will find efforts to review the situation, asking what is to be done in this predicament of expansive global capitalism, corporatization of culture, the specularization of politics, and the marginalization, even criminalization, of the critical left. Discussions range from the spectral form of value, (self)-precarization, deregulation and the privatization of the welfare state to the development of alternative economies and the establishment of various modes of critique and resistance, cartography and historiography, inclination and inquiry, and the politicization of subject positions.

We shall aim to understand the notion of capital, then, as an economic tool, as a measure of exchange and surplus, and as something at once regulated and regulating (by both State and market), as well as a producer of subjectivity (a.k.a. the commodification of everything), but also as a power tool, a force-relation. In an essay called 'Capital as the Integral of Power Relations', the late Felix Guattari provocatively states that capital is primarily about power and only secondarily about profit (and thus, perhaps, touches upon notions of biopower and governmentality). Guattari's text not only points to the changes from the national organization to global capitalism, but also modifies Marx's theories in turn, especially in a reconfiguration of the composition of value. Secondly, Guattari focuses on this change in terms of a 'semiotization' of capital. This notion is crucial for two reasons: firstly in terms of articulation, since the grander motivation behind *Capital (It Fails Us Now)*, is to ask how to go about articulating a contemporary description of capital, which may or may not follow some of the routes pointed out by Guattari *and* how to articulate and imagine a non-capitalistic subjectivity. Guattari obviously takes his cue from the theories of Lacan here, turning his famous idea of the subconscious being structured like a language onto the logic of capital, its expansions and subjectivizations, and claiming that capital is (like) a language. Accounting, measuring and the stock exchange are all linguistic effects, as is the automatization and machinic assemblage of the production and labor process. This notion of semiotization is also a way of describing labor becoming immaterial (and the subsequent dematerialization of value):

> Automatized and computerized production no longer draws its consistency from basic human factors, but from a machinic phylum which traverses, bypasses, disperses, miniaturizes, and co-opts all human activities.[8]

As in the machinic understanding of capital in Marx, technical innovation, including new technologies, is more of a disciplining and alienation of the body and the subject than an aid to it. In other words, the dematerialization of labor and its computerized techniques, as well as its inherent reorganization of leisure and labor time, is not to be considered an emancipation of the working subject and its creativity, but rather as the total co-optation hereof by the machinery of capital.

Guattari's linguistic turn brings about metaphors of grammar and structure, obviously, but perhaps also notions of counter-narrative, incoherent speech, gibberish, lying and *detournément*. And maybe even silence, muting. That is, in the usage of language also lies resistance.[9] Perhaps this was what Michel Foucault was aiming at in his otherwise strangely ambivalent and non-committal preface to another of Guattari's works, *Anti-Oedipus* (co-written with Gilles Deleuze). Foucault famously called the book an introduction and even manual to the "Nonfascist Life."[10] What Foucault was aiming at, was not the historical political formation of fascism, but rather the contemporaneous fascism in our heads. This was something that should be achieved via everyday practice; an ethics and politics of the everyday, but we shall also try to imagine models for a post- or anti-commodified subject position. If Michel Foucault could write about the 'nonfascist life', can we imagine the non-capitalist subject? And what will this entail in terms of economic and social relations living within capitalism? If capital, as was the case with fascism, is in our heads, that is as processes of subjectivization and subjugation, something possessing our very souls, we should perhaps speak more of exorcism than exodus as a political strategy…

A slightly different way of thinking capital as a technology, now that desiring-machines (as posited by Guattari) have to a large extent been smoothly incorporated into global capital, has recently been supplied by Ray Brassier. Writing on Alain Badiou's mathematical ontology, Brassier sees capital as nothing more and nothing less than a huge (accounting) machine, what he calls "…an automated axiomatic system."[11] Brassier sees capital as a machine that can think, fuelled by the very instability and randomness of numbers, rather than countered by it the way Deleuze and Guattari hoped:

> Far from being threatened by its 'contradiction', capitalism thrives on them. It is an open system, an aleatory axiomatic, continually redefining its own structural boundaries, perpetually living off its own impossible limit.[12]

It is thus *not* a determinate, but rather an indeterminate, logic: capital is both the real and the void, and in this sense even the theory that is 'Capital' fails us. Could this then also indicate that refusing to be counted – to stand up and be counted, as it were – is a possible resistance strategy?

This would also mean that the right to work should be changed to the right not to work, not to be counted, stamped, filed, briefed and indexed; that we begin to detach from the notion of work – material or immaterial – as the foundation for (political) identity, and begin to lead truly *unproductive* lives.

* * *

Finally, a note on the format of this book. It is published in conjunction with the two exhibitions, *Capital (It Fails Us Now)* held at UKS in Oslo, Norway and Kunstihoone, Tallinn, Estonia, but it is not an accompanying catalogue. The mode of address in the exhibition is by nature spatial, including specific contingent relationships to the viewer that cannot be documented or reproduced as such in another mode of address such as the book. Instead, the book is a critical reader into the same thematic as the exhibitions: Capital and how it fails us. The essays are thus not catalogue essays explaining and contextualizing the art works, nor the artistic projects illustrations of the text. The essays and projects are parallel to each other and are different ways of investigating and articulating the effects of capital. As such, the art works are also not aesthetic objects in a Kantian or modern sense, but rather aesthetical in the ancient Greek sense of *Aisthésis*, that is, 'felt experience', sensory experiences of living.

Notes:

1. Karl Marx, Capital, vol. 3, London: Penguin/Hammondsworth, 1981, 373.

2. Félix Guattari, 'Capital as the Integral of Power Formations', in *Soft Subversions*, New York: Semiotext(e), 1996, 202.

3. Daniel Bensaïd, *Marx for Our Times: Adventures and Misadventures of a Critique*, London: Verso, 2002, 3.

4. Marx never actually used the term capitalism, but only capital, understood as an economic and social relation of domination, competition and exploitation, rather than as an ideology proper.

5. Here it might be useful to refer to Paolo Virno's definition of post-Fordism not as a general shift from material to immaterial labor, but rather as a reorganization of all parts of the production and labor process, that is, as a shift in the relation between the worker and work: "By post-Fordism, I mean instead a set of characteristics that are related to the *entire* contemporary workforce, including fruit pickers and the poorest of immigrants. Here are some of them: the ability to react in a timely manner to the continual innovations in techniques and organizatorial models, a remarkable 'opportunism' in negotiating among the different possibilities offered by the job market, familiarity with what is possible and unforseeable, that minimal entrepreneurial attitude that makes it possible to decide what is the 'right thing' to do within a nonlinear productive fluctuation, a certain familiarity with the web of communications and information. As one can see, these are generically human gifts, not the result of 'specialization'. What I hold true is that post-Fordism mobilizes all the faculties that characterize our species: language, abstract thinking, disposition toward learning, plasticity, the habit of not having solid habits." Interview with Paolo Virno by Branden W. Joseph in *Grey Room* 21, Fall 2005, 29.

6. I am here referring to Ernesto Laclau's work on the category of the universal within political representation and identification. See, for instance, 'Universalism, Particularism and the Question of Identity' in Ernesto Laclau, *Emancipations*, London: Verso, 1996, 20-35, as well as his dialogue with Judith Butler and Slavoj Žižek in Judith Butler, Ernesto Laclau and Slavoj Žižek, *Contingency, Hegemony, Universalism*, London: Verso, 2000.

7. Commonly attributed to V.I. Lenin, this much quoted phrase is apparently incorrect. The proper quote should read: "Communism is the Power of Soviets plus the electrification of the whole country!" which is slightly more ambiguous and even sinister... I thank Dmitry Vilensky for bringing this to my attention.

8. Guattari, op.cit., 207.

9. This all begs the question, is language the only game in town? And what is the relation between language games and capital as the integral of power relations? (Guattari provocatively states that capital is primarily about power, only secondarily about profit, and thus perhaps touches upon notions of biopower and governmentality). And is language then the site for revolutions rather than the body as Guattari suggests (and as Foucault perhaps suggested in his late works, i.e. 'History of Sexuality')? Is it in the language that we use, as in when we are interpellated by juridico-economic language from state institutions, but also when we respond and react in it? (Not only to these very institutions, but in everyday language. It has, recently, struck how exactly a juridico-economic language is employed by individuals at times of breakdown in, say, friendships, where a sudden turn to such a language capitalizes the relation somehow.) Will the non-capitalistic subjectivity then be achieved through a language of desire, through something non-codifiable? And, given the commodification of everything, how to deal with the problem of co-optation and the state-form as giving and removing rights (to

articulation and participation)?

10. Michel Foucault, 'Preface to *Anti-Oedipus*' (1976), reprinted in *Power, The Essential Works of Michel Foucault 1954-1984*, Volume 3, New York: The New Press, 2000, 106-110.

11. Ray Brassier, 'Nihil Unbound: Remarks on Subtractive Ontology and Thinking Capitalism', in Peter Hallward (Ed.), *Think Again: Alain Badiou and the Future of Philosophy*, London/New York: Continuum, 2004, 52.

12. Ibid.

Invisible States:
Europe in the Age of Capital Failure*
by Brian Holmes

Introduction

After 9/11 and its worldwide consequences, after the travesty of Iraq's supposed weapons of mass destruction, after the collapse of the project for an EU Constitution, after the banlieue riots in France and all they reveal about neocolonial racism on the Old Continent, it might be easier to agree that capital is really failing us, right now. But the most important question is: who are 'we'? And how exactly do we experience the very real breakdowns of that immense and highly abstracted articulation of society which goes under the name of capital? How to map out that articulation, as it changes over time to reach a point of what now appears as permanent crisis? How to locate and name the living flesh of capital failure?

The exhibition of which this book gives an account has its locus in two national states on the northern edges of Europe: Norway, which has declined to be a formal member of the European Union, and Estonia, which is among the new members in the former East. In both these countries (but for very different reasons) the form of the state as a democratic instance and an economic project is intensely at issue.

In what follows I will focus on the changing forms of the capitalist state, within a European context that is structured not only by its shaky supranational architecture, but also by far-ranging transformations of the world economy. The point is not to expect salvation or damnation from what Engels famously referred to as "the ideal collective capitalist."[1] Instead, the point is to create a framework for understanding the transformations of an institutional and legal mix (the state) that attempts to mediate, on the one hand, between the inhabitants of a national territory and the individual capitalist enterprises that organize their productivity; and on the other, between this bounded national territory and the relatively anarchic transnational space into which it is inserted by the constant flux of trade, investment, interstate alliances and relations of force.

Within the world-system composed by the capitalist democracies of the post-WWII era, the state has in effect been called upon to act as a kind of double filter, articulating the specific relations between its various classes of inhabitants, as well as their general relations with the outside world. In this respect, the state is – or more precisely, has attempted to be – the "integral of power formations," to borrow the phrase with which Félix Guattari once described capital.[2] The democratic state, as a crossroads of economic power and popular representation, has at its best been something like the means which society has given itself to make capital visible, to place its operations on the negotiating table. One need not be surprised, then, to find a complex and problematizing exhibition of visual art exploring precisely the ways in which this project of visibility now appears to fail.

Indeed, the postwar democratic state has claimed to be an integrally public and fully transparent articulation between all the conflicting forces at play in the human universe, including not only the powers of capital and its associated imperatives of military production and warfare, but also the expressed needs and desires of populations outside any economic logic or will to domination. It is precisely the existence of this claim, or this aspiration – concretized for a time in what was known as 'the welfare state' – that allows us to speak of the failure of capital. But it is also this democratic claim that is clearly and inexorably breaking down, as the form and function of the mediating national state morphs and reconfigures under the pressure of global economic forces and conflicting wills to dominance. The result of the breakdown is a murky, opaque society, a world of unexpected clashes and fires in the night. What we should then explore – if there is any wish to even begin rediscovering a 'we' – is the very texture of this opacity: the forms of capital failure.[3] Which are also the forms of our lives today.

Metamorphoses of the Welfare State

In an article published in 1982, and destined to become an enduring definition of a fast-disappearing reality, the American specialist in international relations John Gerard Ruggie described the structure of the post-WWII economic compromise as "embedded liberalism."[4] This was before the days of US Army journalism, when one could still aspire to express complex meanings. Ruggie borrowed his key term from an anthropologist, Karl Polanyi, who had maintained that in all known societies prior to that of 19th-century England, exchanges of goods were embedded in an institutional mix, indeed in a human ecology: there was no separation between specifically economic calculations and a broader set of social reciprocities regulating the care and reproduction of land (i.e. the natural environment), labor (the human body/mind) and money itself (whether the cowrie shells of the Trobriand Islanders, or the fiduciary currencies of nation-states). Polanyi showed that the development of English economic liberalism, propelled by the industrial revolution and extended to worldwide dimensions by the gold standard, had effectively disembedded the economy from society, transforming land, labor and money into what he called "fictitious commodities," continuously bought and sold on a supposedly "self-regulating market."[5]

Why are these three commodities any different from the average widget? The thing that makes them 'fictitious', in Polanyi's sense, is that their production and sustainable reproduction is not ensured by market mechanisms. Land that isn't cared for beyond the cycle of a cash-crop or a mineral dig can be durably blighted by misuse; labor with no life-support outside the workplace can be physically destroyed by downward pressure on wages; and the very medium of exchange, money, can be discredited by speculative trading of promissory notes without regard for the institutions from which their value derives. All these phenomena, which had been observed since the Industrial Revolution, were experienced at their cruelest extremes during the early 20th century, and most acutely, during the Great Depression of the 1930s – and Polanyi was hardly alone in identifying the liberal doctrines of free trade and self-regulating markets as the underlying causes of the wars themselves. The essence of the postwar international regime could therefore be convincingly portrayed by Ruggie as an attempt to 're-embed' the worldwide economy of liberalism within territorial systems of checks and balances, regulated at the level of the nation-state.

'Embedded liberalism' described the effort to reconcile the benefits of international trade with the domestic policies for full employment and social welfare that had first emerged (though in disastrously isolationist forms) during the period of closed currency zones and trading blocs in the 1930s. The postwar instruments of this reconciliation were regulated international currency exchange (Bretton Woods), import quotas and tariffs to protect certain productive sectors (the General Agreement on Tariffs and Trade) and labor legislation and social programs (the domestic welfare states). This compromise, striking a balance between the two normative principles of domestic well-being and international free trade, provided what Ruggie called the "generative grammar" of postwar inter-state relations, shaping the possible forms of action by the participating states and contributing to what he called "the internationalization of political authority."

Closer to our time, the regulation-school economist Bob Jessop has developed the most comprehensive description of the general form or ideal-type of the capitalist state that resulted from the postwar compromise.[6] He calls it the 'Keynesian Welfare National State' (KWNS), in reference to the economist and statesman John Maynard Keynes, the English negotiator at Bretton Woods. Keynes was the first to theorize the full employment of the working classes, supported by government debt-financing of works projects, social services and social insurance payments. He saw full employment as the source of "effective demand," which could spur industrial economies to virtuous cycles of continuous growth. The application of this type of policy accompanied the postwar exportation to Canada, Western Europe, Australia and New Zealand of the American Fordist model of industrial development, driven by large, multi-divisional, vertically integrated mass-production corporations. These were the engines of extraordinary economic expansion for some thirty years, in the context of the reconstruction boom in Europe, and at a time when mass production had not yet begun in most other regions of the world (excepting Japan and the Asian 'tiger' economies, which developed more centrally planned or authoritarian variations on the Euro-American model).

The Keynesian pattern of state intervention took on different shapes depending on the size and political culture of the country in question, with the most purely social-democratic forms developing in Scandinavia. The aim (and to some extent, the result) was to create a nexus of supportive and reparative institutions in which competitive economic functions could be embedded, so that their violence could be tempered, softened. Today, for better and often for worse, the KWNS (and the white, male, industrial factory worker who was its privileged subject) still serves as the normative and nostalgic horizon for discussions of public economic policy. But the interest of Jessop's analysis, and of the regulation school more generally, is to help us see how a change in the 'generative grammar' of international relations, from the mid-1970s onward, has provoked a gradual metamorphosis of the forms of the state, which would only be given clear ideological expression with the 'Third Way' programs of the British New Labour party at the very close of the century.

What happened to the compromise of embedded liberalism? As markers of its crisis, all the historians point to the breakdown of the Bretton Woods currency system in the period of 1968–71 and the emergence of the floating exchange regime, the oil shock and recession of 1973–75, and more broadly, the spread of Fordist production through-out the world and the resultant saturation of markets for mass-produced industrial goods. Equally important from a more radical viewpoint were high levels of labor militancy, rejections of bureaucratic normalization and widespread protests against the colonial and imperialist postures of the Western powers.[7] The industrialized countries were beset with persistent conditions of industrial stagnation coupled with inflationary wage-price spirals ('stagflation'), and from the mid-1970s onward, the decline of the United States itself was widely predicted. More recently, however, understanding has grown of the way that the US hegemon was able to convince the rest of the world to go on funding what seemed to be a terminally indebted economy, both by forcing OPEC countries to continue pricing their oil in dollars, and more broadly, by ensuring that dollar-denominated financial markets remain the most highly performing investment destination for global liquidity – among other things, because only those markets are insulated from the violent exchange-rate swings that periodically affect all other currencies with respect to the dollar.[8] The upshot of all this has been to make the US (with its sophisticated financial markets, its control over transnational institutions like the IMF and the World Bank, its far-reaching media sector and its unparalleled army) into the institutional support-structure of what, for all other economic agents, is essentially a stateless world currency, a necessary but uncontrollable medium of exchange. Thus the dollar remained the linchpin of the floating exchange regime, while around it multiplied the sophisticated forms of credit-money (futures, options, swaptions and the entire panoply of derivatives managed by hedge-fund operators like George Soros in direct competition with national fiduciary currencies).

From the early 1980s onward, this new position of the US as an extremely aggressive world financial player, with its industrial production shifting towards a strategic focus on cutting-edge growth technologies (stimulated and directed by lavish defense spending), gave it every reason to force greater trade and investment liberalization on all the countries that wanted access to its gigantic and endlessly debt-financed consumer markets. The IMF emerged as the global prophet and enforcer of this liberalization, which was to be coupled with austerity policies for all governments other than that of the hegemon.[9] The liberalization of foreign direct investment (and the ultimate disappearance of the revolutionary threat posed by really-existing Communism) meant that much more productive plant could be located outside the core countries of the world-system, and therefore, beyond the reach of the national labor and ecology movements. A new pattern of global circulation then took form, where formerly underdeveloped countries (such as China) could export not only raw materials, but also high-level manufactured goods; while the professionals of the former industrial core would focus on financial management, technological innovation, project coordination, and cultural services (including tourism, which has become one of the largest sectors of the world economy). Such was the basic system of constraints – the underlying grammar of international relations – that generated the initial trend toward what Jessop analyzes as the SWPR: the 'Schumpeterian Workfare Postnational Regime', named in reference to the Austrian economist Joseph Schumpeter, who focused on entrepreneurial innovation as the motor of economic growth.[10] What's indicated with that reference is the transformation of the welfare state according to the requirements of the transnational information economy.

The SWPR, also known as the 'competition state', does not represent the clean break with welfare and the eclipse of interventionist 'big government' that is usually evoked in simplistic descriptions of neoliberalism. Instead it signifies a deep and still-ongoing modification in the ways that intervention is carried out, for whom, and to what ends. The former goal of extending employment and benefits programs to all citizens is effectively cast aside, having become impossible under the conditions of functionally borderless economies. The wage is treated, not as a source of effective demand to be propped up for the general good, but instead as a factor of production among others, which can be pushed downward according to the needs of the competitive struggle. The primary focus of intervention now becomes high-quality information access and lifelong education: in other words, the grooming of the most productive citizens for innovation in transnational knowledge and image markets, whose operations can no longer be regulated by a national state, but only adapted to by a postnational regime, which seeks insofar as possible to influence the parameters within which productive individuals make free choices.

A pattern of changes in the forms of state intervention then sets in, which is fulfilled unequally, depending on the specific conditions of each country. These changes are often proposed in the form of 'performance-based contracts' between public administrations and citizens. Automatic unemployment benefits, suspected of encouraging idleness, tend to be scrapped in favor of workfare 'activation' programs that require continuous job searches, compulsory retraining, or community service (with the Danish 'flexicurity' model becoming the new paragon of perfectly calibrated government intervention to meet the needs of a high-turnover job market). In the name of efficiency (but also as a disguised form of societal indoctrination) the former notion of public services provided to citizens is replaced by that of 'public enterprises' competing with each other on subsidized 'quasi-markets' for the patronage of non-paying 'customers'. Vouchers or compensatory tax breaks may also be offered to those who prefer private service-providers, notably in the areas of health and education. Voluntarist or charitable 'third sector' associations (often religious in nature) are called upon to fill in the gaps of stripped-down social programs; while in business operations, centralized state regulation is limited in favor of 'governance' exercised by networks of interested parties or 'stakeholders'. Infrastructures to support high value-adding sectors, which would formerly have been built by employment-generating state agencies as a form of pump priming for the Keynesian economy, are now done almost exclusively by 'public-private partnerships' (PPPs), which are renowned (justifiably or not) for their superior efficiency – and which above all do not create more fiscal liabilities on the state's unemployment or retirement rolls.

This is the basic repertory of the 'New Public Management' that has spread from Britain throughout the formerly social-democratic countries (including Norway in particular), and has also been proposed as a model of state-formation for the post-socialist countries of the former East.[11] The avowed aim of its neoliberal ideologues is to gradually strip the public sector down to the hard-core functions of a night-watchman state: police, justice, diplomacy, army. But for electoral reasons that goal can never be attained, at least not in northwestern European lands, because it would require a break with too many core constituencies, even on the right side of the political spectrum. Full neoliberal 'regime shift' has occurred only in a few countries, primarily the US and Britain. Elsewhere, what results are subtle but far-reaching changes in the way the state socializes its populations, the kinds of expectations it cultivates, the types of subjectivity it fosters.[12] Thus the 'disembedding' of the transnational economy from its sustaining institutional nexus is accomplished under the veil of a persistent, but increasingly attenuated and gradually hollowed-out social democracy.[13] The hope, it seems, is that the gaping zones of exclusion and alienation of entire populations can be covered over for just a little while more – until the productive classes have learned to take responsibility for cultivating their own blindness.

Towards a New Political Ecology

A deeper understanding of the structural transformations that have come to bear upon the European societies obviously requires consideration of the European Union, in its relationship of cooperation and competition with the United States. Postwar European reconstruction was decisively influenced by the US, first via the Marshall Plan, then through the formation of NATO. For the US, Europe was less an export market than a region for direct foreign investment and the implantation of industry. This was chiefly done in Germany, the largest and most industrially advanced European nation, whose postwar constitution had been written by the United States. The creation of the European Economic Community offered an expanded market for US corporations established in Germany, and as such received strong US encouragement.[14] In the 1960s and 70s, only France resisted the fundamental Americanization of Europe; but even there, the resistance was merely gestural and diplomatic. Yet as understanding grew, in the 1980s, of the ways in which the US had succeeded in changing the rule-sets of global production and trade, European elites came to press for a single means of exchange, which would lessen their dependence on the dollar as the *de facto* international reserve currency. Monetary union was proposed in 1986 with the Single European Act, launched in 1992 with the Maastricht treaty, and completed with the introduction of paper notes in 2002. In order to escape similar dependence on the American consumer market, the European Economic Area (EEA) was created in 1994, and has been continuously expanded since then. It should be noted that despite its refusal to be part of the EU, Norway is a fully fledged member of EEA, via the European Free Trade Association (EFTA), of which it was a founding member as far back as 1960. In this way it has become something like an invisible member of a purely functional, non-democratic European economic union.

From 1994 onward, a specular rivalry can be observed between European expansion and the process of hemispherical integration in the Americas. The EU tends to become the distorted mirror-image of NAFTA – though without recognizing itself as such. In many ways, it is again the embedding and disembedding of liberalism that is at stake. From the idealizing perspective of European social democrats, monetary union and the single market should allow the reconstitution of a domestic territory outside the dictates of the world market, so that social relations can be regulated democratically, not just economically. Indeed, the classic European diplomatic posture is to insist on such regulation; and the EU's leading cosmopolitan philosopher, Jürgen Habermas, constantly invokes the normative horizon of a "world domestic policy" (*Weltinnenpolitik*).[15] But one should never forget that the EU only functions as a democracy at one remove, via the Council of Ministers and the European Commission, both of which emanate from the arcana of national administrations, leaving room for only very limited direct representation of the continent's voters in the European Parliament. And behind the internationalist symbols of the Hague Court and the Kyoto climate-control protocols, the EU's tendency toward an objective alliance with the US within the World Trade Organization, against the demands of the Global South, reveals a quite different function of international public law. As Peter Gowan remarks:

> The imperial secret of the whole concept lies in who writes the rules in the first place... The model here is, of course, the European-inspired WTO which presents its rules as rooted in universalist-liberal free trade norms while in fact they are a concoction of positive law rules serving Atlantic capitalist interests.[16]

A similar pattern can be seen within the really-existing domestic territory of the EU, particularly since the ten-member enlargement of May 2004.

The result of the enlargement is a three-part division: Core Europe, New Europe, and what might be termed 'Edge Europe', i.e. the peripheral countries to the south and east of the current borders. Ideally, the social rights of the core countries would be extended through redistribution programs to the new members, while foreign aid and the umbrella of cosmopolitan trading laws would allow the gradual integration of the peripheral zones, whose resources and labor forces are, in any case, streaming into the center. In reality, a hierarchy emerges between the full citizens of Core Europe, who expect some democratic control over the evolution of their societies; the subordinated citizens of New Europe, whose political privileges have been substantively weakened by the loss of economic control over their industries and the westward migration of their younger and more educated people; and the dominated populations of Edge Europe, whose territories and resources are wide open to exploitation by transnational corporations – and whose rights, if they are migrants, can be curtailed arbitrarily, as painfully shown by the experience of French citizens of African origin under the recent state of emergency.

A New Europe country like Estonia exemplifies this three-tiered situation. Its most promising industries and the mainstays of its banking sector were snatched up by corporate investors from the core countries (particularly Finland and Sweden) in the wake of the worldwide financial crisis of 1997–98. Meanwhile, the country's enormous Russian-speaking population – imported from across the empire to work in the Soviet versions of Fordist industry – languishes for the most part without employment and without any right to citizenship and a passport, which are unobtainable without mastery of the complex Estonian language. This means that full-fledged Estonian citizens occupy what at times can seem like a narrow strip of their own small country, between the economic incursions of their more powerful European neighbors and the inconvenient presence of a former working class which they feel they did not ask for, and to whom, in any case, they cannot really speak. The current heroin epidemic among this former working-class population, and the explosion of HIV that inevitably accompanies it, raises the specter of a long-term condition of ghettoization and social exclusion, with the attendant development of the police apparatus and prison complexes that have been characteristic of neoliberal regime-shifts. Under these circumstances, the formation of a state to match far-off Keynesian standards of inclusion and social welfare is more than just difficult. Leaders, parties, political programs succeed each other in a confusing whirl; and what stands out from the rest is the default option of nationalist populism.

But just how far from that same sort of predicament are the hollowed-out social-democratic states of the European core, including Norway and the other Scandinavian lands? The generative grammar of global liberalism – which has structured the development of the EU, and was even written into the articles of its proposed constitution – has given rise to an extraordinarily dynamic upper-middle class, whose members, often involved in the business of culture, are able to switch countries, languages and affective universes with an ease and fluency that could be staggering, if there were any outside perspective from which to judge it. However, the very acceleration of transport and transaction tends to isolate the rarefied upper echelon of the core populations within a highly cohesive network of mobility, insulated from the increasingly heterogeneous composition of the societies they live in (or move through). The decline of the old working classes and the relative eclipse of national traditions in favor of a syncretic, recombinatory culture, coupled with the arrival of new service classes and technology specialists from Edge Europe and beyond, makes it very difficult for the would-be reformers of state services to craft a political platform that can appeal to any kind of majority. The needs of the rising sectors of society and of the financial elites will be satisfied in any case, since these are the foundation stones and principal clients of the SWPR state-form. But to address the people outside the ideal profiles of the knowledge-workers and the corporate financiers, two basic solutions present themselves, which are generally taken together. The first is to cut sectoral deals for specific voting blocs: farmers, unionized industrial workers, functionaries, small businessmen, state pensioners, etc., all of whom still have access to established representational mechanisms dating back to the Fordist era. And the second solution is to cover over those sectoral deals with a broad populist rhetoric of national identity and national dramas, which do not necessarily exist in reality.

The obvious danger in Core Europe today is that of slipping into a new political ecology of fear, which sutures the gaps between diverging social fractions by the knee-jerk scapegoating of the easiest targets, who are the immigrants, the people gathered to do the jobs that aging Core Europeans no longer desire to perform, or are no longer allowed to perform in an economy that needs under-the-table employment as the only possible way to compress the wage-variable, and therefore continue to make a profit in a fiercely competitive economy. To manipulate the figure of the immigrant as a security threat (or even worse, of the Muslim as a civilizational threat) is the most expedient way to cover up much more difficult negotiations over the dismantling of the old welfare state, while avoiding complaints about its replacement by a hodgepodge of changing dispositions that obey no particular sense of justice or even economic rationality. And the problem is that this dynamic of scapegoating and cover-up can only get worse, as core populations grow older and more immigrants are called in to replace them, despite the growing crunch on work permits and residency papers. The question then becomes, why does such an obviously short-sighted tactic seem to be spreading throughout Europe? Why are we looking at the rise of liberal-fascism, and talking about something else? What explains this inability to see the future, when it's already right here before our eyes?

The Chances of Vision
In the finance-driven, networked economy of the postnational compe-tition regimes, it is necessary to add a fourth 'fictitious commodity' to Polanyi's list of three (land, labor and money). This fourth fictitious

commodity is knowledge, in a spectrum of forms ranging from science, technology and law to literature, cooking and everyday know-how. Its production depends on long-term institutionalized learning and teaching experiences, publicly available libraries, archives, museums and data-banks, internalized modes of individual self-cultivation, urban spaces of improvisational or structured group interaction, processes of hybrid-ization between different cultural traditions, the constitution of critical and dissident discourses ranging from punk rock and poetry slams to networks of concerned scientists or alliances of traditional and organic farmers, and so on through a near-infinite spectrum of practices whereby objective observation, theoretical abstraction, individual expression and patterns of social solidarity are laid down in complex traces and artifacts that can be taken up and transformed by successive individuals, groups and generations. The impossibility of completely functionalizing this subtle interweave of practices and motivations is obvious, and was recog-nized throughout the long era of national institution-building, from the early 19th century onwards in most parts of the Western world. As Jessop writes concerning education during the Keynesian period:

> In stylized terms that were never fully matched in reality, we can say that education was expected to promote equality of access and opportu-nity, to create the basis for a talented and just 'meritocracy' that would undermine inherited class and status structures, to create, codify and dis-seminate a shared national identity and culture appropriate to a universal

and solidaristic welfare state, and to develop knowledgeable and critical citizens able and willing to participate in an expanding public sphere as well as a mass plebiscitary democracy.[17]

In terms of practices, values, experiences of time and the other, the educational and cultural spheres undoubtedly formed the most complex institutional mix produced by the era of embedded liberalism.

The expansion of the state's cultural and educational mandate, and its hesitant extension to class, gender and ethnic groups that were formerly excluded from representation, brought new conflicts and challenges to this institutional mix, which undertook a difficult period of transformation in the wake of 1968 and the decade of unrest that followed. It is precisely this 'difficulty of representation', precluding any simple reiteration of supposed national icons and values, that has been the source of most vitally engaging developments in culture over the last thirty years; and the same kind of questioning has even extended into a re-evaluation of certain economic and technoscientific functions. However, with the educational streamlining of the Bologna process, with the corporate sponsorship and instrumentalization of the arts and sciences, with the retooling of national cultural institutions for the transnational tourist market, and with the pervasive trend towards the commodification of knowledge under intellectual property law, what is being challenged right now is the very ideal of the educational-cultural sphere as the locus of a problematic quest for mutual understanding in a pluralist society. Indeed, the commodification of knowledge is the driving force and central goal of the Schumpeterian competition state, to the precise extent that the leading edge of capitalist production is redefined as technological and managerial innovation (particularly in the financial sphere). All the flowerings of human aspiration and experience can then be treated not just as commodities, but as investments in an entrepreneurial self, as the economist Gary Becker has shown with his notion of "human capital."[18] One of the ways Europeans now experience capital failure is when education and culture come packaged with a price tag that disfigures them, even when it doesn't leave them completely out of reach.

Paradoxically, the damage caused by this capitalization of knowledge is at once a primary factor in societal blindness, and a chance to bring the new states of human coexistence under the neoliberal regimes to visibility. The collaboration of artists with social scientists, labor organizations and ecology movements during the recent cycle of anti-globalization counter-summits, and now around the theme of the 'precariousness of existence' in the flexible economy, has marked a step forward in the ability to name and describe the effects of the neoliberal transformation process. Art has become one of the means of investigation, akin to social science, but irreducible to it. Similarly, a transnational organization such as Attac, whose economic critique has gained a certain influence in social-democratic countries like Norway, seeks to make visible the negative influence of a stateless, privatized currency on the fundamental realms of human labor and the natural environment, but also on the cultural-scientific domain that constitutes a second nature or an artificial environment (just as necessary as the air we breathe – and as likely to be polluted).[19] The growth of the Socialist Left Party in Norway (reaching 12.5% of the vote in the 2001 general elections) represents an attempt at a political translation of such investigations. When artists begin to explore the operations of capital, and to point directly to instances of capital failure, they are participating with their own expressive methods in a complex response to the gradual installation of the competition regime, imposed as a single set of exclusive and increasingly intolerant rules for the difficult and irrevocably multiple states of human coexistence in society. The process of exploring and interpellating these currently invisible states is one aspect of the broader effort to constitute social formations that might act in common, having not only shared objective interests but potentially even an interest in each other.

The problem, however, is not only the gradual phasing-out of national cultural institutions, together with their outdated canons of beauty and elitist ideals of identity. The deeper problem is that in order to survive as exploratory and transformative practices, and in order to generate enough interest and involvement to reconstitute a socialized cultural sphere under fresh auspices, the contemporary arts have to throw off their blatant or subtle dependence on the new corporate-oriented institutions that promote an opportunistic and flexible subjectivity. And this is easier said than done, as shown by the ambiguous relations between cultural producers on the museum circuit and activists seeking forms of organization for precarious labor.[20] Because it's easy to invest in a little anguish over the biopolitical instrumentalization of one's own creativity, in order to produce a new niche product for the originality markets. And it's just as facile to criticize that investment. Indeed, hyperindividualization and the capitalization of everything seems to be the very formula for the breakdown of solidarities, and the emergence of liberal-fascism. What's more complicated – as those involved in different aspects of the precarity movements are discovering – is to create lines of invention and critique that reinforce each other in their differences, across professional and class divides. In this respect, the role of knowledge producers in recreating an ability to say 'we' is potentially decisive.[21] By pursuing a new transvaluation of the old national values, it may be possible to arrive at what is now lacking: a sustainable constitution of multiplicity. But there is no assurance whatsoever that this potential will be realized.

The accession of ten new members to the European Union underscores the difficulty. The problem is that none of these countries can find any interest in maintaining the conditions of a welfare state which they cannot afford, and whose restrictions would block their own path to development. One can then only 'join the union' on a battle footing – as proved by the preemptive drafting of certain former Eastern states into the Iraq war. Fighting to support the US petrodollar becomes a paradoxical guarantee of sovereignty, at the very moment of subsumption under a supranational hierarchy. As though the long-held project of becoming a fully fledged member of the EU could only be realized through a dream of the American way of life. To be sure, great dreams are natural, positive, after decades of foreign occupation. But what some Estonian observers consider to be a contemporary culture of wish-fulfilling narcissism (punctuated or punctured by deep mistrust and aggressivity) could also be understood as a way of coping with traumatic change, in the sense of the Polish sociologist Piotr Sztompka, who goes so far as to speak of a "trauma of victory."[22] How to lend tangibility and public visibility to theoretical freedoms that are not always matched by substantive improvements? An entire cartography of existence has been redrawn in fifteen years. The ambiguous class-status and uncertain integration of whole populations along Europe's eastern rim, within and beyond the New Europe, marks the need for lucid and challenging artistic practices that can reveal and transform the unconscious conflicts that lurk beneath the surface of contemporary experience. Ways must be found to carry on this kind of work within the framework of new social relations that are unfolding across the entire European territory, at a time when cultural institutions have no clear mandate or support base for dealing with the difficult questions of identity and difference.

These concerns must surely feel distant to those who live in the state of Norway, outside most of the EU's political constraints, and close to the North Sea oil wells, with a newly elected center-left government coming into power in the fall of 2005. The Norwegians seem to inhabit a different cartography. Yet despite the hopes of intellectuals, the Socialist

Left Party lost ground to traditional Labor in the last elections; while the conservative liberal right-wing Progress Party, with its populist and racist leanings, received 'only' 22% of the vote, making it the second largest force. Is it possible for a small nation to steer itself safely through tumultuous changes in the world-system? For a few weeks that same fall, in the self-run space of the artists' union in Oslo, highly abstracted forms of capital failure were on display. Behind them, one could almost glimpse the invisible states of the union.

I would like to thank all the people, in Estonia and Norway, who generously allowed me to interview them in preparation for this text; as well as Anders Härm and Trude Iversen, for arranging those conversations.

Notes:

1. Friedrich Engels, *Herrn Eugen Dühring's Umwälzung der Wissenschaft* (1878), part 3, chap. 2: "Der moderne Staat, was auch seine Form, ist eine wesentlich kapitalistische Maschine, Staat der Kapitalisten, der ideelle Gesamtkapitalist"; online at www.mlwerke. de/me/me20/me20_239.htm#Kap_II. English version: "The modern state, no matter what its form, is essentially a capitalist machine, the state of the capitalists, the ideal person-ification of the total national capital"; online at /www.marxists.org/archive/marx/works/1877/anti-duhring/ch24.htm.

2. Félix Guattari, 'Capital as the Integral of Power Formations', in *Soft Subversions*, New York: Semiotext(e), 1996.

3. In this text I will use the term 'capital failure' to describe the combined shortfalls in human well-being caused by what sociologists know separately as 'market failure' and 'state failure'. As I will show, the possibility of separating these two categories is increasingly reduced as the entrepreneurial dimension of neoliberal governance comes to predominate.

4. J. G. Ruggie, 'International Regimes, Transactions, and Change: Embedded Liberalism in the Postwar Economic Order', in *International Organization* 36, vol. 2, 1982.

5. Karl Polanyi, *The Great Transformation*, Boston: Beacon, 1957/1944.

6. Bob Jessop, *The Future of the Capitalist State*, Cambridge: Polity, 2002, chap. 2 and *passim*. The introductory chapter can be dowloaded at http://www.lancs.ac.uk/fss/sociology/papers/jessop-future-of-the-capitalist-state-chapter1.pdf.

7. For the crisis of US hegemony in relation to previous world-systemic crises, cf. Giovanni Arrighi, Beverley Silver et. al., *Chaos and Governance in the Modern World-System*, Minneapolis: University of Minnesota Press, 1999.

8. For interpretations of the shift towards a new international regime, cf. among others David Harvey, *The New Imperialism*, Oxford University Press, 2003, as well as Peter Gowan, *Global Gamble*, London: Verso, 1999.

9. For the new role of the IMF since the early 1980s, cf. David Harvey, *A Brief History of Neoliberalism*, Oxford University Press, 2005, chap. 1.

10. Cf. J. Schumpeter, *Capitalism, Socialism and Democracy*, New York: HarperCollins 1975/1942, chap. 7, 'The Process of Creative Destruction', 83: "The fundamental impulse that sets and keeps the capitalist engine in motion comes from the new consumers' goods, the new methods of production or transportation, the new markets, the new forms of industrial organization that capitalist enterprise creates."

11. The term was coined by Christopher Hood, in the article 'A Public Management for All Seasons?' in *Public Administration* 69 (1991). For a critical review of the practices it describes (which date from the 1980s, and betray the influence of the 'Total Quality Management' procedures developed in Anglo-Saxon business circles), see among others Linda Kaboolian, 'The New Public Management: Challenging the Boundaries of the Management vs. Administration Debate', and the articles from the symposium on 'Leadership, Democracy and the New Public Management', in *Public Administration Review* vol. 58, #3, May-June 1998.

12. For an ideal-type of 'flexible subjectivity' in fully neoliberalized societies, see Brian Holmes, 'The Flexible Personality', in *Hieroglyphs of the Future*, Zagreb: WHW, 2002. The text is also available in my archive at www.u-tangente.org.

13. A classic case in this respect is France. For an account of the way the country's economy has been flexibilized around a dwindling core of unionized workers who still serve as representative for the entire labor force, via the classic tripartite state-labor-employer

bargaining structures, cf. Christian Boltanski and Eve Chiapello, *Le nouvel esprit du capitalisme*, Paris: Gallimard, 1999, chaps. 4 and 5 ('La déconstruction du monde du travail' and 'L'affaiblissement des défenses du monde du travail').

14. Consider this quote from Arrighi et. al. (*Chaos and Governance in the Modern World-System*, op. cit., 139), which sums up the perspective of the postwar American elites on European unification: "As John Foster Dulles had declared in 1948, 'a healthy Europe' could not be 'divided into small compartments'. It had to be organized into a market 'big enough to justify modern methods of cheap production for mass consumption'. To this end, the new Europe had to include a reindustrialized Germany. Without German integration into the European economy, remarked General Motors corporation chairman Alfred P. Sloan, 'there is nothing that could convince us in General Motors that it was either sound or desirable or worthwhile to undertake an operation of any consequence in a country like France'."

15. See for example Jürgen Habermas, 'The Postnational Constellation and the Future of Democracy', in *The Postnational Constellation: Political Essays*, Cambridge: Polity Press, 2001.

16. Peter Gowan, 'US Hegemony Today', in *Monthly Review*, vol. 55, #3, July-August 2003, online at: www.mail-archive.com/marxist-leninist-list@lists.econ.utah.edu/msg04762.html.

17. Bob Jessop, *The Future of the Capitalist State*, op. cit. 162-63.

18. GaryBecker, *Human Capital: A Theoretical and Empirical Analysis with Special Reference to Education*, University of Chicago Press, 1993/1964.

19. See www.attac.no and www.attac.org.

20. The missed encounter between artists and activists at the *Klartexte!* conference in

Berlin in January 2005 was an example of this ambiguity. As Marcelo Expósito writes: "It's essential to understand what blocks the compatibility *in practice* between the remarkable work of the *Kleines postfordistisches Drama* and Marion von Osten on the new figures of cultural production, and the necessary process of politically organizing precarious social subjects defended by Alex Foti of Chainworkers." See Expósito's review of the conference, 'Hablando Claro', in *Brumaria 5* (Barcelona, 2005).

21. See the text by the French *intermittents du spectacle*, 'La puissance du nous' [The Power of the 'We'], at www.cip-idf.org/article.php3?id_article=1124. The absolute untranslatability of this text, which is immersed in the remnants of the French welfare state, itself speaks volumes about the difficulty of establishing solidarities on a European level.

22. Piotr Sztompka, 'The Ambivalence of Social Change: Triumph or Trauma?' (2000), online at http://skylla.wz-berlin.de/pdf/2000/p00-001.pdf. Also see Sztompka's contribution to J.C. Alexander et. al., *Cultural Trauma and Collective Identity*, Berkeley: University of California Press, 2004.

Consumerist Interfaces

by Oleg Kireev

*...who burned cigarette holes in their arms protesting
the narcotic tobacco haze of Capitalism...*

Allen Ginsberg, *Howl*

I

Post-Soviet reality provides a perfect angle from which to view capital. First, because many of us had lived in non-capitalist times. I was ten when *perestroika* started and sixteen when the Soviet Union collapsed – I had seen the other reality.

Second, during the 1990s we had the chance to see how capital invades formerly non-capitalist spaces and occupies formerly non-capitalist environments and settles itself in minds.

Third, we'd seen these processes in motion. What took a century in the West, was done here within several years. Some call it 'modernization', or 'catching-up modernization'. The specificity of this kind of modernization is that the modernizing culture absorbs attitudes and values from the culture it takes as a pattern. Like Turkey for example, Russia is prone to absorb the Other's values and to try to deal with what comes out of that.

And, fourth, finally, we'd seen the end of Soviet power – we witnessed the glorious flash of freedom – and if this could happen with the Soviets, why couldn't it with the anti-Soviets? This fourth consideration lets us take it all a bit more easily.

In India there's a tremendous mass movement of farmers against the privatization of natural resources, 'Navdanya', headed by a world-prominent ecologist and an author of many books, Vandana Shiva. In books such as *Biopiracy* and *Patents*,[1] Dr. Shiva shows very clearly that the rules now applied to the economy by transnational corporations operating in India originated in the 'enclosures movement' in Britain's 16th century. Now they form what Dr. Shiva calls 'a new colonialism'. The step from national capitalism to colonialism is described by another female thinker, Rosa Luxembourg. According to Luxembourg, the triumphant worldly parade of capitalism is only made possible by the corruption of a homeland working class at the center of the system, while at the periphery, capitalism inevitably relies on non-capitalist means of production (feudalism or slavery).

Within these theoretical contours, let's take a look at our 'second world' culture. Cultural studies have created various portraits of identities – from an Asian US immigrant to a British football fan. They have mapped the spaces in the 'first world' and 'third world', but the 'second world', which is the post-Soviet space, remains unexplored. Another type should be added, which is a 'post-Soviet man'. This is, first of all, a very disillusioned person. Unlike the 'Soviet man' or 'new Soviet man' who advocated courage, pride, idealism and humanity, the post-Soviets don't trust most idealist arguments. The primary impulse for us was that "everything on this side is defeated," and no one wanted to stay with those who are defeated. That's why Russia, as one Argentinean comrade had said, "became nowadays the most consumerist and religious country." But there was also a secondary impulse, which was an extra-utopian perestroika-times belief that "everything should be built anew and better." We, a generation born in the mid-1970s, were eyewitnesses to millions marching the streets in 1991, and we saw public space, the TV and media completely open – before the propaganda and information wars. And now, under the pressure of capitalism on the offensive, we must also rethink the history of a great 'anti-capitalist experiment' and re-evaluate its essentials. At least we can now understand the starting point of the revolutionaries. It seems to me that we the post-Soviets can valuably contribute to a present international anti-capitalist agenda.

II

Manuel Castells claims that the main feature of an Information Age is 'optimization' in applying knowledge to the cycles of production.[2] In regard to Soviet life, there was no optimization. The economy didn't know what feedback is – the very idea of a five-year centralized plan is contrary to it. Production circles were not optimized because factories could not immediately interact with science, all innovations had to go through various bureaucratic and governmental layers, and even the military complex was functioning quite poorly up to the end of the USSR. Also, Soviet life wasn't optimized because it had no deficit of time. It wasn't 'in a hurry', or 'panicked', as some contemporary thinkers describe the conditions of the information economy. Instead, it had certainty and predictability.

Therefore the change of conditions was for us a change of the *chronos tempos* – we've gotten into a rushing escalation of technologies, goods, needs and desires, news and images. Before, history had a plan – now it's senseless and undetermined. As Susan George argues, "Capitalism is like that famous bicycle that has to keep moving forward or topple over – and corporations are all competing to see who can pedal fastest, straight into the brick wall."

What was the actual historical plan that the Soviet human expected to unfold? A part of this plan had already been fulfilled – the revolution was done. Now there are plenty of obstacles, but they have to be overcome on the way to communism. Communism was considered the next step after socialism. It was declared by Nikita Khrushchev in 1958 that the present generation of Soviet people would live under it.

The Soviet dream of communism was shared by many people. It was expressed perfectly by a 1950-1960s sci-fi writer, Ivan Yefremov.[3] Yefremov's plots take place far into the future, after 4000 A.D. Communism has won on the scale of all humankind. People are into science and space exploration, while also caring about culture. The war against 'gangsterizing capitalism' is won long ago, thereafter the people began to restore natural resources of the planet which had been devastated by the former industrial and military use. Humankind then met the space comrades – other living forms and intellects of the universe. Together they're all very interested in advanced technologies, but the use of technologies, the way in which they are situated in a social system, is totally different from the capitalist way. Their development is more balanced. They correspond to the needs which appear naturally from the growth of a society. Technologies do not hurry up, they don't 'panic'. On the contrary, they're all very friendly and have non-consumerist interfaces. Their interfaces are oriented not towards an ignorant user, but rather towards a skilled and conscious individual.

Buddhists and Hindus would call capitalism 'a realm of ignorance', or *avidya*, because capitalism constantly hides its own sources or grounding in order to mask its primary impulses, and those impulses are greed and profit. The flows of money are the nerves of the social body. Therefore it veils its own basic instincts under the Spectacle, under paradises of advertising, under talk about 'virtuality' and 'post-humanity', and under consumerist interfaces of power. But that's for the inhabitants of the 'first world', of the 'developed countries' with their 'system of values', as George W. Bush likes to point out. In the third-world countries, and also in Russia, it's more likely to show itself unmasked.

"Do you want 50 SMSes for free?" – asks an advertisement. It sounds very friendly. The slogan is usually surrounded by smiles. But if you think about it, the message is not so nice. Each statement of advertising implies the opposite side: pay, and if you don't pay, you will be excluded, there will be no 50 SMSes for free, nor even a single SMS. It directs your attention to a totality of payments you're making – to capital as such. "You will pay now as always, but now thanks to the kindness of a company, you have 50 SMSes for free."

Money is a collective unconscious of capitalist society. People don't usually talk about money – only advertising has this privilege. In order to talk about money and direct the subconscious impulses of people towards consumption, advertising forces a simplification of language and a primitivization of emotions, artificial familiarity and infantile language. It doesn't say that life is difficult and that one should train his skills and gain his own consciousness – no, it says: "You can do it or have it, it's easy, just take out your wallet." Some will not leave satisfied, but that's also welcomed because it will force them to buy more. Also, if we were to look at the way corporations fight for money, we'd find it somehow weird, if not abusive. How many consumers know that printer and scanner producers must pay commissions to publishing industry representatives because their equipment can potentially be used for copying books without buying them? Or look at the actions that the MPAA is taking in respect to file-sharers: a DJ can be arrested by the copyright police just for playing an unlicensed copy of a track at the disco!

Consumerist culture in Russia is in progress. Malls and supermarkets are always full. Their corporate style of service is explicitly impersonal, alien. But the mysterious Russian 'middle class' tolerates it. They must be very depressive people if they like to meet these imagined paradises, imposed identities. And very soon when, as prophets of technocracy promise, personalized advertising will be introduced (the computer scans your electronic ID at a distance and shows you what you like and what is imprinted in your data-body as personal consumerist preferences), the consumer is to feel good about such a 'personal' treatment!

Over the past few years, trade has moved from the center of Moscow to malls situated just beyond the Encircling Road. They build IKEAs and Achanes there in order to pay a relatively low cost to the Moscow region administration instead of the city. Of course, you can acquire everyday food and stuff in your area, but for 'shopping', the new middle-class residents have to get in their cars, preferably on the weekend. They would probably show up at McDonald's on the way. The core idea of 'fast food' is that you can eat quickly, but the very fact of this ordinary food taking is staged with a ceremonial sense of importance. That's why, in our 'post-Soviet' society, boys can solemnly invite girls 'to McDonald's', while the central streets and squares of Moscow are filled with endless boutiques and cafés. The latter replace all kinds of necessary everyday services, for example, in my neighborhood a Japanese sushi restaurant is built instead of a shop for house inventory. Large factories of Coca-Cola, Heineken, etc. appear in suburbs or in the satellite cities like Odintsovo and Solntsevo.

Naomi Klein writes in *No Logo* that her parents, the anti-war US hippies, have emigrated to calm, idyllic Canada in order to be saved from the rush of consumption. Klein mentions how unhappy they were when it very quickly reached them there and even to the mind of their daughter:

The humiliating spectacle of my all-too-real family, so sixties authentic, set against the cascade of inviting plasticity that was the seventies and eighties, was simply too much to bear. 'Stop it, guys, you're embarrassing me!' was the near-hysterical *cri de coeur* of my youth. Even when there was no one but family around, I could feel the plastic world's reproachful gaze.[4]

That's very true for Russian teenagers now, who have grown up on computer games and MTV along with Snickers, Reebok and McDonald's advertisements.

III

Utopia expresses an 'ultimate task', or the dream of society. That's why sci-fi is a part of a national high-tech complex. Richard Barbrook shows it brilliantly in *Imaginary Futures*: the US needed futurology to formulate their 'super-task'. As he says in one interview, "Americans had a nice present, but Russians had a better future, that's the point!"[5] There was a governmental need and a CIA order for creating Daniel Bell's utopia.[6] But, for example, Ivan Yefremov became quite popular, though he was not accepted by the Soviet officials (his last novel's publication being prohibited since his death in 1972). The officials could already recognize a dystopia in it. And some also said that yes, it might be a hidden anti-Stalinist critique. Yefremov was one of the best in the period most interesting to us – a 'thaw' which began in 1956 with Khrushchev's famous speech denouncing Stalin's crimes and ended in 1964 with Khrushchev's involuntary replacement by Leonid Brezhnev. His top hit novel, *Andromeda*, appeared in 1958,

Blade in 1963, *Tais of Athens* in 1973, and the later prohibited, *An Hour of a Bull*, in 1968. Along with the political implications, Yefremov managed to bring other ideas such as cybernetics, psychoanalysis, and even LSD into discussion. His heroes usually talk about history, sociology, technologies and other conceptual issues, and once they say: "Only with the invention of computers could humankind build communism." Somehow he also became a 'Russian new age' oracle, who also introduced yoga, tantra and feminism through his books.

We look back at these times. Yefremov considered the main profession in the future society to be that of the historian, so let us too now take a brief trip into history. In the 1950s the chain reaction after the Third World War liberates third-world countries from colonialism. Very soon 'the world revolution' will be back on the agenda. Meanwhile, in Europe the 'Marshall Plan' invented in America is just brought to life, squeezing all possible commies and SU sympathizers out from any political representation, not to mention parliamentary representation. Still, the European left wing is very strong. Soviet BESM computers are out of factories. Rebels take Cuba. Khrushchev meets Nehru. But after his replacement as a result of a quiet *coup d'etat* in the establishment in 1964, the position of general secretary is taken by the conservative, Leonid Brezhnev. After four years, Soviet tanks enter the Republic of Czechoslovakia. In the same year, 1968, a complete reorganization in Soviet computing is carried out, which destroys the decentralized innovative research and which was called by Edsger Dijkstra "the biggest triumph of the West in the Cold War."

The period of Khrushchev's 'thaw' caused very deep cultural and mental effects. First, it gave a great rise of mass enthusiasm. The state had proclaimed an 'exploration of Siberia' – and thousands of young people, many students among them, came voluntarily to be a workforce on the building of the Baikal-Amur Railroad. Second, culture began to flourish. The golden era of Soviet film dates from the 1960s. It also gives rise to an avant-garde theatre, experimental music and a scientific breakthrough. Communism showed its ability to analyze its own mistakes and to reincarnate! It's still possible to build a true state of workers! But with Brezhnevian stagnation coming, the cultural climate cools down. Only the cinema remained extremely interesting and provocative until the early 1980s, while all other progressive initiatives went underground. There's still sci-fi through the 1970s and 1980s, but now the view of the communist future is much more skeptical. And the most radical part of the intelligentsia stands in a direct opposition to the communist power. With a heroic protest of eight lonely people against the 1968 Prague invasion, the dissident movement begins. This is the first of the disillusioned generations.

However, the boom of the 1960s resulted in many forms of innovative culture, especially in fields remote from politics. There were vast resources of intellectuals not included in the state machine. Many brilliant books of the late Soviet epoch – including sci-fi – praise science, reason, a constructive and positive worldview, and the idea of progress. Such are the most prominent sci-fi books by the two Strugatsky brothers.

But they already keep their distance from the state ideology, even in the their own work, there is an evident gap between the enthusiasm of the 1960s and the disillusionment of the 1970s. Instead of a pathetic Soviet messianism, they rather confess to an abstract romanticism of contributing to human research and the accumulation of knowledge. One of their novels humorously describes the 'Institute for Magic' under which we recognize a Soviet hi-tech institute, and the main hero of it is a programmer…

Still, until 1985, the Soviet state had a much more relaxed style of living than those countries under capitalism. There were tons of dissidents or autonomous individuals who carried out 'inner emigration': while receiving a small amount of money for an easy job, you could spend most of your time on intellectual hobbies independent of the state dictate. Such subcultures in the late SU were those of believers, dissidents, conceptual artists, computer freaks, etc.

Vandana Shiva says that after the fall of the Union there was a big debate over which parts of life should go into the hands of the owners, i.e. be privatized, and what should remain common. Richard Barbrook goes further when he states very clearly that the very idea of a welfare state had been introduced to the Westerners as a reply to the 'Soviet lifestyle'. A prospect of spectacle and consumerism was opened to a Western world inhabitant as an alternative to the utopian perspective of the Soviets. The propaganda just promoted a perspective that was based on different needs and impulses from the ones which the Soviet dream was built on. This also suggests that without the need to compete with opponents, capitalism will very soon denounce its own promises. We can already see this going on with precarisation. Capitalism can compromise its predatory nature only when faced with resistance or danger, otherwise there will be no compromises: the rich will eat everything.

IV

My earliest schooldays had not been the happiest. As a son of nonconformists, I was never at peace with mainstream opinions. Aside from that, the Soviet state was living its last years, and the whole ideological environment seemed really out of fashion, if not to say rotten. With the beginning of *perestroika*, I moved to another school, which was a gathering place for the children of all Moscow intelligentsia. My history teacher influenced me most of all; she was the daughter of a well-known liberal historian who still could very easily publish his books 'under the dictatorship'. My first historical views were therefore inspired by the very basics of the Soviet underground, Western-oriented dissident thought, i.e. Friedrich von Hayek (theory), William Shearer and Alexander Werth (history of the USSR), and Solzhenitsyn and George Orwell, of course. I didn't actually have the chance to come into contact with the communist idea, because it seemed that, apart from the corrupt bureaucrats (*apparatchiki*) and hysterical schoolteachers, there were no communists. 1989-1991 was a perfect time for believing the other truths. The hated system went into crisis and then fell. We in the school saw the rise of a *perestroika* enthusiasm. Pupils supported by the progressive teachers started to create school *soviets* – electoral systems for self-regulation. My school was in the avant-garde of a cultural exchange with America; though I did not, several pupils of mine went to the US, in order to denounce 'an enemy image' of the Cold War. We really believed: from now on, this will all get better.

The negation of the Soviets at this time is quite understandable. But I think the problem was that the dissidents who subverted the power and introduced a new liberal ideology, lacked a critical understanding of capitalism. The market was understood in terms of free competition, *laissez-faire* principles and other dogmatic neo-liberal ideas, but there was no emphasis on monopolization, large capital accumulation, militarization, colonialism etc. Ironically, now we find that these were the hard points of an official Soviet propaganda expressed through posters and political cartoons, which were all familiar from my childhood. This was also a focus of all cultural anti-capitalist critique, from Eisenstein to Yefremov and the Strugatsky brothers. This means that in essence, this critique was true!

At this time the nation put a lot of trust in certain ideas. In 1991, millions of demonstrators supported Yeltsin. He was given the extreme support of the nation, prepared a semi-secret agreement, which dissolved the Soviet Union and let him replace Gorbatchev as the head of the nation. Soon began the propaganda wars, disinformation on TV, and the originating democracy was shut down at the Moscow White House. Activists and politicians who were even just relatively idealistic, wanting a civil society, public opinion and other positive ideas of liberalism were pulled out of the offices by the same old and new *apparatchiki*. A way to privatization of the country was open.

In 1997 when the Radek group was formed, which artistically resisted the power that we didn't know what exactly we're protesting against, it was only obvious that something had gone wrong. Osmolovsky, an initiator of the movement, confessed that he had gotten a first strike of leftist ideas from Jean-Luc Godard's films, not from the Soviet idea. Only now did we start to refer to the Soviet post-war heritage, approve it to our reality, and find its reasons.

These days in Russia, the reactionary state propagandists try to describe a present Russian identity as 'coming back to the sources', to some mythological national identity that existed before the Bolsheviks, was interrupted in 1917, and is back once again now. Also, some Baltic state governments have introduced discriminatory laws against the Russian population, and all Baltic states have included the idea of the 'Soviet occupation' in their state mythology. As in Russia, this idea is being used to ground their identity in an imagined entity. The communist idea is compared to fascism on the level of state propaganda. Governments do so in order to gain votes. But identity is not a pure 'idea' existing in some ideal Platonic realm independent of its historical incarnations. It's shaped by history. What their actions cause are disasters for many individuals, but they can't erase the epoch from history. A Soviet internationalism over the borders is the most powerful antidote to present nationalism, and an argument that "the people of various Soviet republics and ethnicities fought fascism altogether in the same army" is the strongest one until now.

The ideas of communism lived in the SU independently of Stalinist crimes and Brezhnev's stagnant times. This was a belief confessed by most people, that history can be shaped by conscious human will. Traditional religion was replaced by a belief that 'we should be proud to call ourselves human' and that people should do good just because they are humans, never mind gods and rewards or punishments after death. Now these times are over, and the capitalists are back in town, but it's unlikely that humankind will give up the very ideas of historical multi-dimensionality and diverse alternatives. It's unlikely that the perspectives that are still open can be closed.

Notes:

1. Vandana Shiva, *Biopiracy: The Plunder of Nature and Knowledge*, Cambridge: South End Press, 1997; *Patents: Myths and Reality*, Penguin India, 2001.

2. In the third volume of his *Information Age*, entitled *End of Millenium*, dedicated exactly to a history of the late SU: Manuel Castells: *The Information Age: Economy, Society and Culture* (in 3 volumes), Oxford: Blackwell Publishers, 1996-1998.

3. The most interesting of his novels, *Andromeda*, exists in English and can be found at http://lib.sarbc.ru/koi/EFREMOW/tuman_engl.txt.

4. Naomi Klein, *No Logo*, London: Flamingo, 2000, 143-144.

5. L.Levkovitch, R.Barbrook, G.Seaman, *Its comin up!* // *CompuTerra # 560*.

6. Richard Barbrook, *Post-industrial Imperialism: The Imaginary Future of the Information Society* (manuscript).

Meaningful, Meaningless and Free of All Meaning:
Subjects in Spent Time
by Stephan Geene

We understand that keeping production in Germany is increasingly difficult…

> –Mayor of Wolfsburg, Germany, *in defense of the €18 million in tax money invested in the science theme park 'Phaeno'.*[1]

The economic and political elite cannot be dissuaded from the notion of 'work for everyone'. As a result they are blind to the level of hopelessness that is spreading within the ghettos for the superfluous whose inhabitants feel cut off from the existential security of gainful employment. Parties on the right as well as the left, new and old social democrats, neoliberals, and nostalgics for the socialist state refuse to recognize that through conditions of 'jobless growth' work transformed long ago from a 'great integrator' into a mechanism of marginalization.

> –Ulrich Beck[2]

So wrote Ulrich Beck in response to the riots of November 2005 in France, which reached a high point of 1000 burning cars per night, and emergency regulations, which had never before been enforced in France, were invoked. But only this extreme situation brought to public attention, to continue with the car example, the 30,000 cars set on fire since the first of the year, which had become the norm. The media coverage of these events was – for a short time – adequate, if notably uninformed. Suddenly there were no more 'embedded journalists'. Few media crews risked entering the effected 'Banlieus'. And if they did venture in, they went only during the day; continually stressing how impossible these forays would have been without the several strong youths who guided them through the ghettos. For their alleged authenticity the few interviews made relied on stereotype. It is this stereotype that gives a name to Mathieu Kassowitz's 1995 film: *Hate*.

The news features agreed with Ulrich Beck – the angry mob were in the right: they are excluded, they live under segregation, and they have no prospects for work, that is, no hope of integrating. While one simultaneously has sympathy for a (seemingly justified) desperation, the European states are currently in the process of dismantling the welfare state. In this way these societies construct an uncomfortable double bind. One understands that the 'unnecessary' people feel unnecessary, but that cannot be helped. Quite the contrary, as they do not yet know how redundant they will become in the future. After all, in the imminent future, the workers who are becoming fewer and fewer all the time will never be in the position, as common sense would have it, to feed the growing army of non-workers. Most recently Zygmunt Bauman devoted an entire book to this problem. Bauman's *Wasted Lives: Modernity and its Outcasts*, begins with the assertion that "people that are declared superfluous are usually considered financial problems."[3] Superfluousness replaces unemployment, and in this substitution a change – a dissolution – is anticipated for unemployment, but not for superfluousness. In this way Bauman threads this development into the logic of the Modern, and, respectively, its decline.

Ulrich Beck's assumption that burning cars are expressions of desperation and aggression, of 'no longer being necessary', carries with it a number of associations that upon closer examination are not necessarily so self-evident. The 'misfortune of not even being exploited anymore' (Diederichsen) is in any case more of a metaphor than a psychosocial observation. The sudden, ostensible empathy of those 'included' with those 'excluded' is arbitrary and self-righteous. This compassionate understanding, actually ascribing feelings to others, is an appropriative gesture reserved for the dominant group. It has perhaps much more to do with a bourgeois public's ability to 'understand' when confronted with images of people who appear to spend all their time in the streets. And this way of thinking may well become more acute when it is coupled with burning cars. Certainly unemployment, segregation, lack of opportunity and racism are problems, but the way in which they are articulated as problems makes a considerable difference politically. 'Superfluousness' has associations with vegetating, people without the means of agency – images which are only too familiar from the so-called 'drug problem'. In this way the metaphor reproduces a classic social reaction, straight out of the bourgeois inventory, provoked by the 'unusual time management' of the not-regularly-working; namely the implication of 'wasting time'. For while the working consider time valuable, they find nothing more frightening than suddenly having no reason to be busy: a pure *horror vacui*.

When Ulrich Beck ascertains that society can no longer perform the function of integration through work, because there is just not enough, he may well be right. But that does not mean that the lack of work is also responsible for the breakdown of society. After all, even with employment integration does not automatically take place. There is no going back to the joy of work – or the pressure of work – in the Fordist sense. The extreme valuation that newly precious work is experiencing has to do precisely with the fact that post-Fordism is also a crisis for the employed. Employment since 1968 finds itself (justifiably so) in crisis, and work no longer seems by any means to be an incontrovertible interaction with nature.

Beck's critique of the superfluousness of the excluded alleges that all who have work (or know how to keep themselves busy) are necessary. Thus Beck falls victim to exactly that ideological construction, with which the problems and the crisis of social meaning are obscured by the exclusion of some.

Under no circumstances would I disregard the contention that social segregation is murderous. I would however, like to problematize how it is that metaphors are created by those who do not recognize themselves as part of the problematic area, who believe that – as journalists – they can adapt to neoliberal 'working conditions', precisely when (and because) they criticize these conditions. Crocodile tears as politics are of no use.

My main concern here is above all to discuss subjectivity within the horizon of labor and employment and of the social organization of motivation and the promise of happiness. Subjectivity between usefulness and uselessness; subjectivity between consumer gratification and the threat of exclusion.

There Is No Representable Inside of Exclusion / Film

When the film *Rosetta* by the Dardenne Brothers won the Golden Palm in Cannes in 1999, Rosetta became a symbol in France and Belgium: the unemployed society is no fun.[4] Rosetta became a symbol for the individual's struggle for work – a psychodrama of the will to integrate.

This negative image of the 'new economy' heralded the end of the belief, which shortly thereafter seized all of Europe, in self-generated wealth. What still seemed in 1999 to be the audacity of the *nouveau riche*, the neoliberal brutality, has prevailed today as the bankruptcy of public households, as the seemingly unavoidable: the poor state can no longer stop the power of the rich to become wealthier and wealthier.

The film *Rosetta* is at first glance reminiscent of the style of partisanship on behalf of the marginalized well-known since the Italian Neo-Realism of the 1950s: the depiction of the perspective of the poor as a humanitarian claim to better living conditions. The film is in this way a part of the process, especially cultivated in France, of maintaining *l'exception française* as a national sensibility, which is critical. The recognition of this familiar model of social criticism must certainly account for part of the success the Dardenne Brothers enjoy with their films. Still, this recognition is deceptive since today, unlike in the past, the depiction of poverty is in no way something remarkable per se. Poverty is a commonplace element in the entertainment industry. Society considers itself classless; only poverty makes wealth seem nice. Even as there are considerable differences in degrees of realism, *Rosetta* is essentially about other qualities, which can perhaps comment in another way on the meaning of 'exclusion', on what subjectivity in exclusion is. The film develops a method of commenting that does not attempt to let the marginalized speak, to describe the world from the point of view of the poor and under- or de-privileged, but instead it takes the border as its subject. It thereby becomes possible to see that the border is not given 'with them', but is instead an active structural element of segregated societies. The border is not a place, but an activity produced by society in its entirety, undoubtedly with the help of its cultural production: namely, visual communication, or, in other words, visual consumption – accepted as a fundamental life activity in industrial societies.

Rosetta presents the space that opens when the natural given of the Fordist regime fades. The film on the one hand shows the struggle to maintain access to the space of vanishing social necessity that calls itself 'work', while on the other hand it does not seem to give this struggle a psychological, internal space. Thus, *Rosetta* is fundamentally different from socially critical films popular since the 1950s. Moreover, the matrix of labor, employment, money, leisure time and economic macro-structures becomes apparent in a manner specific to the type of commodity by which they appear (film).

Rosetta – The Film

You say that Rosetta is a warrior...

Jean-Pierre Dardenne: With or without work, it is a constant battle that people lead today. Not working, regardless of choice, places you on the margins of society. You lose your reference point, you are unstructured, you don't know your place anymore, or even if you still have one. Work gives you certain duties and rights. When you are no longer working, you lose your rights. Work becomes a rarity. There is nothing left. To get a job you have to take someone else's place, and you have to be prepared to do certain things to get that.

Luc Dardenne: Rosetta is a warrior who never gives up, who is always prepared to attack. She is a survivor who lives in a primary state: water, accommodation, food.[5]

The film is a cry for work that remains heartbreaking. 17-year-old Rosetta lives on the edge of a small Belgian town in a non-place, an empty lot where caravans are parked for the winter. Other than her mother, who is an alcoholic, Rosetta has no one else in the world, except for herself. But Rosetta is obstinate it seems, also when it comes to herself. She is neither a thankful supplicant, nor a clever, compliant service economy worker. She is her own worst enemy. Yet, the first scene already makes clear that she only wishes to have work. In this scene Rosetta learns that she will not be hired on after her probationary period at a bakery. The camera follows her unbridled anger on a rampage through the bakery, assaulting anything in her way as she destroys any chance of being hired there at some point in the future. The camera does not 'look' at Rosetta; it does not intrude on her emotional expression (there are no close-ups of her face). Instead the camera is tied to her physical motion: Rosetta gives new meaning to the 'steadicam', a stabilization device that allows the camera to be mounted on the back of an active performer.

As the film unfolds Rosetta never lets up on her search for work despite her poor communicative and emotional abilities. Finally, she betrays the one friendly offer she receives in order to get a job at a waffle stand.[6]

The specificity of the film lies in the way it brings the leading actress into the center without forcing her to speak (even by way of nonverbal expressions): loneliness without the feeling of loneliness and desperation without the feeling of desperation. In doing so the film leaves open whether or not Rosetta has these 'feelings' at her command or just does not reveal them. Accordingly, the film maintains a degree of discretion, not wishing to intrude. This non-acting gains a certain (philosophical) poignancy as the film itself is not distanced, but instead achieves a physical closeness to the main character, virtually becoming one with her bodily perspective. And this in a time when the exhibition of psychological states of mind has become the basic ingredient in television entertainment. This tension between intimacy and excluded internal state of mind is what makes the meaning of this filmic treatise on social exclusion so relevant.

Rosetta's lacking or concealed inwardness correlates to the important social demand regarding an individual's ability to act, that is, of individual agency. Agency grounds not only the liberal acceptance of market participants, it also plays a major role in the struggle, which is passed off as a cultural struggle, of the ruling economic powers of the USA, Europe, Asia and the Near East under the conditions of globalization. The ability to act and to make decisions, as the basis of democracy and civilization, is pitted against supposedly less developed societies, namely Islamic societies. In this setup, these abilities themselves are thus politicized. This problematic is often simply projected by society onto so-called socially weak milieus. Against this background Rosetta becomes paradigmatic.

She subverts this form of agency; she cannot 'make something' of herself, at least not in the way that economic liberalism demands and has portrayed as the American dream. The marginalized person (paradigmatically, the immigrant) takes hold of his/her chance and works him/herself from the social margin – from temporary job to temporary job

– to the center of society to finally end up rich. On the way to the top, a member of society, a human being, emerges from the indistinguishable mass of nobodies. This person has his/her career, makes plans and sends his/her children to school, all the attributes of civic life, which – at least in retrospect – seem to have been the historical goal of the labor movement since the 19th century.

But Rosetta does not move from margin to center; she lives on the thin line between inclusion and exclusion. When she leaves the campground to go into town, she takes off the rubber boots she needs in the slushy snow and puts on her city shoes. But also in town, at her job (before she loses it) and on her subsequent job search in 'ordinary life', the speechless rush, the anticipation of failure, never leaves her. This thin line not only separates inclusion and exclusion, margin and center; it is also a line of gravitation that determines all that attempts to move away from it. Rosetta fights not only for work, she is fighting to be someone. Perhaps she has internalized the prejudice that society has against people like her; namely, that without work she is nobody. She is 'disposable'.

Although the film is a number of years old, it still is the most accurate 'filming' of the conflict between inclusion and exclusion within the biopolitical regime in societies, which bind migration, work, unemployment, affluence and consumption tightly together. The story the film *Rosetta* tells is not the only point here. Of equal importance is the meaning of film – the meaning of visually processed life under biopolitical paradigms – and perhaps also that of leisure time, to which every element of the entertainment industry belongs.

The filmic gaze upon Rosetta's 'life' is marked completely by a situation, which can no longer be accounted for by a (bourgeois) ordering of her life within a work/leisure time dichotomy. The film brings this gaze to a head, making it unbearable, while also going beyond the overly simplistic commentary: if only Rosetta could find a job, everything would be alright.

Unemployment No Longer Defined through Work, but through Non-Work: Is that 'Life'?

The film provokes an understanding of 'freedom' from work that differs substantially from the way the 'social elite' (Beck) encounter unemployment. They do not want to recognize any solution other than the promise of work – no matter how difficult work is to obtain or even how utterly illusionary it is. Finally, only the image of superfluousness remains. In a critical turn this superfluousness becomes 'you will not be allowed to be unnecessary', but it in fact remains a stigma and an influential image. The implicit knowledge of the impossibility of full, 100% employment transforms the critical position into one that segregates. A crucial link is missing, which Beck has taken into account at other times, specifically, the acceptance of the notion of a work-free society. Only by accepting this premise, can the demand for work as a 'means of existence' be prevented from contributing, because of its unavailability, to the labeling of the so-called superfluous, and hence their being written off.

Hannah Arendt views the concept of superfluity as an essential moment in the fascist crimes characteristic of the 20th century, but for her (as it is also for Agamben), it does not end there: "This 'superfluousness' of human life, whose origins Arendt ascribes to the rise of imperialism, reemerges in those modern democracies that are consumed by automation," writes Julia Kristeva of Arendt.[7] Kristeva goes on to quote Arendt: "...we may say that radical evil has emerged in connection with a system in which all men have become equally superfluous."

In this way Arendt challenges the democracies of human rights, in which the question of the valuation of people through human rights is presumed solved. Human dignity shall be inviolable as defined by law, yet as Ulrike Meinhoff responded, it is violated. In fact state racism makes use of this violation everyday. It practices a clear distinction between those people, who as paradigmatic citizens must be saved – theoretically – at all costs (expensive medical treatments, whose cost well surpass that which the patient in question would ever be able to pay, or costly rescue missions of citizens in danger somewhere in the world) and those for whom other states are responsible. And if those states do not take care of those people, then no one will protect them. But then not only nationals of other states will be excluded from welfare, but those, who have already migrated, who have already completed a great part of their journey towards Europe and the life they dream of, are left completely without rights. And also native citizens, who fall beneath the poverty line, increasingly have less access to education, medical treatment, and job opportunities.

On the History of Work:
Work versus 'Actual Life' as a Form of Subjectivity

> Full employment was not just a worthwhile, as well as achievable, state, it was the highest reason for being. This society cast employment as a key – *the* key – to the resolution of the issues of, simultaneously, socially acceptable personal identity, secure social position, individual and collective survival, social order and systemic reproduction.[8]

That politics and the public persistently refuse to even imagine a society in which work is no longer primary reveals how extensively and fundamentally society is still defined – if not constituted – by the model of labor. Suddenly it is no longer simply a matter of how much work is socially necessary, but rather how essential work is socially. And this goes well beyond the question of whether or not a society without the primacy of work could survive economically; suddenly the question appears on the horizon, of what use is the population if it does not work? But at the present the questions posed are about the utilization of life altogether and who exploits what (or him/herself).

Historically work was never separate from the goal of earning a living or even of survival (for the proletarian classes), as in early forms of capitalism and in many new forms of work in cheap labor zones. In the industrialized states since World War II work has been connected to perceptions of leisure time, consumption, and self-realization, also for broad sections of the working class. Leisure time competed with work, and the protestant work ethic became outdated. Now work has the function of enabling a life that is entitled to meaning and pleasure. Up until the cultural crisis of 1968 entitlement to a certain living standard was tied to family planning. Since then this association of family planning and a living standard has shown itself to be increasingly dispensable as those who are single, in open or childless relationships, or homosexual relationships have been integrated into the logic of post-war society. Where in the past there existed a tendency to privilege evading work whenever possible (the German example would be the 'dropouts' of the 1970s and 1980s), a fundamental change has been undergone. Now, on the one hand many jobs have become more flexible and dispersed within the scope of leisure time, while on the other, work has become so scarce that its value has risen (in a socially aggressive environment).

The meaning of work cannot adequately ground 'society' when there is not enough work for all members of society. Today, in times of mass unemployment and the dismantling of the welfare state, it appears that work has only one value – its opposite – that is, vacation, leisure time and a 35-hour workweek. Yet over a very short span of time, a 180-degree turn has taken place. Until very recently a shorter workweek and early retirement were fought for, while today the retirement age has been raised again. It seems like we are witnessing a crisis of leisure time.[9] Thereby it would in no way be 'economically' reasonable if leisure time were reduced to increase production, since work rendered by one, must be consumed by others (otherwise it would not be offset). The qualified subjects of the new worlds of labor demand a high standard of living but do they not want to spend any 'time' on it.

Between the anti-globalization movement and the New York Times, Antonio Negri has become a symbol for the critique of the late capitalist labor society and the process of globalization accompanying it. In the mid-1990s Negri again took up the position that the Italian *Potere Operaio* (including Negri) had developed in the 1960s: the working class rebels against work. A phase of appropriation of the social means of production – industrial strikes, electrical power theft, student unrest – marked the period. By the 1990s this had transitioned into a phase of the post-revolutionary appropriation of social forces; 'general intellect' became the driving force of the late capitalist economy. While one may certainly doubt whether this new paradigm is as sweeping as Negri argues, less doubt prevails regarding the development of new forms of labor. These new forms of labor are distinguished by their integration of hedonistic elements – they do not exclude desire and pleasure from the working life, and hence appear to be the catalysts for a different relationship to leisure time or in a sense, to life 'time'.

In post-Operaist theoretical discourses, of course, these new forms of labor correlate with new subjectivities. These forms of labor are directly identified with new subjectivities, since the regime of immaterial labor is constituted through their utilization. For instance, if new workers are asked to work with enthusiasm, interpersonal sensitivity, existential zeal, and to be able to take pleasure in their work, then that implies that these qualities are lived out on the job and no longer in leisure time, by going to the movies, taking a walk, etc.

This spirit is exemplified by the self-image of young start-ups going public, transfiguring their initial public offers into veritable rock 'n' roll road shows. Another recent example would be that of the outgoing German chancellor Gerhard Schröder, who – anything but the highest civil 'servant' – had tears in his eyes as a military band serenaded him with Frank Sinatra's 'I Did It My Way' on the occasion of his farewell ceremony. Afterwards Schröder declared that, yes, he felt correctly perceived: a self-image as dissident pop, "Yes, I do it differently."

In post-Operaist discourses this falls under 'production of subjectivity'. Within the logic of Foucault and Judith Butler, for whom subject formation is a discursive effect, the subject proves to be malleable. Despite the obvious fact that the new regime of labor requires new subjectivities à la the 'I Did It My Way' humming Chancellor (what do Tony Blair or Putin hum?), the status of a theory of the subject remains obscure in these theories. In principle these theories treat the subject statistically or as a crowd, mass or group – in short, as multitude. But that does not shed much light upon the status of subject.

In fact, upon critical examination the entire post-Operaist discussion concerning subjectivity is notably weak if not undeveloped. On the one hand, the fact that a 'paradigm of control' has replaced the disciplinary is referred to again and again, and in this respect subjects must no longer be drilled. Instead subjects have internalized the demands of power and, without limit, have made these requirements their own. On the other hand, the question of what this means at the level of the subject is never posed, even though this subject is held to be so central to the new forms of the affective, communicative and social nature of immaterial labor. What does it mean, if this subject considers his/her productivity as his/her own? What about this sense of property? In a text devoted to affective labor, Michael Hardt entitles a section 'Production of Subjectivity' and then proceeds to leave out the word completely, speaking only once of 'collective subjectivities'.[10]

Perhaps one should add that Hardt and Negri already refer to a transcendence of individuality and subjectivity: as if the notion of subjectivity as no different from individuality were overcome, as though the way Hardt and Negri understand economic structure were already a reality; namely, that economic power requires chains, groups and networks of active elements and not building society saving banks, pension fund providers, family starters, multi-millionaires, car owners, etc. However, at best this is only one side of the coin. For even when companies create teams that work non-hierarchically or else when networks of entrepreneurs, by virtue of mutually complimenting each other, form gapless chains, familiar structures of individual motivation, 'me' culture, and clear-cut property relations are still alive in the individual links in the chain. These subjects are not dissolved, being instead very concentrated. And while perhaps they possess fewer automobiles and less property, they have stock options and, more importantly, command over themselves. They know they can fulfill their duties on the strength of their sensitivity, their spontaneity, and their motivation. In short, they have command over themselves. But to what does this practical reflexivity refer? What is its counterpart?

The case of biopolitical entrepreneurs is similar. The subject who appropriates his/her entire social sphere and who invents a structure of his/her own that is productive, Negri's 'biopolitical entrepreneur', is that not also political life? The owner of him/her 'self' and others? A master in the classic sense of the word? Is state racism not exactly this: the denial of someone's power to change his/her living conditions is not deemed scandalous only because these people are not considered to be full juridical subjects.

On the whole, to speak of transcending individual subjectivity, as for instance Deleuze and Guattari do in *A Thousand Plateaus* and *Anti-Oedipus*, is an interesting experiment. However, the implications for people who indeed still perceive themselves as empirical subjects must here be discussed. In other words, what would it mean to apply these theories to political economy, which is bound to the machinations of the market economy, which are also informed by the dynamic of the individual? The market economy is also marked by the pressure state racism exerts upon individual autonomy (since the border of statehood is held up relentlessly as a 'warning'), and in fact, by increased economic pressure of competition, the increased scarcity of work and the dismantling of the welfare state. And yet such a discussion is absent from all texts. This oversight explains how Hardt and Negri can switch so easily from a description of subjectivity as constituted by disciplinary forces to the liberation within the multitude.

In contrast it is more concrete to consider how the form of labor as social, communicative, affective labor impacts the relation of effort to compensation, which marks each individual life. An examination of the theories of subjectivity from this viewpoint is needed, as a theory of subjectivity should hold up when encountered with indexes of individuation and the time management of individuals.

For the worker in post-Fordism the changing nature of work generally does not represent an 'inconvenience', which requires compensation, say via the construction of family/leisure time or shopping/vacation/party. And even if the dichotomy of work (hardship) and its opposite – leisure time, self-realization and family (the justification for this hardship), was never a simple reality, it did supply a practical convention in the 1970s. Work and its compensation provided a kind of system within which to formulate the rationality of the subject. This rationality, or economy, provides a precise set by which to evaluate the neo-bourgeois subject: vacation, education, automobile, consumer goods, marriage and sexual prowess. This inherent patriarchal matrix has been modernized, but persists nonetheless. There is always a male owner (modernized: a potential female owner) of these goods and options for adventure. Althusser paradigmatically theorized this normalization of the individual. The citizen is constituted by the call, and s/he recognizes him/herself in turn in the calling of his/her name. The poststructuralist overcoming of this centrist model of the subject works on the epistemological level (no subject is really centered), but underestimates the centralizing forces that are still effective. A classic theory of the subject, such as Althusser's, for which interpellation or the call isolates or liberates the subject, can never completely characterize the conditions of contemporary subjectivity, yet it still remains appropriate to some extent.

In *La Monnaie Vivante* (*The Living Money*), written at the same time as Althusser's 'Ideology and Ideological State Apparatuses',[11] Pierre Klossowski develops a decentered concept of the subject, which nonetheless acknowledges the activities of a centripetal instance, a 'support', a carrier, a serving medium, in which the powers that contribute in total to the destabilization of the subject confront each other. Of particular interest is Klossowski's inclusion of other economic factors in this economy of the subject and, thus, economic relations of exchange. In contrast to Freudo-Marxism, which merely extends relations of exchange to that which, narrowly defined, is not exchanged economically (love, affection, sex), Klossowski here includes a figure of thought, a concept, namely that the subject itself becomes money. "What if," Klossowski asks, "rather than paying ourselves in money, we paid ourselves in pleasures? Or perhaps if we ourselves were the means of payment."[12]

Here much more is pointed to than within the ideology of market economy, in which the consumer sovereignly decides how to spend his/her money. Klossowski goes beyond this market ideology and also explains more than post-Marxist theories of flows, which effect each other there, where there once were subjects. Most certainly informed by Nietzsche's philosophy of forces, Klossowski consistently ties them back to a budget, that of the subject. Therein the stability of the self is a struggle that is waged against that which seeks to undermine it: affects, moods, desires, distractions, instinctive impulses, coincidences. Klossowski's conception raises the awareness of the addressed self, turns it into a stage that does not just have to be constructed. It becomes a multi-dimensional membrane, a force field on which a fundamentally mercantile character expresses itself. But this mercantile character here implies price- and uselessness, exhaustion and work, so the economy abandons any narrow definition and coincides with life in its totality.

In *La Monnaie Vivante* Klossowski sketches a (impossible) scenario that negotiates an ability to take command over one's own person, in that monetary and mercantile micro-mechanisms take hold. Who owns him/herself, or someone else? Who can give someone something or take something away from someone? Here the body, in Arendt's terms attributed to the 'zoe', to pure life, is no longer the 'paradigm' of private property (Kristeva), and it is no longer that, as Arendt determined: "which one, not even with the best will in the world, cannot own commonly or share with another."[13] Instead the body is imagined as a means of payment. The instrumentality of the market is questioned, which thus makes the dichotomy of subjectivity/one's-own-body ironic.

Qualified life and the stage of the subject

A decisive gain from Klossowski's theory is not the introduction of relations of exchange into the arena of the subject, but the questioning of all strictly economic categories within an intrasubjective economy; namely, the critique of purposefulness, use value, price and pricelessness. His double figure is the following:

1. What would happen if we paid each other not with surrogates, but with satisfaction itself and that not just in a restricted sense, referring to scissors or soap, to simple use values, but one that refers to complicated use values as the more advanced pleasures, such as the sexual ones?

2. Would it follow from there that we ourselves would become money?

Klossowski's successful short-circuit consists of choosing the individual economy of motion of the subject as a starting point for micro- and macro-economic considerations. In contrast, traditional economics pretends to stand outside of the subject, although it is understood that without (individualized) needs, there would be no economy. But the condition *sine qua non* of economics is the whole economy itself and not just its precondition. The entire categories of price, use value, and also of pricelessness become fragile when the purposefulness of actions is questioned – when economy goes beyond whether or not any random product can be produced and sold so that it yields a profit.

Post-Fordism, the so-called 'new economy' consists then in the unfolding of this subjective economy in the macro-economy in which life must be productive. It then can be interpreted as an attempt to understand this tension, between a population not needed for production and the necessity of a population of active consumers, as a crisis. Through the recognition of the crisis in this tension, its escalation may be avoided, and instead the perpetuation of capitalistic value production insured. The 'new' forms of labor, which blur the divisions between leisure time and work, between production, reproduction and consumption, have replaced the old division of production-oriented work and purposeless consumption (i.e. pleasure). Through the immediacy of the act of production, work becomes its own purpose (a phenomenon formerly reserved for artwork). In this way however, the logic of bourgeois life is at risk as it lies in the very movement from means towards ends. Thus the new type of workers lack many characteristics that once defined workers – security, consumption, and meaning.

But what guarantees this 'inside' of society, which qualifies qualified life today? How can an economy be described, which – as has been repeatedly established – utilizes one's entire life? And why is bare life excluded from it with such efficiency?

Holding on to the central paradigm of work may in this sense be seen as a desperate attempt of the individual to imagine him/herself as one of the qualified. And this is perhaps also because the crisis of this imaginary space of bourgeois-capitalist life has a history, which began at least with the social movements, if simultaneously alongside their development, and was already played out in Vormärz (eve of the 1848 German Revolution) and in the Romantic period.

Access to the phantasm of work as a form that generates money that can later be exchanged as one freely chooses, in order to give a topological (a place to live) and temporal (security in the near future) form to an individual interior, becomes impossible in Klossowski's conceptualization. The classical perception of market and money is recognizable as an attempt to give the unstable terrain of subjectivity a fixed setting. The destabilization of the 'I' is countered to that extent through stabilization.

Klossowski's concept shows that the fluctuations and ambivalences of the ability to determine one's own life and its appropriation create a terrain that is essential for the individual economies. This term 'individual economy', derived from Klossowski, definitely can be seen as constitutive for individuation and may be compared with Althusser's fundamental claim to describe the constitution of the economic subject. The extensive appropriation of the right to self-determination enforced by the state by means of deportation camps and residency requirements is an extremely violent invasion in the sensitive fabric of individuation. According to Giorgio Agamben, the state's intervention does not begin when individuals are robbed of their autonomy, their self-determination (as in camps), but even earlier: the very possibility of the isolation of a pure life which has been reduced to pure existence constitutes sovereign power.

Its counterpart for Agamben is the so-called qualified, political life, "for which what is at stake in its way of living is living itself"[14] (something not made possible for the excluded). This opposition explains Agamben's provocation, according to which life for a person living in a deportation camp is analogous to that of a person in a coma, as both are unable to act.

Non-Subject and its Life: Biopolitical Exclusion from the Subject Position
Rosetta is excluded from access to qualified life and to the micro-economy. Rosetta is not shown as someone who wants to work in order to have money: she wants a connection to a life of her own, or even just to a life.

Rosetta is not a subject who wants compensation for work in her life as for her work appears to be a scarce commodity in itself and is thus in itself valuable. But Rosetta is not in a position where she can reflect upon her efforts. For the time being she has left behind – in film or as film – this dichotomy. Her relationship to work destroys any sort of 'I' that could formulate itself as a difference to the demands of the drive to work. Rosetta is not a bourgeois subject; in other words, interpellation (in Althusser's sense) has not been successful.

As a subject Rosetta has nothing that allows her to say, "Stop, what do I need to do to achieve my goal in the long term?" The film does not put any inner life at Rosetta's disposal: No conversation with herself, no – even visually communicated – internal monologue, no reflection. In this way the film denies its main character the typical hallmark of art-house films – specifically, the sensitivity of the main character with which the audience identifies. Rosetta remains as silent as otherwise only a person as other, as not-myself, can remain. In this way the film positions its main character as an emblematic excluded person, between a fundamental pull towards subjectification and its denial – through (state) racism. An asymmetry between subjectivity (as one's relationship to one's self) and all 'others' can be understood as the basis for all subjectifications. Still, intersubjectivity consists of the presumption that the others possess that quality of subjectivity, which cannot be 'seen' directly. That this subjectivity does not function without some conflicts and inconsistencies has been discussed in diverse theories of subjectivity from Sartre to Lacan or Levinas.

Of course, empirically there is no such being without subjectivity, or, at least, it is not connected to migration. On the contrary the act of migration is already a project, a result of organization and discipline, of various aspects of the subject's relationship to his/her self. Nonetheless, this lack of subjectivity can be represented easily in film. The entire history of film is haunted by this subjectless other – humans who are no longer themselves: body snatchers, automatons, monsters, the dead, the undead.

From this perspective it is relevant that the representation of excluded migrants remains trapped in an aporia. This representation can only ever switch between a representation of the migrant as subject – as a person in terms of civic rights, who actually suffers under the current revocation of his/her civic rights – a revocation that can only be imposed on him/her from the outside – and another representation, in which migrants are no more than objects, figures passing though the picture. In this case the film can only affirm, even if it takes a critical stance, that which it intends to denounce; namely, that these people are 'bare', deprived of any meaning that their internal emotional life could possess. They have lost possession of their bodies.

Biopolitics – as Film – as Visual Consumption

Rosetta, the film, fuses with the physicality of the struggle. The camera is glued to Rosetta and becomes the motive force of the main character. Only in fragments does her body become an object of the gaze. Its breathlessness, its non-reflexivity is not shown, but reproduced.

The film does not simply show the fusion of vital energy and the work regime in the state of its dissolution, but attempts to abandon mere exhibition, to become its own subject matter. As in the action genre, the film strives to become energy, adrenalin, or fear. Quoting Douglas Sirk, Fassbinder insisted that motion pictures are not made about blood, love, and so forth, but *with* blood and love.

Thus the film modifies an elementary paradigm of film: we watch a person. As viewers we watch a person, finding ourselves in the familiar regime of everyday life in which we also observe people – strangers as well as those with whom we are acquainted. A circumstance whose intensification thanks to modern means of transportation and urbanity increased alienation, as Benjamin wrote. But in film the camera, which represents the viewer, does not exist. The absence of the viewer from this arrangement makes possible what is referred to in classical film theory as 'identification'. Whatever the exact requirements for identification are,[15] a contradictory intimacy, a deviation from the everyday relationship to the self is contained in film. This relationship to self consists basically in the ability to be alone with oneself, to be subject and object for oneself. Film fundamentally transforms this relationship to 'self', which is spatialized in this (imaginary) self-conception: in film a person is seen from the outside in a way one could never observe oneself, but one is this person in so far as one is alone with him/her, as there is no one else present. To be alone with someone in a space where only one person is present is the aporia of film. This is the type of internal mental space, which falls into one with the bourgeois subject. This space is not given to Rosetta. She is alone, but not with herself.

Yet, the relationship between film and spectator is by no means cognitive or paradigmatic. The play between subject and screen or monitor acquires its political dimension because, on the one hand, film (and visual production in general) is a central element of the entertainment industry (whose capacity for production is the last remaining growth factor increasing the GNP). On the other hand, it is important for the way of life in the industrialized states, but it is also exported globally via visual imagination. Thus it represents the fundamental ingredient of 'desirable' life, of the living standard, of the telos of labor and effort. It is the ultimate good of the production of goods, which are no longer objects, but time, and their only remaining use value would be to be 'good for amusement', to be a good 'way of killing time' (as one said in the 1970s), to be good for contributing to recuperation (i.e. to the reproduction of the workforce, if the consumers were workers). A third factor strengthens the special place visual products inhabit in the macro-economy, as well as in the micro-economy of most individuals in consumer societies. Visual production and consumption can only exist if these images and trends in fashion – the novelty-factor – are socially produced. That does not only apply to the concrete production of films, for example, but also to the consumer's labor, to show openness vis-à-vis those machines of difference, to be able to understand novelty, or respectively to develop curiosity.

To put it differently: the investment of one's own life in visual production consists in the triangle of the lifetime the producer has invested (which is more than just work time, but also affective labor),[16] of the lifetime the consumer has invested and not least of visual production's importance as a cipher of leisure time, that is, compensation for the exertions of life (where appropriate: work).

One must confront these thoughts with the 1970s critique of consumption, with the 'domination of life by spectacle' (Debord) or the culture industry (Adorno/Horkheimer), which as it were, induces false needs and which makes people believe through 'structures of delusion' that industrial leisure time is the meaning of life, which in reality, according to that critique, it is not. Klossowski had already noted: "Anathemas have been hurled since the middle of the last century against the industrial civilization in the name of emotional life." But under this "pretext of denunciation" considerable moral power is attributed to the industry's means of production.[17]

This overestimation of the culture industry makes clear the extent to which consumer goods are part of life and leisure time, and accordingly transcend the distinction of work and leisure.[18] If one subtracts the preconception that products of the entertainment industry are 'alienated', as is their reception (a Disney film is a waste of time or mind numbing, while reading a fairy tale aloud is not), then all assets or liabilities of the culture industry become elements of life in the industrialized states – not more and not less. Interesting from this perspective are clichés of cultural critique, such as apathy, wasted time, and vegetating as a 'couch potato'. At the same time furnishings such as a television set, refrigerator, stereo system (in the 1970s) and Dolby Surround Sound home theatre, are the epitome of a cozy home, the secure basis of the bourgeois lifestyle. This interior is still the ideal image of affluent societies, which are in the process of dissolution.

The critique of culture finds its own confirmation in the fact that the 'couch potatoes' have nothing better to do than, spend their alienated lives, via visual consumption, watching other people's lives – lives in which something happens – in which there is action, experience, adventure, in short: everything that a life without experience can no longer offer.

Today it is easy for us to acknowledge that youths addicted to consumption do not automatically get bogged down in passivity. Instead they may develop profit-driven business ventures out of sheer enthusiasm for goods or savvy *à la* Adbuster. In this way, as all producers and consumers, they are busy with the politicized question of what life is. A question, it is said, but actually a force field, and the drawing and shifting of boundaries makes those forces effective.

APPENDIX

Biopolitics – A Discourse

Several current types of discourse relate to biopolitics, but they actually differ quite a bit. Amongst them is Deleuze's paradigm of control, which differs from the historically preceding paradigm of disciplinarity. Society is not controlled, it controls itself. Governmentality, as developed by Lemke, Bröckling and Krassmann, at this point follows the same direction. Here too, the regime of a mentality of being governed is instilled into the subjects and 'steers' them from within. What Foucault analyzed from the context of Christian pastoral ethics and liberalism, is here extended to the conditions of neoliberalism. With the term 'immaterial labor', post-Operaists like Antonio Negri and Maurizio Lazzarato have taken on a central term of neoliberal economic theory and developed it, following diverse political currents arising since the 1960s. Their idea of labor, which no longer orients itself by the production paradigm of the classical factory, responds to the feminist accomplishment that acknowledged reproduction as a socially necessary labor (which is also production), but also to conceptualizations like those developed by Situationists or other avant-gardes, whereby the constitution of a product of reception needs a co-producer to succeed. In a similar sense, artworks of the avant-garde don't make sense by the materialization of the work but by the labor of the museum's visitor, the work of the TV-program's direction cannot be isolated from the labor of the consumer who accepts or rejects the novel formats. Both cases require people who will view the program. With this new notion of labor, affective labor, social labor and the labor of love all become part of the concept of production. For Hardt and Negri this is not only about the effects of this adjustment in relation to production, but also about the effects on power and governance. While Foucault's theory of power relocates it in institutions and social acts, thereby decentralizing it and thus making it difficult to ask the question about power and resistance, Hardt and Negri ontologize what falls under the more recent total annexation of capital, namely life itself, in its totality, as the actual core of the annexed. But the annexation is what it 'eats' or consumes. Power, in the times of biopower, consists entirely of what it subjugates, but it is this very power that the subjugated then 'has'.

Neither the scientific-rational abstraction nor the capitalist-false conception can be made responsible as agents for social development. The actually active, to put it oddly, is life, or 'more precisely', the multitude, or life in its communicative, non-subjective, non-biological, productive energy.

This account is 'unjust' or perhaps even academic, because it cuts Hardt and Negri's book off from its political connection. It is not limited to contemplating the primacy of chicken or egg in a philosophical way, but to understand the primacy of the impelling power of the multitude as a heuristic operation. And this is with sound philosophical reasons, because the question of what is primary is a historical and not a philosophical one, which means that the question itself must first appear. And where the historical perspective on History (at least that of capitalism) has difficulty deciding the contest between liberation/struggle and its monopolization, the future stays open to the extent that the essentialism of any form of historic determinism is mistrusted and thus approached skeptically.

It is only in relation to this debate that Giorgio Agamben's theory can be discussed here. Indeed, he is concerned with the connection of power (sovereignty) and life, but he chooses a completely different focus, which leads him to different conclusions. For him there is no ultimate integration of the entire life of individuals, precisely because he finds instead a separation. Central to his theory is power's compartmentalization of life. Power is exercised to the extent that it separates forms of life from a (pure) life that is not allowed to take form. Here Agamben makes use of different examples, of which I choose two, because they indicate the range of his theory. Migrants in camps are radically cut off from their potential to lead or develop a qualified life. They cannot do anything but wait/survive. They are not enemies of the State, who are to be killed; they are simply abandoned – not allowed. Here they are not just excluded, but, with Agamben, included as excluded. For Agamben this operates under the same paradigm as the inclusive exclusion of bare life in coma patients. This separation can happen in 'the citizen' as well, as in the case of non-admission to 'citizenship'. Therefore migration is something essentially different for Hardt and Negri, who recognize in it an element that is productive for power. For Agamben, it is a constitutive element of power but decidedly not a productive element in Hardt and Negri's sense. Agamben also sees a functionality, namely for the constitution of absolute sovereignty also in so-called human rights regimes.

If one looks at this discussion from the perspective of the control paradigm, that is from the demand on individuals to be intensive, make sense and be systematic, then according to Agamben's terminology this would mean that governance consists in connecting with forms of life. The paradigm of control as well as the theory of governmentality acts on the assumption that the obligation of individuals to a kind of 'dignified' life is the essence of the new government. The theory of immaterial labor is more in line with economical theories, but shares the assumption of a necessity for turning individuals into 'biopolitical entrepreneurs', namely into entrepreneurs of one's own life, in all its parameters. Agamben's camp paradigm, by contrast, speaks of life that is excluded, not admitted to this 'dignified' life and not directly about this life with dignity, this form of life.

Agamben's theory says, bare life is excluded from its opposite, the political life, which he defines as the life, which is concerned with the good life, with its own happiness. And this is, in its current form, the world citizen, the individual of liberalism. What is excluded is the bare life of the other (migrants for instance) or one's own life (like the biological body, which keeps on existing in a coma, like that which catapults one into illness or one should put it better: that by which one falls) which brings one into the state in which the pragmatic logic of the political is not valid anymore, the logic of what is useful to one other than pure (bare) survival.

At this point Agamben introduces a theoretical construction, whose main features are well established, but which he uses in a specific way, namely the inclusive exclusion. Agamben only presents this figure at this point and doesn't elaborate upon it further. What does it mean for qualified life that bare life is included as excluded in it? Does it mean that bourgeois life or so-called normality is haunted by the fact that bare life is the suppressed; that this ambivalence of the bourgeoisie is – its uncanny, or its incontinence – the absent presence, the blind spot of bourgeois self-construction, the inescapability of ideology? But we have seen all of this before and thus I believe that when one is interested in Agamben's theory, it is from this point that one has to work.

Agamben does not pursue this question; he investigates something else, namely sovereignty, power. But what does this mean for the questions raised here? Power is, he says, with the beginning of modernity, connected to the inclusive exclusion of bare life. Hereby, we are bound to bare life as included members, as acknowledged citizens, as actors in our life bound to the bare life. But why? And does this really hit the mark? Agamben's theory states here that differentiation itself implies the generation of sovereignty. But does Agamben not re-write Althusser's theory on ideology, as the interpellation in Althusser is, in a way, the constitution of qualified life (the status of the subject). To be excluded from the status of subject, thus not to be interpellated, therefore means bare life, a possibility which Althusser's master text does not foresee. But Agamben's theory of ideology revision – were one to follow this analogy of the theories of biopolitics and ideology – would write something additional into the status of the subject, namely that bare life separates from itself through language and it remains active in this separation.

Agamben takes up sovereignty because for him, bare life is connected to sovereignty while the qualified life is not. If one tries to construct the relationship of bare to political/qualified life from his text, one must try to describe in exactly which way qualified life is connected to sovereignty. How does the bourgeois individual relate to the state? Or perhaps sovereignty is not always embodied by the state, but in other 'powers', in the mountains, the sea, airplanes. What connects the individual to the state? Or what connects the individual with him/herself via the state? Similarly, it relates to Althusser again, but the self-constitution here considerably limits what is being sought-after, as sovereignty then becomes something inseparable from the individual.

What concrete meaning does sovereignty have for the head of purchasing or the head of marketing? How is this meaning (theoretically) to be constructed? Do they need (state) power? This question is not so easy to answer, because it touches on the core political belief of liberalism, socialism, etc. It is obvious anyhow, that the existence of sovereignty, not relative power, is what structures the terrain upon which meaning and purpose are oriented. To lead a successful life is unthinkable without order. Why not otherwise take the most direct way (fraud, murder, etc.) to one's own goals. All the *relative* joy (money, security, love, intensity, beauty, health, family, sex, entertainment) has meaning only in relationship to sovereignty. But then the term sovereignty would not primarily mean governmental power, but contingency, finitude, violence – violence as power and as magnitude. And this is organized by state power, if only through representation. It can be represented by other powers or even manage without these powers. If a state power democratically organizes these forces, it gives the impression that random forces are out of its reach. And the state then *compensates* for the negative consequences of these forces. In a totalitarian state on the other hand, sovereign power *competes* with the so-called natural factors (catastrophes) by directly forming contingency as finitude and violence.

Translated from the German by Christine Wolfe

Notes:

1. *Tagesthemen* television news programme, November 23, 2005.

2. *Süddeutsche Zeitung*, November 15, 2005.

3. Zygmunt Bauman, *Verworfenes Leben* [*Wasted Lives. Modernity and its Outcasts*], Hamburg: 2005, 21.

4. That year one spoke in Belgium of a '*Loi Rosetta*'.

5. Interview in *artificial eye*: http://www.artificial-eye.com/video/ART184/inter.html.

6. "Before falling asleep, Rosetta utters in voice-over (even as we see her on screen) the following mantra of reassurance, words that at the same time painfully attest to the degree of her alienation from a self that she has nearly objectified in an effort to steel her humanity against the world's cruel indifference: 'Your name is Rosetta. My name is Rosetta. You've found a job. I've found a job. You have a friend. I have a friend. You have a normal life. I have a normal life. You won't fall into the rut. I won't fall into the rut.' To indicate the relative normality that Rosetta has achieved, the Dardennes film most of this scene at Riquet's apartment in a static, becalming long take, with the camera in medium shot. Much of the rest of Rosetta, by contrast, is photographed with a hand-held camera that remains disorientingly close to the heroine as she dashes about, with a twofold effect. On the one hand, the restless, uneven camerawork of Alain Marcoen (who was also the director of cinematography for La Promesse) creates the visual equivalent of the instability and uncertainty in Rosetta's life; on the other hand, the handheld camera seems to dog Rosetta with an angry intensity that matches her own, as it were her doppelganger-cum-guardian angel or, antithetically, the devil of destiny in disguise." From Bert Cardullo, 'Rosetta Stone: A Consideration of the Dardenne Brothers' Rosetta', *Journal of Religion and Film*, Vol. 6 No. 1, April 2002.

7. Julia Kristeva, *Das weibliche Genie Hannah Arendt* [*Female Genius: Hannah Arendt*], Berlin, 2001, 30.

8. Zygmunt Bauman, *Verworfenes Leben*, 18.

9. The lives of a large part of the world's population are treated as though they were redundant. One has only to think of working conditions in the global periphery, where workers barely have time to recuperate from work, much less to lead their own lives in any form. Clearly no value is placed on the 'real' lives of these people. But this is a result of racist divisions of the world's population, rather than the increasing redundancy of the category of consumption, etc.

10. "In the production and reproduction of affects, in those networks of culture and communication, collective subjectivities are produced and sociality is produced – even if those subjectivities and that sociality are directly exploitable by capital. This is where we can realize the enormous potential in affective labor." Michael Hardt, 'Affektive Labor', in Marion von Osten (Ed.), *Norm der Abweichung*, Vienna/New York, 2003, 220.

11. Louis Althusser, 'Ideologie und ideologische Staatsapparate' [Ideology and Ideological State Apparatuses], Hamburg/Berlin 1977.

12. Pierre Klossowski, *La Monnaie Vivante* [*The Living Money*], Paris, 1994.

13. Hannah Arendt, *Vita activa oder Vom tätigen Leben* [*The Human Condition*], Munich: Piper, 2005, 132.

14. Giorgio Agamben, *Means without End: Notes on Politics*, Minneapolis: University of Minnesota Press, 2000, 4.

15. While Laura Mulvey's extremely influential feminist film theory of the 1970s presumed that the viewer identified with the omnipotent perpetrator, she herself later modifies this position. Authors like Linda Williams inverted this presumption, arguing that

identification lies with the passive object, the victim (see Nabakovski, *Frauen in der Kunst*, Frankfurt, 1976, Linda Williams, *Hard Core*, Frankfurt, 1995, Steven Shaviro, *The Cinematic Body,* Minnesota, 1993).

16. Compare Maurizio Lazzarato, *Videophilosophie*, Berlin: b_books, 2002, 132.

17. Pierre Klossowski, *La Monnaie Vivante* [*The Living Money*], 9.

18. Visual consumption (being influenced by television, advertising or going to the movies) leads to the center of qualified life for many reasons that are not easy to uncover and distinguish. Visual consumption, unlike other forms of consumption, requires time or rather it consists in spending time. Beyond that it is tied substantially to the exertion of wealth. Although it works in ways that must be specified, since, interestingly, visual consumption is possibly the most widely distributed form of goods. Television is available even to those without means. Advertising is distributed free anyhow, and even the movies are affordable, since they can be rented from video stores and copied illegally. Visual consumption is the most practical answer to the question of why one lives (or works). This, however, presumes that there is a question regarding the possibility of consumption itself becoming work.

It is now obvious, although perhaps not very enlightening, to locate the parameters of biopolitical regulation within visual consumption. These parameters are hallucinated normal life, violence, sex effects, the face, the body as product and death. But what does it mean to reproduce these parameters visually? The intuitive explanation would be to assume that this is just what interests people. But one need not contradict this assumption, to nonetheless want to know more about it, such as why these things maintain such a constant and high presence. The traditional answer is: we are seduced by it and, therefore, miss out on life. But what does it mean, beyond moralistic speculation about the 'actual'?

A biopolitical discussion of visual consumption would have to be interested in the inclusionary exclusion of bare life; visual consumption as a technical apparatus through which the position of the subject within the field of sovereignty (i.e. factuality of the world) and bare life are acted out. The political does not only consist in the isolation of bare life, as Agamben suggests, but also in the interpretation of sovereign power.

Governmentality and Self-Precarization:
On the normalization of cultural producers

by Isabell Lorey

For some of us, as cultural producers the idea of a permanent job in an institution is something that we do not even consider, or if so, for a few years at most. Afterward, we want something different. Hasn't the idea always been about not being forced to commit oneself to one thing, one classical job definition, which ignores so many aspects; about not selling out and consequently being compelled to give up the many activities that one feels strongly about? Wasn't it important to not adapt to the constraints of an institution, to save the time and energy to be able to do the creative and perhaps political projects that one really has an interest in? Wasn't a more or less well-paying job gladly taken for a certain period of time, when the opportunity arose, to then be able to leave again when it no longer fit? Then there would at least be a bit of money there to carry out the next meaningful project, which would probably be poorly paid, but supposedly more satisfying.

Crucial for the attitude suggested here is the belief that one has chosen his or her own living and working situations and that these can be arranged relatively freely and autonomously. Actually, the uncertainties, the lack of continuities under the given social conditions, are also consciously chosen to a great extent. Yet the following is concerned not with the questions, 'When did I really decide freely?' or 'When do I act autonomously?' but is concerned instead with the ways in which ideas of autonomy and freedom are constitutively connected with hegemonic modes of subjectivation in Western capitalist societies. The focus of this text is accordingly on the extent to which 'self-chosen' precarization contributes to producing the conditions for being able to become an active part of neoliberal political and economic relations.

No general statements about cultural producers, or all of those currently in a situation that has been made precarious, can be derived from this perspective. However, what becomes apparent when problematizing this 'self-chosen' precarization, are the historical lines of force of modern bourgeois subjectivation, which are imperceptibly hegemonic, normalizing, and which can possibly block resistance.

To demonstrate the genealogy of these lines of force, I will first turn to Michel Foucault's concepts of 'governmentality' and 'biopolitics'. We will not focus on the breaks and rifts in the lines of bourgeois subjectivation, but instead, on their structural and transformative continuities, including the entanglement in governmental techniques of modern Western societies to this day. What ideas of sovereignty arise in these modern, governmental *dispositifs*? What lines of force, i.e., what continuities, self-evidences, and normalizations can be drawn to what and how we think and feel as 'self-chosen' cultural producers that have been made precarious in neoliberal conditions, how we are in the world, and more specifically in so-called dissident practices? Do cultural producers who are in a precarious state embody a 'new' governmental normality through certain self-relations and ideas of sovereignty?

With the genealogy of the lines of force of bourgeois subjectivation, in the course of the text I will differentiate between precarization as deviance, and therefore as a contradiction of *liberal* governmentality, on the one hand, and as a hegemonic function of *neoliberal* governmentality on the other, to then finally clarify the relationship between the two based on the example of the 'free' decision for precarious living and working.

Biopolitical governmentality

With the term 'governmentality', Michel Foucault defined the structural entanglement of the government of a State and the techniques of self-government in Western societies. This involvement between State and population as subjects is not a timeless constant. That which had been developing since the 16th century first took root in the 18th century: a new government technique, more precisely, the lines of force of modern government techniques up to this day. The traditional sovereign, for whom Foucault introduces the character from Machiavelli's *The Prince* from the 16th century as a prototype, and Hobbes' contract-based voluntary community of subordinates from the 17th century, were not yet concerned with ruling 'the people' for the sake of their welfare, but instead, they were primarily interested in dominating them for the welfare of the sovereign. It was in the course of the 18th century, when liberalism and the bourgeoisie became hegemonic, that the population first entered the focus of power and along with it, a governing that was oriented to the life of 'the people' and the making of that life better. The power of the State no longer depended solely on the size of a territory or the mercantile, authoritative regulation of subordinates, but instead, on the 'happiness' of the population, on their life and a steady improvement of that life.

In the course of the 18th century, governing methods continued to transform toward a political economy of liberalism: self-imposed limitations on government for the benefit of a free market on the one hand, and on the other, a population of subjects that were bound to economic paradigms in their thought and behavior. These subjects were not subjugated simply by means of obedience, but became governable in that, on the whole, "their life expectancy, their health, and their courses of behavior were involved in complex and entangled relationships with these economic processes."[1] Liberal modes of government presented the basic structure for modern governmentality, which has always been biopolitical. Or, in other words: liberalism was the economic and political framework of biopolitics and, equally, "an indispensable element in the development of capitalism."[2]

The strength and wealth of a state at the end of the 18th century depended ever more greatly on the health of its population. In a bourgeois liberal context, a government policy oriented towards this means, to this day, establishing and producing normality and then securing it. For that, a great deal of data is necessary; statistics are produced, probabilities of birth rates and death rates are calculated, frequencies of diseases, living conditions, means of nutrition, etc. Yet that does not suffice. In order to manufacture a population's health standard, and to maximize it, these bio-productive, life-supporting biopolitical government methods also require the active participation of every individual, which means their self-governing.

Foucault writes in *The History of Sexuality*:

> Western man was gradually *learning* what it meant to be a living species in a living world, to have a body, conditions of existence, probabilities of life, an individual and collective welfare, forces that could be modified, and a space in which they could be distributed in an optimal manner.[3]

Here, Foucault describes two things that I consider essential: the modern individual must first learn how to have a body that is dependent on certain existential conditions, and, second, he or she must learn to develop a reltion-ship with his or her 'self' that is creative and productive, a relationship in which it is possible to fashion his or her 'own' body, 'own' life, 'own' self. Philipp Sarasin shows the emergence, in the context of the Western hygiene discourse of the waning 18th century and early 19th century, of "the belief that the individual was largely capable of determining its health, illness, or even the time of death."[4] This idea of the ability to shape and fashion one's self never arose independently of governmental *dispositifs*.

In the context of liberal governmental technologies of the self, the attribute 'own' always signifies "possessive individualism."[5] Initially however, self-relations oriented on the imagination of one's 'own', were only applicable to the bourgeoisie, then gradually towards the end of the 19th century their applicability was extended to the entire population. At issue here is not the legal status of a subject, but the structural conditions of normalizing societies: one must be capable of managing oneself, recognizing oneself as subject to a sexuality, and of learning to have a body that remains healthy through attentiveness (nutrition, hygiene, living) and that can become sick through inattentiveness. In this sense, the entire population must become biopolitical subjects.[6]

With reference to wage workers, such imaginary self-relations mean that one's own body, constituted as the property of the self, becomes an 'own' body that one must sell as labor power. Also in this respect, the modern, 'free' individual is compelled to co-produce him- or herself through such powerful self-relations, that the individual can sell his or her labor power well, in order to live a life that steadily improves.

Therefore, in modern societies, the "art of governing" – which was another name given by Foucault for governmentality[7] – does not primarily consist of being repressive, but instead, of 'inwardly held' self-discipline and self-control. It is the analysis of an order that is not only forced upon people, bodies, and things, but in which they are simultaneously an active part. At the center of the problem of government ruling techniques is not the question of regulating autonomous, free subjects, but instead, of regulating the relations through which so-called autonomous and free subjects are first constituted as such.

Already in the second half of the 17th century, John Locke who, according to Karl Marx, "demonstrated that the bourgeois way of thinking is the normal human way of thinking,"[8] wrote in *The Two Treatises of Government*, that man is "master of himself, and proprietor of his own person, and the actions or labor of it."[9] At the beginning of the modern era, property acquired a supposed "anthropological meaning"[10] for both the bourgeois man, as a prerequisite for his formal freedom as a citizen, as well as for the worker, who owns his own labor power and must sell it, freely, as wage labor. It seemed to be the prerequisite by which the individual could become independent and free from the traditional system of subordination and security. With a biopolitical governmentality perspective, the meaning of property, however, surpasses the limited levels of citizenship, capital, and wage labor and is, in fact, to be understood as something entirely general. For in a biopolitical *dispositif*, relations of bodily ownership apply not only to citizens or workers, but to the entire population as governmental self-governing. The modern person is, accordingly, constituted through possessive individualistic self-relations, which are fundamental for historically specific ideas of autonomy and freedom. Structurally, modern self-relations are based – also beyond an economic interpellation – on a relation to one's own body as a means of production.

In this broad sense of economy and biopolitics, the lines of the labor entrepreneur, "the entrepreneur of one's self"[11] as a mode of subjectivation, reach back to the beginnings of modern liberal societies and are not an entirely neoliberal phenomenon. This type of genealogy of course skips over the era of the social, the welfare state since the end of the 19th century, and ties together the, for the most part compulsively constituting, self-entrepreneurs in the current reconstruction and deconstruction of the social/welfare state, with fundamental liberal governmental methods of subjectivation since the end of the 18th century. With the injunction to be responsible for one's self, something that had already failed in the 19th century seems to be repeating itself now, namely, the primacy of property and the construction of security associated with it. Property was introduced in the early stages of bourgeois rule as a form of protection against the incalculability of social existence, as security against vulnerability in a secularized society and the domination of the princes and kings. Ultimately this applied to only a limited few, and at the end of the 19th century the nation state had to guarantee social security for many. However, it does not automatically follow from this that today the State must once again take on a more comprehensive social function of protection and security.[12] For this would quickly reproduce the utterly flexible, Western nation state nexus of freedom and security with similar structural inclusions and exclusions, rather than break through it.

Normalized free subjects
In biopolitical governmental societies, the constitution of the 'normal'

is always also woven in with the hegemonic. With the demand for an orientation around the normal – which could be bourgeois, heterosexual, Christian, white male, white female, national – in the course of the modern era, it was necessary to develop the perspective of controlling one's own body, one's own life, by regulating and thus managing the self. The normal is not identical with the norm, but it can take on its function. Normality is, however, never anything external, for we are the ones who guarantee it and reproduce it through alterations. Accordingly, we govern ourselves in the *dispositif* of governmentality, biopolitics, and capitalism in that we normalize ourselves. If this is successful – and it usually is – power and certain relations of domination are barely perceptible, and extremely difficult to reflect upon, because we take part in their production, as it were, in the ways we relate to ourselves, and own our bodies. The normalizing society and the subjectivation taking place within it are historical effects of a power technology directed at life. The normalized subject itself is, once again, a historical construct in an ensemble of knowledge forms, technologies, and institutions. This ensemble is aimed at the individual body as well as at the life of the population as a whole. Normalization is lived through everyday practices that are perceived as self-evident and natural.

Additionally, the normal is naturalized with the effect of actuality, of authenticity. We thus believe, for example, that the effect of power relations is the essence of our self, our truth, our own actual core, the origin of our being. This normalizing self-governing is based on an imagined coherence, uniformity and wholeness, which can be traced back to the construction of a white, male subject. Coherence is, once again, one of the prerequisites for modern sovereignty. The subject must believe that it is "master in its own house" (Freud). If this fundamental imagination fails, then usually not only do others perceive the person in question as 'abnormal', but the person also has this opinion of him- or herself.

Let's remain with the learned way of self-relation, which is so existential for the biopolitical governmental modern era, and which applies to the entire population in very different ways. This relationship with one's self is based on the idea of having an inner nature, an inner essence that ultimately makes up one's unique individuality. These kinds of imagined 'inner, natural truths', these constructions of actuality, are usually understood as unalterable, only capable of being suppressed or liberated. To this day they nourish the ideas of being able to, or having to fashion and design one's self and one's life freely, autonomously, and according to one's own decisions. These kinds of power relations are therefore not easy to perceive as they commonly come along as one's own free decision, as a personal view, and to this day produce the desire to ask: 'Who am I?' or, 'How can I realize my potential?' 'How can I find myself and most greatly develop the essence of my being?' As mentioned, the concept of responsibility of one's own, so commonly used in the course of neo-liberal restructuring, lies within this liberal line of force of possessive individualism and actuality and only functions additionally as a neo-liberal interpellation for self-governing.

Basically, governmental self-government takes place in an apparent paradox. Governing, controlling, disciplining, and regulating one's self means, at the same time, fashioning and forming one's self, empowering one's self, which in this sense, is what it means to be free. It is only through this paradox that sovereign subjects can be governed. Precisely because techniques of governing one's self arise from the simultaneity of subjugation and empowerment, the simultaneity of compulsion and freedom, in this paradoxical movement, the individual not only becomes a subject, but a certain, modern, 'free' subject. Subjectivated in this way, this subject continually participates in (re)producing the conditions for governmentality, as it is first in this scenario that agency emerges. According to Foucault, power is practiced only on 'free subjects' and only to the extent that they are 'free'.[13]

In the context of governmentality, subjects are, thus, subjugated and simultaneously agents, and in a certain sense, free. This freedom is, at the same time, a condition and effect of liberal power relations, i.e. of biopolitical governmentality. Despite all of the changes that have occurred from the end of the 18th century to the present, this has remained as one of the lines of force through which individuals in modern societies can be governed.

This normalized freedom of biopolitical governmental societies never exists without security mechanisms or constructions of the abnormal and deviant, which likewise have subjectivating functions. The modern era seems unthinkable without a 'culture of danger', without a permanent threat to the normal, without imaginary invasions of constant, common threats such as diseases, dirt, sexuality, or the 'fear of degeneration'.[14] The interplay of freedom and security, self-empowerment and compulsion, with the help of this culture of danger, drives the problems of the political economy of liberal power.

Against this backdrop, all of those who did not comply with this norm and normalizing of a free, sovereign, bourgeois, white subject including its property relations, were made precarious. Furthermore, in the context of the social state, which was meant to guarantee the security of modern insecurity, not only were women made structurally precarious as wives, through the normal labor conditions oriented on the man, but also those who were excluded as abnormal and foreign from the nation state compromise between capital and labor were likewise made precarious. Accordingly, precarization has always been, until now, an inherent contradiction in liberal governmentality and, as abnormal, disturbed the stabilizing dynamic between freedom and security. In this sense, it was often the trigger for struggles and resistance.

Presently, normal labor conditions oriented on a male breadwinner, a situation largely accessible only for the majority society, is losing its hegemony. Precarization is increasingly a part of governmental normalization techniques and as a result, in neoliberalism it transforms from an inherent contradiction to a hegemonic function.

Economizing of life and the absence of resistance

The talk of 'economizing of life', a discussion often struck up in the past several years, provides only very limited explanations of neoliberal transformation processes: not only due to its totalizing rhetoric, but also because of the associated proclamation of what is supposedly a new phenomenon. 'Economizing of life' usually refers to certain simplified theses: no longer only work, but also life has fallen prey to economic exploitation interests; a separation between work and life is no longer possible and in the course of this, an implosion of the distinction between production and reproduction has also taken place. Such totalizing implosion theses speak of a collective victim status and distort the view of modes of subjectivation, agency, and ultimately of resistance.

However, the thesis of the 'economizing of life' does make sense from a biopolitical governmentality perspective. It points to the power and domination relations of a bourgeois liberal society which has, for more than two hundred years now, been constituted around the productivity of life. In this perspective, life was never the other side of work. In Western modernity, reproduction was always a part of the political and the economic. Not only reproduction, but also life in general was never beyond power relations. Instead, life, precisely in its productivity, which means its design potential, was always the effect of such relations. And it is precisely this design potential that is constitutive of the supposed paradox of modern subjectivation between subordination and empowerment, between regulation and freedom. A liberal process of constituting precarization as an inherent contradiction, did not take place beyond this subjectivation; it is an entirely plausible resulting bundle of social, economic and political positions.

In this sense, the currently lamented 'economization of life' is not an entirely neoliberal phenomenon, but instead, a force line of biopolitical societies, which today perhaps becomes intelligible in a new way. The associated subjectivations are not new in the way that they are usually claimed to be. In fact, their biopolitical governmental continuities have hardly been grasped.

Were the living and working conditions that arose in the context of social movements since the 1960s really in no way governmental? Indeed, the thoroughly dissident practices of alternative ways of living, the desire for different bodies and self-relations (in feminist, ecological, left-radical contexts), persistently aimed to distinguish themselves from normal working conditions and the associated constraints, disciplinary measures, and controls. Keywords here are: deciding for oneself what one does for work and with whom; consciously choosing precarious forms of work and life, because more freedom and autonomy seem possible precisely because of the ability to organize one's own time, and what is most important: self-determination. Often, being paid well hasn't been a concern as the remuneration was the enjoyment of the work itself. The concern was with being able to bring to bear one's many skills. Generally the conscious, voluntary acceptance of precarious labor conditions was often also an expression of the wish for living the modern, patriarchal dividing of reproduction and wage labor differently than is possible within the normal work situation.

However, it is precisely these alternative living and working conditions that have become increasingly more economically utilizable in recent years because they favor the flexibility that the labor market demands. Thus, practices and discourses of social movements in the past thirty to forty years were not only dissident and directed against normalization, but also at the same time, a part of the transformation toward a neoliberal form of governmentality.

But to what extent are precarious modes of living and working, formerly perceived as dissident, now obvious in their hegemonic, governmental function? And why do they seem to lose their potential for resistance? The following will offer a few thoughts without any claims of presenting a comprehensive analysis.

Many of the cultural producers who have entered into a precarious situation of their own accord, the people of whom we are speaking here as a whole, would refer consciously or unconsciously to a history of previous alternative conditions of existence, usually without having any direct political relationship to them. They are more or less disturbed by their shift to the center of society, i.e. to the place where the normal and hegemonic are reproduced. That does not mean, however, that former alternative living and working techniques will become socially hegemonic. Instead, it works the other way around: the mass precarization of labor conditions is forced upon all of those who fall out of normal labor conditions, along with the promise of the ability to take responsibility for their own creativity and fashion their lives according to their own rules, as a desirable and supposedly normal condition of existence. Our concern here is not with these persons forced into precarization, but with those who say that as cultural workers they have freely chosen precarious living and working conditions.

It is amazing that there are no systematic empirical studies of this. The common parameters of cultural producers, however, should be that they are well or even very well educated, between twenty-five and forty years-old, without children, and more or less intentionally in a precarious employment situation. They pursue temporary jobs, live from projects and pursue contract work from several clients at the same time, one right after the other, usually without sick pay, paid vacations, or unemployment compensation, and without any job security, thus with no or only minimal social protection. The forty-hour week is an illusion. Working time and free time have no clearly defined borders. Work and leisure can no longer be separated. In the non-paid time, they accumulate a great deal of knowledge, which is not paid for extra, but is naturally called for and used in the context of paid work.

This is not an 'economizing of life', that comes from the outside, overpowering and totalizing. Instead, these are practices connected with desire as well as adaptation. For these conditions of existence are constantly foreseen and co-produced in anticipatory obedience. 'Voluntary', i.e., unpaid or low paying jobs in the culture or academic industries, for example, are all too often accepted as an unchangeable fact, and nothing else is even demanded. The necessity of pursuing other, less creative, precarious jobs in order to finance one's own cultural production is accepted. This forced, and simultaneously chosen, financing of one's own creative output constantly supports and reproduces precisely those relations from which one suffers and of which one wants to be a part. Perhaps those who work creatively, these precarious cultural producers by design, are subjects that can be exploited so easily because they seem to bear their living and working conditions eternally due to the belief in their own freedom and autonomy – due to self-realization fantasies. In a neoliberal context they are exploitable to such an extreme that the State even presents them as role models.

This situation of self-precarization is connected to experiences of fear and loss of control, feelings of insecurity through the loss of certainties and safeguards, as well as fear and the experience of failure, social decline and poverty. Also for these reasons, 'letting go' or forms of dropping out and dropping off of hegemonic paradigms are difficult. Everyone has to remain 'on speed' otherwise you might fall out. There are no clear times for relaxation or recuperation. This kind of reproduction has no clear place, which in turn results in an unfulfilled yearning and a continuous suffering from this lack. The desire for relaxation, to 'find oneself', becomes insatiable. These kinds of reproductive practices usually have to be learned anew. They are not self-evident and must be fought for bitterly against oneself and others. In turn, this makes the yearning for reproduction, for regeneration, extremely marketable.

As a result, not only has the side of work, of production, become precarious, but also the so-called other side, which is often defined as 'life', the side of reproduction. Do production and reproduction therefore coincide? In these cultural producers, in an old new way, yes. What they reveal is that, in a neoliberal form of individualization, parts of production and reproduction are deposited 'in' the subjects. Panagiotidis and Tsianos also argue along these lines when they state:

> The progressive vanquishing of the division of production and reproduction does not occur at home or at the workplace, but instead, through an embodiment of the work itself: a reflexive way of precarization![15]

Though what is materialized in the bodies, beyond the work, is also always the governmental life, as biopolitical governmental power relations function doggedly through the production of hegemonic, normalized bodies and self-relations.

The function of reproduction consequently changes in the present context of precarious, immaterial, usually individualized, work and 'life'. It is no longer externalized with others, primarily women. Individual reproduction and sexual reproduction, the production of life, now becomes individualized and is shifted, in part, 'into' the subjects themselves. It is about regeneration beyond work, also *through* work, but still, quite often beyond adequately paid wage labor. It is about regeneration, renewal, creating from one's self, re-producing one's self from one's own power, of one's own accord. Self-realization becomes a reproductive task for the self. Work is meant to guarantee the reproduction of the self.

Presenting 'precarized' cultural producers (that is, cultural producers who have been made precarious) in their entire heterogeneity in such a uniform fashion, it is possible to say that their subjectivation in neoliberalism has obviously been contradictory: in the simultaneity of, on the one hand, precarization, which also always means fragmentation and non-linearity, and on the other, the continuity of sovereignty. The continuity of modern sovereignty takes place through the stylizing of self-realization, autonomy, and freedom, through the fashioning of and responsibility for one's self, and the repetition of the idea of actuality. An example of this is the (still) widespread idea of the modern male artist subject, who draws his creativity from himself, because it supposedly exists within him, there where Western modernity also positions sex and has made it the nature, the essence of the individual. In general, for the cultural producers described here, sovereignty seems to rest mainly in the 'free' decision for precarization, therefore, self-precarization. Yet this could, in turn, be a central reason for why it is so difficult to recognize structural precarization as a neoliberal governmental phenomenon that affects the entire society, and is hardly based on a free decision. Cultural producers therefore offer an example of the extent to which 'self-chosen' ways of living and conditions of working, including their ideas of autonomy and freedom, are compatible with political and economic restructuring. How else can we explain that in a study of the living and working conditions of critical cultural producers, when asked what a 'good life' is, they had no answer? When work and life increasingly permeate one another, then that means, as one interviewee expressed: "work seeps into your life." But obviously, not enough ideas of a 'good life' seep into the work, whereby this could then, in turn, transform into something that could collectively signify a 'good life'. Resistance with the view to a better life, which has less and less of a governmental function, is missing.

Apparently, the belief in precarization as a liberal governmental oppositional position can be maintained with the help of contradictory subjectivation, between sovereignty and fragmentation. However, in this way, continuing relations of power and domination are made invisible and normalization mechanisms become naturalized as the subject's self-evident and autonomous decisions. The totalizing talk of the 'economization of life' only contributes to this by causing the effects of hegemony to disappear from view and with them, battles and antagonisms. One's own imaginations of autonomy and freedom are not reflected on within governmental lines of force of modern subjectivation; other freedoms are no longer imagined, thus blocking the view of a possible behavior contesting the hegemonic function of precarization in the context of neoliberal governmentality.

What is the price of this normalization? In neoliberalism, what functions as the abnormal? As the deviant? What can't be economically exploited in this way? Rather than focusing on the messianic arrival of resistance and new subjectivities, as Deleuze rhetorically questions: "Do not the changes in capitalism find an unexpected 'encounter' in the slow emergence of a new self as a centre of resistance?"[16] I believe that it is necessary to continue to work further and more precisely on the genealogies of precarization as a hegemonic function, on the problem of continuities of bourgeois governmental modes of subjectivation, especially in the context of notions of autonomy and freedom that see themselves as dissident.

Translated from the German by Lisa Rosenblatt and Dagmar Fink

Notes:

1. Michel Foucault, *Geschichte der Gouvernementalität II. Die Geburt der Biopolitik. Vorlesungen am Collège de France 1978-79*, Frankfurt/M: Suhrkamp, 2004, 42; own translation.

2. Michel Foucault, *The History of Sexuality, Volume I: An Introduction*, New York: Vintage, 1980, 141-42.

3. Ibid., 142, emphasis I.L.

4. Philipp Sarasin, *Reizbare Maschinen. Eine Geschichte des Körpers 1765-1914*, Frankfurt/M: Suhrkamp, 2001, p. 19. See also Hannelore Bublitz, Christine Hanke, Andrea Seier, *Der Gesellschaftskörper. Zur Neuordnung von Kultur und Geschlecht um 1900*. Frankfurt/M./New York: Campus, 2000.

5. Crawford Brough Macpherson, *Political Theory of Possessive Individualism: Hobbes to Locke*, Oxford University Press, 1962.

6. See Isabell Lorey, 'Als das Leben in die Politik eintrat. Die biopolitisch gouvernementale Moderne, Foucault und Agamben', in Marianne Pieper, Thomas Atzert, Serhat Karakayali, Vassilis Tsianos (Eds.), *Empire und die biopolitische Wende*, Frankfurt/M./New York: Campus, 2005.

7. Michel Foucault, 'Governmentality', in Graham Bruchell et al. (Eds.), *The Foucault Effect: Studies in Governmentality*, University of Chicago Press, 1991, 87-104.

8. Karl Marx, *A Contribution to the Critique of Political Economy* (1859), http://www.marxists.org/archive/marx/works/1859/critique-pol-economy/index.htm, 1999.

9. John Locke, *Two Treatises of Government*, 'Concerning the True Original Extent and End of Civil Government §44' (1823), in *The Works of John Locke. A New Edition, Corrected. In Ten Volumes, Volume V*, London, http://socserv2.mcmaster.ca/~econ/ugcm/3113/locke/government.pdf.

10. Robert Castel, *Die Stärkung des Sozialen. Leben im neuen Wohlfahrtsstaat* (2003), Hamburg: Hamburger Edition, 2005, 24.

11. Katharina Pühl, 'Der Bericht der Hartz-Kommission und die "Unternehmerin ihrer selbst": Geschlechterverhältnisse, Gouvernementalität und Neoliberalismus', in Marianne Pieper and Encarnación Gutiérrez Rodríguez (Eds.), *Gouvernementalität. Ein sozialwissenschaftliches Konzept im Anschluss an Foucault*, Frankfurt/M./New York: Campus, 2003, 111-135.

12. e.g., Robert Castel, *Die Stärkung des Sozialen. Leben im neuen Wohlfahrtsstaat.*

13. See Michel Foucault, 'The Subject and Power', in Hubert L. Dreyfus and Paul Rainbow (Eds.), *Michel Foucault: Beyond Structuralism and Hermeneutics*, University of Chicago Press, 1983, 208-226.

14. Michel Foucault, *Geschichte der Gouvernementalität II. Die Geburt der Biopolitik. Vorlesungen am Collège de France 1978-79*, 101f.

15. Efthimia Panagiotidis and Vassilis Tsianos, 'Reflexive Prekarisierung. Eine Introspektion aus dem Alltag von Projektlinken', in *Fantômas. Magazin für linke Debatte und Praxis: "Prekäre Zeiten"*, No.6 (Winter), 2004/05, 19.

16. Gilles Deleuze, *Foucault*, Minneapolis: University of Minnesota Press, 1988, 115.

The Spectral Form of Value:
Ghost-Things and Relations of Forces

by Katja Diefenbach

As Derrida was kind enough to tell us, Marx, in the first chapter of *Capital,* wrote a spectral theory of the commodity-form as social relation, according to which the social appears to man as phantasmatic, while it is actually a set of "material relations between persons and social relations between things."[1] Here we have an interesting form of a real insanity, which inhabits things without being at home in them. This insanity is not a natural character of these things. It appears at the moment of exchange and expresses the social character of labor. A social form is embodied in the commodity. This form expresses a relation of substitution, abstraction and reification. Marx calls this real abstraction – as actual as it is fantastic – a specter that must be driven out. In commodities you can touch what is otherwise untouchable: the mode of production of capitalism. Commodities are in this sense, sensuously supersensible things; they are social crystals. This is the secret of commodities, a secret that shows itself by not showing, a mysterious mirror. People don't get the mysticism of the commodity, they think that it is quite normal that things have a value and are exchanged. Marx reveals this as a mystery. He is a decipherer who makes it clear that the phantasmatic will not vanish by interpreting it. It will not dissipate until we pass into another mode of production. It will not be until then – and this is a passage in *Capital*, beautiful in its clarity, while remaining mystical regarding the rationality of the revolution:

> the whole mystery of commodities, all the magic and necromancy that surrounds the products of labor as long as they take the form of commodities, vanishes therefore, so soon as we come to other forms of production.[2]

Marx holds this lesson on specters in the fourth section of the first chapter of *Capital*: 'The Fetishism of Commodities and the Secret thereof'. Conjuring the magic of the commodity, Marx operates with a religious and fantastic vocabulary:

> Here it is a definite social relation between men, that assumes, in their eyes, the fantastic form of a relation between things. In order, therefore, to find an analogy, we must have recourse to the mist-enveloped regions of the religious world.[3]

His pathos of truth is that of an exposing, an unveiling critic of religion. His problem is that his critique is still dominated by a religious spell (that he would like to get rid of) because he forgets to reflect upon whether the sharp distinction between a rationality of use and an irrationality of exchange is in itself spectral, mysterious and fantastic.

We are now at an intersection of theoretical and political questions. Derrida's book, *Specters of Marx*, culminates in deconstructing the concept of a phantasmatic form of the commodity and Marx's strategy of driving out the specters, making them dissipate, vanishing into a communism of the pure use of things and planned work. This Marxist mythology of truth reverberates in the structuralist cinema of the 1960s and 1970s, in its anti-fetishism, in its will to show things behind the things, and its suspicion of the gaze and the image. With his first remarks on biopower in *The History of Sexuality, Volume 1*, Foucault implicitly and radically differs from this idea of truth and of work.

To put it directly: 'doing' is not the essence of man. The body – as working, as fucking – could never be liberated; it is an effect of power, and communism should question how we can alter our bodies so that they are not time bombs of mobilized discipline, of the wish to work, the wish to confess, to be creative, to do something, to have sex. "When did you shoot your last movie?", "When did you go to the gym?", etc. This symptom is most evident in certain segments of urban youth under the age of forty-five. It signals a development in the mode of socialization, a simultaneity that is coming to a head: both the mobilization of forms of life and the attack on them, this ticking make-something-of-yourself, get out of normality (even the trashy promise of becoming a superstar), and at the same time, the expansion of mechanisms of exclusion and valorization: super-poverty, super-deportation, super-control. There is an increasing anxiety among urban youth, having to do with the need to have a deviant lifestyle, while still being successful. With this biopolitical imperative of our societies, both the norm and deviation have been occupied. In a certain sense this could be described as the successful failure of 1968 or perhaps as a sort of paradoxical "communism of capital," as Paolo Virno has put it.[4] In 1968, activists fought for a revolutionary change that does not stop in front of everyday life, feelings, sexualities and living conditions. Step by step this minoritarian politics has become detached from the question of socialism. It has become a biopolitical building block of an expanded capitalist life. This is not to say that the greater variety of forms of life are just bullshit, or that things were better in the 1950s – quite the contrary. And, of course, this ideological amphetamine – less sleep, more Open Source – only suits the lives of certain people: the coke-sniffing creative bourgeoisie, or the hippie version: Green party voters who shop in health food stores and dress casually. And it has ultimately led to a growing number of advertising films in which one can observe fast-cut, blurry footage of people in track suits in their hip, disorderly, daily lives. Today advertisements no longer directly praise the commodity-object, but rather, they praise forms of life. And if there is something like a spectral commodity-life, we should not try to drive out the specters in the belief that there is a previous pure life.

Form

Marx deciphers a social form in the commodity. The bourgeois political economy had already developed the theory of labor-value. In 1817 Ricardo wrote that,

> the value of a commodity, or the quantity of any other commodity for which it will exchange, depends on the relative quantity of labor which is necessary for its production, and not on the greater or less compensation which is paid for that labor.[5]

That's not the news of Marx's critique of political economy; the news is that the commodity form is the form of a commodity producing society itself. Let's reconstruct the scene: Marx starts from the elementary exchange of products: *x* amount of commodity A is exchanged for *y* of commodity B, for example 20 yards of linen are worth 1 coat. That is to say: the social form does not hide in the money-form, but in the elementary value-form in the exchange of one commodity for another. Here we have a double methodological hint: first, Marx recognizes an embryonic form that already incorporates its ultimate breakdown, a fictional germ,[6] and, secondly, this embryonic form expresses no substance and no essence, but a relation which, again, will be one of the starting points of the poststructuralist discussion.

According to Marx, the commodity-form is determined by substitution and a double abstraction (from use and from concrete labor). When linen is exchanged for coat, the coat acts as a mirror to the value of the linen. In a certain sense, according to Marx, its material purity vanishes together with its possibility of use. As soon as the commodity enters the market and transforms into the form of value, it becomes its own specter. As a good pupil of Hegel, Marx claims that use-value becomes the form of appearance of its opposite: value as such. As this unit of the contradiction of matter-object and value-form, the commodity could be called a sensuously supra-sensuous thing, "abounding in metaphysical subtleties and theological niceties,"[7] a bodiless body. This spectral incarnation only works because, in the exchange, labor is reduced to an abstract quantum. What counts is the average time that is necessary to produce a commodity. Marx is not just politically accusing capitalist society of ignoring the working conditions, poverty, and the 12-hour workday, but also, and more profoundly, of not regarding the mode of its expenditure. He constructs a theoretical method in which the commodities themselves incorporate a form which determines, moves, and limits historical development. This is the social: the form of a movement of advancing contradictions, into which crisis and breakdown are already written.

Let's get that briefly and schematically: The fundamental principle of a capitalist society is reducing costs and increasing profit. This is only possible because of surplus value. People earn less than the value of the products that they are manufacturing. Lowering wages or prolonging working hours has absolute limits. But the development of big industries and the automatization of the factory opened up huge possibilities to relatively increase surplus. Less and less work time is needed to produce goods, but as we know, this time does not go into communist holidays of disposable time or a 3-hour workday, being used rather to reduce wage costs. This means that at the same time, according to Marx, each commodity has less value because less work is contained in it. From a certain moment on, the conditions of capitalist development become its own fetters. It then generally tends toward a drop in profit margins and then to over-production and crisis.

Marx is fitting a political collective-subject into that objective movement of capital in which the horizon of crisis is always present. The problem with this is that it presupposes the sublation (*Aufhebung*) of capitalism and the passage to another mode of production as something inherent to the very movement of capital itself; that is, it sees the abolition of capital as inevitable. The working class will realize the abolition of capitalism; it stands potentially at just that time-place in which the movement of contradictions leads to crisis. Like hare and hedgehog,[8] one moment the movement of capital is the hedgehog, the other it is the working class. The whole thing is a circular argument. Capitalism needs the working class: there must be people who have nothing other than their own labor to sell. Capitalism produces the working class: poverty and class consciousness increase and, at last, capitalism will be abolished by the working class; it will be the last obstacle for its movement. Showdown of history. This finely balanced political-economic movement of Marxist theory has been sharply criticized. This criticism opened up a new way of thinking for the new left of the 1960s, new social movements, non-dogmatic Marxism and poststructuralist theory.

The multitude of social relations does not hide a contradiction in its heart that determines and figures its limits. The social is not the effect of a form that explains the social. Foucault and Deleuze break with this theoretical figure. End of dialectics. Period. History is not a movement of negation, negation of negation and sublation. Deleuze once said that "A social field does not contradict itself, but what is primary is that it flees."[9]

Relations of forces

One of the problems of Marxist theory is the vanishing of the social event. If the dynamics of capitalist development are determined by a form-law (*Formgesetz*), changes can be anticipated. They waver between modernization and revolution. According to Marx, the contradictory builds a higher unity: an individuality. With poststructuralism, the materialism of an antagonistic form is no longer the starting point, it is rather the materialism of an irreducible multitude of practices that have an effect on bodies, populations and forms of life. In that sense the historicity of one contradiction is replaced by the idea of a contingent historical event, and that event is a kind of improbable effect of strategies of power which constitute subjectivity along with many diverse moments of resistance. The forces that clash in a strategic conflict – and the social is a strategic conflict – influence each other, that is, they neutralize, intensify or destroy each other, but they are not reigned or determined by a structuring form.[10]

Foucault's work is characterized by a kind of genuine struggle with Marx, which has been one of the principal sources of its productivity. In

The History of Sexuality, Volume 1, Foucault poses the question of why power is so persistent, to which he will answer that the expansion of capitalism coexists with the mobilization of bodies in a way that is as productive as it is disciplining. Biopower means enabling and regulating life, which radically questions our political idea of autonomy. There is nothing that represents the determining kernel, foundation, or source of emancipation – not human practice or human activity, not the body, not the libido, not the truth, not life, love, laughter and struggle – nothing. While in the theory of Marx the relations of forces are internalized by a form, Foucault suggests an extreme exterior figure of power. It does not express itself through a form, being rather a force that stands in relation to, and has effects on, other forces. Using the term 'form', Foucault means the historical stratifications of knowledge and institutions. He speaks of power in an almost nominalist way; the term is very much emptied out. Power is just a diagrammatic fitting-in of different *dispositifs*. A *dispositif* connects the discursive with the non-discursive, the development of knowledge and the development of institutional strategies: science of law and prison, psychology and clinic, always "the sayable and the visible."[11] You can't reduce one to another or derive one from the other. In a way, power is just the name – this is what is meant by nominalism – of the mobility of the *dispositifs* on which it is based and which it stratifies. Power is nothing other than an actual cross-section of the mobility of social processes, like increasingly intensifying the strongest element of a social situation, reversing it or increasing both poles at the same time.

From a law of form determining and limiting the movement of advancing contradictions to a complex strategic situation of mobile *dispositifs* modifying each other and modified in turn by acts of disagreement, revolt, and deviation that power tries to anticipate. From Marx to Foucault. The spectral figure of real-abstraction has vanished into the figure of the relation of a relation that is never fully present. This could be called the virtuality of the social, which would be its spectral aspect in a positive sense.

Foucault develops this position step by step. In *Discipline and Punish*, he represents the prison as sort of universal form of a *dispositif* in which the panoptic model of power expresses itself. Here we come across remaining pieces of an unexpressed teleology: If all of society has become a prison, the prison will open its doors, Foucault indicates at the end of *Discipline and Punish*. These are remaining pieces of an unexpressed law of form, therefore it is not "surprising that prisons resemble factories, schools, barracks, hospitals, which all resemble prisons."[12] In *The History of Sexuality, Volume 1*, Foucault revises this position. The prison is not the big model anymore. The *dispositifs* do not express an internal determining form. Just as there is no homology between the micro- and the macro-level: the family is not an embryonic form of the state, while the state does not imitate the family. Instead, Foucault radicalizes the idea of differential relations of forces. The social articulates through bodily, economic, sexual and discursive lines. They do not maintain a dialectical relation – a mutual one, yes, a spiral one, yes, sometimes an antagonistic one, but never a dialectical one.

And now the next question: Do we recognize anything in these relations of forces? Foucault analyzes a differential field of relations by starting with the local unstable subjectifying strategies that effect bodies. He does that mostly by reading the prescriptive discourses of a specific time, looking for the cross-sections of knowledge and power. The school, the prison and the state are already end-forms of infinite clashes. This is his Nietzschean side. Especially until the mid-1970s, Foucault sees the central mode of power not in law and consensus, but in war and struggle. Later on he concentrates on the question of how integrated strategies emerge out of this mobile field of the social, how more stable strategies of governing and regulating the population have been established, always focusing on their coexistence at a given moment.

Today workfare strategies making labor precarious and economizing health care coexist with a strong call for making provisions and having medical check-ups: stop smoking, keep fit. And not just on the level of the mass trim trail of the 1970s, but professionalized: Nordic walking, gyms and fitness centers for exquisite taste. It is possible to deduce one from the other. If health care is capitalized, it will be even more necessary to stimulate people to make their precautions, to prompt them to be responsible for themselves, to take care of their bodies, to become self-entrepreneurs of their health. That would determine the character of biopolitical measures by the regulation of capital. In this sense, Antonio Negri and Michael Hardt identify the movement of capital with the development of biopower. Until capitalism begins to help itself to those forms of life that valorize emotions, creativity, and not just the six or eight hours a day of wage labor – they call that the real subsumption of society under capital – until then, they say, capital is biopolitical. Yes, so far as they would like to remark that the strategies of valorization and of biopower modify each other increasingly, in spiral forms. No, so far as they would like to suggest a single tendency in the social, namely, the mode of biopolitical production. Then, simultaneity is deduced, the difference of strategies that calculate profits and of strategies that regulate bodies is deduced and again a teleology is induced. Let's face it: in contrast to the metaphorical qualities of the term 'society of control', we do not live today in the Sci-fi of computerized control. In our societies, high security prisons coexist with electronic collars for inmates of jails, post-trauma therapy with the internment of refugees, the increasing of supernational law standards alongside a politics of emergency. We are not racing into the horizon of a pure, fully deterritorialized capitalism. We are not rushing through the narrow channel of a one-way progress.

Ghost-Things

The spectacular element of Marx's comments on the character of the commodity lies in his strategy to shift the form of the social into the form of the commodity. There it emerges: a mysterious incorporation. The secret is not hidden behind the phenomena, it is *in* the phenomena. This shift begs the question of the state of the things. What's up with commodities? Marx autonomizes the commodity. It becomes a contradictory individuality, a para-subject, a thing that is illuminated by the social. Marx often speaks about the commodity as if it were a living thing, a twisted thing that has a commodity-soul: it dances, it stands on its head, as "soon as [a trivial table] steps forth as a commodity, it is changed into something transcendent [...] and evolves out of its wooden brain grotesque ideas, far more wonderful than 'table-turning' ever was."[13] Marx says, if the commodity would speak, it would say..., if the commodity could walk it would..., etc. Resolutely and categorically ignoring what it has to do with constituting the body, with constituting sex, with the population, Marx lends the things a fetishistic force. Crystallizing the social, they incorporate exchange-value; they are just jellies of value, spectral objectivity. Marx wants to get the phantasmatic out of them again. Therefore he operates with the idea of material, actual, present objectivity: that is, the simple trivial thing – a value in use. He permanently identifies reality with rationality, presence and use. Of course, this is crazy in itself. Even if it's pointing towards something important, something irreplaceable and valuable, still a jewel of social theory: capitalism is not a natural necessity.

Here Marx gives us a critical ontology of presence as actual reality, as purity of use and as objectivity. A chair is for sitting. It is what it is, identical with itself. This was in the beginning. It was intact. But there is nothing like the real reality of things and the simple rationality of use and production. This idealism of use and utility characterizes the romantic anti-capitalist mourning for things that have lost their original state. It still reverberates in the new social movements rejecting consumerism, in this disgust for all these false things, the abundance of things, trumpery and glitter of the commodity-world. And often enough, the body of the woman is chosen as a metaphor for this fetishism of things. That shows a huge and dark lack in Marxism concerning the constitution of the body, sexualities and affects. In romantic anti-capitalism, the woman must lend her body to the commodity, until she herself becomes, in a certain sense, a commodity. Eye shadow of blindness. Anti-fetishism wants to show something behind the deception of the commodity, something true, something simple concerning the woman, it is the female worker, the mother, menstruation, the not-made-up woman. Therefore the secret relationship of *ungeschminkt* and *wahr* in German (*ungeschminkte Wahrheit*), without makeup and true (the naked truth). The analysis starts to become interesting when the series of stratifications are reconstructed in which the female body of consumption has been constituted. How did that work? The sexualization and refinement of femininity: How many practices of housekeeping, educating a girl, taking care of health and sexuality, how much the visual politics of advertisement and movies have become sedimented in the female body. Linda Singer writes, in her book *Erotic Welfare*, about the ensemble of bodily strategies, consumer practices and the effect of a commodity that is perceived as fetish.

Marx's strong rhetorics of the secret, which shows itself by not showing itself, strengthened the gesture of the critique of ideology in

Marxism. In part, materialist aesthetic theory established that idea: to ban the fetish, to smash the mirror, to lift the veil, to unmask reality. This line of young-Hegelian critique of religion was inherited by the structuralist cinema of the 1960s and 1970s. Laura Mulvey writes, in her introduction to *Fetishism and Curiosity*, about this position in Marxist and feminist movies. She writes about the primacy of showing and, at the same time, the suspicion of the gaze in a world of blindness. The work, the daily routine at the factory, the social conditions should be dragged out, should step out of the shadow of the glitter of distraction around the commodities that have been worshipped by Hollywood and its studio interiors and middle-class stories. The feminist movie made an analogy between the commodity-fetishism and the beauty-fetishism of the female star. Here, again, there is a strong deciphering gesture and a will to show: images of vaginas, menstruation, close-ups of skin – what was considered as the abject inverse of normative beauty. The menstruating star. Why not? But it should not be linked with the truth of the non-artificial, the not-made-up, with dis-alienation. Slowly the vogue of romantic anti-capitalism and essentialist feminism has come to an end. The anti-fetishist impulse weakens. Camp has been actualized again: the gesture of dis-identification, repeating and displacing the sex-self-fame-money equation. The question is less whether – in the representation and incorporation of beauty and sex, fashion and porn – a powerful form of sexist alienation and substitution is hidden and expressed, and more a question of how fetishistic practices are carried out, with which other practices they are linked, in what ways do they have effects on forms of life, what is their relation of forces? Not deciphering, but analyzing. When the Canadian queer porn filmmaker Bruce La Bruce left the film university of Toronto, he decided to de-program the entire Marxist-feminist discourse of movie theory, in the first place its anti-fetishism, carrying on with what Kenneth Anger and Jack Smith, Andy Warhol and John Waters had begun. A remark on one point concerning the social relation of forces in which the pro-fetishist and the pro-porn attitude emerge: a potential blockade and retortion it could meet would be the mainstream desire for trash and the anti-left *ressentiment* with which one line of love for artificiality, fashion, and glamour is connected.

At the end of the section entitled, 'The Fetishism of Commodities and the Secret thereof', Marx presents a short version of communism as:

> a community of free individuals, carrying on their work with the means of production in common, in which the labor power of all the different individuals is consciously applied as the combined labor power of the community.[14]

Producing what is needed and what is possible, the result is social. One portion serves as fresh means of production, the other portion is shared justly and consumed by the members of the community. Marx writes: "The social relations of the individual producers [...] are in this case perfectly simple and intelligible."[15] Doing, being active, emerges here as a natural character of human beings. Man is active and practical. Against this idea, Foucault develops the concept of biopower. Activity is not the essence of human beings; the horizon of a community of free individuals carrying on their work in common is not a free horizon. The horizon of work is an effect of modern power. Marx thinks that overcoming capitalism means overcoming the spectral incarnation of the form of value. This is problematic on a theoretical level because truth is equated with utility and objectivity (*Gegenständlichkeit*), while it is problematic on a political level because it fails to question how it is that the constitution of an active, mobilized, working subjectivity coexists with capitalism.

For Marx, the commodity-form is phantasmatic because it is irrational. But knowledge and truth are not simply measures of the degree to which a form corresponds to an object. The object as matter is not separable from its frame as form, through which and in which the object is recognizable. Communism doesn't imply the separation of simple matter from its false capitalist form. The correspondence between truth and emancipation is cut. The idea of a non-correspondence between truth and objects does not imply that there is no truth, but rather, that truth has a normalizing rather than a rational character. Communism must question the state of the body and the form of life that demands that you make-something-of-yourself, that you be active, creative, have sex, and make sense. The most recent conception of a communism of autonomous activity can be found in the book *Empire*, which I mentioned above. The authors, Antonio Negri and Michael Hardt, claim that a proto-communist collective subjectivity has emerged due to the following changes: with the class struggles and confrontations of the 1960s and 1970s, the factory diffused into society and all of society became a factory; the feminist perspective of counting non-paid work as part of social productivity became true historically on an expanded level; capital eats more and more through bodies, valorizes the knowledge of the working process, valorizes the ability to cooperate, the ability to self-organize, the affects, the subcultures, compelling subjects to become entrepreneurs of their own existence. Negri and Hardt suggest that the mode of being of subjects in late capitalism is so refined that it has become precious and autonomous. Capitalism is now only a passive machine of profit-robbery. Activity – that is the multitude. Potentially it knows how it wants to live, to work, to have relationships, etc. This forgets about the constitution of a postfordist form of life; it does not see that autonomy is always an effect of power. Ability in discipline. We find this idea of a happy communism of autonomy in the concept of Open Source programming as a proto-communist activity. Again, the situation of the body in front of the screen – its being-engendered, its non-social loneliness, its 24-hour-online-guard – is forgotten.

The promise of the commodity
Walter Benjamin is far away from the politics of truth and presence. He is turning back all the time; he speaks with the past. He was inspired by Marx's works and historical materialism for different reasons: Benjamin

hated capitalism and Marx's theory promised to give his hatred materialist sharpness and clarity. Benjamin was a friend of Brecht and while he was working on *The Arcades Project*, both Adorno and Horkheimer advised him to read especially the first chapter of *Capital, Volume 1*, on commodities. Upon the announcement of the Hitler-Stalin Pact, Benjamin wrote, in shock, "the experience of our generation: that capitalism will not die a natural death."[16] Therefore, revolution is not a final goal of history, it is an interruption and a redemption of the past. As a political author, revolution is the locomotive of global history for Marx, while with Benjamin revolution is a pulling of an emergency brake. It delivers us from the pain and defeat of the past, from catastrophe: the angel of history would like to wake the dead and join together what has been smashed to pieces.

Analyzing the fading fashions of the 19th century, Benjamin insists on the actuality of the past in the present – the presence of what is not present. He refers to Marx's chapter, 'The fetishism of the commodities and the secret thereof', shifting or displacing the question that is posed there. Detecting another (utopian) aspect of commodities – not just the crystallized form of private expended labor – Benjamin does not want to exorcize the spectral. He does not want to return to elementary use as he does not identify truth with rational production. No hunger, no poverty, communality of production forces, just distribution, etc. are preconditions for another society, which must be there, but as a revolutionary spiritualist, he is searching for the promise of what a life could be in the tiny things, the short seconds of bliss, the fragile beauty.

Marx was analyzing a crystallized form in an antagonistic movement. After doing so he does not really care about the experience of that thing, the commodity, to which he had given an autonomous existence as spectral. He does not speak much about the aesthetics, perception, or glam of the commodity. What's up with consumption? What kind of a practice is it? Benjamin speaks about the puppet-like entity and its enthronement. He recognizes in the commodity the sign of a standstill of what is happening. What a figure! In the *dernier cri* of yesterday, in the most recent crystal of commodity Benjamin finds the irredeemable of an epoch and its dark deception. Sex-appeal of the anorganic. According to his messianic understanding of revolution as something sudden – something that happens now, like a shot on the clock tower – there trembles, in the commodities' glitter of distraction, a possibility of that which has not yet been actualized.

And now? What can we do with Benjamin's crazy mixture of messianism, romanticism and materialism? What is our 19th century? How could we describe the experience of the commodity? The methodological figure of a 'dialectics at a standstill' does not seem so appropriate. It is related too much to the Hegelian idea of a unity of contradictions. Like use-value and exchange-value, utopia and cynicism take their respective sides, facing each other in the commodity. In his book, *Stanzas*, Giorgio Agamben criticizes Marx's opposition between the enjoyment of use-value as something natural and the accumulation of exchange values as something aberrant. As Derrida in *Specters of Marx*, Agamben notices that

> the whole [Marxian] critique of capitalism is conducted on behalf of the
> concreteness of the object of use against the abstraction of the exchange
> value [and that] Marx's critique is limited in that he does not know to
> separate himself from the utilitarian ideology, which decrees that the
> enjoyment of use-value is the original and natural relation of man to
> objects.[17]

Agamben looks for the possibility of a relation to things that goes beyond
both the enjoyment of use and the accumulation of exchange value. He
takes the artificiality of the commodity-thing, the will to fashion, the
distinguished gesture of the dandy who is a connoisseur of the speciality
of the commodity world, as starting point. He is looking for a way of
redeeming things from the imperative of use – for the possibility of an
impossible movement: the appropriation of unreality. But Agamben's text
still remains deconstructive poetry. He remains far away from the everyday experience of capitalism. Agamben, for example, takes Baudelaire as
an early witness of struggling against triviality. The *flaneurs* who, around
1840, set the tempo by walking turtles through the arcades on glittering
leashes held in their pink-gloved hands, testified to an early gesture of
pop cultural peculiarity: the loneliness of sensation-seeking and the
aristocratic distinction of the last dandies in contrast to the coming
world of salaried employees.[18] Since then, the strategy of coolness and
beautiful emptiness, open to impressions from commodified things, has
been repeated a thousandfold and failed successfully – as real capitalist

pop strategy it ran aground because of the pressure for subjectivization, outdoing oneself, anti-bourgeois excess, fucking as desire for transgression, the de-socialization of revolt, etc.

The poststructuralist term 'singularity' understands experience as an ensemble of pieces of things, parts of subjects, certain practices and certain situations. A singularity is more individual than a subject or an object. Hence Deleuze's quote of Lewis Carroll's paradox of "a grin without a cat,"[19] an intensity that does not refer to a subject or an object.

I would like to ask if the experience of the commodity is a real capitalist intensity of what Benjamin called now-time (*Jetztzeit*): the intensity of a promise of sudden change that until now just crystallizes itself in a newly bought thing. We should show this experience no disgust for alienation. If we take Benjamin without dialectics, without setting utopianism and cynicism opposite each other, we have to ask first for the relation into which the commodity-experience enters, that is to say, which non-actualized options does it have? That would again be the spectral aspect of social experience, and secondly, how could these intensities potentially escape the capitalist horizon?

And using Benjamin today: from which dream will we one day awake? Is it the past of Fordism? Which promise, which irredeemable expresses the mass goods that have been piled up in warehouses since the end of the Second World War? What does it mean that today the commodity-thing steps into the background? The experience of commodities becomes more and more immaterial and biopolitical. The image of the commodity altered: we now see clips out of casually professionalized life-forms, stills of casual bodies, flashlights on deviant forms of life. This has become the primary image of commodity: an affect, a lifestyle, sometimes a sub-cultural one. We can see it in advertisements all the time. What's up with the biopolitical commodity? Perhaps it incorporates the experience of how capitalist consumption occupies norm and deviation at the same time.

Notes:

1. Karl Marx, *Capital, Volume One* (1867), http://www.marxists.org/archive/marx/works/1867-c1/index.htm.

2. Ibid.

3. Ibid.

4. See Paolo Virno's 'Ten These on the Multitude and Post-Fordist Capitalism' at the end of his book, *A Grammar of the Multitude* (2002), Cambridge: MIT Press, 2004.

5. David Ricardo, *On the Principles of Political Economy and Taxation* (1817), London: John Murray, 1821. http://www.econlib.org/library/Ricardo/ricP.html.

6. Karl Marx, *Capital, Volume One.*

7. Ibid.

8. See The Brothers Grimm's Fairy Tale of *The Hare and the Hedgehog,* in which the hedgehog always wins the race; when he arrives at full speed at the lower end of the field, the hedgehog meets him with the cry, "I am here already." (http://fairytales4u.com/story2/hare.htm).

9. Gilles Deleuze, 'Desire and Pleasure' (1994) in Arnold I. Davidson (Ed.), *Foucault and His Interlocutors*, Chicago: University of Chicago Press, 1996.

10. For this debate, see the exciting article by Étienne Balibar, 'Foucault and Marx, the Question of Nominalism' (1989), in Timothy J. Armstrong (Ed.), *Michel Foucault: Philosopher*, New York and London: Harvester Wheatsheaf, 1992.

11. See Gilles Deleuze, *Foucault* (1986), Minneapolis: University of Minnesota Press, 1988.

12. Michel Foucault, *Discipline and Punish: The Birth of the Prison* (1975), Harmondsworth: Peregrine, 1977.

13. Karl Marx, *Capital, Volume One*.

14. Ibid.

15. Ibid.

16. Walter Benjamin, *Gesammelte Schriften*, with Theodor W. Adorno and Gershom Sholem, Rolf Tiedemann and Hermann Schweppenhäuser (Eds.), Frankfurt/M: Surkhamp, 1972-1999, V, 819.

17. Giorgio Agamben, *Stanzas: Word and Phantasm in Western Culture*, Minneapolis: University of Minnesota Press, 1993, 48.

18. Benjamin notes that "it was briefly fashionable to take turtles for a walk [...] The [dandy] liked to have the turtles set the pace for him. If he had his way, progress would be obliged to accommodate itself to this pace" in 'On Some Motifs in Baudelaire', in *Illuminations*, edited and introduced by Hannah Arendt, New York: Schocken, 1968, 197.

19. See Gilles Deleuze, *Difference and Repetition*, where he is referring to *Alice's Adventures in Wonderland*: "'Well! I've often seen a cat without a grin', thought Alice; 'but a grin without a cat! It's the most curious thing I ever saw in my life!'"

A Few Fragments on Machines
by Gerald Raunig

In the history of philosophy the problem of the machine is generally considered a secondary component of a more general question, that of the *techné*, the techniques. Here I would like to propose a reversal of the view in which the problem of technique is a part of a much more extensive machine issue. This 'machine' is open to the outside and its machinic environment and maintains all kinds of relationships to social components and individual subjectivities. It is hence a matter of expanding the concept of the technological machine into one of the machinic assemblage...[1]

Félix Guattari describes here in a few words the extent of one of the main and frequently misunderstood concepts of his heterogeneous theory production. Like many terms from the Guattarian concept forge, the machine is quite intentionally far removed from everyday language. In the reception of his theory, this practice of bending and inventing terms led to widespread, polemic attacks on Guattari and his colleague Gilles Deleuze as "hippies."[2] Yet the reinterpretation of the machine concept is not so new and radical as to be attributed solely to the French poststructuralists. Even at the time of the final expansion of the industrial revolution throughout Europe, a clear movement in the direction that Guattari took towards an extended machine thinking, could already be found in Karl Marx's *Grundrisse der Kritik der politischen Ökonomie*, drafted in 1857/58, in the 'Fragment on Machines'.[3]

In this section of the *Grundrisse* Marx developed his ideas on the transformation of the means of labor from a simple tool (which Guattari later called a proto-machine) into a form corresponding to fixed capital, in other words into technical machines and 'machinery'. In addition to the central concept of the machine, to which Marx was later to devote considerably more attention in *Capital*, here a second concept is treated on the side, which had a greater impact on further currents of post-Marxist theory. The concept of the 'General Intellect', which Marx introduced as a secondary concept, was the explicit starting point for the Italian (post)-Operaists, also for their ideas on mass intellectuality and immaterial labor.[4] The mutual references between French poststructuralism and Italian post-Operaism are generally just as manifold as the ways both currents refer to Marx and simultaneously distance themselves from him, however the concrete relation between the two aspects of the small Marx fragment (machine – General Intellect) is lost on both sides.[5]

Marx on Machines

In general, Marx sees the machine succinctly as a "means for producing surplus-value,"[6] in other words, certainly not intended to reduce the labor effort of the workers, but rather to optimize their exploitation.

Marx describes this function of 'machinery' in Chapter 13 of *Capital* with the three aspects of enhancing the human being utilizable as labor power (especially women's and child labor), prolonging the working day, and intensifying labor. Yet the machine also appears as an ever new effect of ever new workers' strikes and protests, as capital confronts them not only with direct repression, but especially with new machines.[7]

In the 'Fragment on Machines', Marx especially addresses the negative aspects of a historical development, at the end of which the machine, unlike the tool, is not at all to be understood as a means of labor for the individual worker: instead it encloses the knowledge and skill of workers and scholars as objectified knowledge and skill, opposing the scattered workers as a dominant power. According to Marx, the division of labor is the specific precondition for the rise of machines. It was only after labor was transformed into work that was still human, but increasingly mechanical, mechanized, that the condition was created for these mechanical tasks of the workers to be taken over in a further step by machines:

> But, once adopted into the production process of capital, the means of labor passes through different metamorphoses, whose culmination is the *machine*, or rather, an *automatic system of machinery* (system of machinery: the *automatic* one is merely its most complete, most adequate form, and alone transforms machinery into a system), set in motion by an automaton, a moving power that moves itself; this automaton consisting

of numerous mechanical and intellectual organs, so that the workers themselves are cast merely as its conscious linkages.[8]

This passage from Marx indicates that the machine itself, in the final stage of the development of the means of labor, not only structuralizes and striates the workers as automaton, as apparatus, as structure, but it is also simultaneously permeated by mechanical and intellectual organs, through which it is successively further developed and renewed.

On the one hand, Marx here formulates the workers' alienation from their means of labor, how they are (externally) determined by the machines, the domination of living labor by objectified labor, and he introduces the figure of the inverted relationship of man and machine:

> The worker's activity, reduced to a mere abstraction of activity, is determined and regulated on all sides by the movement of the machinery, and not the opposite. The science which compels the inanimate limbs of the machinery, by their construction, to act purposefully, as an automaton, does not exist in the worker's consciousness, but rather acts upon him through the machine as an alien power, as the power of the machine itself.[9]

The inversion of the relationship between workers and means of work in the direction of the domination of the machine over the human being is defined here not only by the hierarchy of the labor process, but is also understood as an inversion of the disposal of knowledge. Through the process of the objectification of knowledge forms in the machine, the producers of this knowledge lose undivided competence and power over the labor process. Labor itself appears as separated, scattered among many points of the mechanical system in single, living workers. "In machinery, knowledge appears as alien, external to him [the worker]; and living labor [as] subsumed under self-activating objectified labor."[10]

Even for Marx in the 'Fragment on Machines', however, the huge, self-active machine is more than a technical mechanism. The machine does not here appear limited to its technical aspects, but rather as a mechanical-intellectual-social assemblage: although technology and knowledge (as machine) have a one-sided effect on the workers, the machine is not only a concatenation of technology and knowledge, of mechanical and intellectual organs, but additionally also of social organs, to the extent that it coordinates the scattered workers.

Hence the collectivity of the human intellect is ultimately also evident in the machine. Machines

> are *organs of the human brain, created by the human hand*; the power of knowledge, objectified. The development of fixed capital indicates to what degree general social knowledge has become a *direct force of production*, and to what degree, hence, the conditions of the process of social life itself have come under the control of the general intellect and been transformed in accordance with it. To what degree the powers of social production have

been produced, not only in the form of knowledge, but also as immediate organs of social practice, of the real life process.[11]

I will come back to the significance of the General Intellect later, but at this point the aspect should be emphasized that productive force not only corresponds to new technical machines, not even only to the concatenation of 'mechanical and intellectual organs', but also and especially to the relationship of the producers to one another and to the production process. Not only is the inside of the technical machine permeated by mechanical and intellectual lines, but social linkages and relationships are also evident on the outside, which become components of the machine. The 'Fragment on Machines' not only points to the fact that knowledge and skill are accumulated and absorbed in fixed capital as "general productive forces of the social brain"[12] and that the process of turning production into knowledge is a tendency of capital, but also indicates the inversion of this tendency: the concatenation of knowledge and technology is not exhausted in fixed capital, but also refers beyond the technical machine and the knowledge objectified in it to social cooperation and communication.

When Theater Becomes Machine...[13]

Building upon early attempts at mass staging, biomechanics and constructivist stage mechanization by Vsevolod Meyerhold, in the 'Moscow First Workers Theater' Sergei Eisenstein and Sergei Tretyakov developed the 'eccentric theater' and the 'montage of attractions' between 1921 and 1924, from which separate versions of art production strategies later emerged in film, theory and operative literature. In the Soviet Union in the early 1920s the inclusion of elements from circus, revue and film still signaled an attack on the pure practice of bourgeois theater, carried out especially by means of the 'attraction'. The 'Theater of Attractions' involved aggressive and physical moments of theater, the effects of which were intended to disrupt the mechanisms of illusion and empathy. At the same time, the montage of attractions did not signify an accumulation of tricks and artifices designed for effect, but rather the further development of circus and vaudeville elements for a materialist, 'natural science' theater. What the *Proletkult* theater took over from the circus was the approach of the *artiste*, but also the fragmentation of its structure of numbers, the sequencing of "individual attractions not con-joined by a subject matter":[14] with Eisenstein and Tretyakov, this apparent deficiency of disconnectedness became a weapon against empathy. To counter the totality of the subject matter, they mounted and molecularized the piece as a piecework of single attractions. Eisenstein wrote:

> I define an attraction in the formal sense as an independent and primary element of the construction of a performance – as the molecular (i.e. consti-tutive) unity of the impact of theater and of the theater in general.[15]

The attraction is thus more than just a circus number, it is a situation that, as a molecular unit, contains conflicts. Eisenstein and Tretyakov's intention was to create a collision with the audience.

The 'Theater of Attractions' did not conceal this assault on the audience as the "main material of the theater."[16] Contrary to the theater illusion inviting the audience to take part in an experience in a pseudo-participatory manner, the 'Theater of Attractions' sought to establish a process of fragmented excitement. The aspect of montage did not determine the macro-structure of the piecework here, but was instead applied to the composition of the individual attractions. "The actors, the things, the sounds are nothing other than elements, from which an attraction is constructed":[17] an interweaving of actors, who do not portray, but work – and of things, constructive frameworks and objects that the actors work with instead of decorations and props.[18]

> The illusory action of the theater is regarded as an inherently coherent manifestation; what we have here, however, is a conscious expectation of incompleteness and of major activity on the part of the viewer, who must be able to orient himself to the most diverse manifestations that are played out before him.[19]

In his writings on the 'Theater of Attractions', Tretyakov indicates the direction that the relationship of human machines, technical machines, and social machines should take:

> The work on the scenic material, the transformation of the stage into a machine that helps to develop the work of the actor as broadly and diversely as possible, is socially justified if this machine not only moves its pistons and holds up to a certain workload, but also begins to carry out certain useful work and serve the ongoing tasks of our revolutionary era.[20]

Above and beyond the aestheticizing use of technical machines and constructions as decoration, attempts were undertaken to make the stage machinery of the theater transparent as a model for technicization and to create flowing transitions between technical machines and the constructive scaffolding and stage sets. Beyond Meyerhold's biomechanics, which trained rigid self-discipline of the human body as a machine, but easily deteriorated into danced sculpture, the actors and actresses became elements of the attraction. And finally, Taylorist ideas of the scientific administration of work and the reversal of the man-machine relationship led to the development of a concatenation of technical machines (the things), the bodies of the performers, and the social organization of all participants, including the audience. These ideas of the interlocking of technical and social structures in the 'Theater of Attractions' remain only superficially bound to a 'theater of the scientific age'. The attempt to also 'calculate' machines this complex, as proposed by Eisenstein and Tretyakov, goes beyond a relationship of the exteriority of technical machines and social collectives and beyond purely mathematical, technical considerations.

Eisenstein described the attraction as being based solely on something relative, on the reaction of the viewers. The representation of a given situation due to the subject matter and its development and resolution through collisions that are logically connected with this situation, subordinated to the psychologism of the subject matter, is replaced by the free montage of attractions, which are mounted to achieve a certain final effect and thus carry out a work on the audience. Eisenstein and Tretyakov wanted to change the order of emotions, to organize them differently. The audience was to become part of the machine that they called the 'Theater of Attractions'. Through "experimental testing" and "mathematical calculation," they wanted to produce "certain emotional shocks" among the audience.[21]

The emphasis here is on *certain* emotional shocks: contrary to the total management of emotions in bourgeois theater, this meant an excitement determined by utility and precisely demarcated by exactly mounted impulses. This attempt to 'exactly calculate' emotions was the attempt, contrary to the bourgeois strategy of aesthetic fiction, to steer and test the cited reality of signs, the body work of the performers and the bodies of the audience in their interplay. However, a clear distinction must be made between the means of the old theater model and that of the new. Although the theater performance was not explicitly defined as a "process of working on the audience with the means of the theater effect"[22] in bourgeois theater jargon, the intention of 'aesthetic educa-tion' implicitly had a similar effect. The 'Theater of Attractions', however, sought to *calculate* its audience. This also meant that "the attractions are calculated *depending on the audience*."[23] In other words, every performance required new considerations, in fact the performance found its purpose in the audience, its material in the context of the life of the audience. It is not known how far Eisenstein and Tretyakov took their calculation experiments; surveys were taken among the viewers, their reactions meticulously observed and the results carefully evaluated. The fact that their calculations had to/were intended to take a considerable goal-consequences difference into consideration, certainly a far greater uncontrollability than the performance practices of the 19th century, was due not only to the audience classes newly won for the theater, but also to the experimental format of the attraction.

The performances of Tretyakov's *Moscow, Do You Hear Me?* must have been a pinnacle in this context, resulting in partly tumultuous situations in the theater.[24] Written, organized, and produced extremely quickly as a mobilization and agitation play for a possible German revolution following the Hamburg revolt in late October 1923, it premiered on the sixth anniversary of the October Revolution on November 7, 1923. From a superficial perspective, Eisenstein and Tretyakov's play failed on two levels: on one level, it failed on account of the occasion, since the revolution, as we know, did not take place. On another level, its self-reflexive theme, inciting a revolution through art, also holds the entire problematic issue of overestimating artistic practice. The revolution was to be set off not solely by the representation of situations, but by converting the situation through intervention and the abrupt transformation of the bourgeois theater into a revolutionary theater. Just in the specific performance context of the socialist society in Moscow, however, this representation of revolution was to have a different impact than in a revolutionary situation. Tretyakov and Eisenstein made use of the increasingly mounted attractions with an accentuation such that more and more excitement spread through the audience: more and more frequent heckling, viewers reaching for weapons, and fist fights with extras getting involved in play fights must have resulted in an impressive chaos. And the inflamed viewers were reported to have reacted heatedly not only in the theater, but also in the streets of Moscow afterward: "after that they moved through the streets, wildly beating against shop windows and singing songs."[25]

The question can probably not be answered as to what extent the 'Theater of Attractions' intended to 'calculate' with the spontaneity described above, outside the space of the theater as well. The *calculation* of the audience may well have gone so far as to seek to plan for, calculate, and evaluate even chaos and tumult. With their demands for exact definitions of social tasks and scientific methods, Eisenstein and Tretyakov certainly succeeded in shifting the theater machine to a terrain so unstable that no other artistic practice would soon be able to match it.

Re-inventing the Machine

In the 'Appendix' to *Anti-Oedipus*, Gilles Deleuze and Félix Guattari not only develop a 'Programmatic Balance for Wish Machines',[26] but also write, in contrast to Marx's ideas on machinery,[27] their own machine concept. What this involves is an expansion or renewal of the concept, but not at all a metaphorizing of the machine. Deleuze and Guattari do not establish a 'figurative sense' of the machine, but instead attempt to newly invent the term at a critical distance from both its everyday sense and that of Marxist scholars:

> We do not presuppose the metaphorical use of the word machine, but rather an (indistinct) hypothesis about its origins: the way in which arbitrary elements are made to be machines *through recursion and communication*.[28]

Marx's machine theory is introduced here with the cipher, "that classical schema" and is only explicitly named in the third and final part of the appendix.[29] Whereas Marx, in the thirteenth chapter of *Capital*, addresses the question at some length of "how the instruments of labor are converted from tools into machines, or what is the difference between a machine and the implements of a handicraft,"[30] Deleuze and Guattari find the linear conception of the first question particularly insufficient in many respects. What they question here is less the immanent logic of the transformation of the machine as described by Marx, than the framework that Marx presupposes as the basis of this logic: a dimension of man and nature that all social forms have in common. The linear development from tool (as an extension of the human being to relieve strain) toward an upheaval, in the course of which the machine ultimately becomes independent of the human being, so to speak, simultaneously determines the machine as one aspect in a mechanical series. This kind of schema, "stemming from the humanist spirit and abstract," especially isolates the productive forces from the social conditions of their application.

Imagined beyond this evolutive schema, the machine is no longer only a function in a series imagined as starting from the tool, which occurs at a certain point. Similar to the way the *techné* concept of antiquity already meant both material object and practice, the machine is also not solely an instrument of work, in which social knowledge is absorbed and enclosed. Instead it opens up in respectively different social contexts to different concatenations, connections and couplings: "There is no such thing as either man or nature now, only a process that produces the one within the other and couples the machines together."[31]

Instead of placing tool and machine in a series, Deleuze and Guattari seek a more subtle differentiation, and in this way their query corresponds to Marx's second question about the distinction between machine and tool. Indeed, this distinction could be explained in the form of a different genealogy than the one followed by Marx, such as one that refers to the pre-modern understanding of the *machina*, in which the separation between the organic and the mechanical was irrele-vant. In *Anti-Oedipus*, however, this difference is treated conceptually/theoretically: the machine is a communication factor, the tool – at least in its non-machinic form – is, on the other hand, a communication-less extension or prosthesis. Conversely, the concrete tool in its use for exchange/connection with the human being is always more machine than the technical machine imagined in isolation: "Becoming a piece with something else means something fundamentally different from extending oneself, projecting oneself or being replaced."[32]

By distinguishing the machine from something that simply extends or replaces the human being, Deleuze and Guattari not only refuse to affirm the conventional figure of the machine's domination over the human being. They also posit a difference from an all too simplistic and optimistic celebration of a certain form of machine which, from Futurism to cyber-fans, is in danger of overlooking the social aspect in ever new combinations of 'man-machine'.[33] The narrative of the human being's adaptation to the machine, the replacement of the human by the machine, misses the machinic, according to Deleuze and Guattari, not only in its critical, Marxist articulation, but also in its euphoric tendency.

> It is no longer a matter of confronting man and machine to estimate possible or impossible correspondences, extensions and substitutions of the one or the other, but rather of conjoining the two and showing how man becomes a piece with the machine or with other things in order to constitute a machine.[34]

The 'other things' may be animals, tools, other people, statements, signs or wishes, but they only become machine in a process of exchange, not in the paradigm of substitution.

Consider the fable from *The Third Policeman* by Flann O'Brien, in which the Irish author presents precise calculations of the point in time when, due to the flowing of molecules, people on bicycles turn into bicycles and bicycles into people and in what percentage – with all the problems resulting from this, such as people falling over if they are not leaning against a wall and bicycles assuming human features. For an investigation of the machine here, it is specifically not a question of changing quantities of identity on both parts (20% bicycle, 80% human or – even more alarming – 60% bicycle, 40% human), but rather of the exchange and the flux of machinic singularities and their concatenation with other social machines:

> On the contrary, we think that the machine must be grasped in an immediate relation to a social body and not at all to a human biological organism. Given this, it is no longer appropriate to judge the machine as a new segment that, with its starting point in the abstract human being in keeping with this development, follows the tool. For human being and tool are already machine parts on the full body of the respective society. The machine is initially a social machine, constituted by the machine-generating instance of a full body and by human being and tools, which are, to the extent that they are distributed on this body, machinized.[35]

Deleuze and Guattari thus shift the perspective from the question of the form in which the machine follows the simpler tool, how human beings and tools are machinized, to that of which social machines make the emergence of specific technical, affective, cognitive, semiotic machines and their concatenations possible and simultaneously necessary.

The main feature of the machine is the flowing of its components: every extension or substitution would be communication-lessness, and the quality of the machine is exactly the opposite, namely that of communication, of exchange, of openness. Contrary to the structure, to the state apparatus, which tends toward closure, the machinic tends toward permanent opening. From the text 'Machine and Structure', written in 1969, to 'Machinic Heterogenesis', published in 1992, Guattari repeatedly pointed out the different quality of machine and structure, machine and state apparatus:[36] "The machine has something more than the structure."[37] It is not limited to managing and striating entities closed off to one another, but opens up to other machines and moves with their machinic assemblages. It consists of machines and penetrates several structures simultaneously. It depends on external elements in order to be able to exist at all. It implies a complementarity not only with the human being that fabricates it, allows it to function or destroys it, but also by itself in a relationship of alterity with other virtual or actual machines.[38]

In addition to this theoretical approach to a simultaneously indifferent and ambivalent machine concept in *Anti-Oedipus* and several older and more recent texts by Guattari, however, it is important not to omit the historical context of a normative turn to the machinic. Guattari had already started to develop his machine concept in the late 1960s, specifically against the political background of leftist experiments in organizing. These endeavors were initially directed against the hard segmentarity of Real-Socialist and Eurocommunist state left-wings, were further explored on the basis of the experiences of diverse subcultural and micropolitical practices – in Guattari's case especially on the basis of anti-psychiatric practice – and ultimately flowed, even after 1968, into efforts to resist and reflect on the structuralization and closure of the 1968 generation in cadres, factions, and circles.

The problem that Guattari deals with in his first machine text, written briefly after the experience of 1968, is the problem of a lasting revolutionary organization:

> the problem of establishing an institutional machine distinguished by a special axiomatic and a special practice; what is meant is the guarantee that it does not close itself off in the various social structures, especially not in the state structure, which seems to form the cornerstone of dominant production conditions, although it no longer corresponds to the means of production.[39]

Not only the 'dominant production conditions', but also the current forms of resistance have assumed machinic form; structuralization and closure as gestures of (self-)protection bypass this fact. Machinic institutions cannot reproduce the forms of the state apparatus, those provided by the paradigm of representation, but produce new forms of 'instituent practices':

> The revolutionary project as the 'machine activity' of an institutional subversion would have to uncover these kinds of subjective possibilities and ensure them ahead of time in every phase of the battle against being 'structuralized'. Yet this kind of permanent check of the machine effects that affect the structures could never be satisfied with a 'theoretical practice'. It requires the development of a specific analytical practice, which immediately applies to every step of organizing the battle.[40]

General Intellect and the EuroMayday Machine

Much of what Guattari formulated in his thoughts on the machine against the background of experiences of May 1968, has been updated in recent years – perhaps even more so than during the 1960s and the 1970s – in the forms of non-representationist movements that have become active against migration and border regimes, economic globalization and the precarization of work and life.[41] The latter is the main issue especially of the EuroMayday movement,[42] which started in Milan and has sought to re-appropriate May 1st, particularly in recent years. Quite similar in this respect to the theater audience revolutionized and animated by Tretyakov and Eisenstein's play *Moscow, Do You Hear Me?*, the EuroMayday activists today also move through the streets, sometimes "wildly beating against shop windows and singing songs;" specifically through the streets of about twenty European cities, including London, Copenhagen, Maribor, Barcelona, Hamburg and Vienna.[43] Sometimes the shop windows are broken, but more often they are painted over, sprayed and covered with a layer of new signs.[44] The EuroMayday Parades not only renew the revolutionary traditions of May 1st, but also oppose the privatization of urban public spheres with their bodies, images, signs and statements. This kind of reappropriation of the city is consistently played out without stages and podiums, in the endeavor to counter the paradigm of representation with the paradigm of the event.

Yet the EuroMayday machine has two temporalities. Not only that of the event, but also the long duration of instituent practices, in which the connection between the machine as movement against structuralization and the machine as 'social productive force' becomes clear. Organizing for May 1st is not the only dimension of the Mayday activists: even though limited by the wish and time resources of the activists, throughout the year there are micro-actions and discursive events, regular communication on mailing lists and meetings in various European cities for transnational exchange. In addition, an increasingly dense network of addressing the issue of the precarization of work and life is growing, not only in Europe.

However, this formation of instituent practices is only incipiently evident. According to the post-Operaist philosopher Paolo Virno, the movement has "not yet sufficiently bundled the forms of battle that are suitable for transforming the situation of precarious, temporary and atypical work into a subversive political asset."[45] This kind of bundling starts less with the old forms of organization by 'state apparatuses' than with the concatenation of machinic forms of movement and post-Fordist forms of work and life. In his texts on this theme, especially in *A Grammar of the Multitude*, Virno picks up directly from the 'Fragment on Machines' and the concept, casually introduced there by Marx, of the General Intellect. Even if social knowledge was really ever fully absorbed in the technical machines in the era of industrialization, this would be completely unthinkable in the post-Fordist context:

> Obviously, this aspect of the 'general intellect' matters, but it is not everything. We should consider the dimension where the general intellect, instead of being incarnated (or rather, *cast in iron*) into the system of machines, exists as attribute of living labor."[46]

As post-Operaist theory formulates, following Guattari, due to the logic of economic development itself, it is necessary that the machine is not understood merely as a structure that striates the workers and encloses social knowledge in itself. Going beyond Marx's idea of knowledge absorbed in fixed capital, Virno thus posits his thesis of the simultaneously pre-individual and trans-individual social quality of the intellect:

> Living labor in post-Fordism has as raw material and means of production: thinking that is expressed through language, the ability to learn and communicate, the imagination, in other words the capacity that distinguishes

> human consciousness. Living labor accordingly incarnates the *General Intellect* (the 'social brain'), which Marx called the 'pillar of production and wealth'. Today the *General Intellect* is no longer absorbed in fixed capital, it no longer represents only the knowledge contained in the system of the machines, but rather the verbal cooperation of a multitude of living subjects.[47]

By taking up Marx's term, Virno indicates that 'intellect' is not to be understood here as the exclusive competence of an individual, but rather as a common tie and a constantly developing foundation of individuation, as a social quality of the intellect. Here *pre*-individual human 'nature', which lies in speaking, thinking, communicating, is augmented by the *trans*-individual aspect of the General Intellect: it is not only the entirety of all knowledge accumulated by the human species, not only what all prior shared capability has in common, it is also the in-between of cognitive workers, the communicative interaction, abstraction and self-reflection of living subjects, the cooperation, the coordinated action of living labor.

Finally, on the basis of Virno's writings we are able to connect General Intellect as a collective capability and a machine concept in Guattari's sense. Knowledge as collective intellectuality is complementary to the machinic quality of production and social movement. General Intellect, or the 'public intellect', as Virno further develops the concept, is another name for Guattari's expansion of the machine concept beyond the technical machine and outside its realm: "Within the contemporary labor process, constellations of concepts exist, which function as productive 'machines' themselves, without needing a mechanical body or a little electronic soul."[48]

For suggestions and critical advice, I would like to thank Martin Birkner, Isabell Lorey, Birgit Mennel and Stefan Nowotny.

Translated from the German by Aileen Derieg

Notes:

1. Félix Guattari, 'Über Maschinen', 118, in Henning Schmidgen (Ed.) *Ästhetic und Maschinismus. Texte zu und von Félix Guattari*, Berlin: Merve, 1995, 115-132.

2. Cf. for instance Richard Barbrook, 'The Holy Fools', in *Mute* 11, London: Mute Publishing, 1998, 57-65 and Oliver Marchart, 'The Crossed Place of the Political Party', http://www.republicart.net/disc/empire/marchart02_en.htm, *accessed 16/10/2005.*

3. Karl Marx, *Grundrisse der Kritik der politischen Ökonomie*, MEW 42: Dietz, 2005, 590-609 [http://www.marxists.org/archive/marx/works/1857/grundrisse/ch13.htm#p690].

4. For a brief outline of the various references from Operaist and post-Operaist generations to the machine fragment, see Paolo Virno, 'Wenn die Nacht am tiefsten … Anmerkungen zum General Intellect', in Thomas Atzert and Jost Müller (Eds.) *Immaterielle Arbeit und imperiale Souveränität*, Münster: Westfälisches Dampfboot, 2004, 148-155.

5. In Toni Negri's early book, *Marx beyond Marx*, for instance, which resulted from his Paris seminar on the Outlines in 1978, there is no discussion of the machine. An exception here is Maurizio Lazzarato, who continued the idea of both aspects in his work on immaterial

labor on the one hand and video philosophy on the other.

6. Karl Marx, *Das Kapital*, MEW23, Berlin: Dietz, 1998, 391 [http://www.marxists.org/archive/marx/works/1867-c1/ch15.htm#S1].

7. Cf. Marx, *Das Elend der Philosophie*, MEW4, Berlin: Dietz, 1990, 174 [http://www.marxists.org/archive/marx/works/1847/poverty-philosophy/ch02e.htm]: "In England, strikes have regularly given rise to the invention and application of new machines. Machines were, it may be said, the weapon employed by the capitalist to quell the revolt of specialized labor. The self-acting mule, the greatest invention of modern industry, put out of action the spinners who were in revolt."; Marx, *Das Kapital*, 459 [http://www.marxists.org/archive/marx/works/1867-c1/ch15.htm#S5]: "Machinery [...] is the most powerful weapon for repressing strikes, those periodical revolts of the working-class against the autocracy of capital..."

8. Marx, *Grundrisse*, 592 [http://www.marxists.org/archive/marx/works/1857/grundrisse/ch13.htm#p692].

9. Ibid., 593 [http://www.marxists.org/archive/marx/works/1857/grundrisse/ch13.htm#p693]

10. Ibid., 595 [http://www.marxists.org/archive/marx/works/1857/grundrisse/ch13.htm#p694]

11. Ibid., 602 [http://www.marxists.org/archive/marx/works/1857/grundrisse/ch14.htm#p706]

12. Ibid., 594 [http://www.marxists.org/archive/marx/works/1857/grundrisse/ch13.htm#p694]

13. This fragment is an abridged version of the section 'Theater Machines Against Representation. Eisenstein and Tretyakov in the Gas Works' from Raunig, *Kunst und Revolution*, 134-147 [http://www.republicart.net/publications/artandrevolution.pdf].

14. 'Ein Experiment der Theaterarbeit', in *Proletkult 2. Zur Praxis und Theorie einer proletarischen Kulturrevolution in Sowjetrussland 1917–1925*, Peter Gorsen and Eberhard Knödler-Bunte, Stuttgart: Frommann, 1975, 111-116.

15. Sergei Eisenstein, 'Die Montage der Attraktionen', 118, in *Proletkult 2. Zur Praxis und Theorie einer proletarischen Kulturrevolution in Sowjetrussland 1917-1925*, 117-121.

16. Ibid.

17. 'Ein Experiment der Theaterarbeit', 112.

18. The concatenation of events and of players, things, sounds and audience, as described here, comes surprisingly close to Guattari's machine concept. In *Anti-Oedipus* Deleuze and Guattari mention that, in Russian Futurism and Constructivism, certain production circumstances remain, despite collective appropriation, "external to the machine," yet the practice of the 'Theater of Attractions' seems to contradict this.

19. 'Ein Experiment der Theaterarbeit', 116.

20. Sergei Tretyakov, 'Theater der Attraktionen', 68, in *Proletkult 2. Zur Praxis und Theorie einer proletarischen Kulturrevolution in Sowjetrussland 1917-1925*, 121-127.

21. cf. Eisenstein, 'Die Montage der Attraktionen', 119.

22. 'Ein Experiment der Theaterarbeit', 112.

23. Tretyakov, 'Theater der Attraktionen', 69.

24. cf. 'Hörst du, Moskau?', 128f., in *Proletkult 2. Zur Praxis und Theorie einer proletarischen Kulturrevolution in Sowjetrussland 1917-1925*, 127-129.

25. Tretyakov, 'Notizen eines Dramatikers', 99, in *Gesichter der Avantgarde. Porträts, Essays, Briefe*, Berlin: Aufbau, 1985, 98-101.

26. Gilles Deleuze and Félix Guattari, *L'Anti-Oedipe*, 463-487, Paris: Les Éditions de Minuit, 1972: The appendix was not published in the English version of *Anti-Oedipus*.

27. In *L'Anti-Oedipe* Deleuze and Guattari seem to consistently refer to *Capital*; in 'Capital as the Integral of Power Formations' (205), for instance, Guattari also refers to the machine fragment.

28. Deleuze/Guattari, *L'Anti-Oedipe*, 464.

29. Ibid., 465 and 481ff.

30. MEW23, 391 [http://www.marxists.org/archive/marx/works/1867-c1/ch15.htm#S1].

31. Deleuze/Guattari, *L'Anti-Oedipe*, 8.

32. Ibid., 465.

33. At this point it should be noted that Deleuze and Guattari's use of the machine concept is consistently indifferent to ambivalent. At the same time, the dark sides of machinization come up regularly, such as in reflections on fascist and post-fascist forms of the war machine in *A Thousand Plateaus* (especially 420-421) or Guattari's concept of 'machinic enslavement' in 'worldwide integrated capitalism', as Guattari called the phenomenon in the early 1980s that is today framed as globalization. Unlike Marx, here 'machinic enslavement' (Guattari, 'Capital as the Integral of Power Formations', 219-222) does not mean the subordinated relationship of the human being to the technical machine that objectifies social knowledge, but rather a more general form of the collective management of knowledge and the necessity of permanent participation. It is the machinic quality of post-Fordist capitalism – here Guattari is close to the theories of neoliberal governmentality developed from Foucault – that adds a palette of control mechanisms to the traditional systems of direct repression, which requires the complicity of individuals.

34. Deleuze/Guattari, *L'Anti-Oedipe*, 464.

35. Ibid., 516.

36. The relevant concept of the state apparatus goes far beyond conventional concepts of the state; as the opposite of machines, state apparatuses are characterized by structures, striated spaces and hard segmentarity.

37. Guattari, 'Über Maschinen', 121.

38. Cf. Guattari, 'Machinic Heterogenesis', 37.

39. Guattari, 'Maschine und Struktur', 137f, *Psychotherapie, Politik und die Aufgaben der institutionellen Analyse*, Frankfurt/Main: Suhrkamp, 1976, 127–138 (The original French version of this article was published in Félix Guattari, *Psychoanalyse et transversalité*, Paris 1973).

40. Ibid., 138.

41. The category of 'non-representationist practice' does not include the Social Forums movement, which has not met its own claims, as defined in its statutes, of rejecting representation in form and content.

42. On the issues addressed by this movement (especially the precarization of work and life), cf. the articles of the eipcp Web Journal entitled precariat http://www.republicart.net/disc/precariat/index.htm, particularly Mitropoulos, 'Precari-Us?' on the question of terms.

43. cf. http://www.euromayday.org and the links on this site to the various local EuroMayday sites.

44. On these aspects of the reappropriation of the city in the course of EuroMayday parades, cf. Raunig, 'La inseguridad vencerá. Anti-Precarious Activism and Mayday Parades', http://www.republicart.net/disc/precariat/raunig06_de.htm.

45. Paolo Virno, 'Eine performative Bewegung', 6, in *Kulturrisse* 02/2005, 6-9.

46. Paolo Virno, *A Grammar of the Multitude*, Los Angeles/New York: Semiotext(e), 2004, 65.

47. Paolo Virno, 'Der Engel des General Intellect', 174, in *Grammatik der Multitude*, Vienna: Turia & Kant, 2005, 165-188.

48. Paolo Virno, 'Wenn die Nacht am tiefsten … Anmerkungen zum General Intellect', 154.

Autonomy and the Administration of Aesthetics

by Trude Iversen

Marx's theory of alienation is both well-known and debatable, as its point of departure is that the organization of labor is the impetus of history, the history of the modes of production. For certain Marxists, alienation is therefore the central starting point of an analysis of society and a critique of the system. Alienation from one's labor (product) damages one's cognition, because labor is a cognitive activity; both self-cognitive and cognitive towards things and surroundings.

Based on this model, the artist is perceived as free from capitalist accumulation; an autonomous producer. This is because the artist is not producing under the yoke of profit. But how does this comprehension of autonomous production affect the possibilities for counter-strategies and critique? And does a (relatively) autonomous art production always necessarily imply a liberating aspect? When does the category of autonomy act as ideology, and how does art act as pure productive force? Some of these are not new questions, and they are in part discussed by Peter Bürger in his book *Theory of the Avant-Garde* from 1974,[1] by Theodor W. Adorno in his *Aesthetic Theory* (1970)[2] and by Jay Bernstein in *The Fate of Art: Aesthetic Alienation from Kant to Derrida and Adorno* (1992).[3]

According to Bürger, the autonomy of art must be understood as a historical phenomenon, and must not to be mistaken for something inherent in the essence of art or as art's self-realization. Paradoxically, art is *integrated* as autonomous in the bourgeois-capitalist society to a greater degree than in earlier organizations of society. For the aesthete of autonomy, the important thing is that art becomes socially relevant by taking an antagonistic stance towards society, something which can only be done in a state of autonomy. Adorno therefore uses art as an example of something which performs social critique merely by existing: When art becomes self-legislative, it gains the opportunity to "yield to existing social norms and qualify as 'socially useful'," and thereby it rejects the "debasement by the situation which moves toward the total exchange society." As autonomous, art has become pure productive force, and thus it exists as "the objective counter-image to the chained."

In contrast to Adorno, Bürger claims to be able to demonstrate that the historical Avant-Garde movement in the beginning of the 20th century revolted towards what they saw as art's *limited* function and marginalization by virtue of its autonomy. Marginalization as a consequence of autonomy has proved to be difficult to account for theoretically. Attempts to understand the implications of autonomy and art often lead to an exaggeration of art's self-legislation. The history, logic and beauty of art are frequently regarded as separate from other social mechanisms, and the contexts in which art is involved are lost, out of sight. According to Bürger, "Even if it is necessary to determine what art is in bourgeois society, the concept of autonomy distorts the social conditions of art so that they become invisible." It is therefore necessary to break with the aesthetic which understands autonomy as "the essence of art" or "the self-realization of art" or as something which is determined by the consciousness of the artist. A materialist model of interpretation perceives autonomy in art as a historical phenomenon, and undertakes the charting of the historical prerequisites for how this change could happen.

The category *bourgeois autonomy*, which describes art's *relative* independence of society, is easily transformed into the false concept of *total* independence. Hence, autonomy is also ideology, because of the failure to recognize the category as a historical entity. The category of autonomy, Bürger claims, contains both an aspect of truth, in art's detachment from the life praxis, and an aspect of untruth, in the hypostasis of the autonomy.

Only art which has been totally separated from the life praxis of the existing society – something art, according to Bürger, accomplished in aestheticism – can be the focal point of the organization of a new life praxis. Bürger sees the *self-critical* aspect of the Avant-Garde critique as a manifestation of the attempt to overcome the dialectical one-sidedness of the construction of the past as the prehistory of the present. Marx's concept of the self-critique of the present is involved and employed in the art field. The pre-Avant-Garde art movements performed a critique on previous art production that became immanent in the system: critique that only deals with artistic means. Only when art becomes self-critical does it have the possibility to grasp the development of art, while at the same time acknowledging that this comprehension isn't independent of the current standpoint of the onlooker; according to Bürger, "insight in the collective process to the degree to which it has come to an – always temporary – conclusion in the cognitive subject's present time."

The analysis that the historical Avant-Garde was the first to be able to make this self-critique owes alot to Marx, who asserted that the self-critical is only possible when the *part* of society to which it is directed is totally detached and has acheived a state of autonomy. By not having any social function, the art production of aestheticism could lay the foundation for the self-critique of the historical Avant-Garde.

Today, the works of the Avant-Garde are received and exhibited *as* art. This also applies to the works of the neo-Avant-Garde. Bürger's function analysis brings forth the notion that when the neo-Avant-Gardists demand that the their work be received as art, they reject the intentions of the historical Avant-Garde: the Avant-Garde is institutionalized, and thereby its intentions are *negated*.

Autonomy as ideology is related to an exaggeration. This exaggeration exists on several planes: as an argument for reactionary institutional practice (for example, claiming that artists shouldn't be subject to the same laws on minimum wages as the rest of society), as an argument for conceptions of the essence of art and its history, and as an argument for other unsocial practices. Reproduction of the conception that the art world exists as something other than the 'real world', claims Andrea

Fraser, conceals exactly the economical, intellectual and political interests that are invested in art productions (works, exhibitions, books and events).[4] This concealment turns artists and art workers into false beacons of neoliberalism, because of their 'voluntary' freedom, creativity and entrepreneurship.

Reactionary exploitation of the concept of the autonomy of art can only exist if we accept this exaggeration as an argument, and accept that autonomy has become ideology. The notion of the art space as a free space in an otherwise control-orientated society (Adorno) must be revised, but the exaggeration of the autonomy of art is also related to the plane of thought on which we place the insights of art. It is not an unknown conception that specific works of art can be perceived as "more truthful than empirical truth [...], more rational than methodical reason, more just than liberal justice, more valuable than principled morality or utility."[5] By hypostasing the autonomous status of art, however, this is hard to demonstrate and display, because the aesthetic experience becomes unique. For Jay Bernstein it is a historical fact that art was alienated in the moment it became aesthetic: "it denominates art's alienation from truth which is caused by art's *becoming* aesthetical, a becoming that has been fully consummated only in modern societies."[6] For Bernstein, art's severance from religion is the story of the aesthetical alienation of art. Hence, it is not an unproblematic separation where different modes of experience live side by side in a language game. For Bernstein, perceiving art as alienated means experiencing it "as acting in excess of its excluded status."

As opposed to what has been the case in recent discussions on whether art should recapture the concept of beauty, we should bear in mind the consequences of aestheticizing art's status. The different planes on which the discussion of autonomy exists makes it difficult to defend the autonomy of art per se. If Peter Bürger is correct in claiming that the self-critique was possible only after a total separation of the art field, and that the ambition of uniting art and practice failed with the incorporation of the neo-Avant-Garde, we have reason for a self-critique[7] where both joint responsibility and complicity may be among the ingredients.

It is obvious that continuing to maintain autonomy for autonomy's sake is an outdated standpoint today. The notion that the art world is something other than the world in which we exist on a daily basis must be reconsidered and turned down. The fact that art is part of a million-dollar industry today makes it difficult to construe art production as independent of the mechanisms of capitalism. This doesn't mean that art isn't at all separate from other things. It only means that the field which defines what is art and what's not doesn't exist outside or above an alternative, more 'real' world; it means that the art field exists as a field among many other 'real' fields of praxis.

Notes:

1. Peter Bürger, *Theory of the Avant-Garde* (1974), Minneapolis: University of Minnesota Press, 1984.

2. Theodor W. Adorno, *Aesthetic Theory* (1970), Minneapolis: University of Minnesota Press, 1998.

3. J.M. Bernstein, *The Fate of Art: Aesthetic Alienation from Kant to Derrida and Adorno*, Cambridge: Polity Press, 1992.

4. Andrea Fraser, 'From the Critique of Institutions to an Institution of Critique', *Artforum*, September 2005, XLIV, No. 1, 278-83.

5. J.M. Bernstein, *The Fate of Art: Aesthetic Alienation from Kant to Derrida and Adorno*.

6. Ibid.

7. The neo-Avant-Garde's erroneous 'maintenance' of the Avant-Garde's intentions of uniting art and life praxis is, according to Andrea Fraser, the very foundation of Institutional Critique.

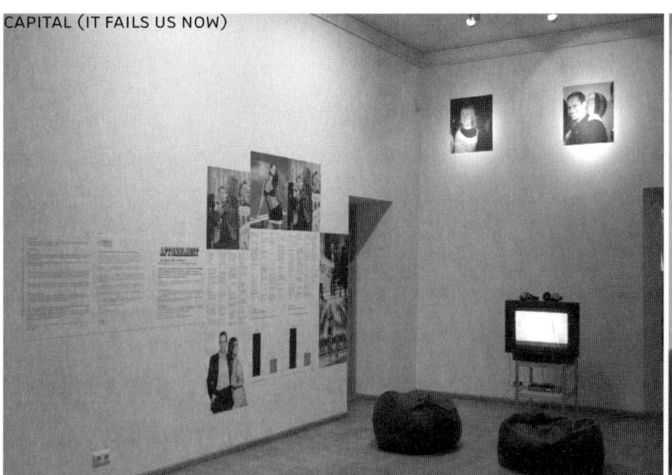

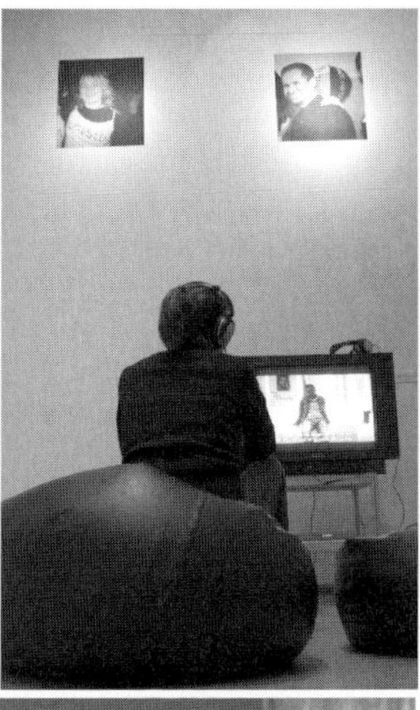

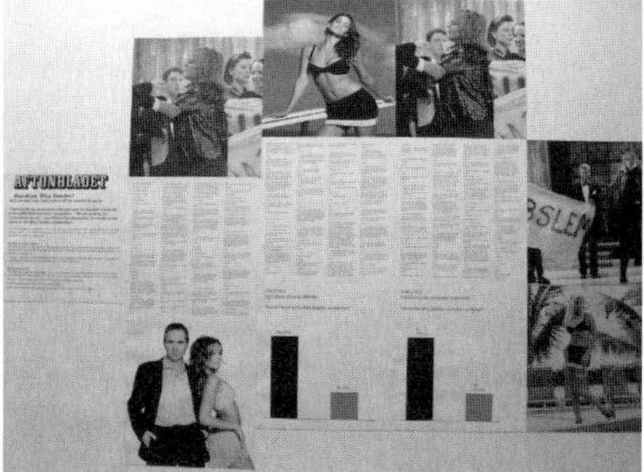

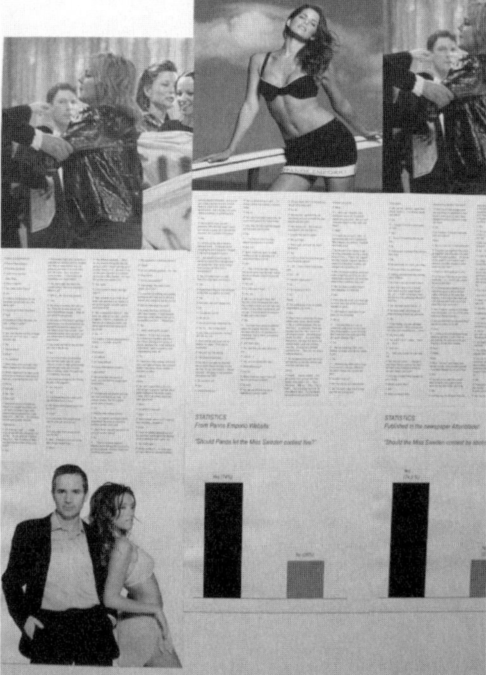

Installation shots from exhibition Capital (It Fails Us Now), Tallinn, Jan.-Feb. 2006: My Business with the Bikini-King, Fia-Stina Sandlund.

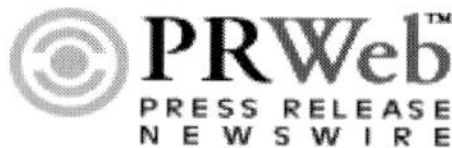

Sweden without Miss Universe Contestant for the First Time Ever

When the Scandinavian swimwear company Panos Emporio last year purchased the rights to the Miss Sweden pageant from TV3, the intentions were to bring the contest back to its original high status. Harassment from feminist organizations has however forced the company to put the competition on hold. This has led to the fact that in 2005 Sweden will not send a contestant to the Miss Universe pageant for the first time ever.

(PRWEB) April 14, 2005 - Panos Emporio announced in August of last year that the new plans for the competition would be presented during the fall, but after having been harassed by feminist organizations the decision to wait was made.

"Feminists forced me to cancel. I was surprised that, in a country as far developed and as liberated as Sweden, women's rights movements receive so much attention in the media regarding an issue like this," says Panos Papadopoulos, CEO of the company. At first he saw the response as negative, but then he realized that Sweden now has the chance to create something new and astonishing in the field of beauty contests, and become a role model for others to follow.

"I am the kind of person to listen to the opinions of others in our society, and I show humility towards them," Panos continues. "Therefore the contest will rest for a year for us to have enough time to look into the possibilities of creating something new that will take Miss Sweden to a whole new level.

"The future of the contest depends on whether I can create a program that is accepted by most people in our society. It is important to create a contest that emphasizes the dignity as well as the beauty of the woman", he ends.

This means that in 2005 Sweden will not send a contestant to the Miss Universe pageant for the first time. Sweden is one of the very few countries that have never failed to participate in the contest.

For more information and pictures, please contact
Johan Jihde
Panos Emporio AB
E-mail: email protected from spam bots
www.panos.com

# # #

Contact Information
Panos Emporio
PANOS EMPORIO AB
http://www.panos.com

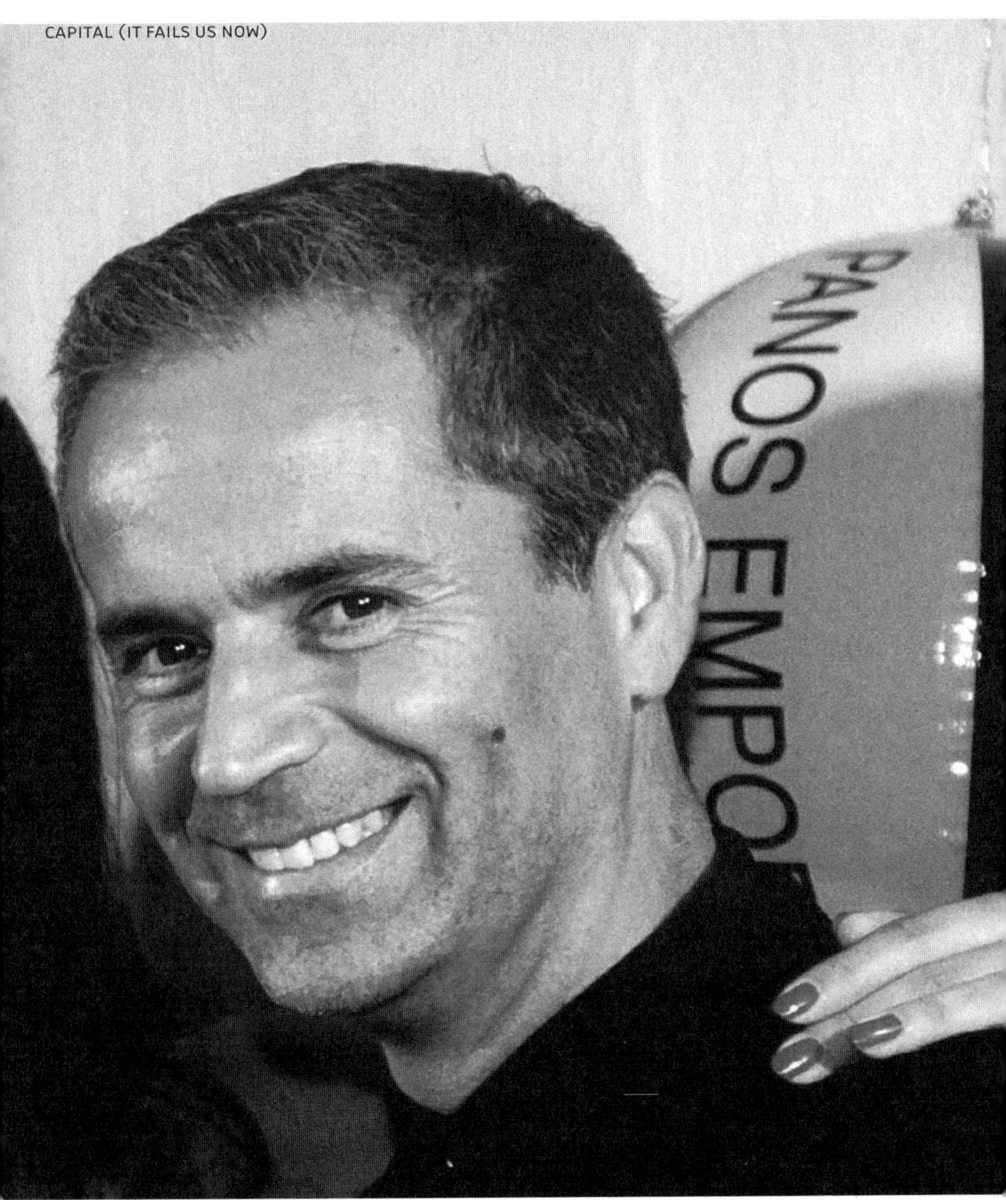
ANOS EMPO

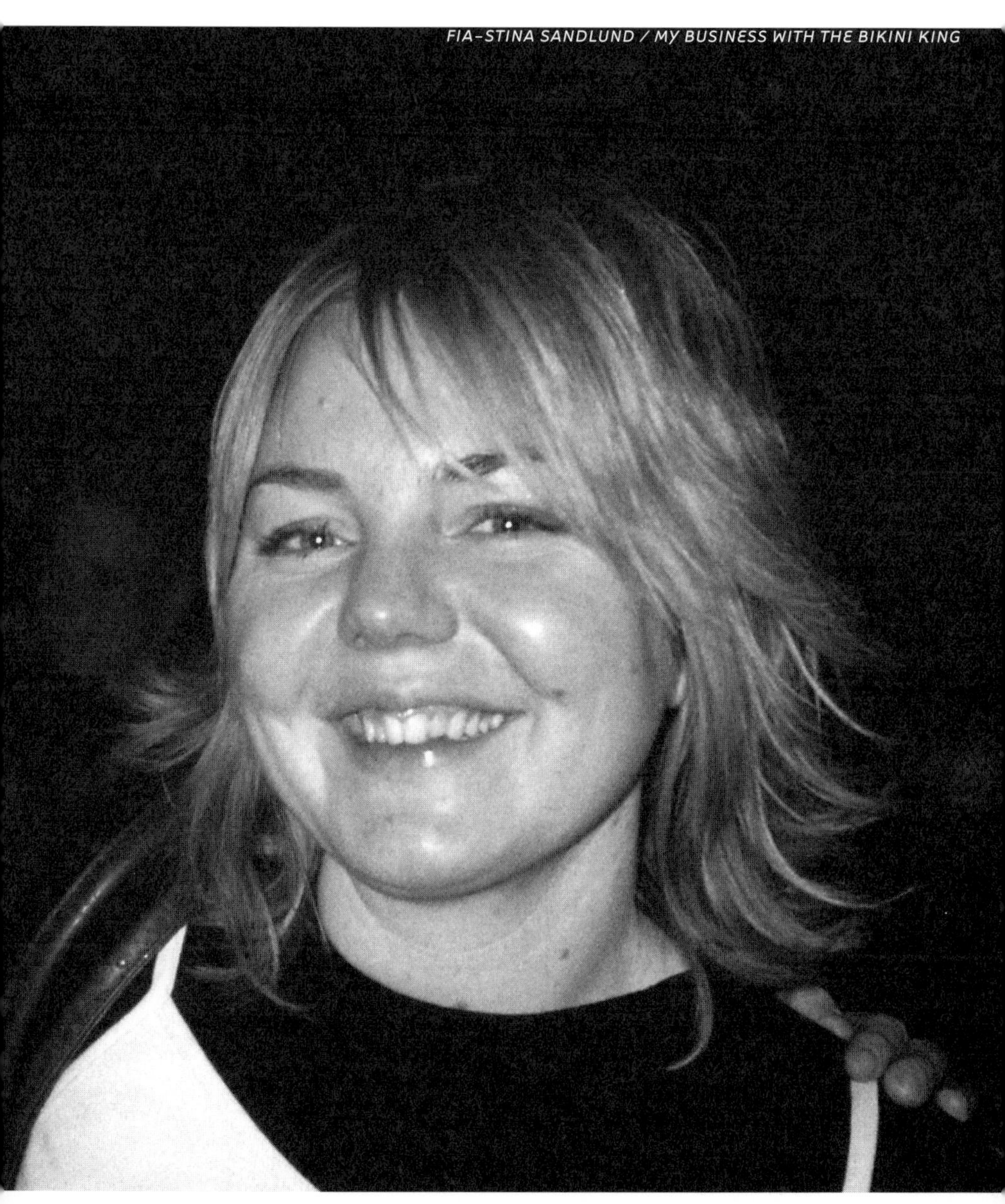

FIA–STINA SANDLUND / MY BUSINESS WITH THE BIKINI KING

Phone conversation

F=Fia-Stina Sandlund

P=Panos Papadopoulos

F: God, I'm so nervous.

…Ring, Ring…

P: Panos Emporio!

F: Yes, hello. Is this Panos?

P: Yes.

F: Hi this is Fia Sandlund, do you remember you phoned me a few weeks ago?

P: I've just gotten in from Stockholm.

F: Yeah.

P: I've still got it from the plane, my ears… What's it called?

F: A bit blocked…?

P: Yes, a bit blocked and lots of things to sort out, yes now I know, it was a long time ago.

F: Yes.

P: You vanished?

F: What?

P: You vanished!

F: Have I been gone too long? Ha ha. What's happened in the meantime?

P: What's happened? You were going to treat me to dinner or I was going to treat you, or something like that, eh?

F: Ha ha.

P: Nah nah…

F: Hee hee.

P: Nah, nah.

F: Well what can you do? How are things? I've thought about you such a lot since you called. I was really pleased that you phoned me, it was really cool… hee hee… You phoning me and asking what I thought.

[short pause]

P: Eh, what can I say? …I usually moan at my staff and colleagues and the like… You've got to be a human being first… and I'm willing to listen and get inspiration from others, you know?

F: Yes.

P: And maybe that's why I've done so well with my business and my designs and why so many women love my products and want to be associated with the brand. There should be some content… Or there has to be something in it, hasn't there?

F: *Yes, that's right. But how's the contest going? Have you reached a decision yet?*

P: ...no, it's a long process...

F: *I see.*

P: We keep on working. And not just me. There are several people and we've had different people... What do you call it? Focus groups...

F: *But what do* you *think? Last time I spoke to you, you mentioned that you wanted to revamp the pageant and you talked about it being more, I can't remember exactly what you said, but you talked about it being less about appearance...*

P: You could say that for me, the way you look is the person.

F: *Yes.*

P: I see a lot of really good-looking girls who are really ugly, eh, quote unquote, or lots of really good-looking guys who are really ugly, because there is nothing inside! The light's out or something, you know.

F: *But could you imagine, like, having fat girls in the pageant?*

P: Yes, why not?

F: *Yes?*

P: I don't think they'd be ruled out for, say, five kilos here or there.

F: *But do you think people would vote for them?*

P: Sorry?

F: *Do you really think people would vote for a fat girl, for instance?*

P: Er.

F: *Do you really think people would vote for her?*

P: Well... It depends how you do the other things around it all.

F: *Mmm...*

P: The different elements... What do you show to the people who are going to vote? I haven't got any good solution how to do it... Because if you put the same question to a politician as you put to Miss Sweden, he'd look like an idiot too, wouldn't he?

F: *Yes, really.*

P: I don't know. It doesn't feel right, does it?

F: Nah, but what do you think about what I said last time, that maybe it is wrong having girls compete against each other at all?

P: Yes, a competitive element... Has been, eh, what do you say... Can be negative... Can be... It depends on how you do it, what you mean, and some want to do it and some don't, you know?

F: Yes...?

P: It leads to a certain development in society... For better or worse.

F: Yes.

[short pause]

P: It's difficult.

F: It's really difficult...

P: A very philosophical question...

F: Absolutely!

P: But going back thousands of years, you see there've always been competitions...

F: Yes.

P: I thought a lot about what you said last time, and tried to see how... In ancient Greece. The first Olympic games were in beauty...

F: Oh.

P: And that was Ancient Greece!

F: Yes, but how do you imagine them competing? Because you intend to hold the contest, don't you?

P: I don't know, I haven't decided if I'm going to run the contest...

F: No...

P: ...there is so much material missing, we're looking into it and we've got focus groups, how they view it and one thing and another...

F: My suggestion is that you cancel it.

P: Great!

F: As you perhaps guessed... hee hee.

P: How simple...

F: You're not surprised?

P: How simple. You make it very simple, don't you?

F: I could see something very positive coming out of it. Not just for me as a woman and a feminist, but for you too.

P: But isn't that what I've done?

F: In a way, but if you continue to call it Miss Sweden, it might become something totally different that isn't a competition and isn't... Without you...

P: Yes.

F: ...doing anything for equality?

P: Mmm... It's like this, you know, I try to keep out of politics, because I don't think I belong to that group of people. Because I've never wanted to understand, I won't succeed in ever understanding them, eh.

F: No.

P: I have been very socially committed and I see, right or wrong, that it doesn't matter if the color of your politics is red, blue or yellow.

F: Mmm?

[pause]

P: You can't expect that a 25- or 23-year old girl, or anyone, can talk about global matters for the whole society. I mean, first of all, where would you learn about that?

F: Mmm.

P: On what TV channel?

F: Mmm.

P: Which media, where is it? I haven't seen anything... anywhere...

F: Nope.

P: There are global catastrophes and the headlines are all about Big Brother Linda or whatever their names are...

F: Yes, that's right...

P: Really exciting! It... In some way you can't take it for granted that they get any decent information, and you've got to take that into account. And it's better to avoid world matters, and world politics, than think that they can solve Africa's problems or something else.

F: Yes.

P: We've got to solve our own problems. Why do it far away? I see it as a whole in a way, as a question for mankind, not a question for a group. [pause] I did this survey about the Miss Sweden brand... I'd thought about changing the brand because I thought it had such a negative ring to it.

F: But doesn't it cost a load of money to contact those ad agencies and everything? How much money have you put into this? Isn't it unnecessary?

P: Yes, if it doesn't turn out well... Then it is a bad deal, and that's it.

F: Yes.

P: It just shows that you love what you do and that you want to do it well...

F: Yes.

P: And then, you can't always win...

F: No.

P: I usually do, but okay...

F: Okay, ha ha.

P: You've got to lose sometimes too...

F: Ha ha... Yes, I understand.

P: Just think if you become my best fan? Oh my God.

F: Can't that be your goal? Ha ha... Making me happy? Then you've succeeded.

P: Yes, but I try. I try and try...

F: The greatest opponent...

P: You fall in love with my idea and the complete Panos ideology so you say that "It's our new religion... For all feminists... We're going to call ourselves Panos-feminists" Okay?

F: Do you think so?

P: Yes.

F: Panos-Feminism?

P: Yes, or whatever we'll call it... Or Panos-Democracy instead, it sounds better.

F: Ha ha.

P: Yes, but if you have a good idea, let it out! Don't save it, it's Friday today!

F: Hee hee. Okay this might be utopian but I've really tried to think:

P: Mm.

F: ...I've told you that I'm really against competitions in general...

P: Mm, mm.

F: But if I reach out, and I've really

reached out far, by agreeing to a competitive element at all...

P: Mm.

F: ...then I think that Miss Sweden, the actual name, must be kept, seeing as you've already tested it at your ad agencies...

P: Yes, yes.

F: Or, wherever it was?

P: Yes, yes.

F: Mm, so you've got to keep that... But then I think that despite the name, the contest could be open for men and women, of any ethnic background, and any age. Everyone would be welcome to take part in the contest...

P: Mm.

F: ...And then there would be different criteria for judging. And then I think the basis should be the qualities you mentioned, that is, talent, competency and charisma?

P: Mm, that's right.

F: Yes, and then you and I sit on the jury...

P: Just us...?

F: Yes, and we decide who wins...

P: What democracy!?

F: Ha ha.

P: Where have you been? Have you been in old Russia or what?

F: Or what...

P: Yes, we can do that; I've got a majority, so it doesn't matter.

F: Do you think? But if it's me and you, we get 50% votes each.

P: Ah, ah.

F: We say that I represent the old opponents and you represent the man who bought the rights.

P: Yes, but you, er... You know you must agree? We can't fall out...

F: Exactly! We have to agree!

P: We can't fight...

F: That's right, and when we reach agreement...

P: Yes.

F: Don't you think that then, then we'll have found the winner?

P: ...Eh... I didn't intend to be on the jury.

F: No... okay...

P: I wouldn't have done it...

F: No...

P: I'm not going to do it...

F: No.

[pause]

P: The contestants, if you set quality requirements, you know...

F: Mm.

P: They'll have to show that they have some quality, quote, talent, interest in life, or in plain language, they live their lives... in some way. Those who live their lives like "Yes, I work in an old people's home – look what good deeds I've done"... You could follow that person. See how she works over several weeks, what she achieves, how she... It would be a fantastic contest for me... Then you can show a waitress working...

F: So the beauty thing won't be in it at all? Will they be like fully clothed, with short hair and dikes and...

[silence]

P: Ehhh... Beauty contest... You go by their face, by their skin, their bodies, their posture, etc ... They... You mean... Will we... They... This is hard... You sometimes see it on TV or in different films... It's not always the prettiest one you fall for, but the charmer, you know...

F: Mmm.

P: ...who's got charisma. Live characters above all. I'm tired of people who just exist... But you don't know why they're on this earth, you know?

F: Well?

P: I'd really like to have... Ehh... A real feminist with lots of opinions as Miss Sweden, for instance. That'd be absolutely great!

F: But wouldn't it be smarter to get rid of the competition and do a media thing of it like, "Panos has stopped the Miss Sweden pageant. Sweden is ahead of all the other countries and changes the competition for..."

P: Mm, the media would go along and make a big thing out of it if you did a bimbo-style competition; it's what they have in their headlines every day.

F: Yes, but there's another thing in their headlines. It's feminists.

P: Mm.

F: If you stop the event, you would get so much cred from all the feminists in Sweden so you'd...

P: I don't want to count what I'd get back. It's not of interest.

F: Oh no.

P: ...The best thing is if I can do something really good out of it? And then, if the headlines or the feminists like it, then that'd be really good that you could combine it but...

F: Yes.

P: ...but you could say, that I don't believe, no matter what words I speak to you...

F: Yes.

P: ...because you really want to bury it so it doesn't make any difference. You won't change your opinion will you?

F: You don't think so?

P: No, I try and try but it seems hard.

F: Yes. It is hard. I find it hard to see how this can turn out well.

[short pause]

P: Mm, but we – almost – agree that I should cancel it... I've already, quote, cancelled it.

F: Um.

P: ...Though if I let the contest carry on, then...

F: Mm.

P: ...it won't be anything like the old one...

F: No.

P: There wasn't anything in the old one that I liked.

F: No.

P: Me personally, as a man, you know.

F: What was it that you didn't like?

P: Nothing, actually there was nothing I

liked. Nothing...

F: But how come you bought it then?

P: Well, that's what a lot of people have asked and I've asked myself too... eh... I think it is because I see the chance to do something different. I think that.

F: Yes, and what would that be...?

P: Ah, that's what I don't know yet... What I'm trying to work out, you know.

F: Yes.

P: If you're making up a new alphabet, it takes time and a lot of courage and resources and everything else... Work.

F: Yes, that's right.

P: Yes, and if I find it... Wow... That'd be... Uhum...

F: Yeah, but I...

P: ...That's why I asked for your help too...

F: Yes, that was lovely... I thought it was lovely that you phoned me. But I still don't quite understand what you are after. What's your goal?

P: Let's say a modern Miss Sweden to put it simply.

F: What's modern then?

P: Mm?

F: What is modern? What characterizes modern? Our time?

P: Well I don't have answers and the only thing I've answered is that it hasn't been good. It hasn't been adapted to today's society in a way, you know.

F: No.

P: Is it modern if only feminists take part, for instance?

[pause]

F: But isn't your aim to sell swimsuits?

P: They don't go together! They don't go together! Lots of people, I've been asked the same question... Of course, it'd be great if I could sell an extra swimsuit, and why shouldn't I when everyone else does?

F: Hold on, I don't quite get it, why?

P: Let me put it like this, if I sell more swimsuits... Er... And if I did, what'd be wrong with that?

F: I'm thinking about wanting to do something good for the world and selling swimsuits at the same time. Hee hee, I can imagine that there are a lot of people who think you're only doing this to sell swimsuits?

P: Yes, of course, seeing as it is linked to me personally, and I've got the other trademark, Panos Emporio...

F: But you think that the swimsuit thing

has got something to do with...

P: Sure.

F: ...being a bit undressed and being attractive and that? I took a look at your website, the pictures of the girls. They are a bit like Miss Sweden...

P: Mmm.

F: Really...

[pause]

P: Mmm. I've been very happy over the last months, since it came out that I'd put Miss Sweden on ice, you know.

F: Yes?

P: I've had phone calls from people who I've never met or would never have met anytime in life, you know.

F: Yes.

P: And they say: It's fantastic that you have taken over Miss Sweden, if it's in the right hands, if you can make something good out of it. Only you can do it, Panos! And it's anything from politicians to, what can I say, junkies, you know...

F: Yes.

P: The entire spectrum and it is great to hear it, you know. So expectations are high.

F: Yes, that's great. And I'm hoping for a

funeral...

P: Uh... funeral, sure...

F: A nice funeral... And then...

P: ...How many feminists will be at the funeral then?

F: Loads of them! I can fix as many as you want, and you'll sell so many swimsuits you won't believe it... You won't believe how many feminists who will buy your swimsuits! Ha ha ha.

P: Ha ha ha, *wow!*

[laughing together]

P: Wow! I'd like to see that... I'd like to see that!

F: Wouldn't you? Hee hee!

[laughing together]

P: ...I want to see that.

F: It'd be one of those win-win situations, you know.

P: Yes sir! ...But, you know... Can you order a plot in a cemetery in Stockholm then...? Ha ha ha ha.

F: Yes, that's what we'll do: put it to rest there... Yes, it'll be really good. It'll be really popular internationally, too, I promise.

P: Yes, no, the next ad will have to come from results, not from... If you knew a little more about me... If you could look below the surface you can interpret it like some people interpret it, but...

F: Mm.

P: There are a lot of media people in this country... who will do anything to be seen, you know... They are...

F: Mm, but it's not your thing?

P: ...My brand name has to be visible, but I've never wanted to be exposed in contexts that would sell my family or my private things or my... my mistresses or...

F: Oy... Your mistresses?

P: Yes, or... whatever, my ex-mistresses then, or ex-girlfriends or having sex on the train like lots of people come out and say, "I've had sex there" just to get a few pages of newsprint, you know? It is, it has never, you will never see that...

F: Yes.

P: It's not my thing, you know...

F: That sounds cool, you know. It's the result, then, that we get to see? I believe, like I said, in cancelling it and starting something new but I'll think about it more...

P: You... How many meters under?

F: Ha ha, I don't know. Two – three might be enough.

P: Okay.

F: But don't dig it up again, keep it buried forever.

P: Mm, mm.

F: We can plant something nice on top of the grave that'll flourish; it could be very poetic.

P: We can plant a nice plant...

F: Yes, right, we'll each go and look in a gardening magazine, ha ha.

P: Promise?

F: Promise.

P: OK, keep in touch, don't disappear. Okay?

F: Nah, take care!

P: And if you're down in the country, call me.

F: Yes, I will.

P: Promise?

F: Okay, I promise.

P: Bye .

F: Bye.

[click – phone is put down]

F: Hee hee hee.

Report on: *Better for Alexandra without Birgitta and Carolina Getting it Worse, Better for Birgitta without Carolina and Alexandra Getting it Worse, Better for Carolina without Alexandra and Birgitta Getting it Worse.*

On September 26th I sent out an invitation to the following fourth-year students at the Academy of Fine Arts, Umeå University: Jill Blomqvist, Aldis Ellertdottir, Johan Hallberg, Isaskar Jerrhage, Tove Kleist, Andreas Kurtsson, Ylva Landoff-Lindberg, Solveig Lindgren, Lisa Manner, Åsa Norberg, Mikael Näsström, Gustav Sparr, Radek Stypczynski, Jennie Sundén och Helena Sundin. The invitation was as follows:

Hi,
With this letter I would like to invite you to take part in an experiment in dividing a set of resources.
16 persons take part in the project. Once a month each participant contributes with €25 which is put in a pot. All participants receive the full pot of €400 one time during the 16 months of the project.
Set up of the project:
** Recruiting participants and presentation of the set-up of the project.*
** Introduction, discussion and eventual changes of the set-up of the project.*
** Continuous documentation of the project in text and images.*
** Presentation of the project at* Capital (It Fails Us Now), *Oslo, 2005.*
** Presentation of the project at* Capital (It Fails Us Now), *Kunstihoone, 2006.*

Hope you are interested in participating, I'm happy to answer questions. Please confirm you have received this mail. I need your answer by October 1 at the latest.
All the best,
Elin Wikström

I chose to work with an already existing group of people with whom I would be in regular contact over the next two years because of my teaching job at the school. I made it clear to the students that the project I had invited them to participate in wasn't a part of my teaching. The invitation was followed by talks and meetings. The following topics were discussed:

* The project in relation to the exhibition *Capital (It Fails Us Now)*.
* Reciprocity (an important ingredient in collaborations).
* The principle of reciprocity (between states and between individuals).
* Different forms of reciprocity (generalized, balanced and negative).
* Two examples of strong and weak reciprocity (my contribution to *Capital (It Fails Us Now)*, Oslo and my contribution to *Capital (It Fails Us Now)*, Tallinn)
* How to measure trust? What is game theory?
* Two examples from game theory (the dictator-game and the ultimatum game).
* Three different forms of capital (financial, human and social).
* Two perspectives on social acts (the social and the economical).
* Darwin's survival of the fittest and Kropotkin's ravens.
* James Coleman and the term social capital: We are not completely profit maximizing being and not only products of cultural factors.
* Robert Putman and different types and functions of social networks.
* The Prisoner's dilemma (reasons for why collaborations fail).
* The use of the term social capital in four different fields (economy, social science, sociology and health).
* Positive and negative aspects of the use of the term 'social capital'.

Big questions were posed at the meetings: What is a good collaboration?

What is a just collaboration? What is a good person? What is a just person? What is a good society? What is a just society? What is a good world? What is a just world? As well as logistical, for example: Would the possibilities for a good collaboration increase if a reward or punishment in some form were added?

Per Nilsson, philosopher and a colleague of mine at the Academy of Fine arts, contributed to the discussion with a local example of a similar social act. One of the dads at his daughter's day care center had told him about it. Twelve men, originally form Ethiopia and now living in Umeå, put €100 in a pot once a month. In connection to the handing out of the pot, a ritual is carried out: a party is given by the next man receiving the €1200. That information made us aware of the importance of having some kind of ritual in relation to the collecting and handing out the pot. One of the students added that he had seen a TV documentary about microcredits and made us interested in finding out more about it.

At one of the meetings less than half of the class turned up. "I would have liked to participate said one of them, but after the rent is paid I only have €100 to live off, so to put €25 would be impossible for me." At the meeting it was decided that there was no interest in being part of the project if the pot was to be used individually. On the other hand there was an interest if it was to be used collectively. So the students came up with following idea:

16 persons participate in the project. Once a month each participant contrlbutes with €25 which is put in a pot. At the end of the 16 months of the project, the common pot of €6400 is used collectively for producing an exhibition.

At the time of writing the student's extended version of the project is still in progress. In November the concept of the project was reworked a bit and a revised invitation was sent, this time to colleagues of mine.

Hi,

With this letter I would like to invite you to participate in a project.

The project directs attention to microcredit – a form for saving built on solidarity.

16 women are invited to participate in the project. Once a month each woman contributes with €25 which is put in a pot. All participants receive the full pot of €400 one time during the 16 months of the project.

Loans of a few thousand can change women's life – during 2005 the issue of micro-credit is raised all over the world. Microcredit is called so because the loan is small but can generate big advantages. The saving's social meanings are of more importance than the economical. It's mostly women in developing countries who are using microcredit as a tool to fight poverty. The method is worth notice also here as a step on the way to better status for women in the family, in the society and in the world – saving money together is more fun than saving money alone!

Method: The participants each deposit their part (€25/month) in the project's bank account during the 16 months of the project. Before the start of the project lots will be drawn for the order of the payment of the common pot. It's possible to change payment times with each other. The common pot (€400) is paid out, month by month, respectively to each participant's bank account.

The invitation has been sent out to the following artists: Anna Brag, Catti Brandelius, Johanna Billing, Maria Bjurestam, Carin Ellberg, Ingrid Eriksson, Meta Isaeus Berlin, Erla Haraldsdottir, Ilona Huss Wallin, Pia König, Anna Kindgren, Gunilla Klingberg, Anna-Lena Lundmark, Fia-Stina Sandlund, Paula von Seth and Lena Ylipää.

The title of the project is:

Better for Alexandra without Birgitta and Carolina getting it worse, Better for Birgitta without Carolina and Alexandra getting it worse, Better for Carolina without Alexandra and Birgitta getting it worse.

Hope you are interested in participating. I'm happy to answer questions. Please confirm you have received this mail. I need your answer by January 7 at the latest. All the best,
Elin Wikström

Today is the 15th of January and the result is that 14 of the invited artists are interested in participating and I'm working on recruiting two more persons and having the project running in the next two or three weeks.

I would like to thank everyone who during the carrying out of the project, has contributed with their advice, reactions and interesting comments, but special thanks to the following persons:
Jill Blomqvist, Aldis, Johan, Isaskar, Tove, Andreas, Ylva, Solveig, Lisa, Åsa, Mikael, Gustav, Radek, Jennie Sundén, Helena Sundin, Anna Brag, Catti Brandelius, Johanna Billing, Maria Bjurestam, Carin Ellberg, Ingrid Eriksson, Meta Isaeus Berlin, Erla Haraldsdottir, Ilona Huss Wallin, Pia König, Anna Kindgren, Gunilla Klingberg, Anna-Lena Lundmark, Fia-Stina Sandlund, Paula von Seth and Lena Ylipää.

Elin Wikström, Umeå, January 2006

Report on: *Does Annika Believe That Bianca Rejects an Equal Split?*

With the help from Anders Härm, curator at Kunstihoone, Tallinn, two persons were invited to participate in the project. The rules Anders got for how to choose the two persons were:

* They must not have heard about or read the description of the project.
* They should not have met before.
* They should not be connected to Kunstihoone, Tallinn.
* They must be over 18.
* The only information you can give to them about the project is that it is an experiment in dividing a given set of resources.
* They must agree to the carrying out of the project being documented with video and still images.
* They must have time to participate in the project on the 5th of January. The carrying out of the project will take approximately 2 hours.

The two participants, Ege Raudsepp and Mattias Luha, arrived at Kunstihoone and were given a short presentation of the exhibition by Simon Sheikh, curator of *Capital (It Fails Us Now)*. The experiment was carried out in an apartment in the same building as Kunstihoone. We drew lots on who should have the role as person A and person B. Ege got role A and Mattias got role B.

Excerpts from the transcription of the documentation of the project:

Elin: The project is an experiment in dividing a given set of resources and the title of the project is *Does Alexandra Believe That Birgitta Rejects an Equal Split?* Person A (Ege) will get 6000 EEK (Estonian crowns) but to keep the money she has to come to an agreement with person B (Mattias) about the division of the money in a special way. Ege has to offer Mattias a part of money but if Mattias doesn't accept the offer, neither A (Ege) or B (Mattias) get the money.

Elin: Let's start. Do you have any more questions?
Mattias: Do we have to use the money for something specific?
Elin: No, no, no. It's totally up to you how you will spend the money. If you get the money… I also would like to inform you that it's not my personal money. The money comes from the production of the show. The money comes from NIFCA. NIFCA is…
Anders: It's Finnish money. Finnish tax payer's money.
Ege: Can we keep the money afterwards?
Anders: Yes, yes.
Ege: Really?
[Ege laughs]
Elin: Yes, good that you asked! I don't want to make you nervous, but take your time and think a bit before you make your offer to Mattias.
Ege: Mm.
[Ege thinks]
Ege: I would suggest fifty-fifty. 3000 and 3000.
Mattias: Are you sure?
Ege: Yes, I'm sure.
Elin: So Mattias, what do you say? Will you agree on Ege's offer?
Mattias: I think it is even more than fair.
[Mattias thinks]
Mattias: I think you should have kept a bigger part.
Anders: But would you have accepted it? Do you accept the offer now?
Mattias: Yes, of course.

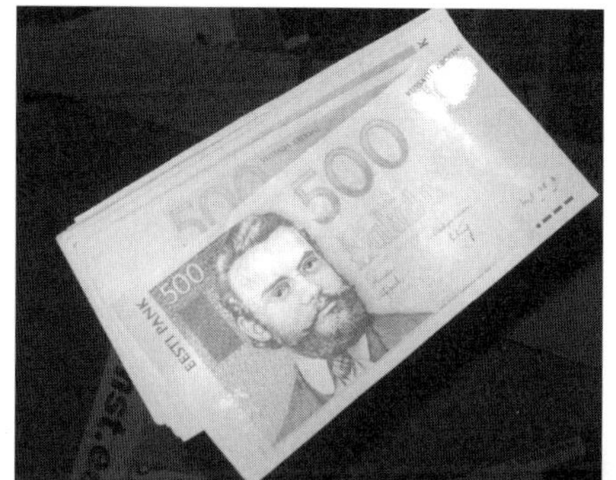

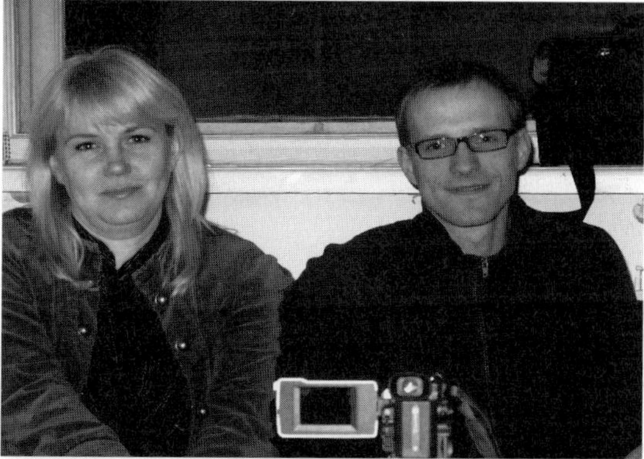

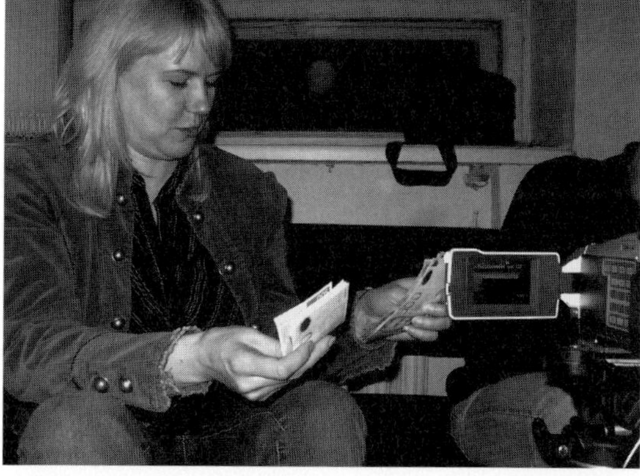

Snapshots from Tallinn, Jan. 2006, where one experiment was carried out in relation to the exhibition Capital (It Fails Us Now).

Ege: I made my offer.

[Ege laughs]

Elin: You made your offer. Here is your money. Divide it!

Ege: Okay… Fifty-fifty!

Mattias: Thank you very much.

Ege: You are welcome.

Anders: Hmm. What if it would have been your own money?

Ege: Well.

Anders: And you should have shared it with a total stranger under the same circumstances.

Ege: I don't know. It isn't my own money.

Anders: But would you have acted differently?

Ege: Yes.

Anders: Could you imagine what your offer would have been?

Ege: Maybe 1000 Estonian crowns.

Anders: Oh, yeah? That's a big difference!

Ege: Yeah!

Anders: And you, Mattias?

Mattias: I was just thinking one good offer could be: I offer you 1000 plus I buy you a dinner.

[Laughter]

In game theory, several attempts have been made to measure trust. The most well known example is called *the dictator game*:

Person A gets a sum of money and is asked to share the money with an anonymous person B. Person A has the possibilities of giving a part of the sum to person B or keeping the whole sum for herself.

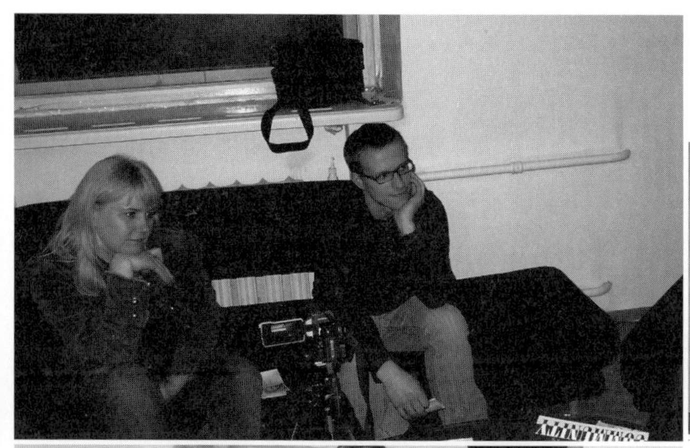

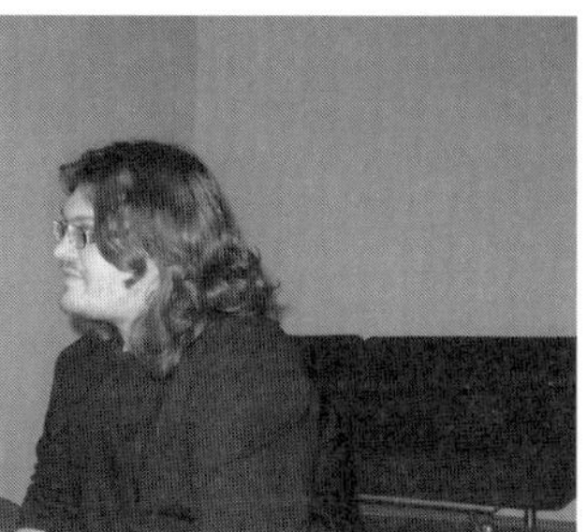

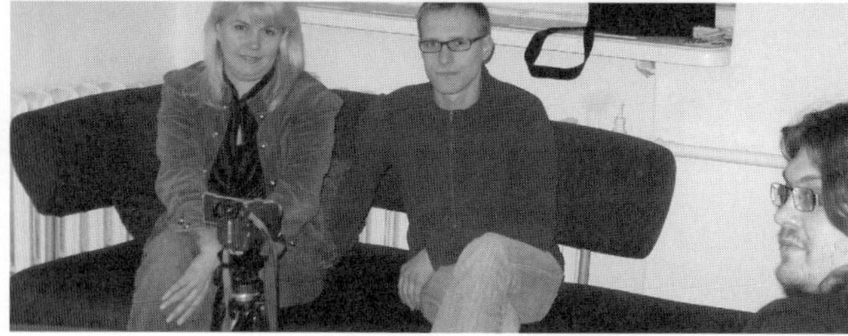

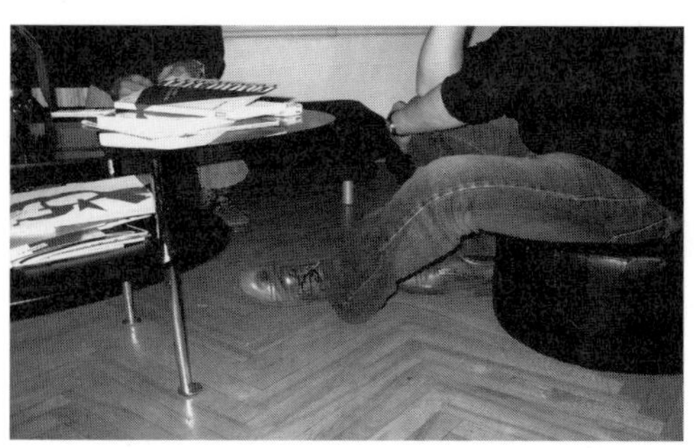

The result is that most persons tend to share the sum and give between 20% – 60% to person B.

In *the ultimatum game* person A in general offers person B between 40% – 50% of the sum. If person A proposes a smaller part of the sum, for example 10%, person B often rejects the offer and punishes person A for having made an unjust offer and both lose the money.

Person A's actions could be explained by self-interest, the fear of losing the pot, but person B is acting irrational in accordance to the tight economical perspective of social acts. The purpose of person B's actions are not following the principle of profit maximization and as person A and B don't know each other from before, they couldn't be linked by a psycho-logical mechanism attached to affinity, gratitude, identification or any other loyalty as result of years of reciprocal exchanges either. The result of the game admits that there are aspects of social justice that are built more on common interest than on self-interest. If there is a set of resources which no one can claim to have an individual right to – something one receives from outside so to say – and have good reasons to regard as common, they should be divided equally. To demand more would be nabbing at the expense of others, to demand less would be unjustified and compliant.

I would like to thank everyone who contributed with their advice, reactions and interesting comments while carrying out the project and special thanks to Ege Raudsepp and Mattias Luha.

Elin Wikström, Umeå, January 2006

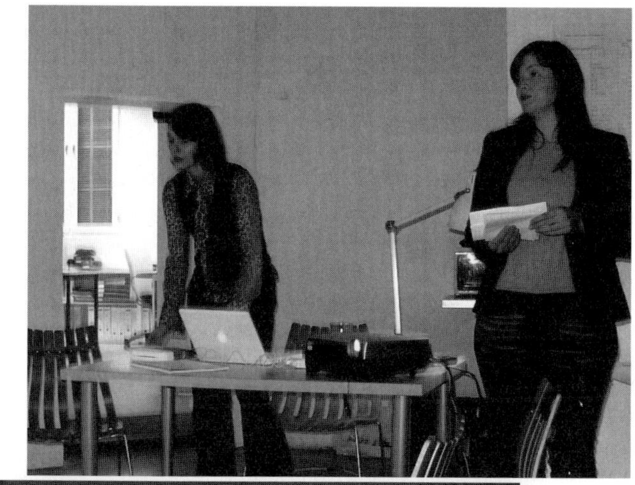

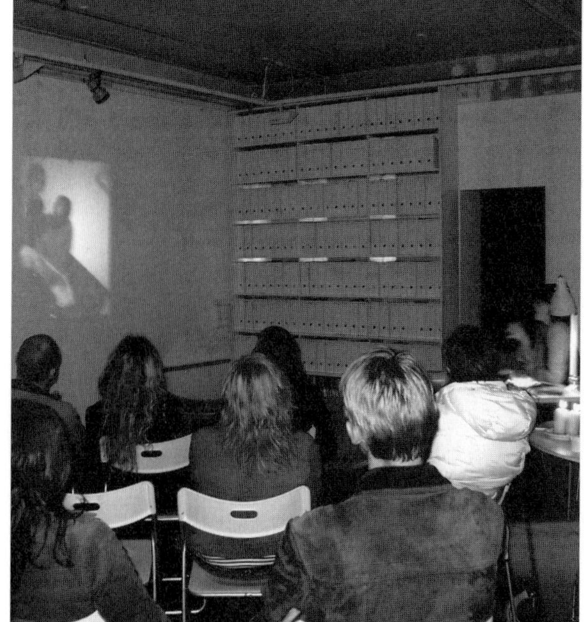

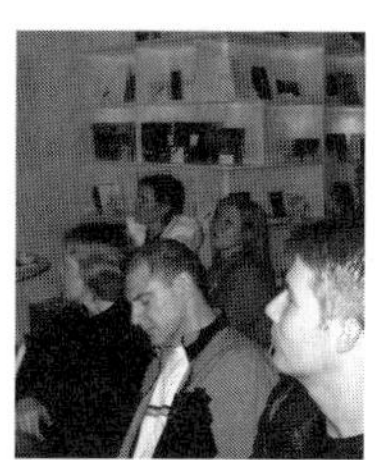

Snapshots from exhibition Capital (It Fails Us Now) where Elin Wikström gave talks presenting her project and the research behind it. Shots from UKS, Nov. 2005.

**...deeply ________ to the notion that the ____ world is ________ to the observer...
(committed) (real) (external)**

Immateriality and Oil

In 1973 the world was confronted with the first global energy crisis. The so-called oil crisis is usually explained by the Yom Kippur War. But there are clues indicating that the scarcity of oil was fabricated, for reasons other than that, which are well documented. The crisis was related to several economic, political, and cultural paradigm shifts and was, or is to be regarded as part of a larger crisis.

At the time of the so-called oil crisis, the discourse concerning virtual money, immaterial labor, and Conceptual Art intensified on different levels. The value of the dollar was no longer based on the gold standard, which had been in effect since the Bretton Woods conference that followed the Second World War. It now became a virtual currency, secured only by the oil industry, but remained the key currency. The oil industry was an adequate safeguard for currency, because the need for oil is inflexible and therefore can act as a stabilizing factor.

The industries did not want to meet the growing wage demands of workers. But they could not confront the unions' power, only circumvent it and therefore looked for possibilities for automation and outsourcing of capital and production. An intensification of the third sector, which is primarily service related, was the result. So-called immaterial labor is based on changing conditions of production within this relocation. The main resource is not land, natural resources or labor anymore, but knowledge.

In art, the notion of object within modernity became discredited or was declared uninteresting. What counted from then on was the idea. Works were produced, which now, in part, only existed in the mind. All of these levels were connected to a changing understanding of production and added value. At the same time they indicated a crisis situation. In order to understand this crisis it is not only necessary to look at the Bretton Woods system and the role of the US dollar in the global economy, but also the rebounding cultural discourse of the impairment of the object and the growing interest in the idea of immateriality and dematerialization. This idea contained a great utopian potential, and only seems to be in opposition to the ruling power. In fact, the different levels combined constitute the paradigm shift towards immaterial and dematerialized production. The energy crisis was the turning point and catalyst for this change. The immense profits called 'petrodollars', which were realized in a short time with the rise of the oil price by 400% in 1973, were the planned financing for this.

Experience Versus Knowledge

> I remember this moment. I was still very small. It was cold, because I was dressed warmly. My sister was too. Her arms were sticking out, because she had so much stuff on. I believe she had just learned to walk, I had it drummed into my head that one shouldn't run onto the street for any reason. And suddenly everything was changed. I went off… waddling in the middle of this big street in front of our house with my sister. We weren't the only one. Everybody was outside. Like in a state of emergency. But a good one. That made an impression on me.

On November 25, 1973, the so called oil crisis led to the first car free Sunday in the history of the Federal Republic of Germany. The travel ban effected around 13 million drivers. Exceptions applied to emergency vehicles and certain professions. The regulation was extended to three further Sundays in the winter of 1973/1974. The empty or pedestrian filled streets were discussed in the press, and were often paired with threatening analyses of an international crisis and the scarcity of the oil deposits. On the one hand, this led to anxiety and uncertainty because the basic value of modern industrialized business was, along with other things, expansion and mobility. These suddenly appeared to be limited.

On the other hand, there was the experience of being able to walk on an empty street and to experience the place of the street completely differently – an initial experience of an ecological consciousness and emancipating approaches to the use of street space. To this day there are countless initiatives for car free streets, that refer back to this first car free Sunday.

Plot of an action

Several people, activists, cultural producers and such like, have gathered material on the political, economic, and cultural background of the oil crisis in 1973. They collected the material on a portable billboard, which they want to place outdoors. The billboard folds up and one can carry it as a backpack. Two of them walk along a street. It is a big street, probably an 'Autobahn'. The street is empty. No cars are driving by. One of the women, let's call her A, carries the billboard. The other woman, K, films with a small video camera. They decide to set up the billboard for the documentary. A jams her finger while unfolding it and therefore takes over the camera, while K sets up the billboard. Afterwards K is rolling a cigarette for A and herself. They smoke, sit on the street and look at their billboard. After a while they fold it up again. A straps it on her back and K takes the camera again. Another camera records everything the whole time it's happening.

More information at: www.possest.de/notaboutoil.html

An Ounce of Gold (Krügerrand 2001)

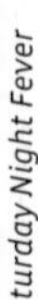

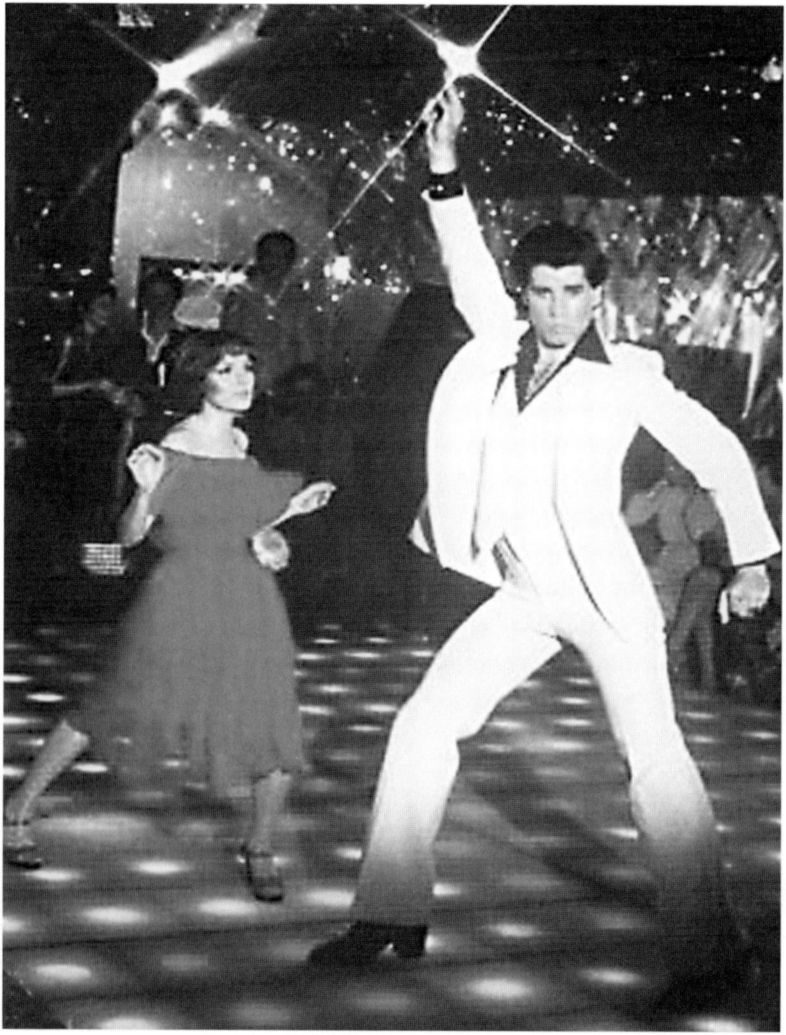

Saturday Night Fever

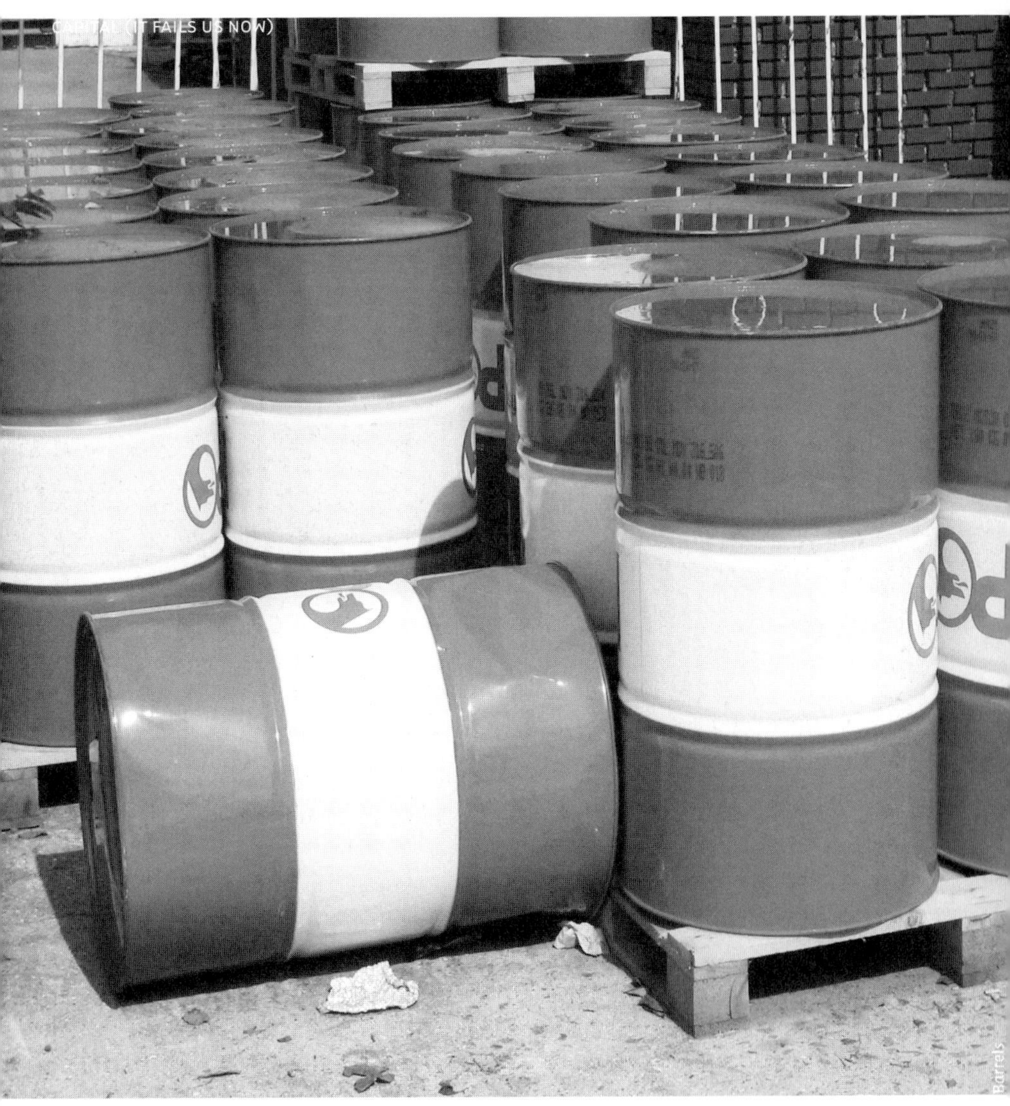

CAPITAL (IT FAILS US NOW)
Barrels

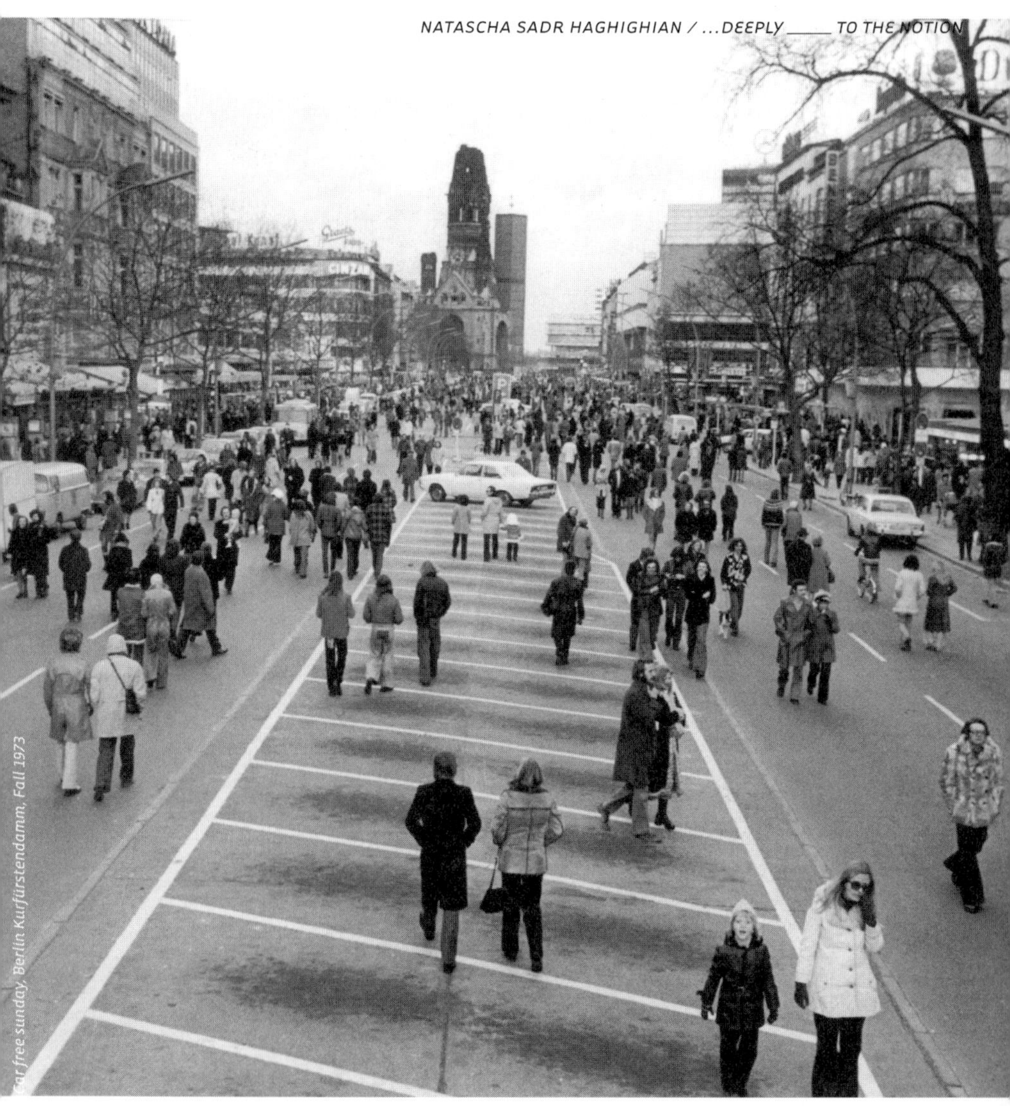

Car free sunday, Berlin Kurfürstendamm, Fall 1973

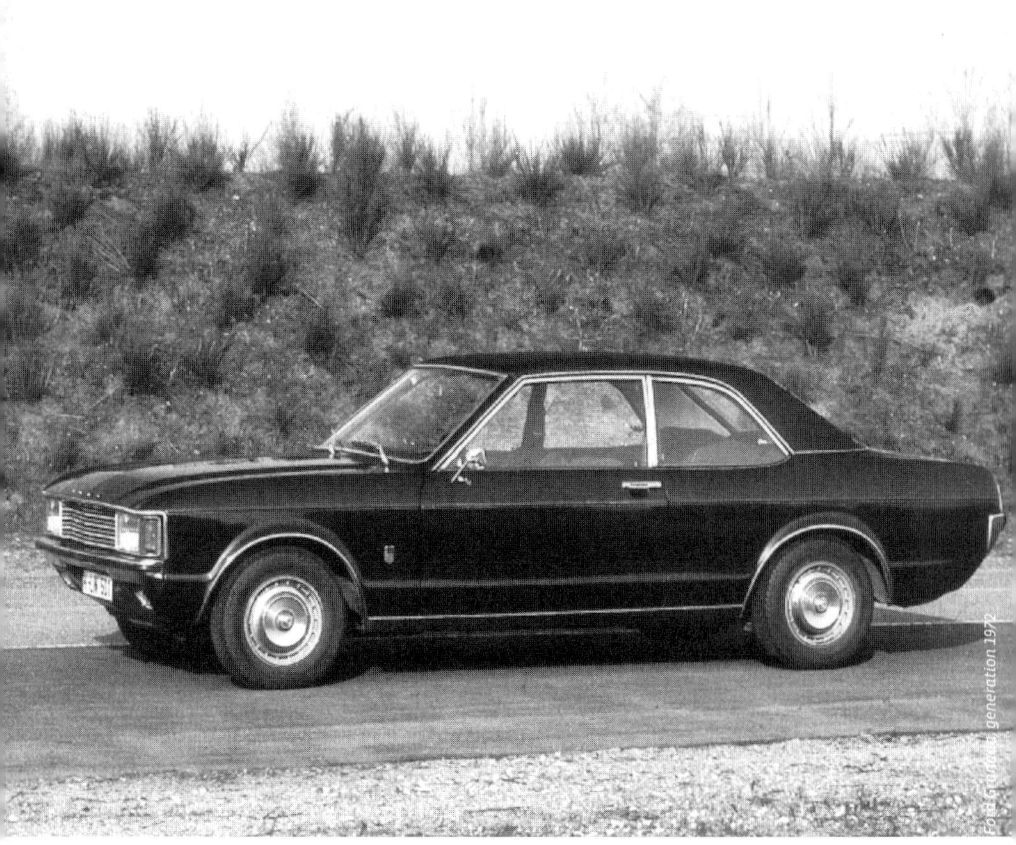

Ford Granada, generation 1972

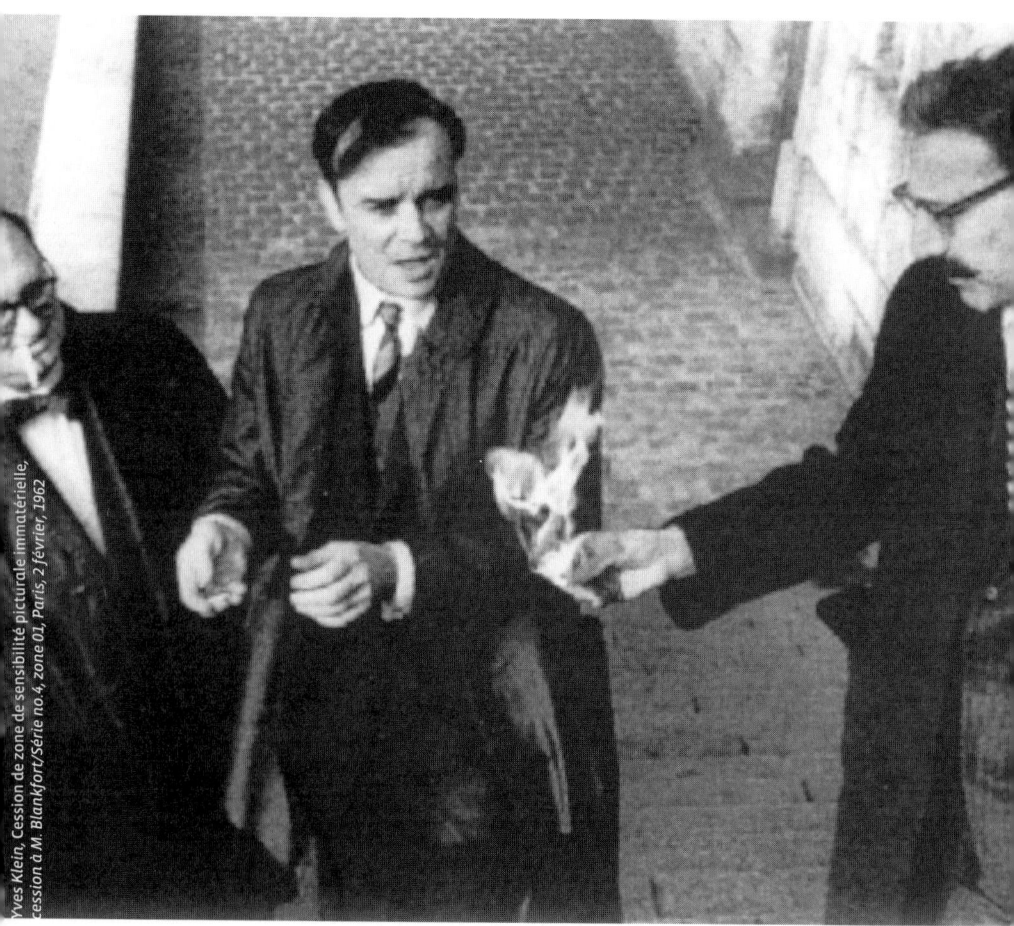

Yves Klein, Cession de zone de sensibilité picturale immatérielle,
cession à M. Blankfort/série no.4, zone 01, Paris, 2 février, 1962

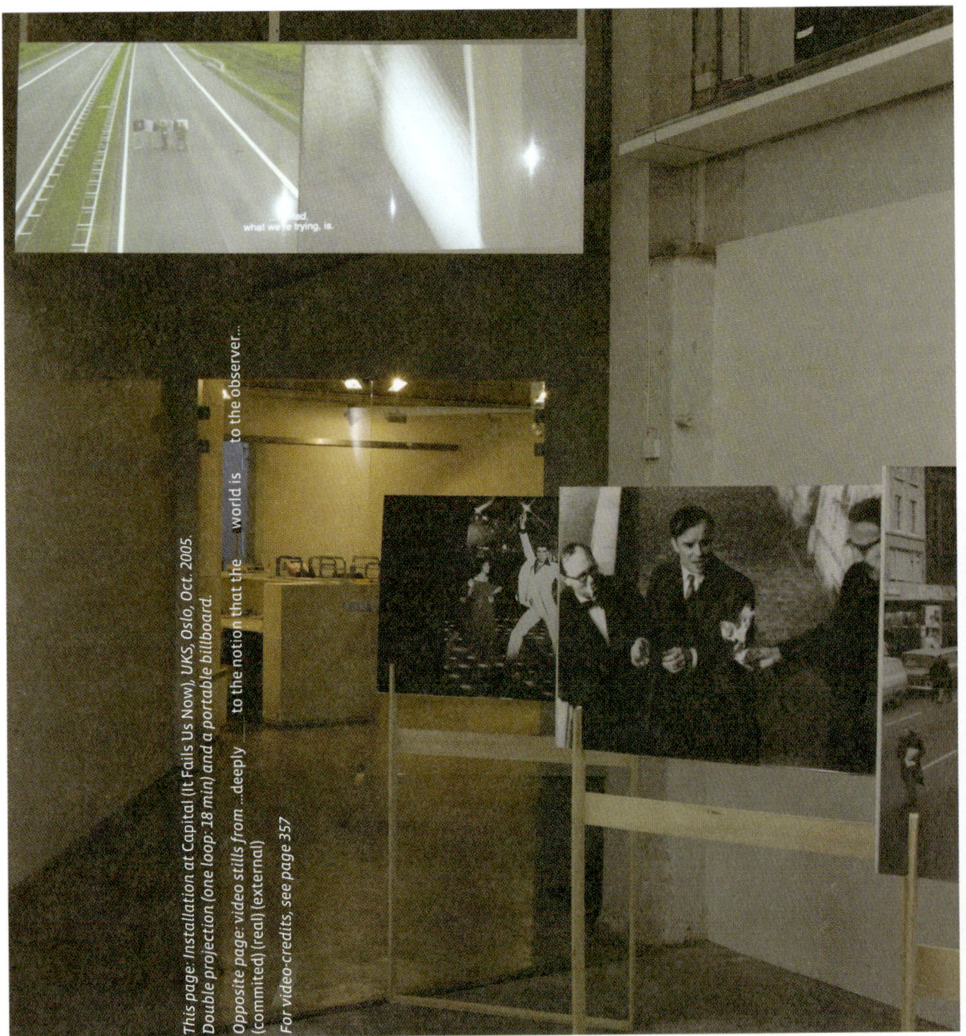

This page: Installation at Capital (It Fails Us Now), UKS, Oslo, Oct. 2005.
Double projection (one loop: 18 min) and a portable billboard.

Opposite page: video stills from ...deeply
(commited) (real) (external)

For video-credits, see page 357

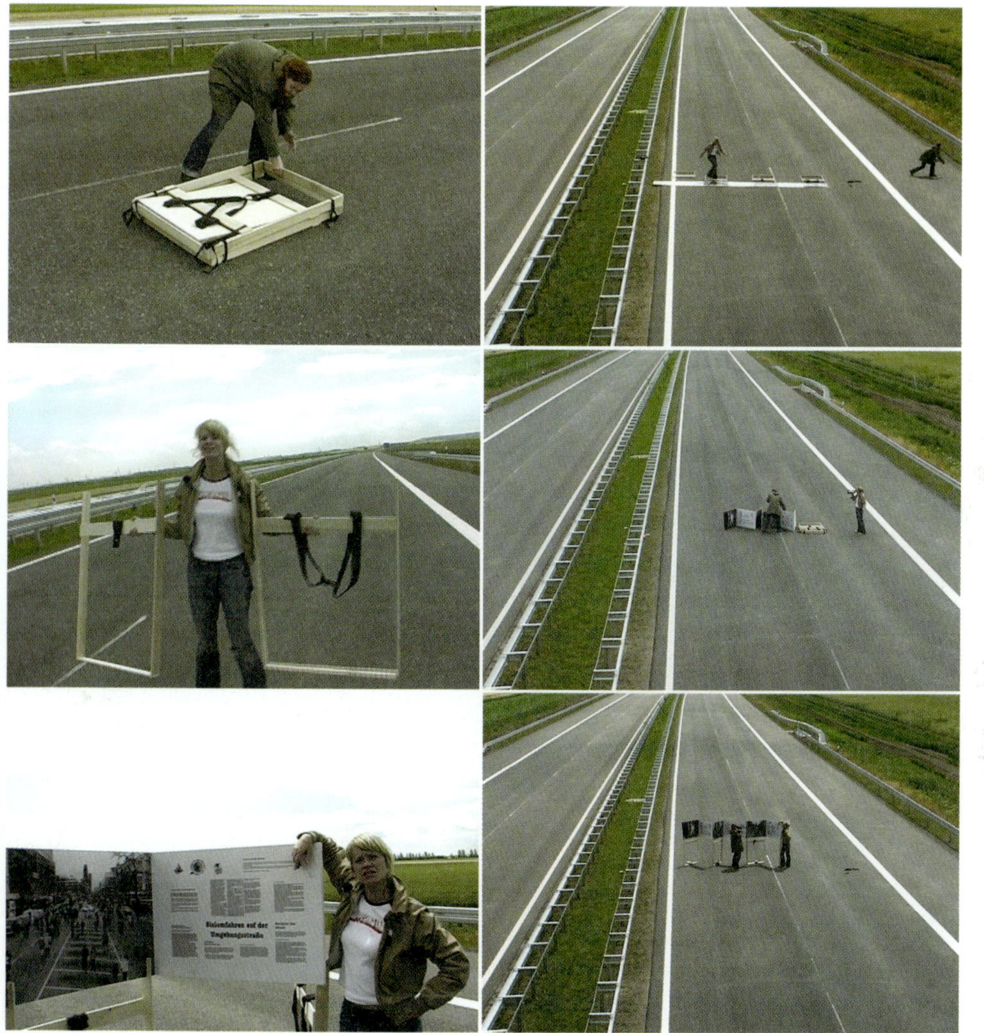

Dancing Structural Changes

A choreography based on a text from Terje Vassdal,
a professor at the Norwegian College of Fishery Science, at the
University Tromsø.

Actor: Nic G. V. Arnevåg

Part 1

In 1950 about 100,000 fishermen were registered. Of these almost
70,000 had fishing as sole or main occupation. Fifty years later,
in 2000, Norway had about 21,000 registered fishermen. Of them
about 15,000 with fishing as their sole or main occupation. During
a period of fifty years the number of fishermen had been reduced
to one-fifth.

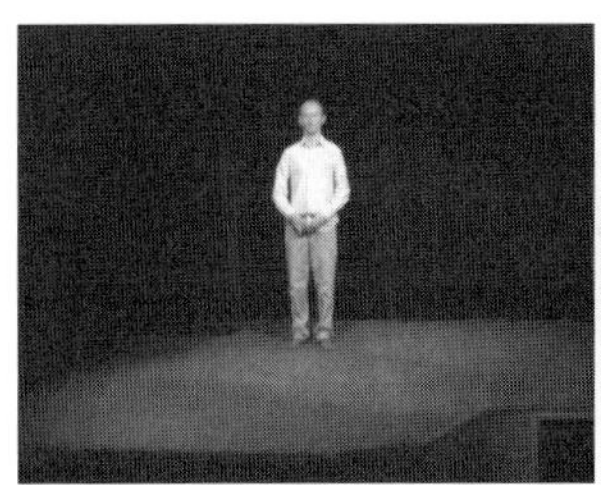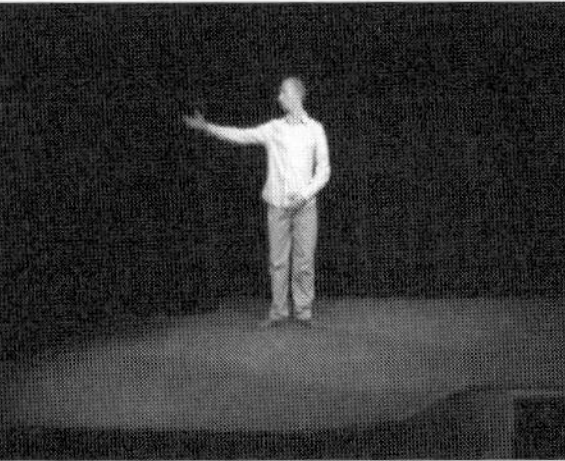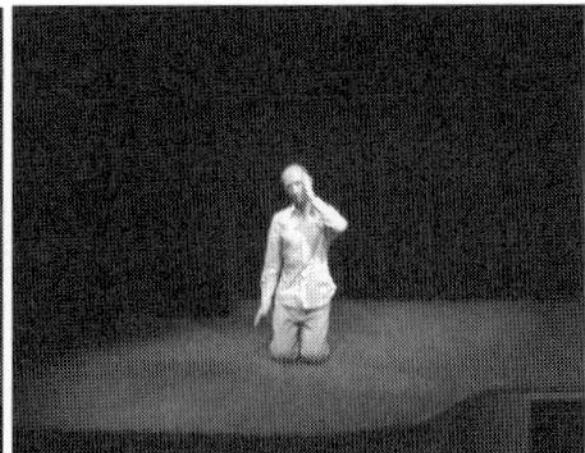

Part 2

First, one should always keep in mind that about 90% of Norwegian fish are exported in some way. This large export share is nothing new. A trade regime with minimal restrictions has always been a preferred goal for Norwegian authorities when working within the framework of the WTO (World Trade Organization).

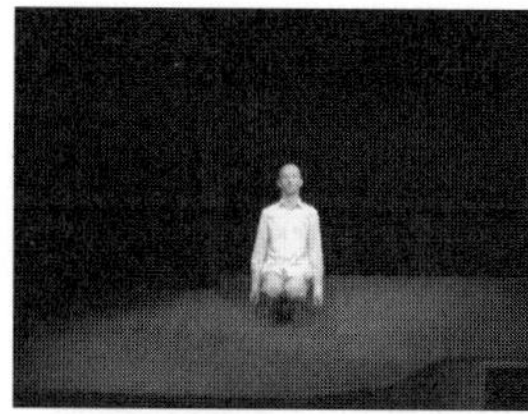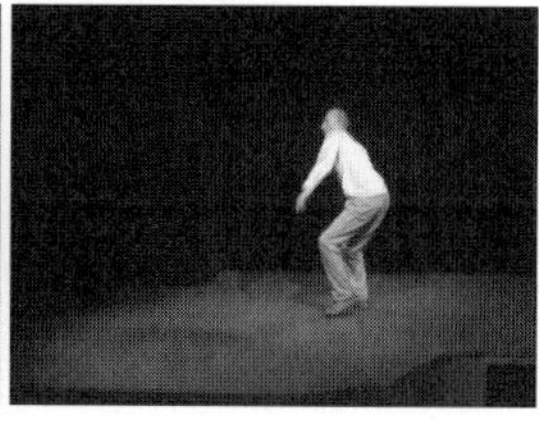

Part 3

After the collapse of the Soviet Union, Norway started importing large quantities of unprocessed cod fish from Russian vessels. In the top years, the import exceeded 100,000 tons, but are now less, and declining. The imported raw materials were produced in Norway by a modern and efficient fishing industry, and have contributed to profit and value adding in Norway while likewise resulting in a loss for Russian workers.

Part 4

Recently one may have observed, as a consequence of globalization and international trade, that some countries with extremely low labor costs build processing plants producing imported fish for immediate export. China is such a country. Fish are being imported, processed, and then exported again. Most of such fish are being caught in north Pacific waters and could be Alaska Pollock or Pacific cod.

Part 5

Compared to most countries, a Norwegian worker earns more per hour. In many regions of Norway, working in the fish industry is not a popular activity. Working on the floor in the industry is linked to low status, this in contrast to working on a fishing vessel. When an employee is paid the same amount in another industry, he (or she) may not prefer the fishing industry.

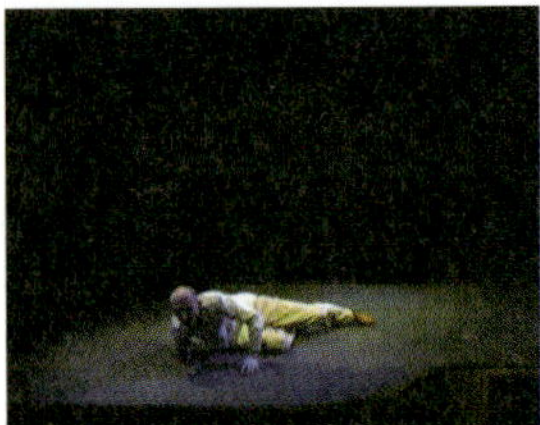
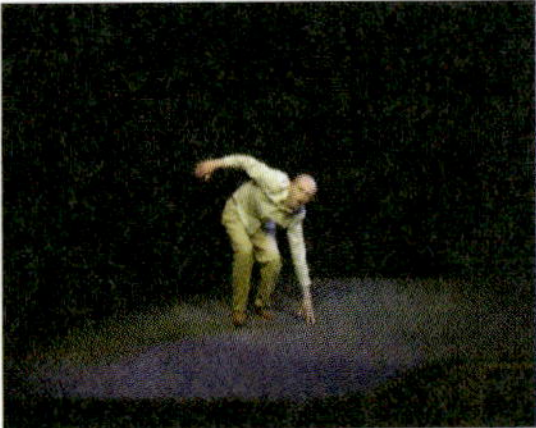

Part 6

The fishing industry is known for having a high turn-around for labor. Many foreign seasonal workers are employed in the industry. In North Norway this has traditionally been young women from Finland and North Sweden, but now increasingly people from the Baltic countries are recruited. Also workers from far away, like Tamils from Sri Lanka, have found their work in the industry.

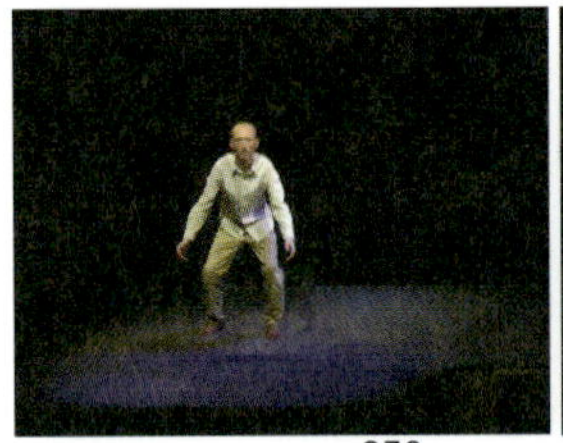
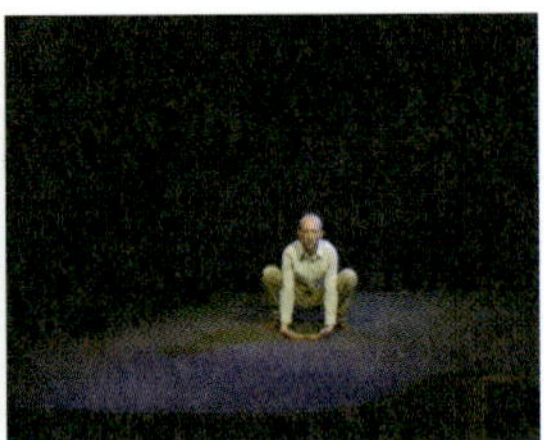

Part 7

Improved profitability is the result of price increase, productivity increases, and a changed product mix. Cost reductions are, in this industry, often synonymous with less employment. As much of the industry is located in coastal communities with little alternative employment, this development can have serious local repercussions.

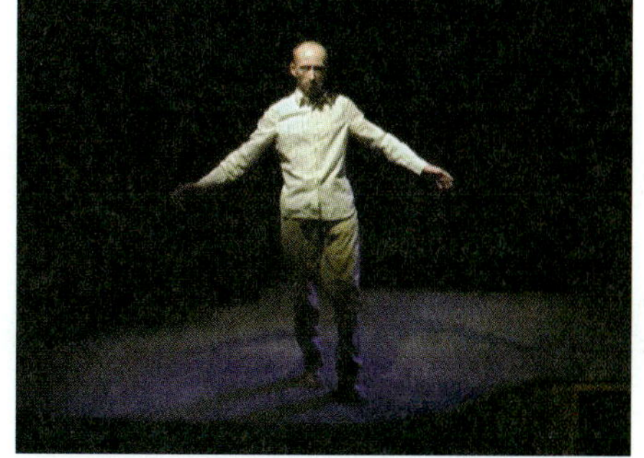

Part 8

It may be rather safe to say that the activity around fishing and the fish vessels will continue and may most likely stay profitable. The problem arises in the processing on shore after fishing. One possibility will be that Norway may switch to distributing fish with little processing to the closest markets in the form of fresh fish. This is mainly what the salmon aquaculture sector has been doing, and with considerable success.

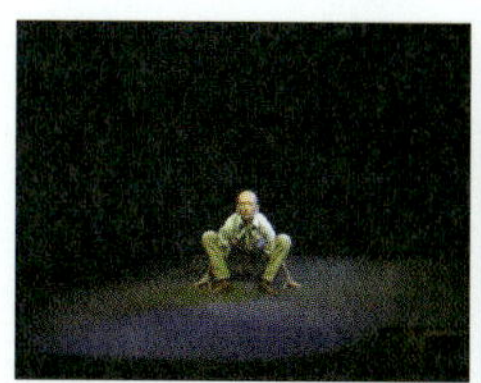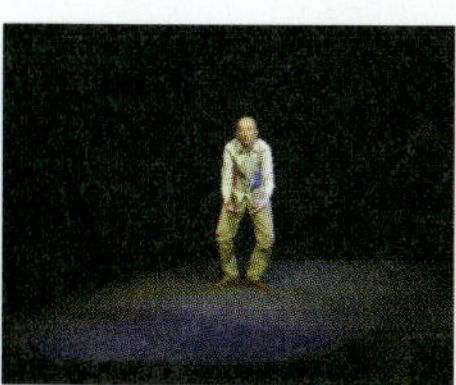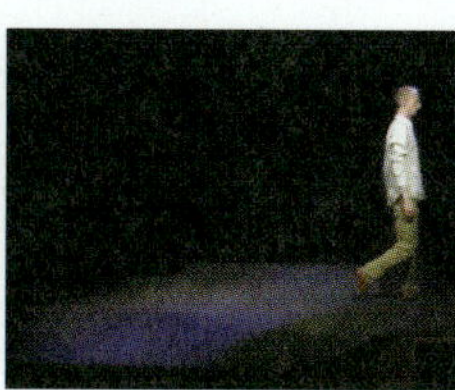

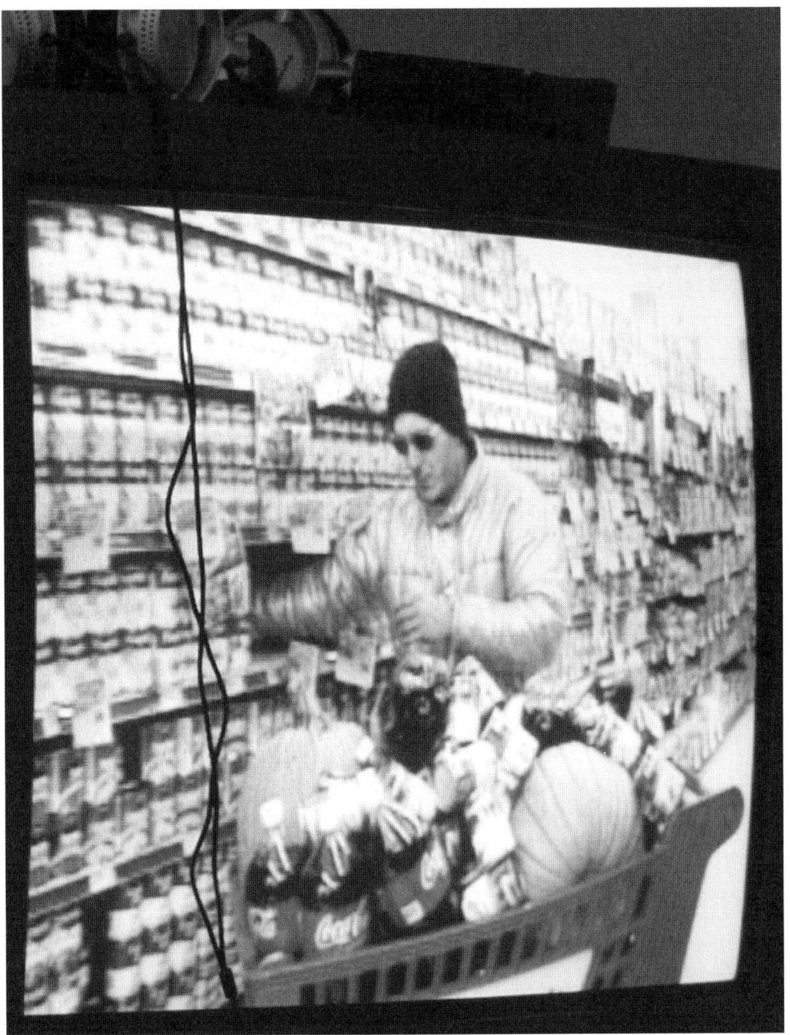

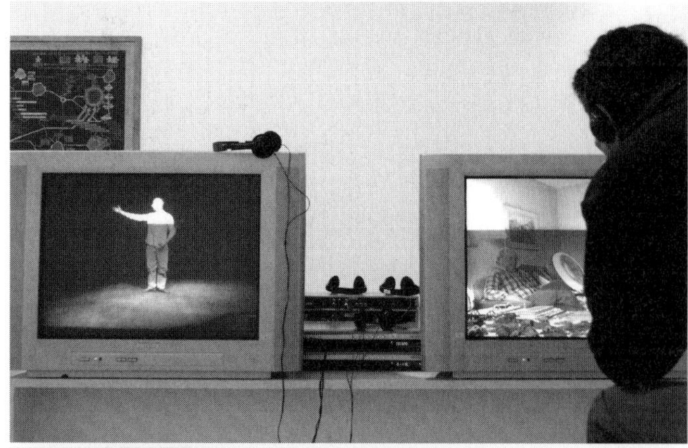

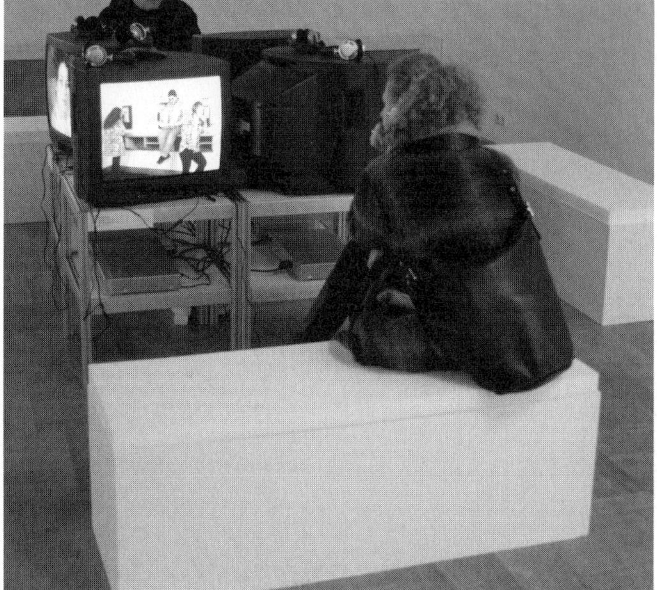

Installation shots from Capital (It Fails Us Now) at (top) UKS, Oslo, Oct. 2005 and (bottom) Kunstihoone, Tallinn, Jan.-Feb. 2006. Opposite page: Screen with still from Wandering Marxwards by Michael Blum.

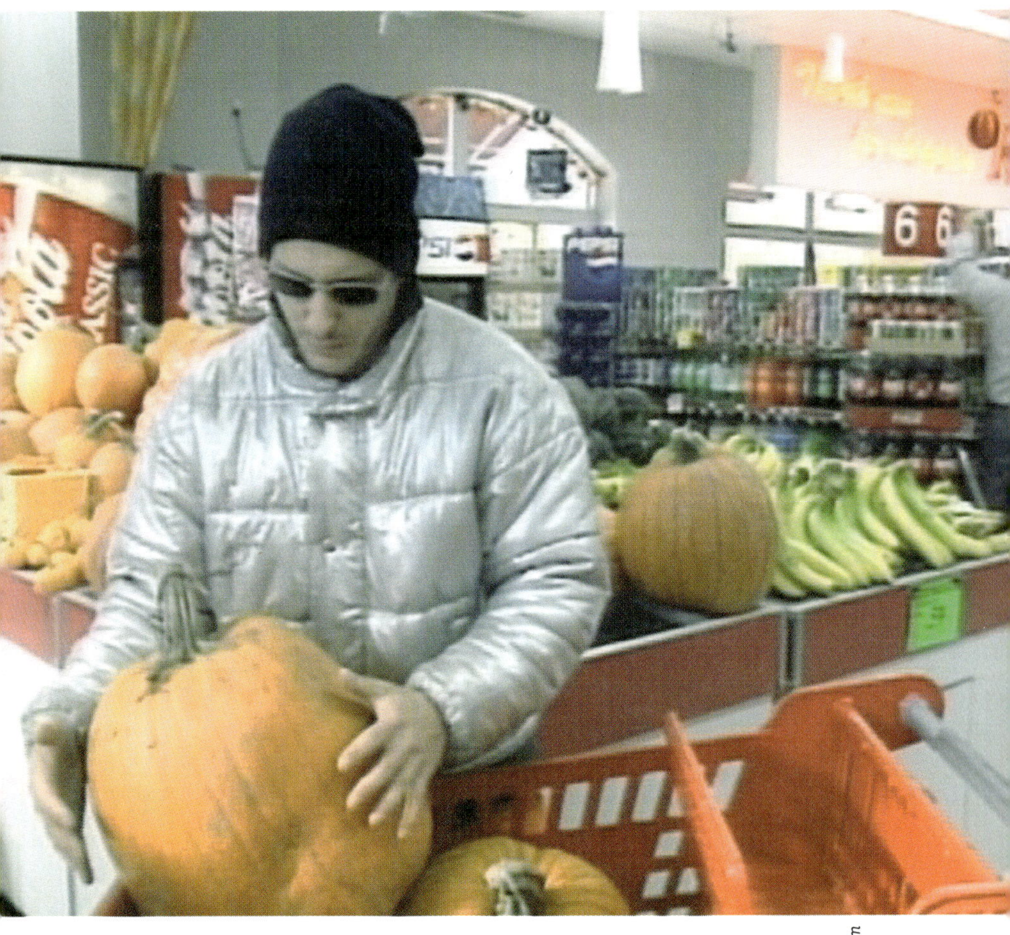

Michael Blum, stills from Wandering Marxwards, video, 19' 23", 1999. Courtesy of the artist.

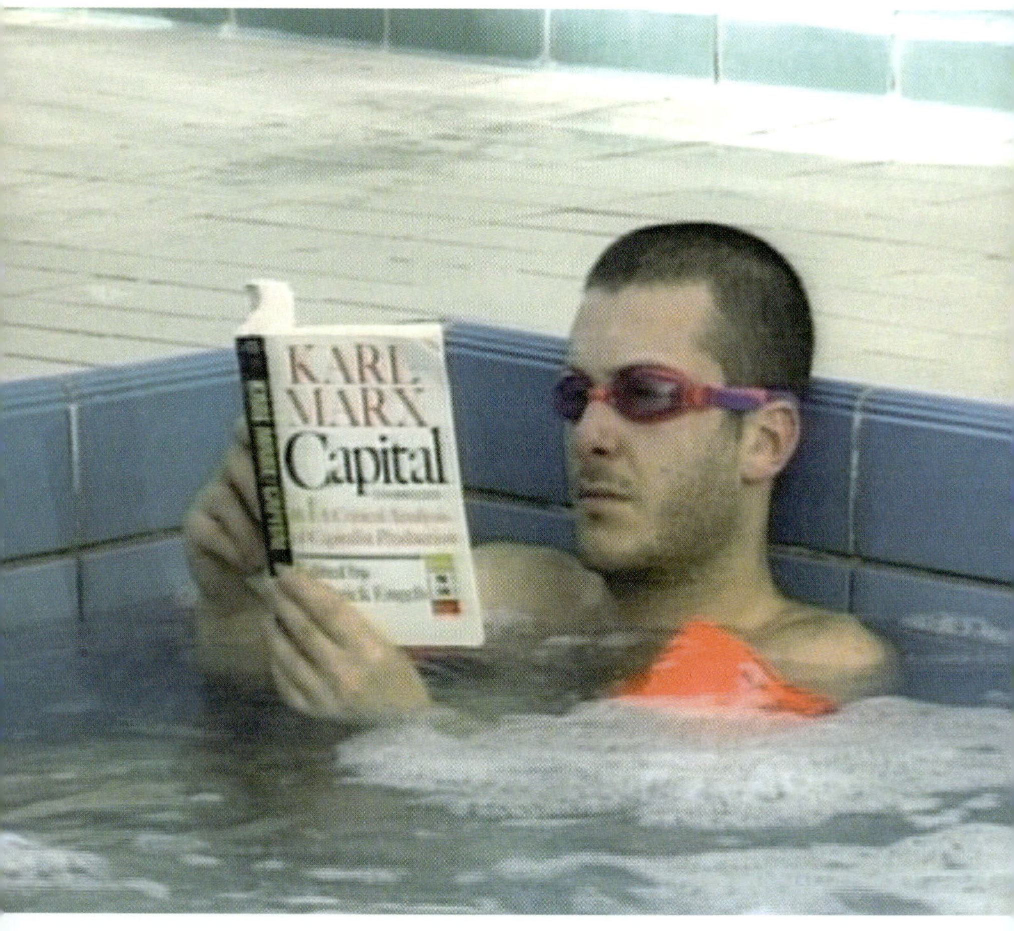

KARL
MARX
Capital

I began to read Marx in Paris for my project *Movements of Capital*, a contemporary re-reading of the general formula of capital expressed by Marx. Then, I had to displace myself, go into an exile that was as comfortable as Marx's wasn't, in order to induce a distance, or even a gap in-between myself and the world. With both my project and a copy of *Das Kapital*, I never began to think about the ways to represent capital. And I was really scared when I realized that the only person who'd been thinking of such an ambitious subject was the inventor of modern cinema himself. In effect, there are some notes that Eisenstein wrote during the editing process of *October*, from October 1927 to April 1928, and which attest that he had the project to film Marx's *Capital*. But the project, even articulated by such an extraordinary intelligence, was bound to fail anyhow. This statement wasn't exactly the most encouraging I could receive. Filming *Capital* was too much for me, or I was too little for filming *Capital*. At this point, I remembered a Persian proverb which says: *when you're entering a house / make sure you know how to get out*.

Excerpt from Wandering Marxwards *by Michael Blum*

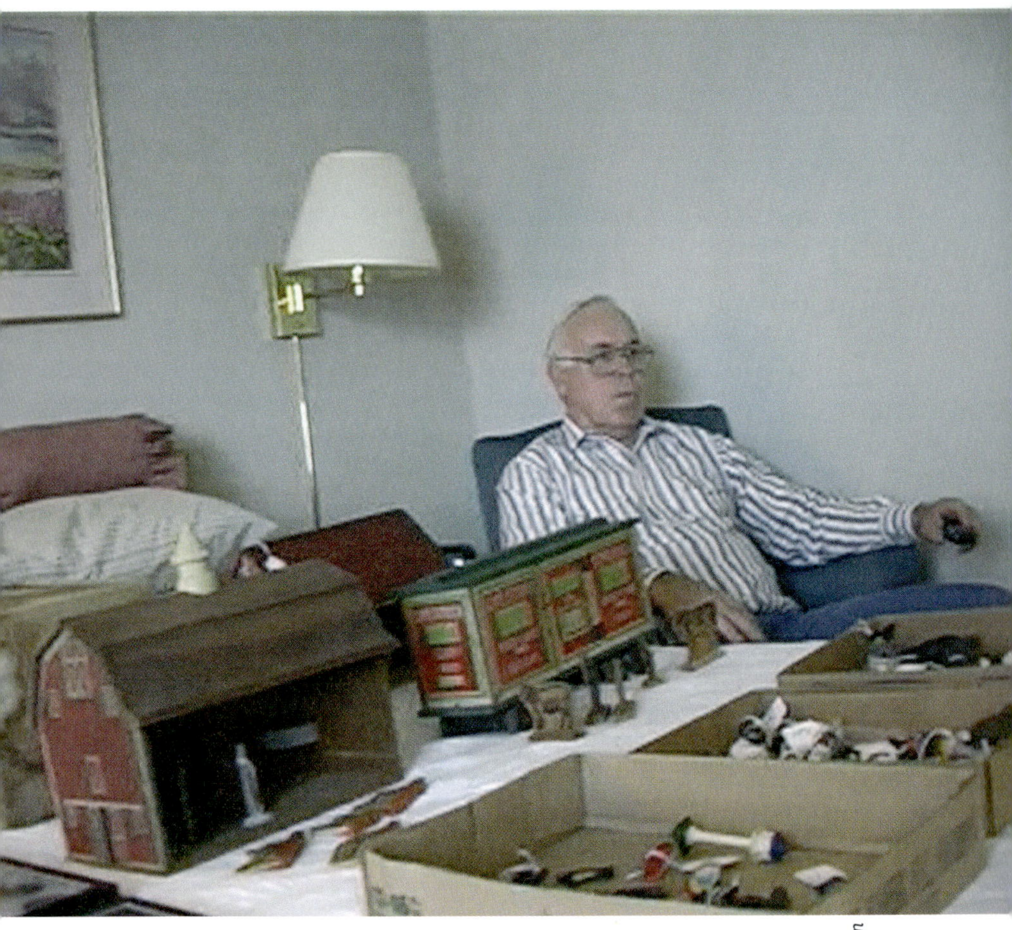

Michael Blum, stills from Old Boys and Toys, video 39' 33'', 2005. Courtesy of the artist.

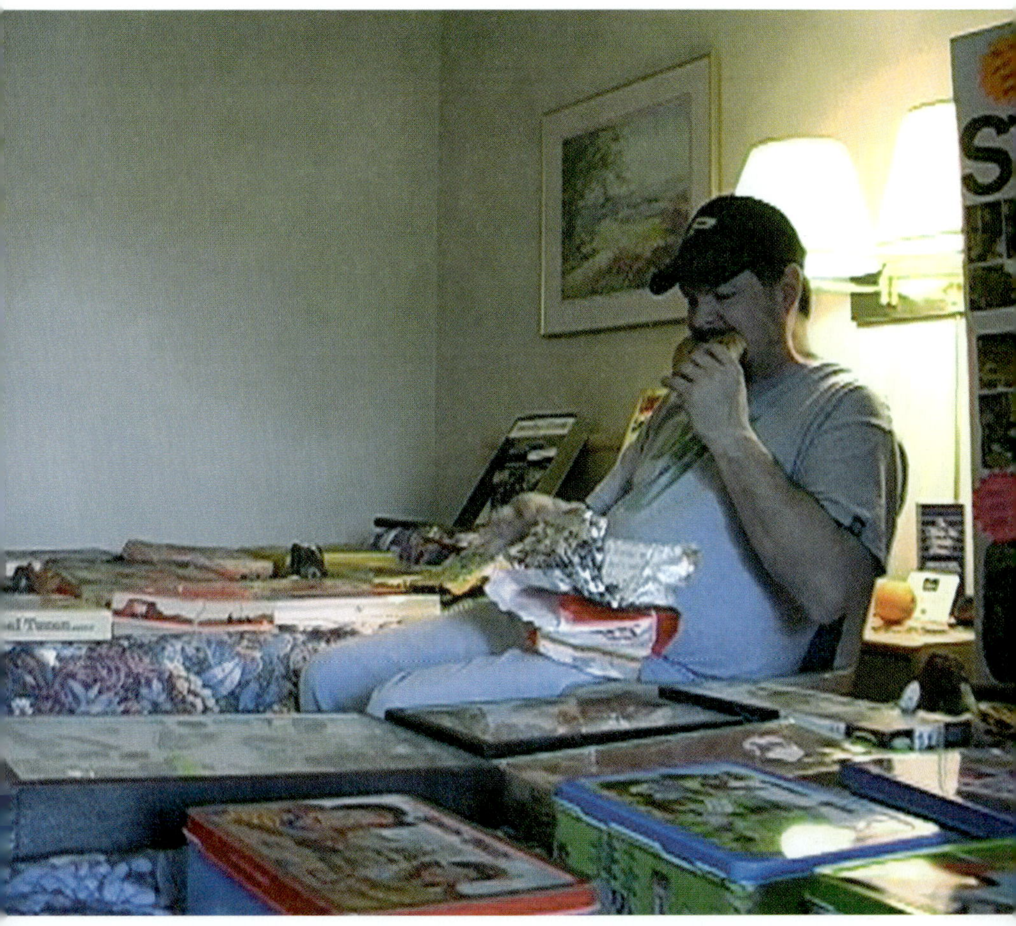

Every year in April, the *Antique-Collectible Toy & Doll World Show* is taking place in seven halls located in a field 50 miles West of downtown Chicago. It is the leading event of the collectible toy community and the biggest fair of this kind in North America.

During the 3 days prior to the fair, toy dealers, mostly white men over 60, rent rooms and display their collection at the local Holiday Inn, leaving the door open for other members of the community – potential buyers.

Since a few years, the sales volume is dramatically decreasing at the fair – and increasing on e-bay. In ten years, the fair will probably cease to exist.

Michael Blum, Chicago, August 2005.

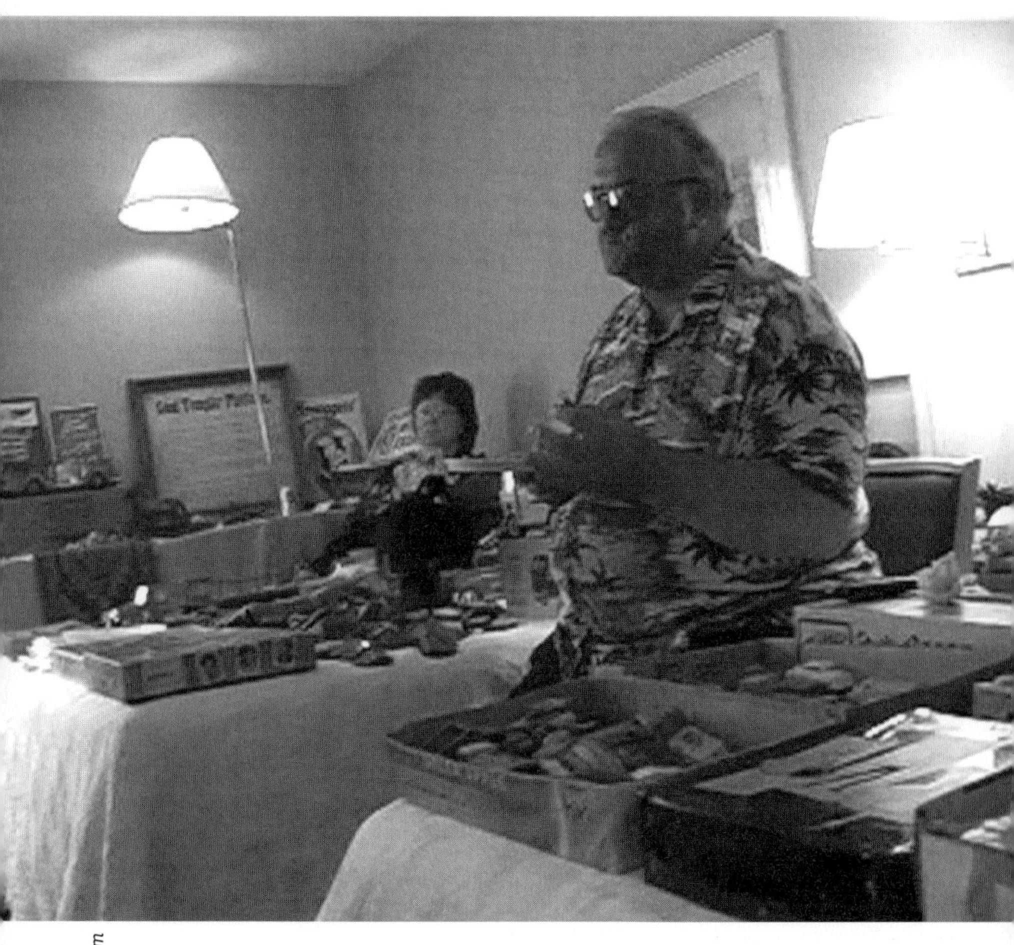

Michael Blum, still from Old Boys and Toys, video 39' 33", 2005. Courtesy of the artist.

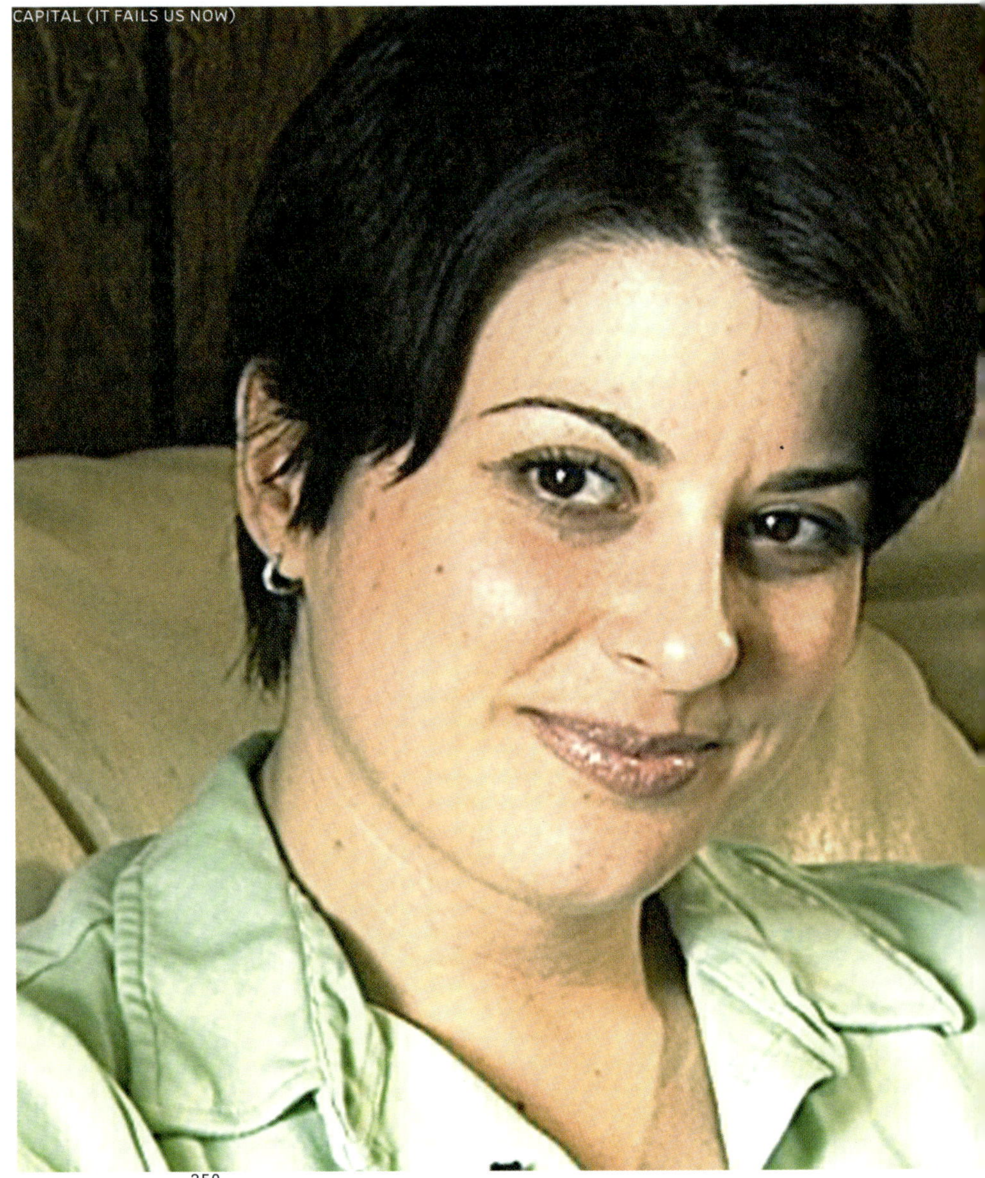

Still from Vera, by Jason Simon, 25 minutes, 2003, digital video.

Vera is an assisted self-portrait of consumption. The subject is a woman whose passions and compulsions are of spending and loss, taste and subjectivity. This conceptual document is both a study of our moment of economic abandon and of the dynamics of narcissism. Using both psychoanalytic and documentary tools, the video returns to earlier media strategies of minimalism and duration to bring its subject and its audience to a moment of recognition.

Vera, by Jason Simon, 2003, 25 minutes, digital video

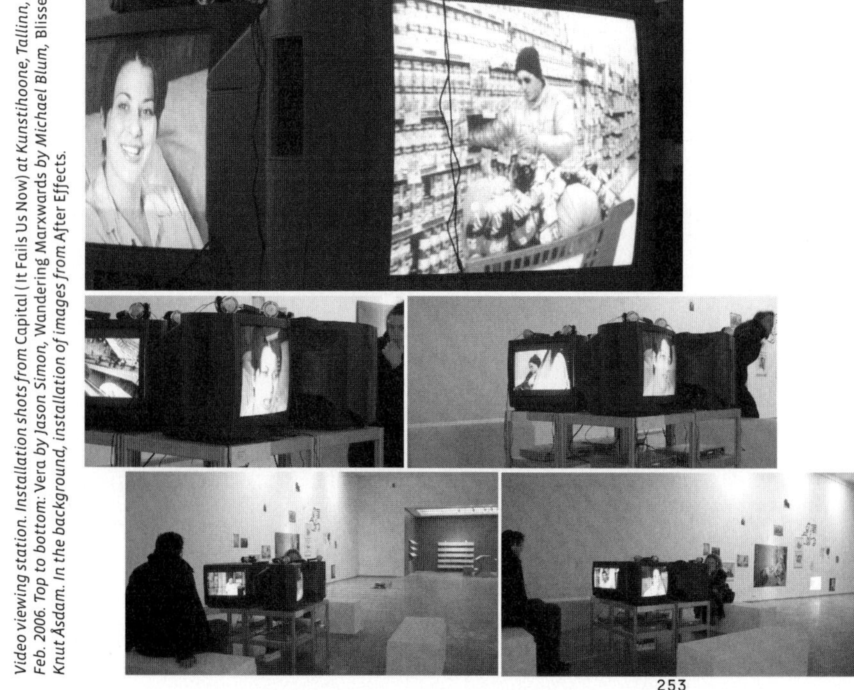

Video viewing station. Installation shots from Capital (It Fails Us Now) at Kunstihoone, Tallinn, Jan.-Feb. 2006. Top to bottom: Vera by Jason Simon, Wandering Marxwards by Michael Blum, Blissed by Knut Åsdam. In the background, installation of images from After Effects.

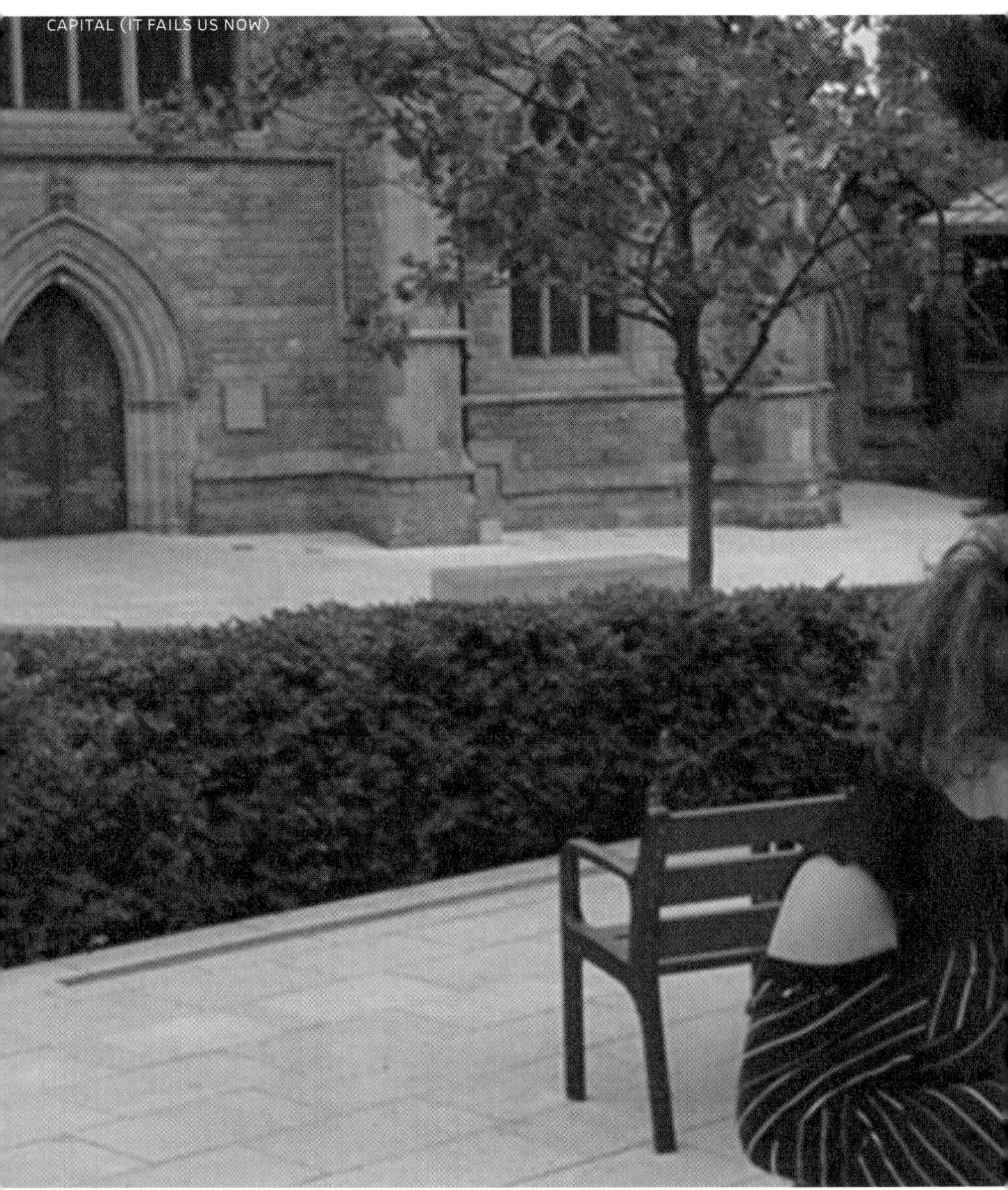

CAPITAL (IT FAILS US NOW)

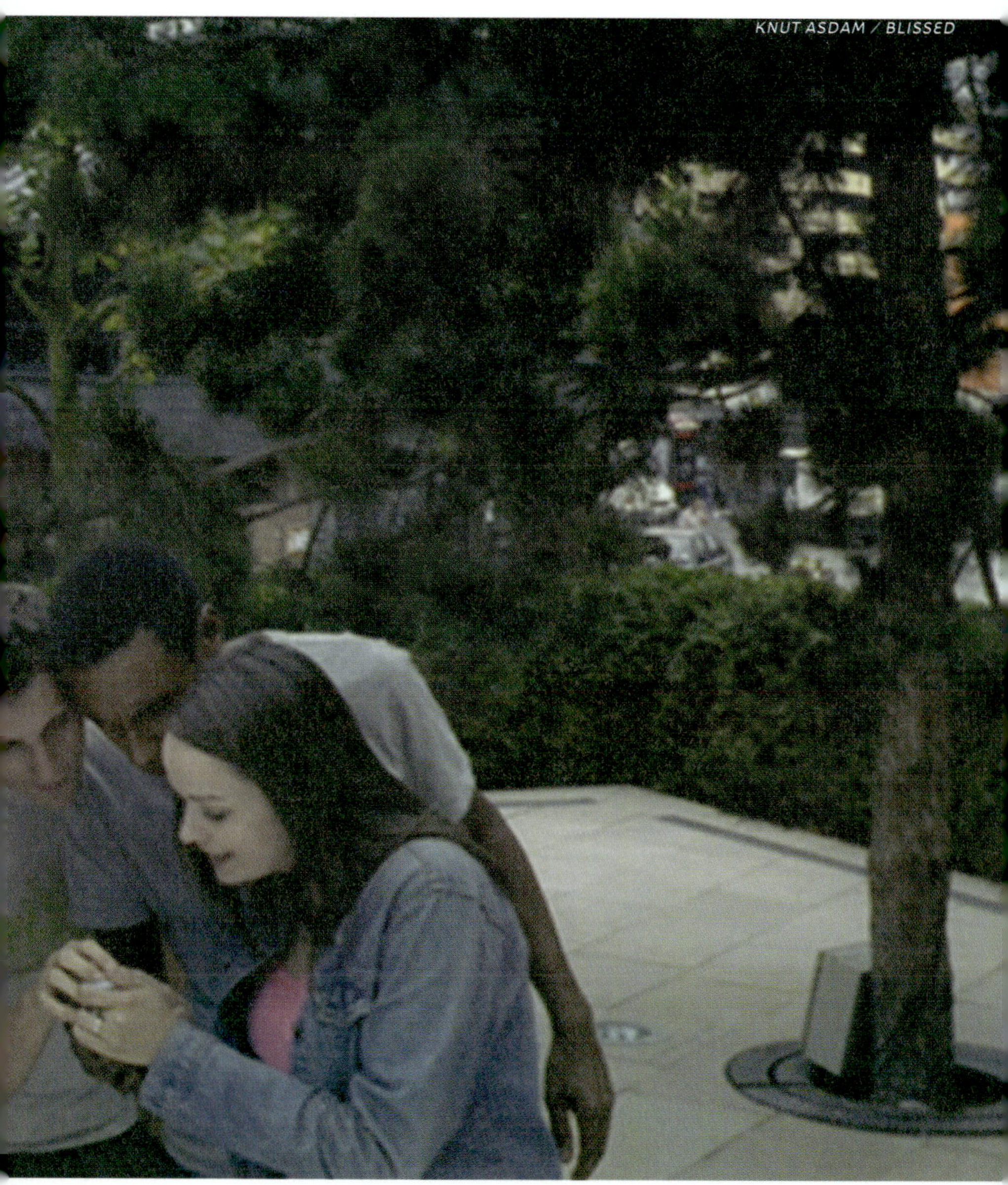

Blissed, 2005, follows four people in interaction within an urban environment. The film was motivated by two tropes: One is that of friendship manifested through language, and another is economy as manifested through the environment, architecture and through manners of speaking. In the film, the dialogues and the environment might seem oblivious to each other, but they are in fact closely intertwined. *Blissed* is rhythmically constructed in a series of actions, pauses, breaks and transitions.

Blissed, 2005

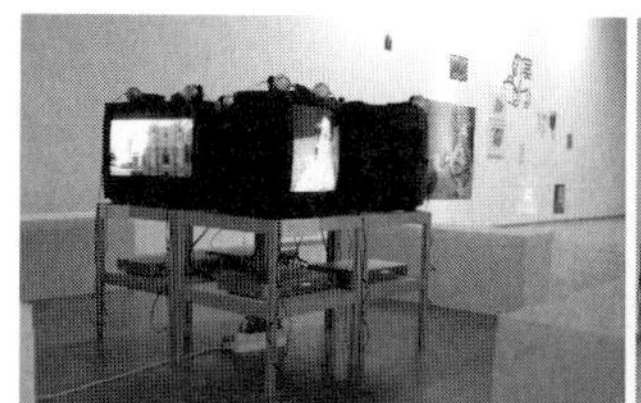
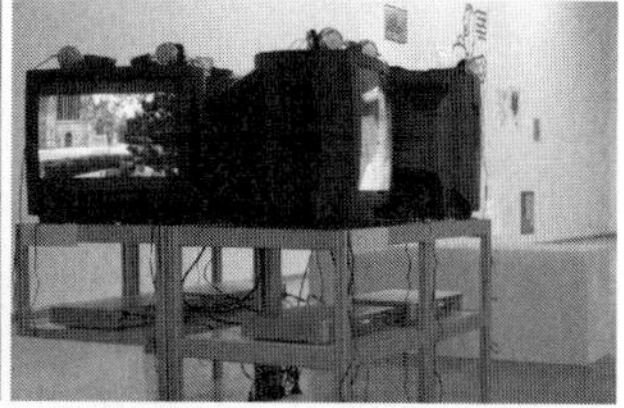
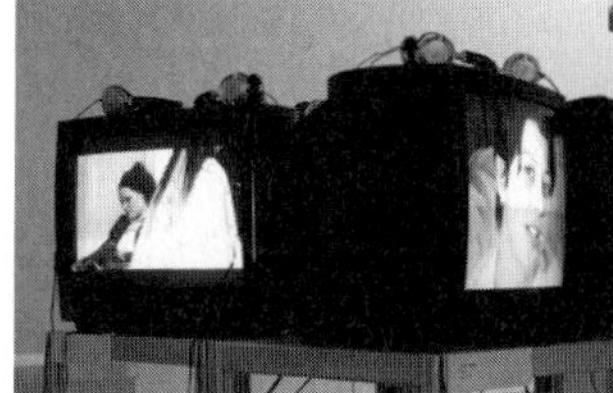
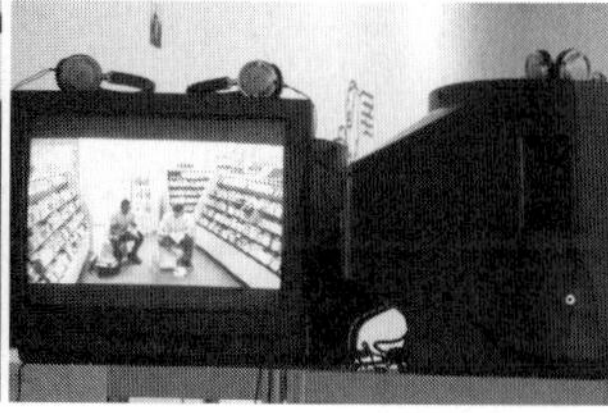

Installation shots from Capital (It Fails Us Now) of video-viewing station at Kunstihoone, Tallinn, Jan.-Feb. 2006.

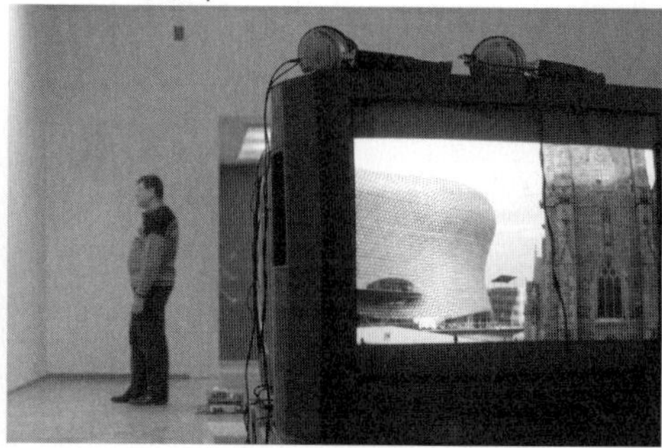
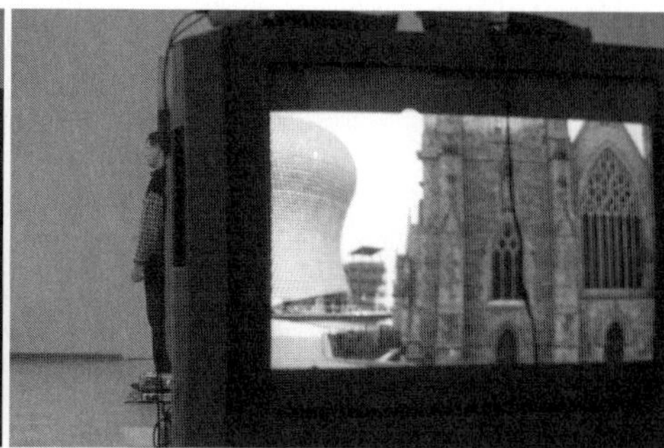

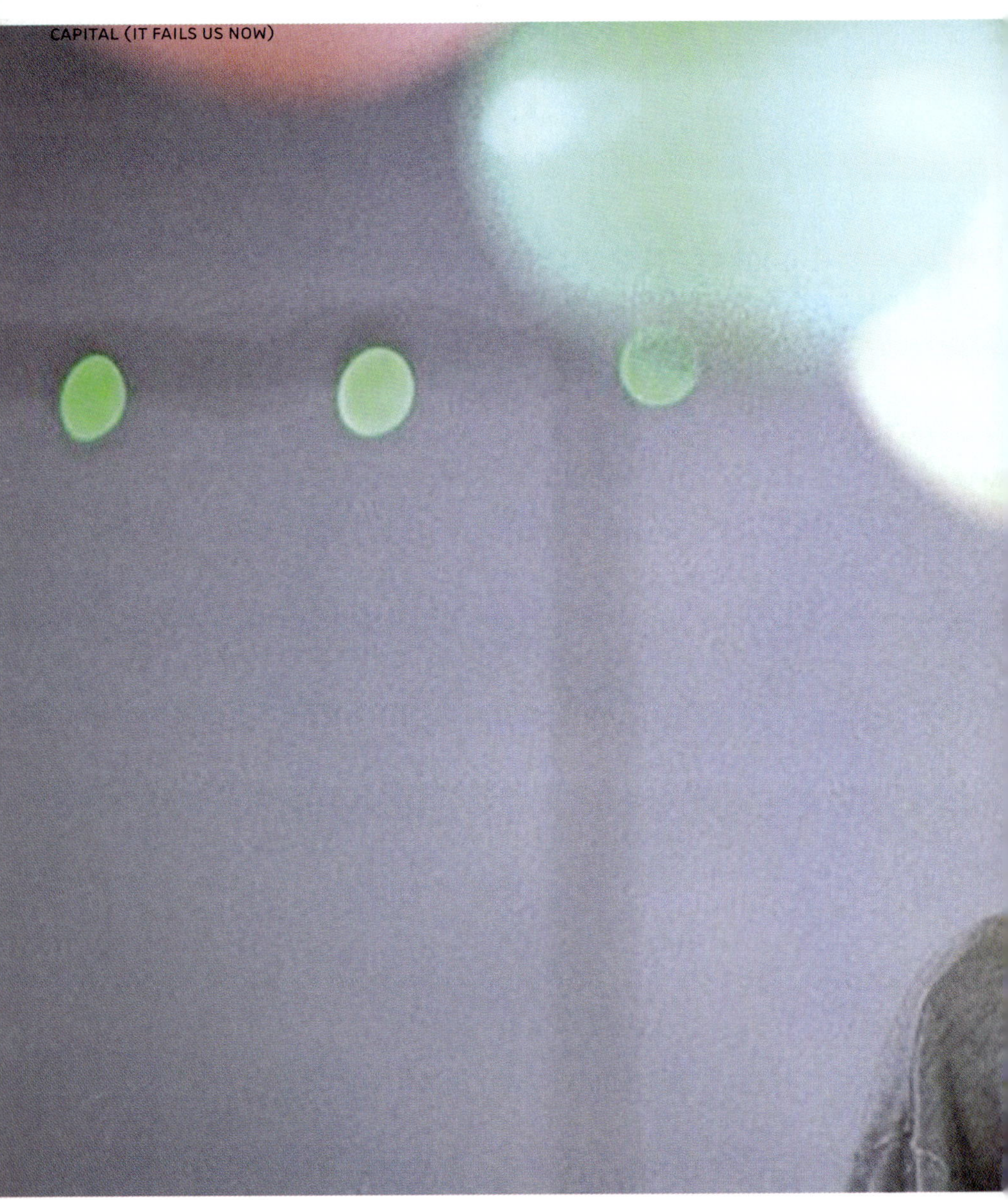

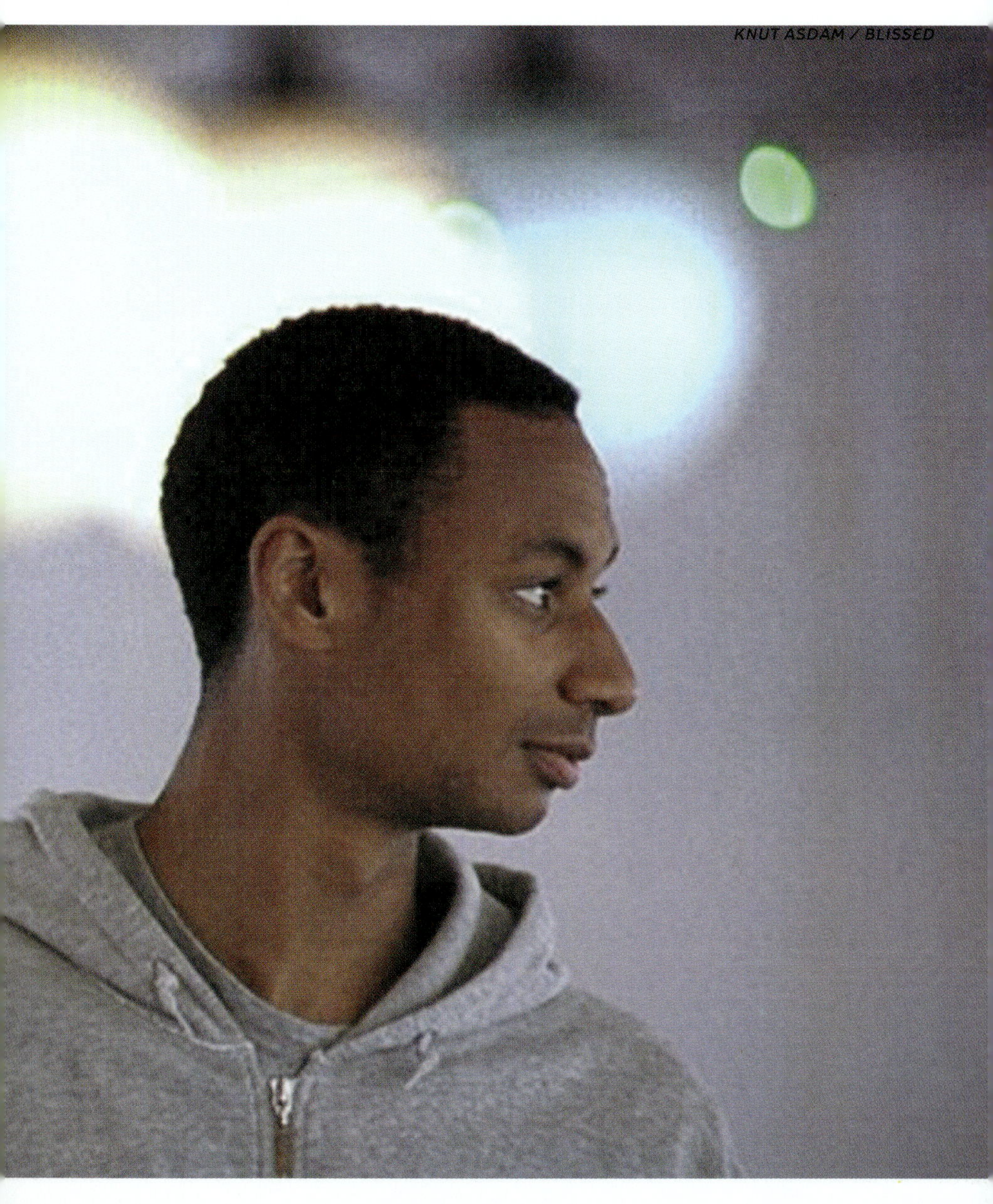

I was just finished work, and I was on my way home. I needed to go to the bank, to get some money out. I was gonna get some groceries and that from Sainsbury's. There was this guy standing there, and he looked, like, homeless, and he was really like aggressive. He had, like, swollen eyes, they looked really wet and he was maybe like a scaggard or an alcoholic or something because he had all these scabs on his face. He was like, still looking at me, yeah, and I slowly brought my eyes to him and looked at him back, and all he did, yeah, was put his hand out like that, –as if to say, you know, "where is my money?", and I am like: I am going to the bank mate, you know, to get my money, I am not going to give it to you. Anyway, so I walked past him and I was quite faced by him really. I went to the bank, got some money, and suddenly, yeah, I hear this "WACK" and like, I turned around, and the same guy, yeah,

Excerpt from Blissed, 2005. 12 min. 35mm and DVD, colour and sound. By Knut Åsdam.

that I was just talking about – with the scabs on his face and that – he had fallen flat on his face, but the thud that I heard was, like I could hear the slap of his flesh and then I could hear his brain inside bouncing about in his head, and I was, like, Wooow, you know, what was going on there? Seeing him earlier, I wouldn't have gone near him, I wouldn't have touched him, but when I saw him laying there I put out my hand and tried to help him up, and then this old lady was there as well, and she was just shouting and anything and everyone in the street. It made me feel quite bad really, that, you know…, I am not saying that if I had given him some money it wouldn't have happened, but I don't know… Eventually, we rounded up the police and stuff and then I went to the grocery store and I was just, you know, like, getting my pesto and getting my pasta and stuff.

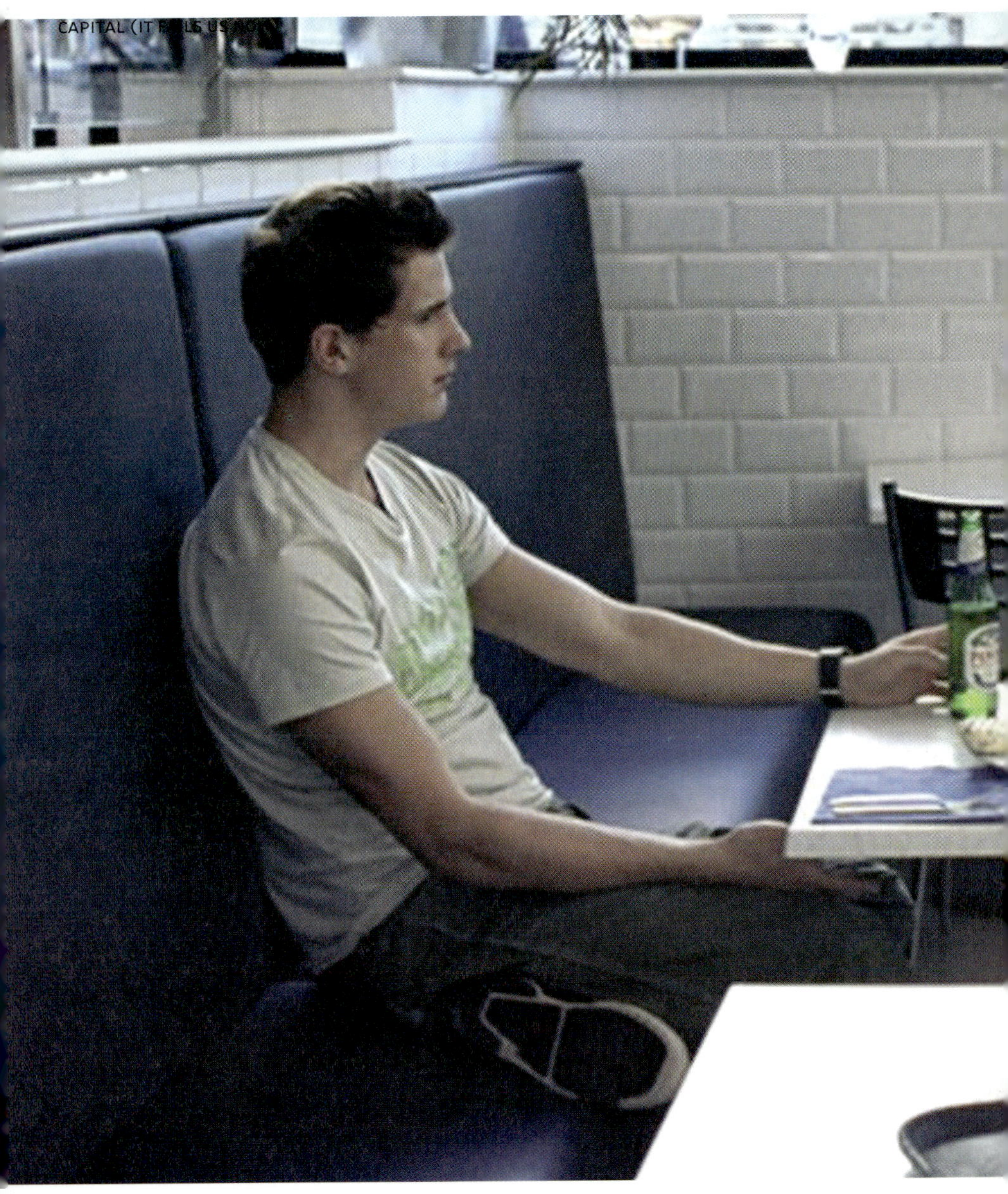

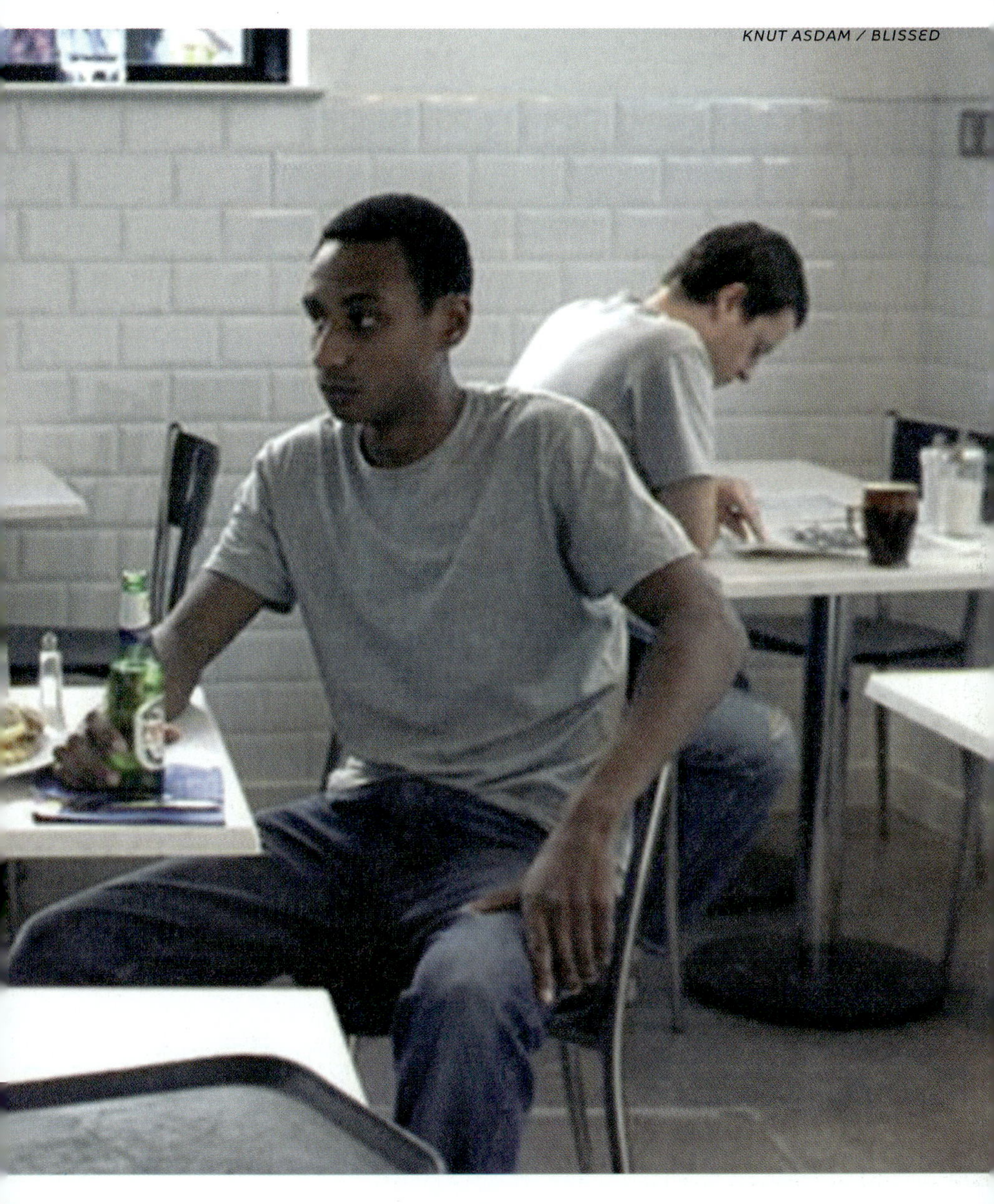

CAPITAL (IT FAILS US NOW)

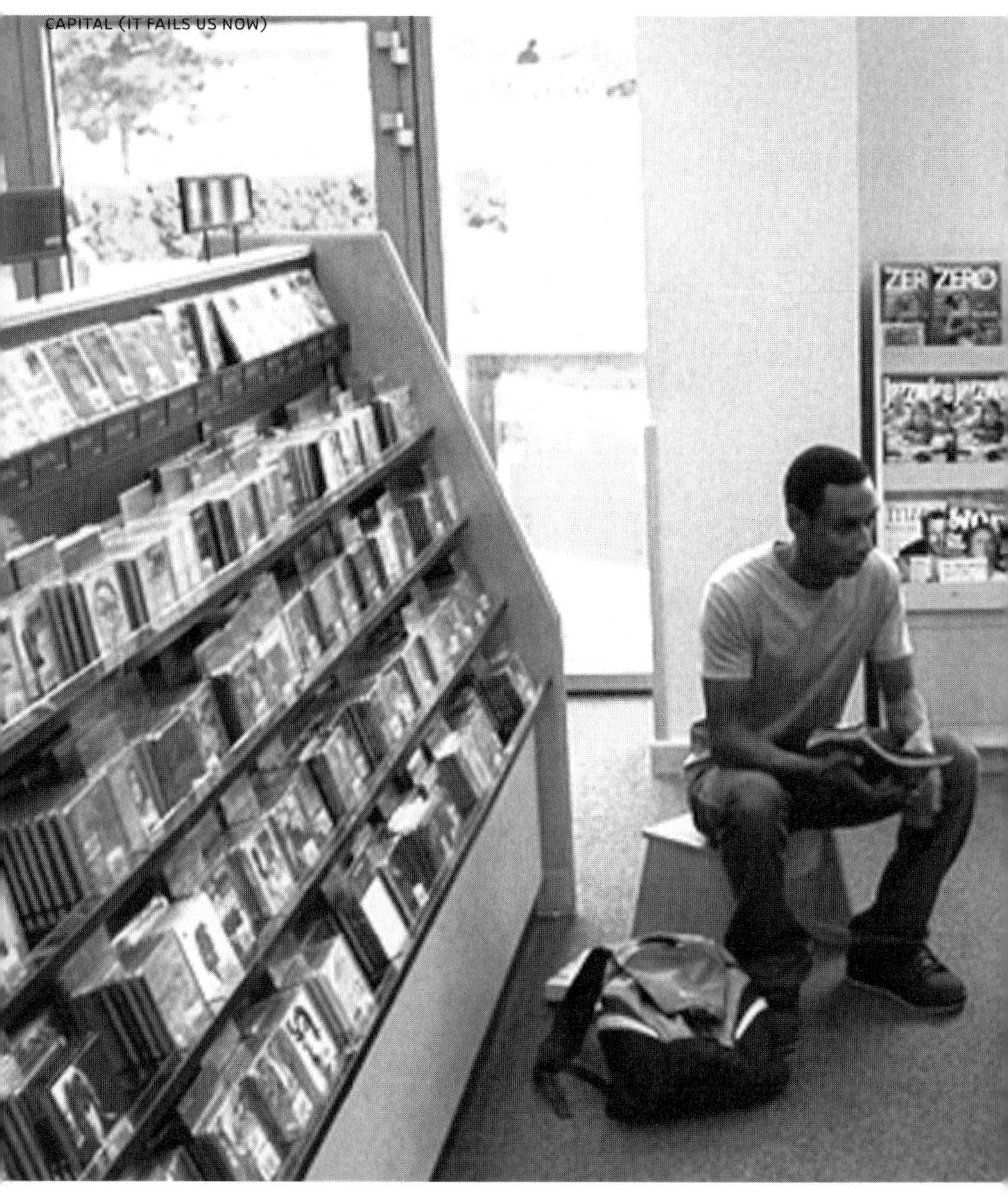

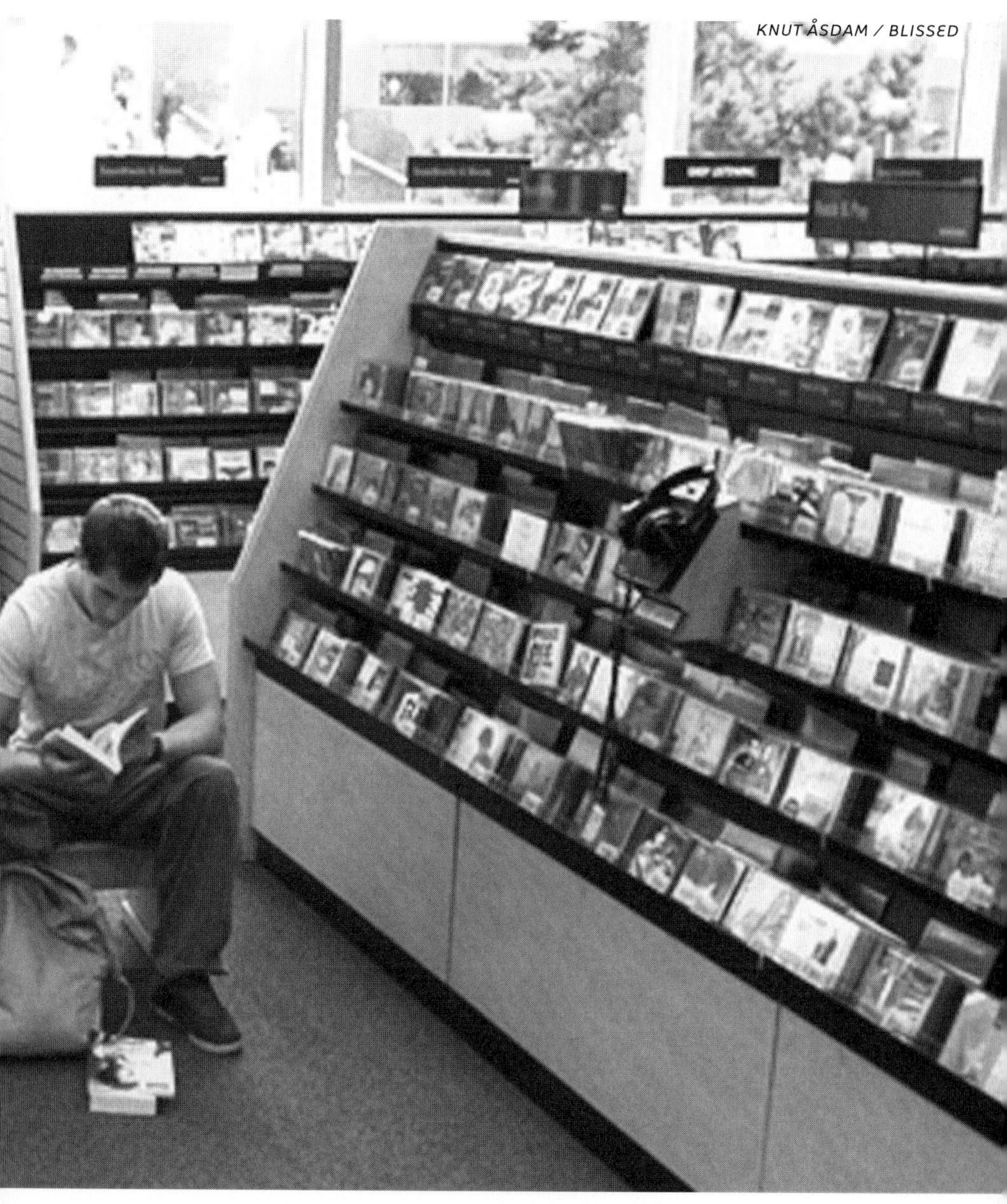

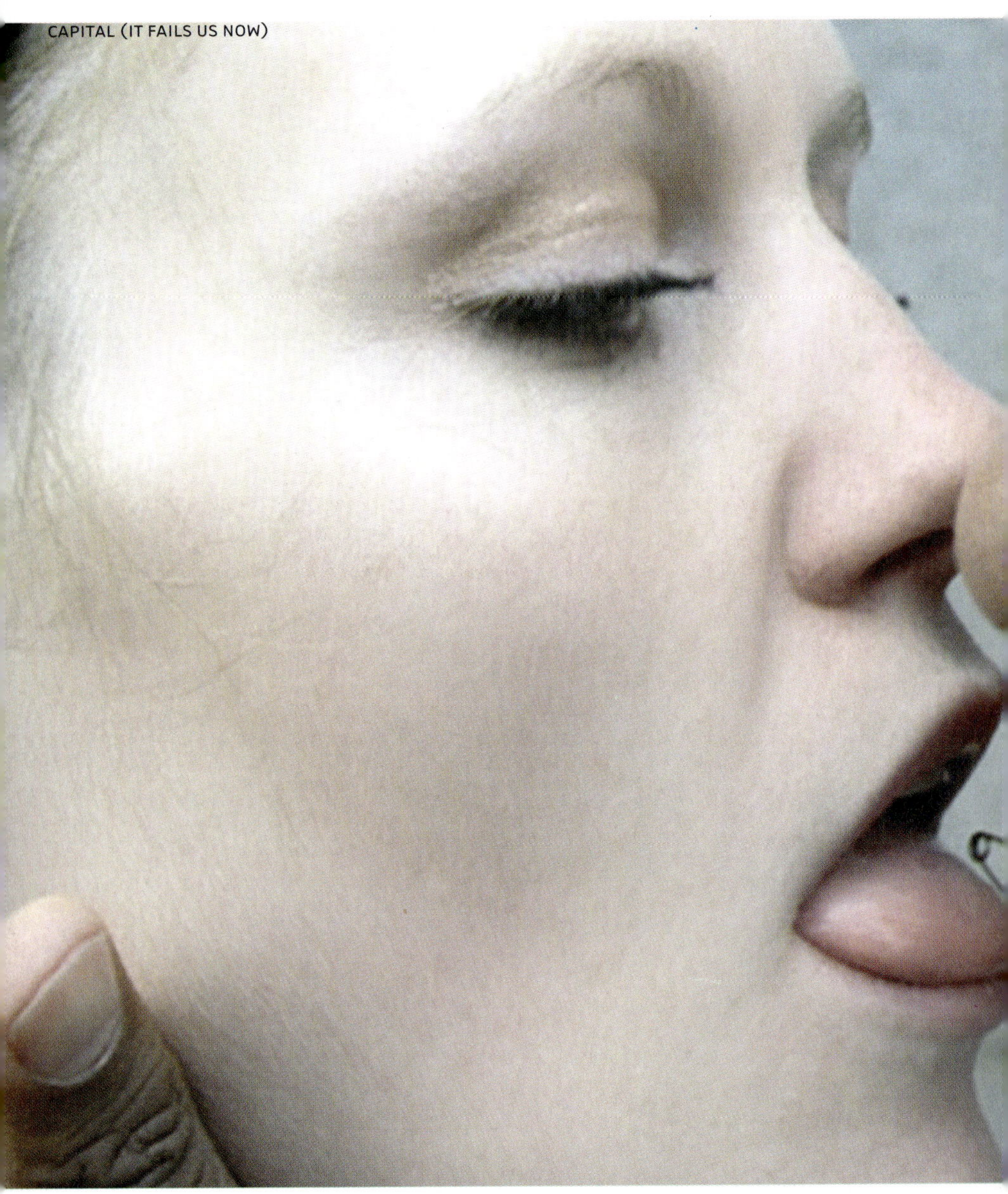

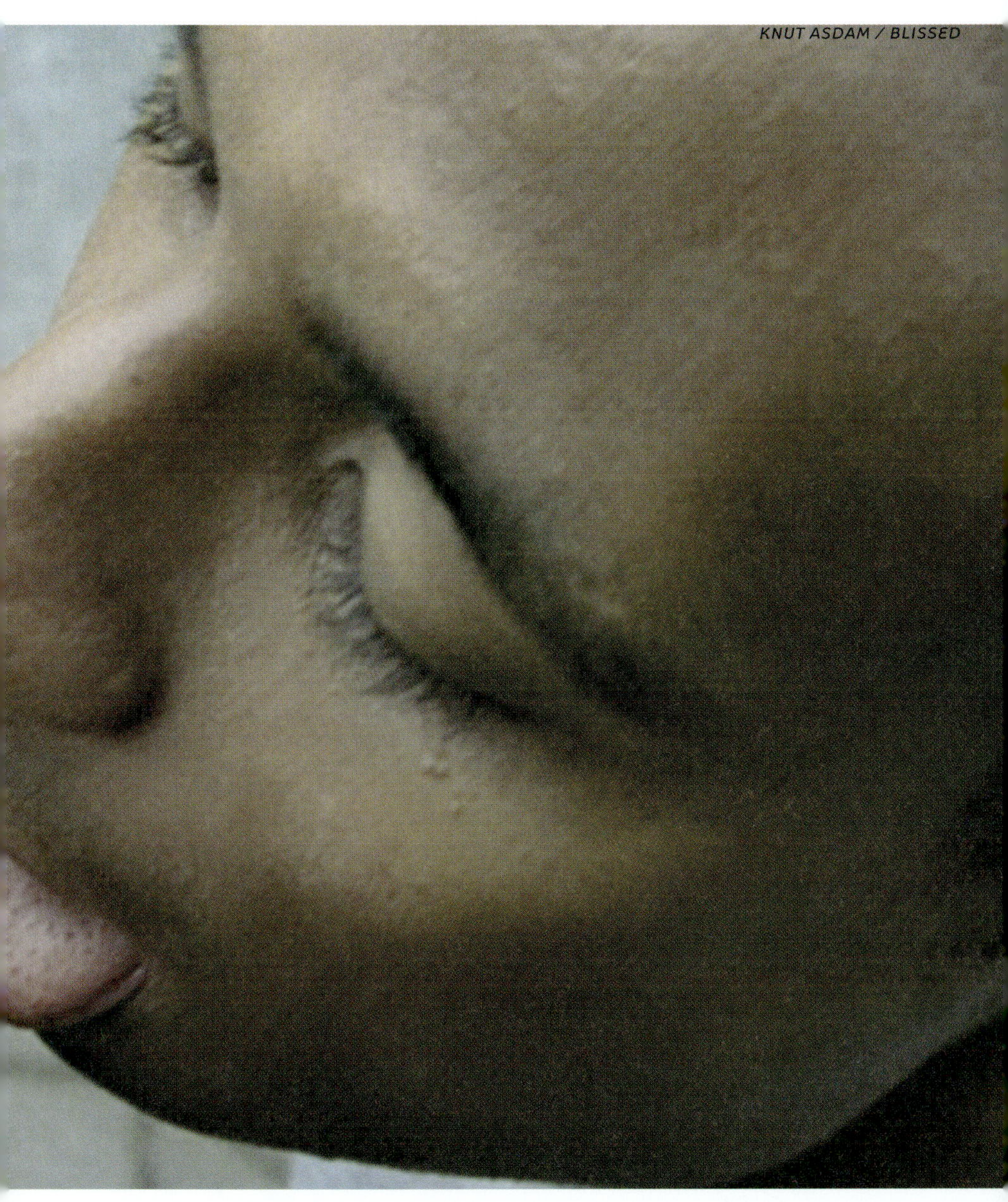

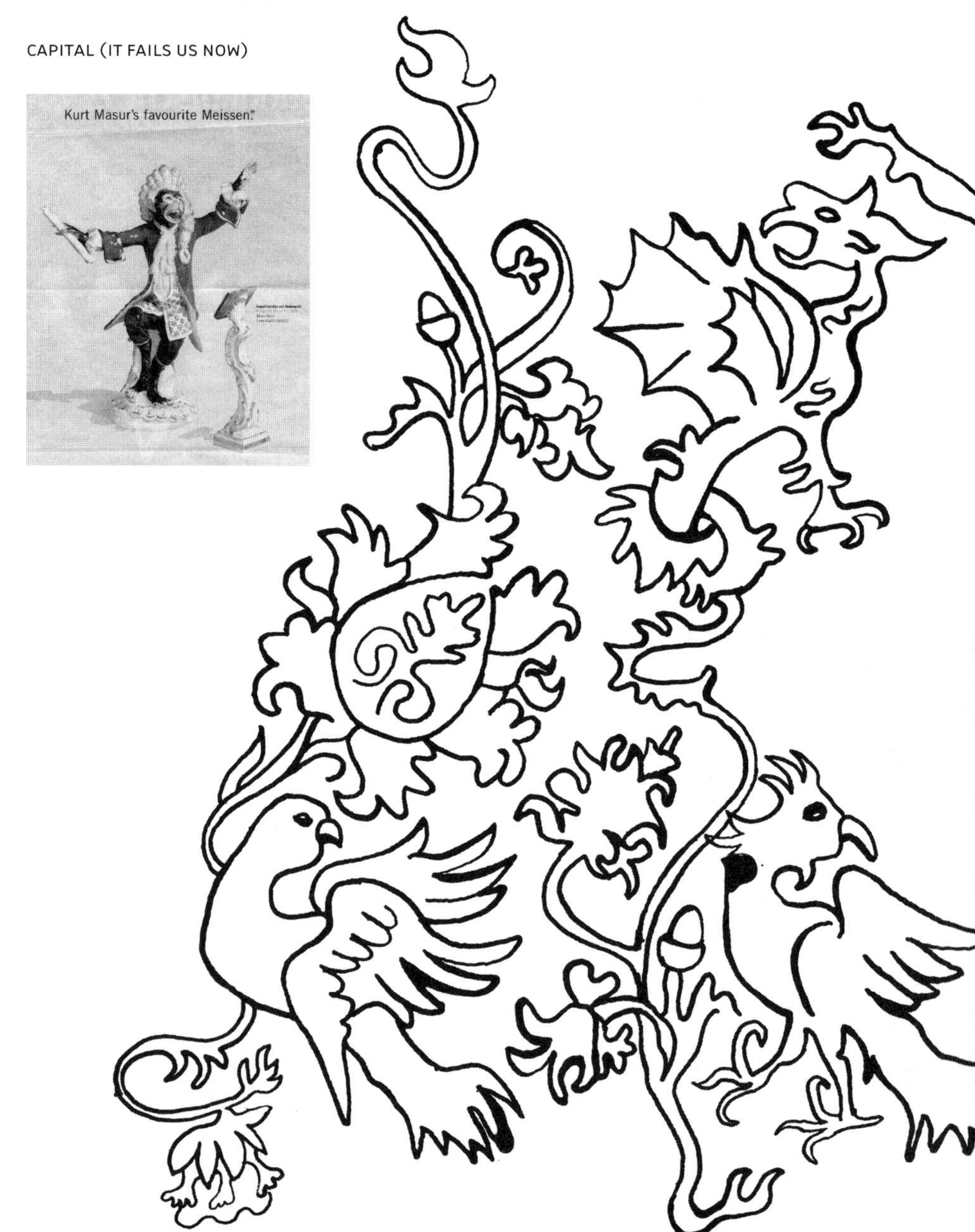
Kurt Masur's favourite Meissen.

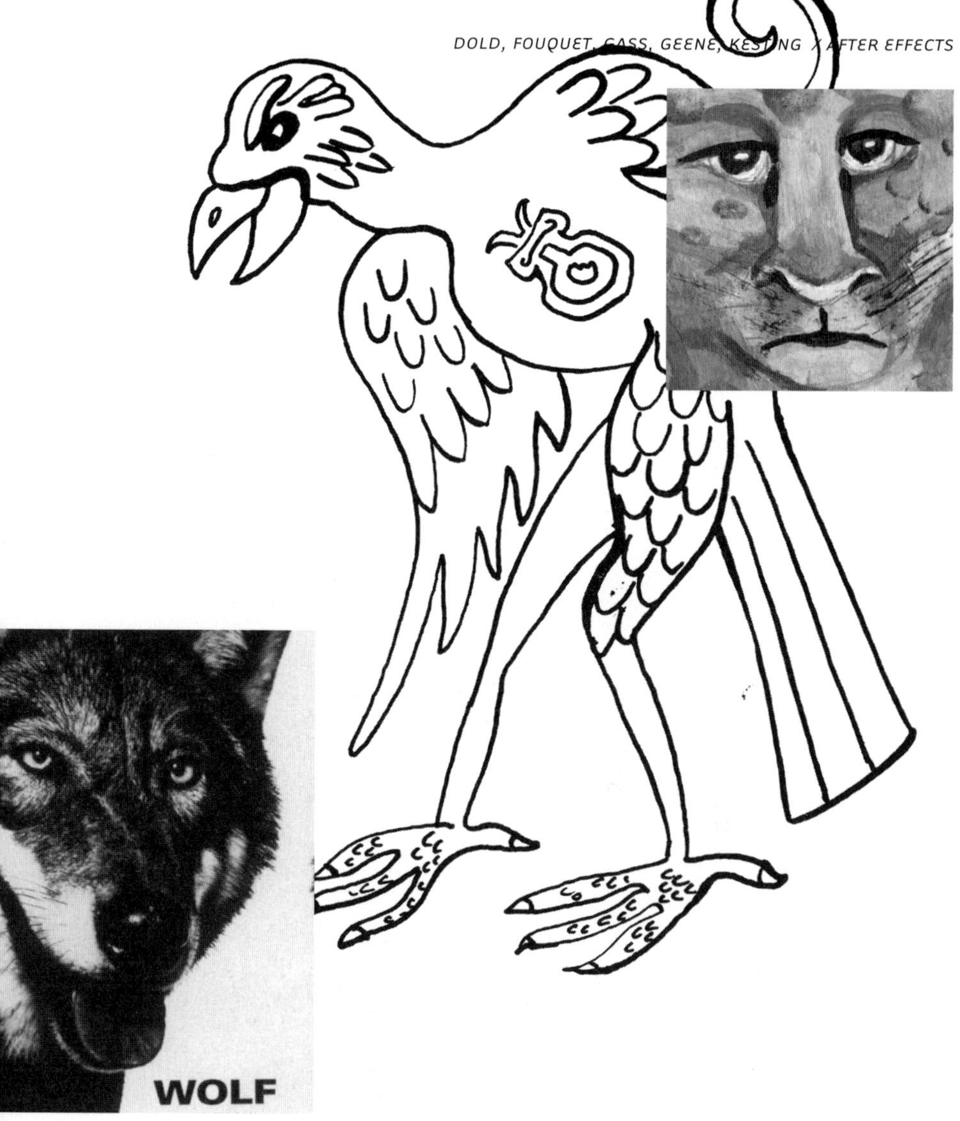

WOLF

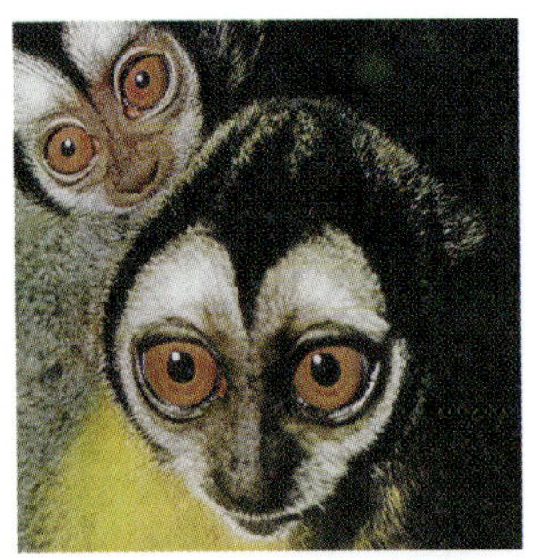

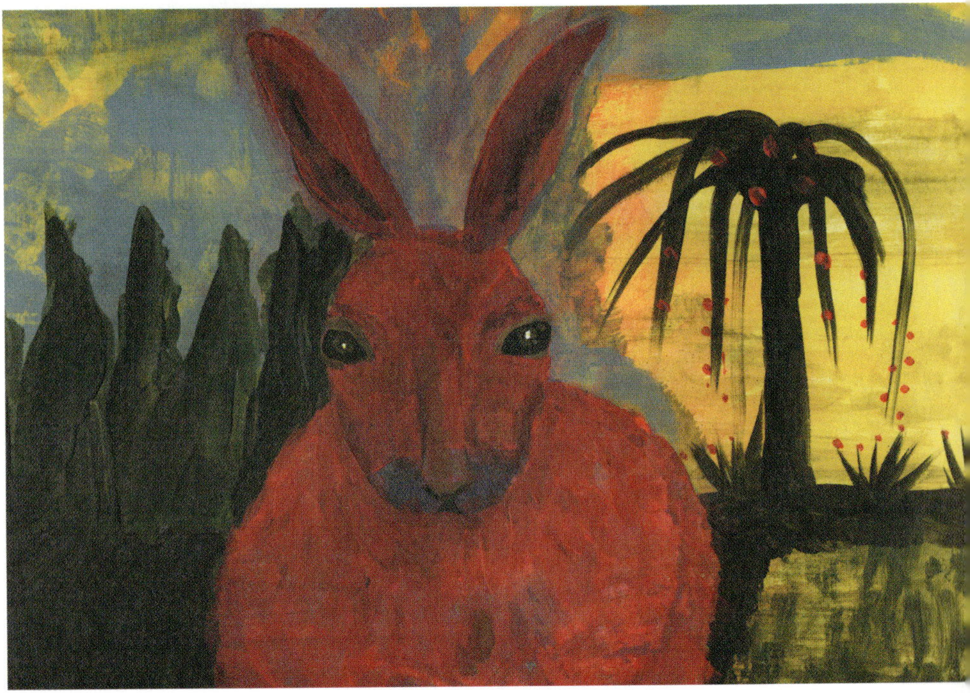

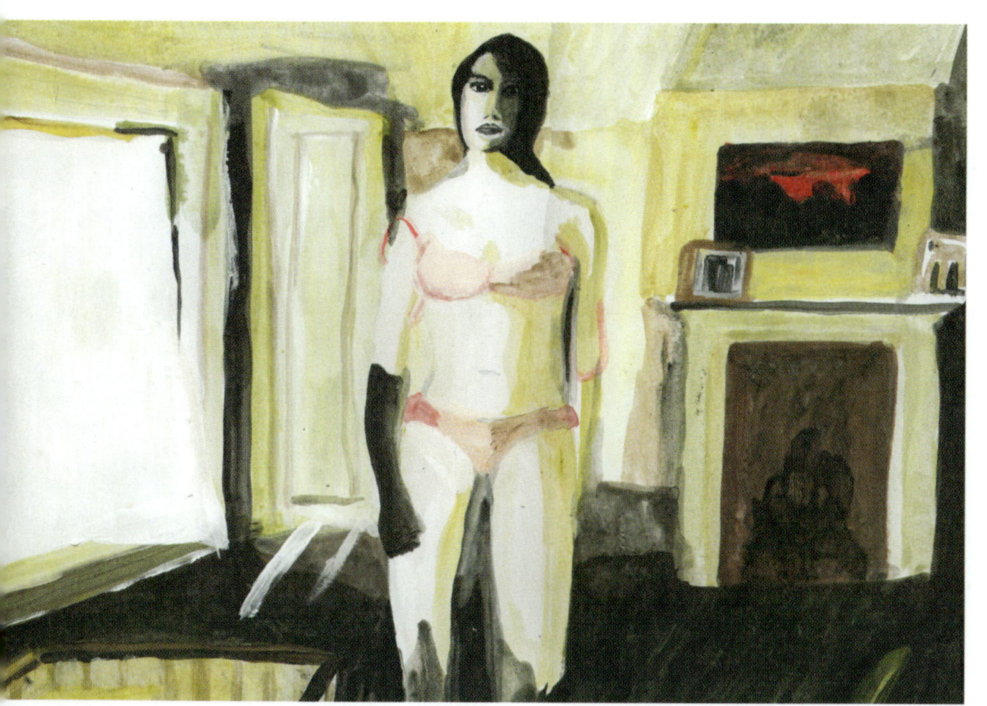

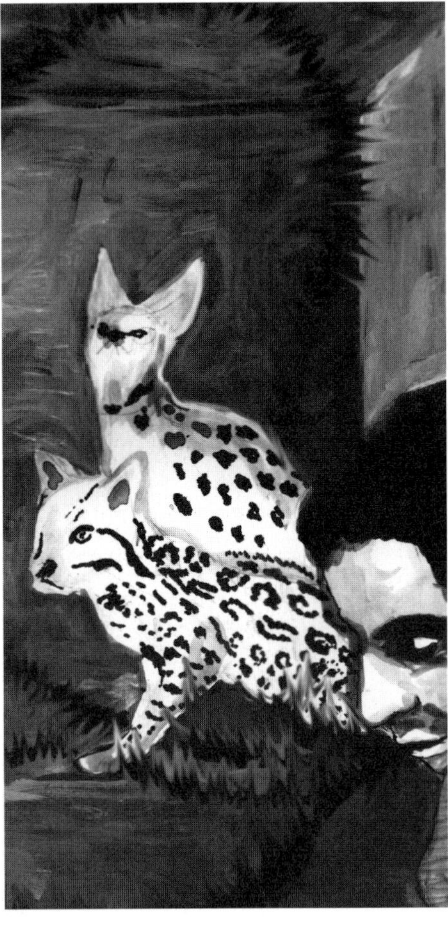

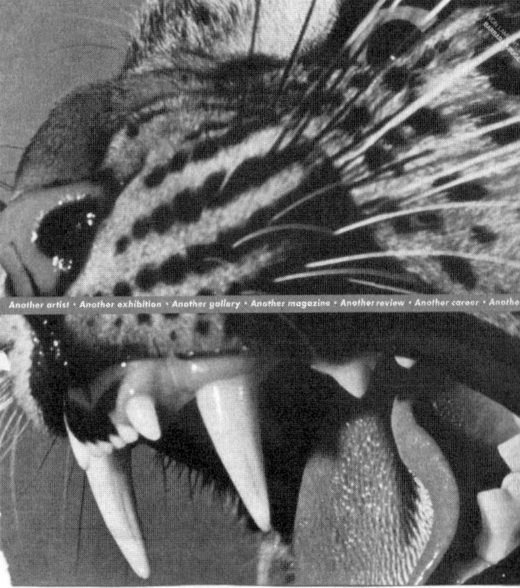
Another artist · Another exhibition · Another gallery · Another magazine · Another review · Another career · Anothe

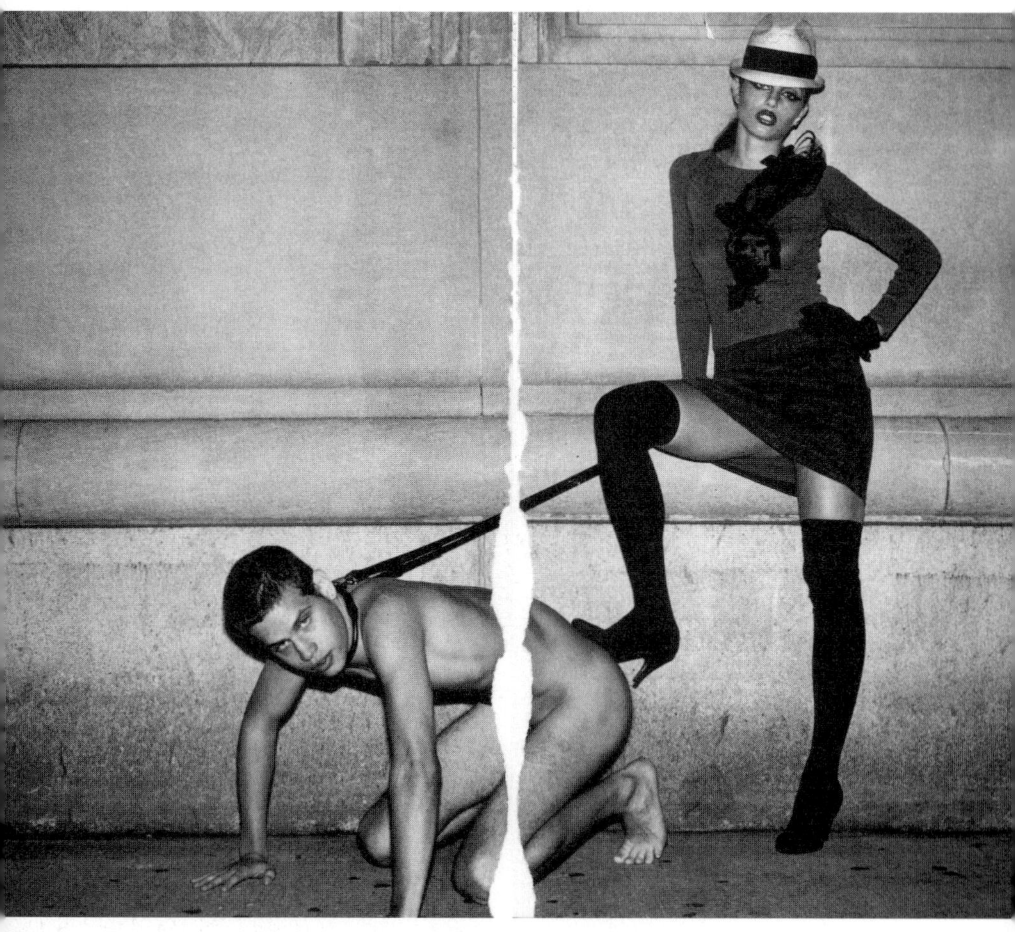

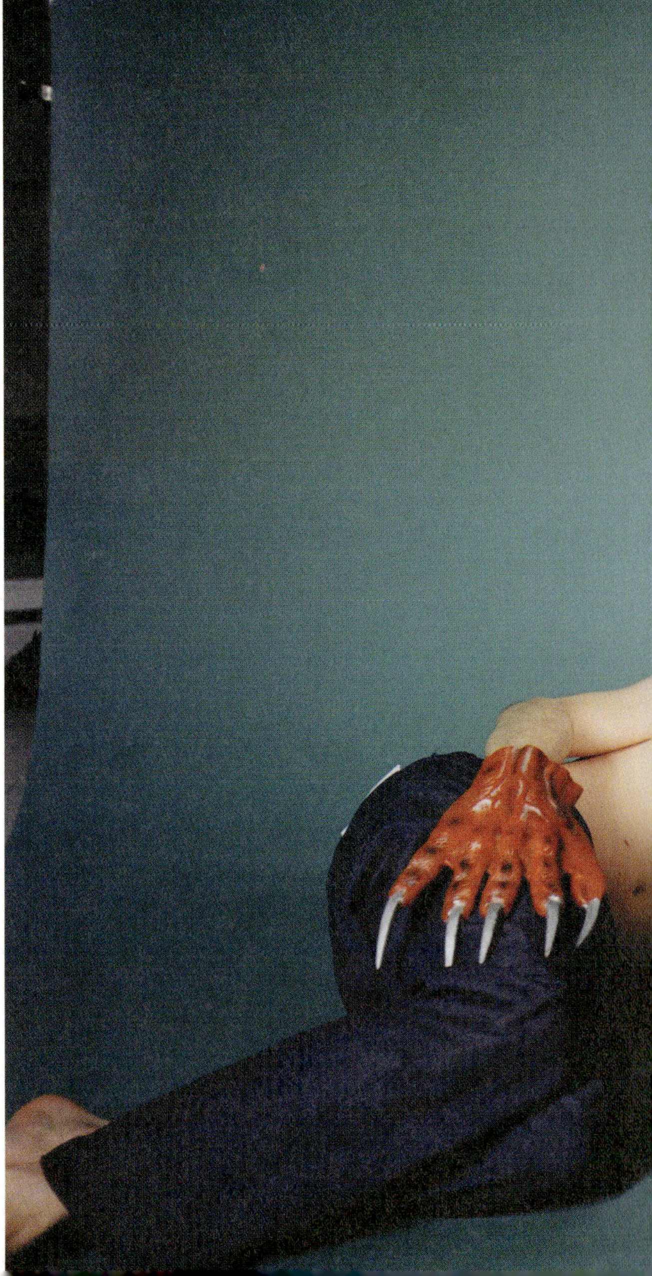

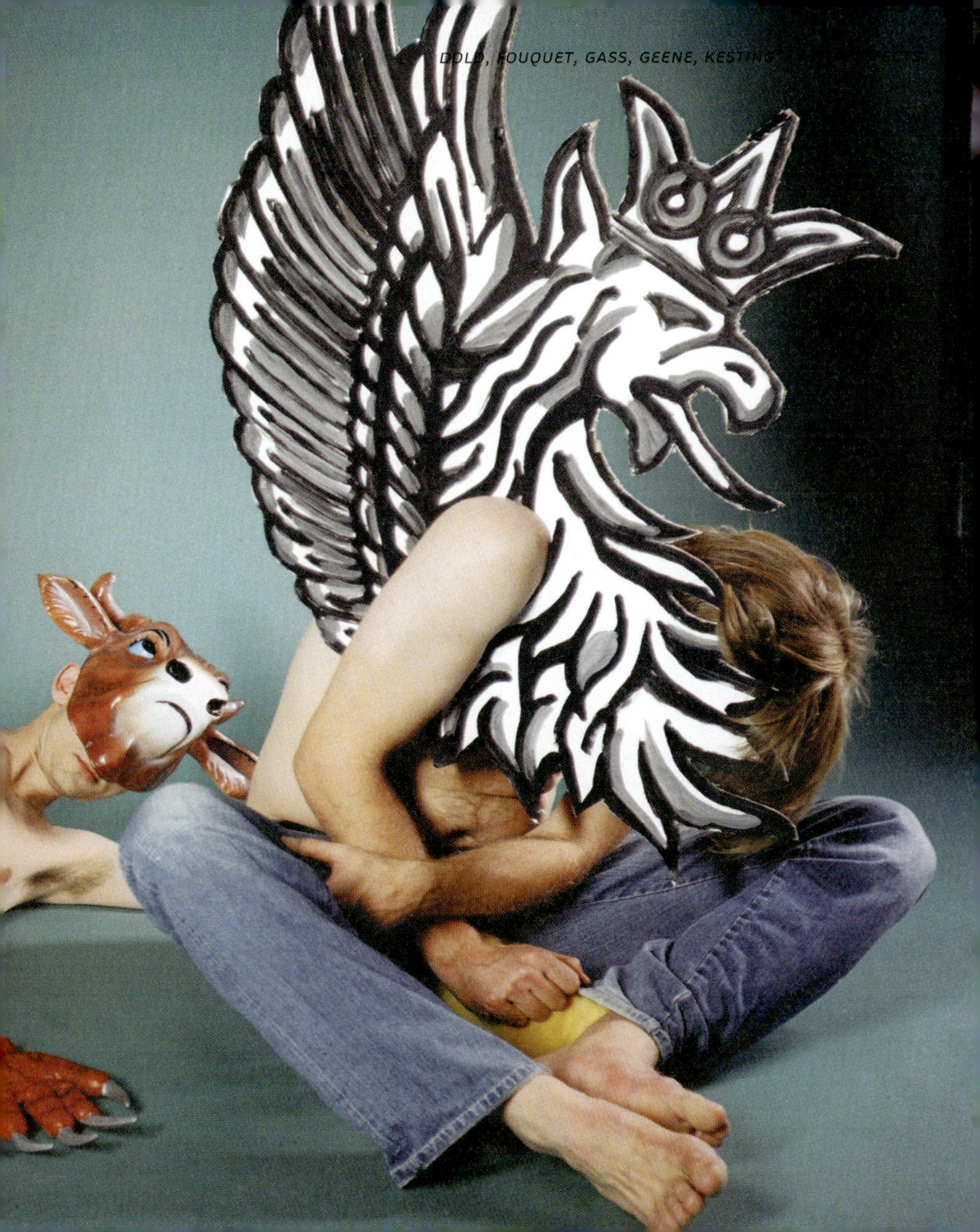
DOLD, FOUQUET, GASS, GEENE, KESTING

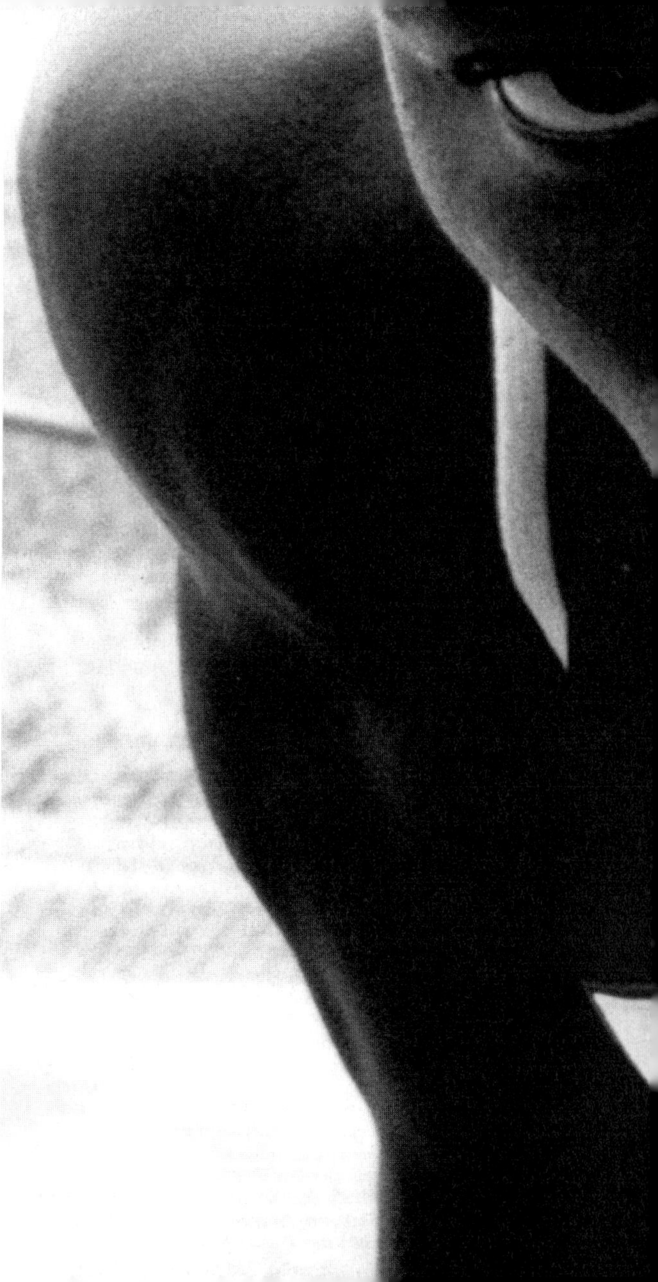

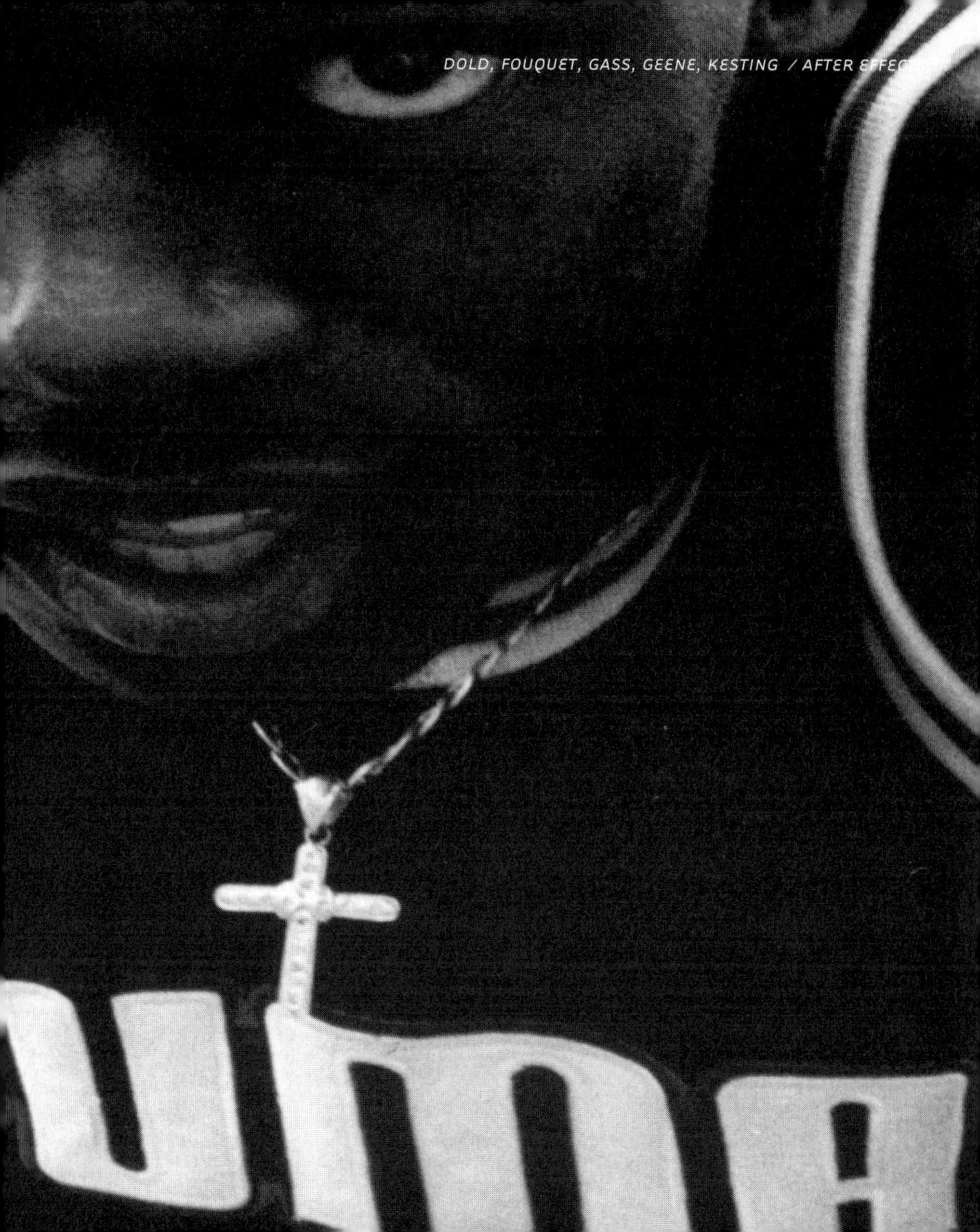

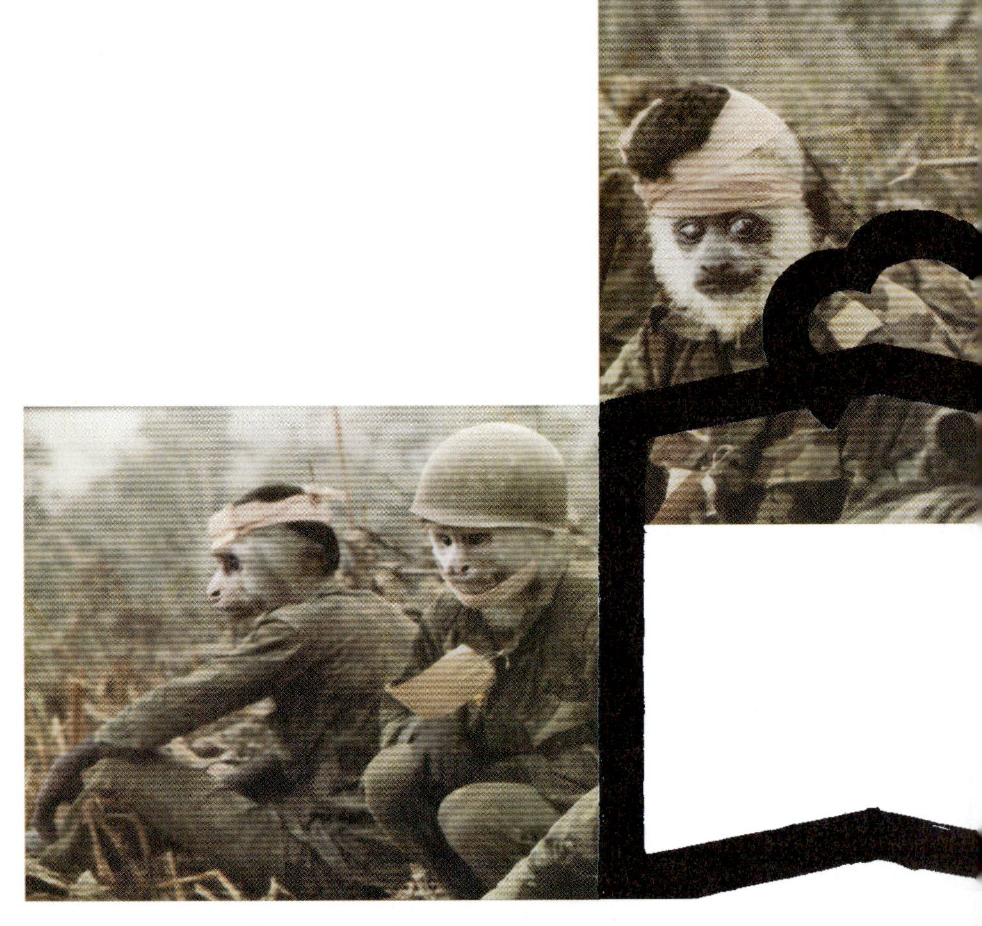

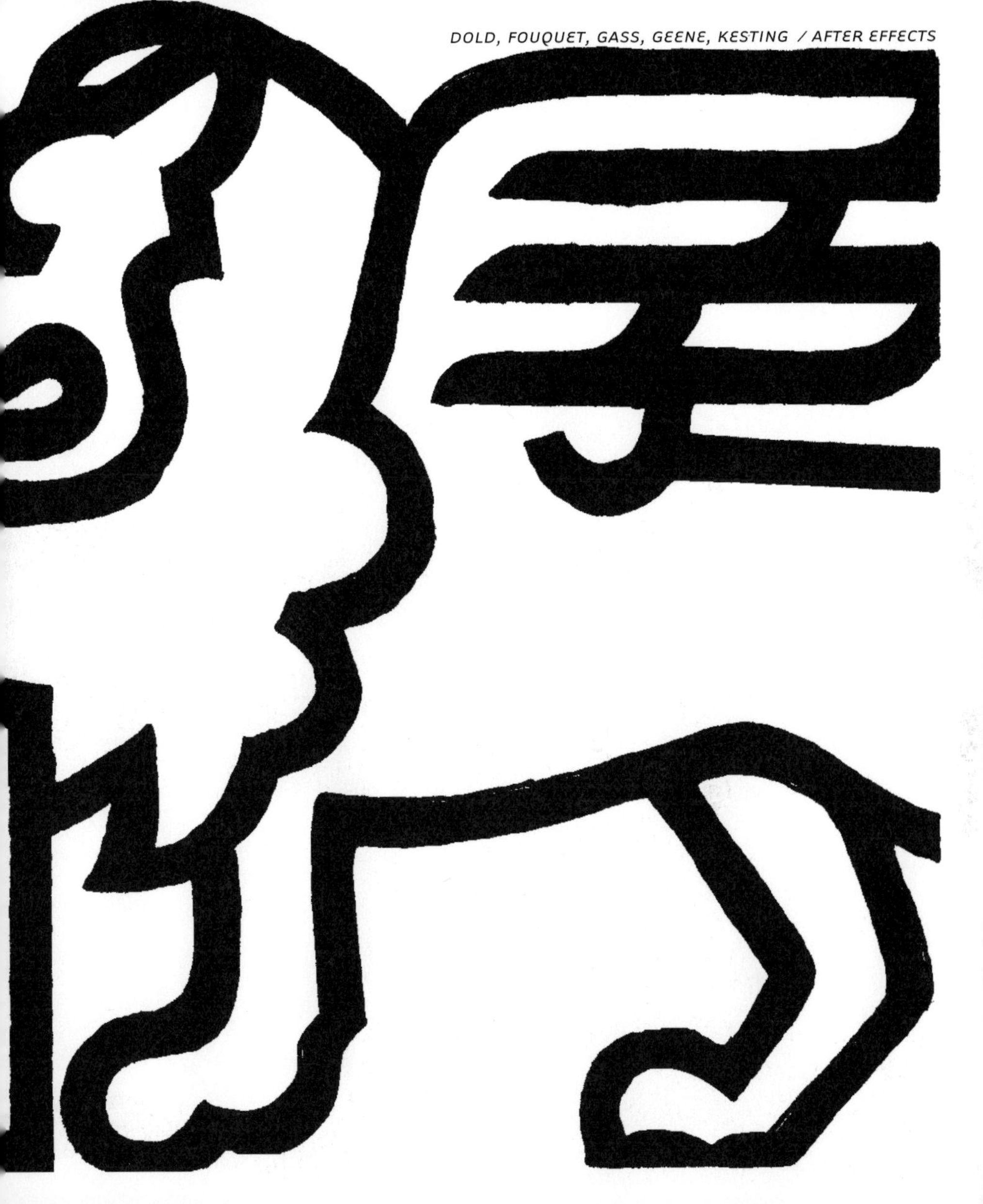

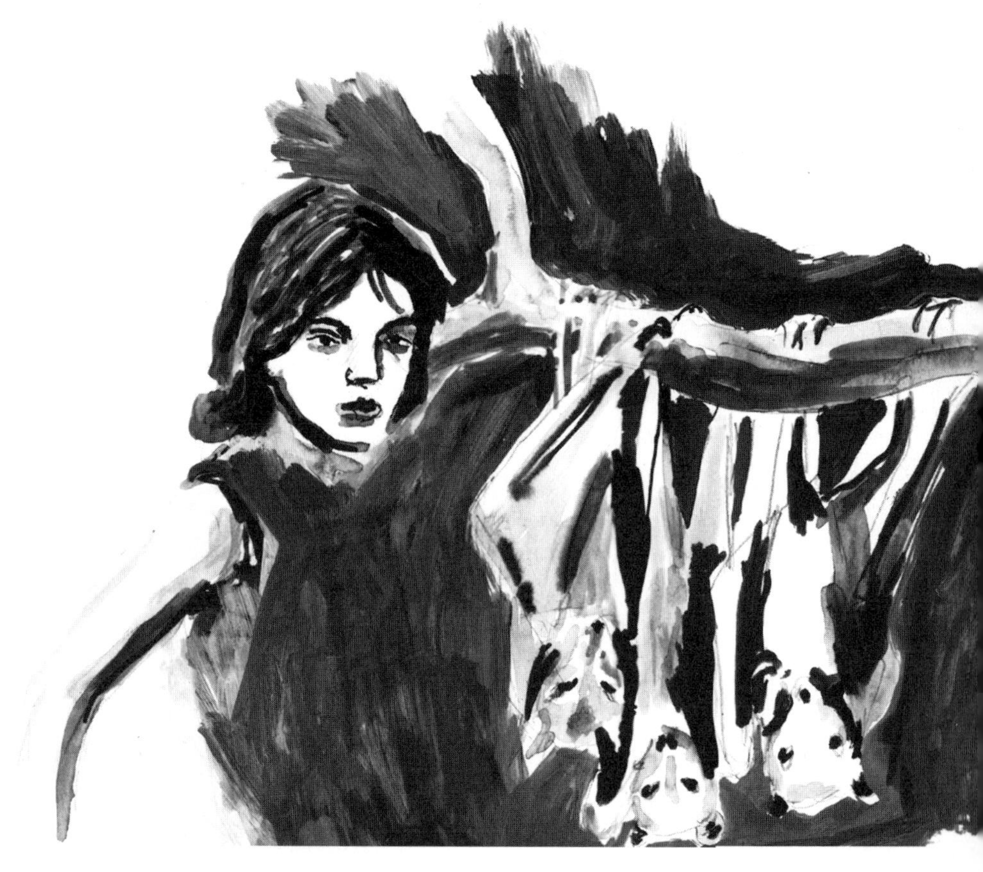

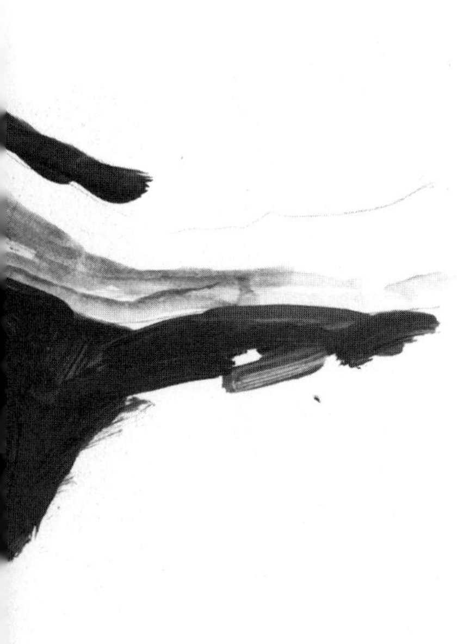

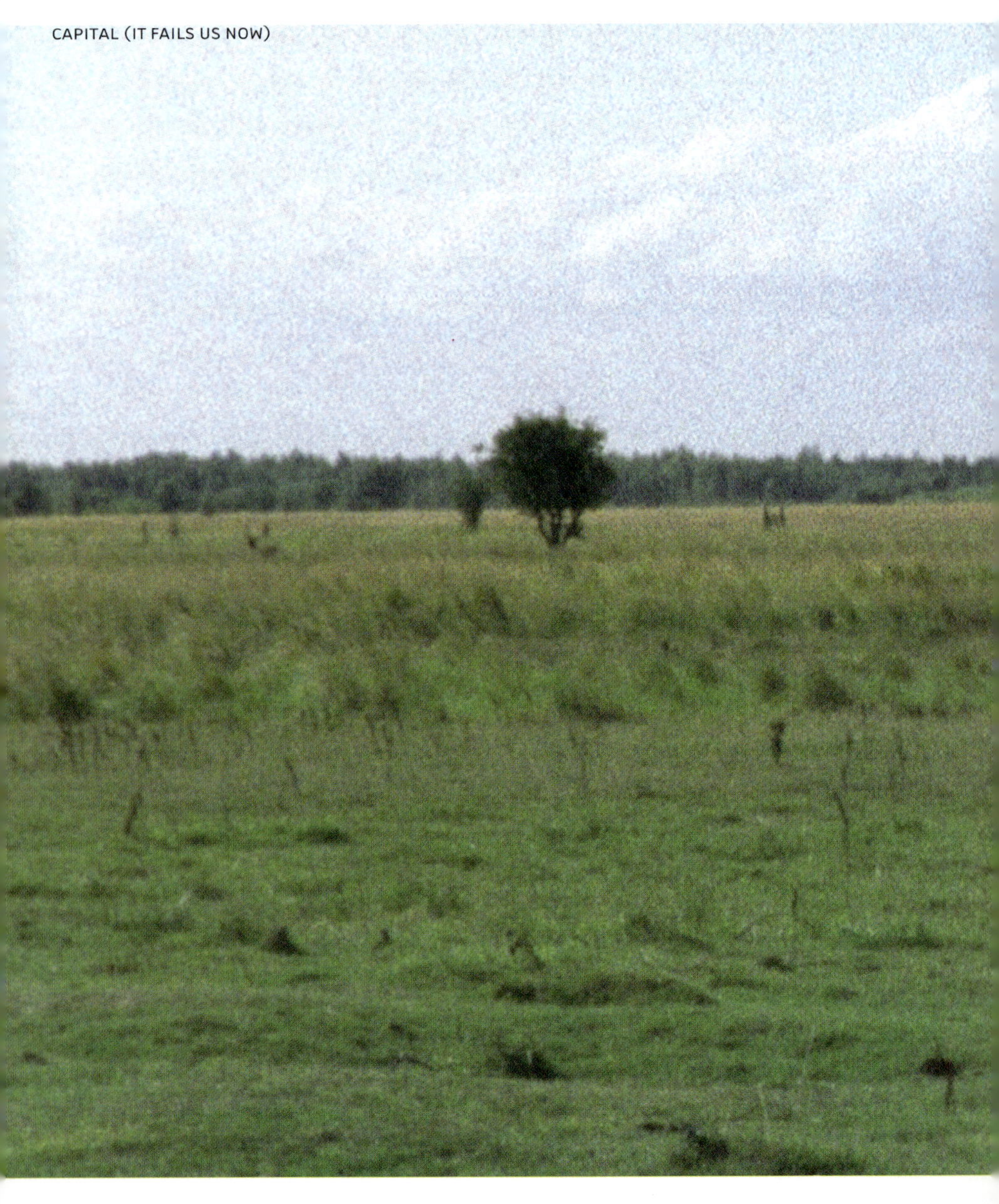

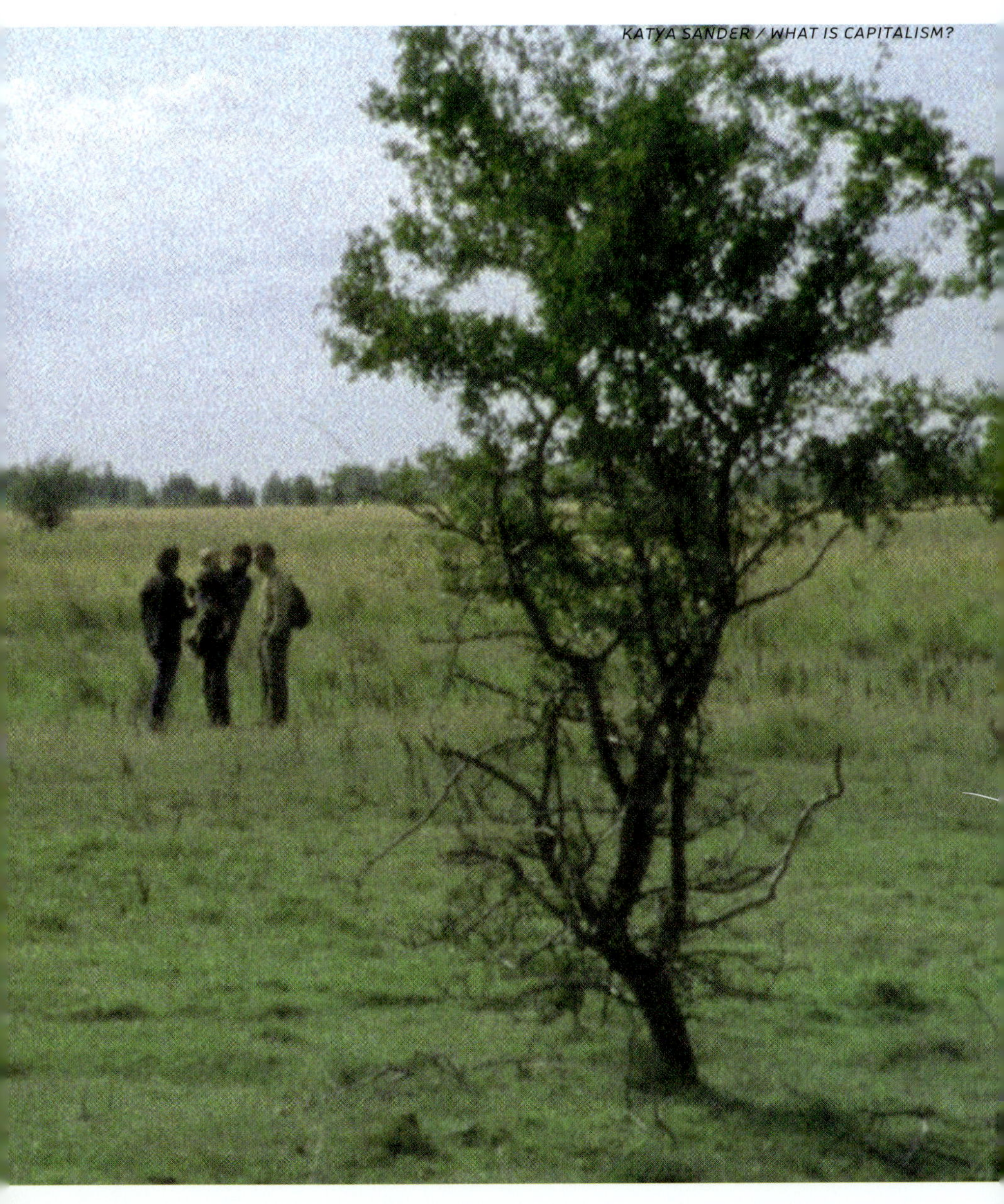

[Darkness. Then lens cover is removed. Close-up of face covers the view.]

Interviewer: Okay, okay... how is the image?

Voice behind camera: Yes, we are rolling.

Interviewer: And sound?

Voice behind camera: Sound is coming through fine, yes.

Interviewer: ...Can you then please give me the mic? Thanks.

[Person 1 enters]

Interviewer: Uh, excuse me... 'scuse me, can I ask you something? Ehm.. What is... I'd like to know what is capitalism?

Person 1: Ha... ehm... it's... well, it's a word, it's a word that we use to describe... ehm, to name a system... a kind of ordering system, which is a social system where... Okay, you know, it's a way to make things equal, to make things equivalent. But it's a social order that then of course is also an economic ordering, because... I don't know. Let's see you have an example, like you have a coat. You have a coat and... I can't remember. Something else... a coat and – shit – a coat and a house. A coat and a house. So you need to figure out how the coat and the house relate to each other in this system, how they are equal, so you need to figure out how many coats for a house... So it's about making things the same...

Interviewer: Okay! Thanks. Thank you!

[Person 1 exits]
[Person 2 enters]

Interviewer: Excuse me, can I ask you a question? What is capitalism?

Person 2: Capitalism? ... That's a good question... well, I suppose some would say it's an ideology, but I... well, if you're asking me, I guess... I guess I'd rather say that it's a sort of a translation... a translation of relations between people... capitalism... well... it's something that has happened, right? It's not something anyone has thought up. I think it has become a translation... of values and desires and... between people.

Interviewer: Okay. Thank you, thank you very much.

Person 2: You're welcome.

[Person 2 exits]
[Person 3 enters]

Interviewer: Excuse me, eh, excuse me, but can I ask you a question? What is... what is capitalism?

Person 3: Capitalism? Umm... I think it is a principle of expansion... that is... in the sense that it can only exist as expansion, as movement. – It needs to expand and expand, constantly needing new markets, new colonies and new factories, new ideas, new labor... kinda like a bubble that keeps getting bigger... capitalism. Hm... it leads... only to itself... and it draws along and displaces its own limits in its movement... like an enormous flow of interest... which can only from time to time implode in on itself,

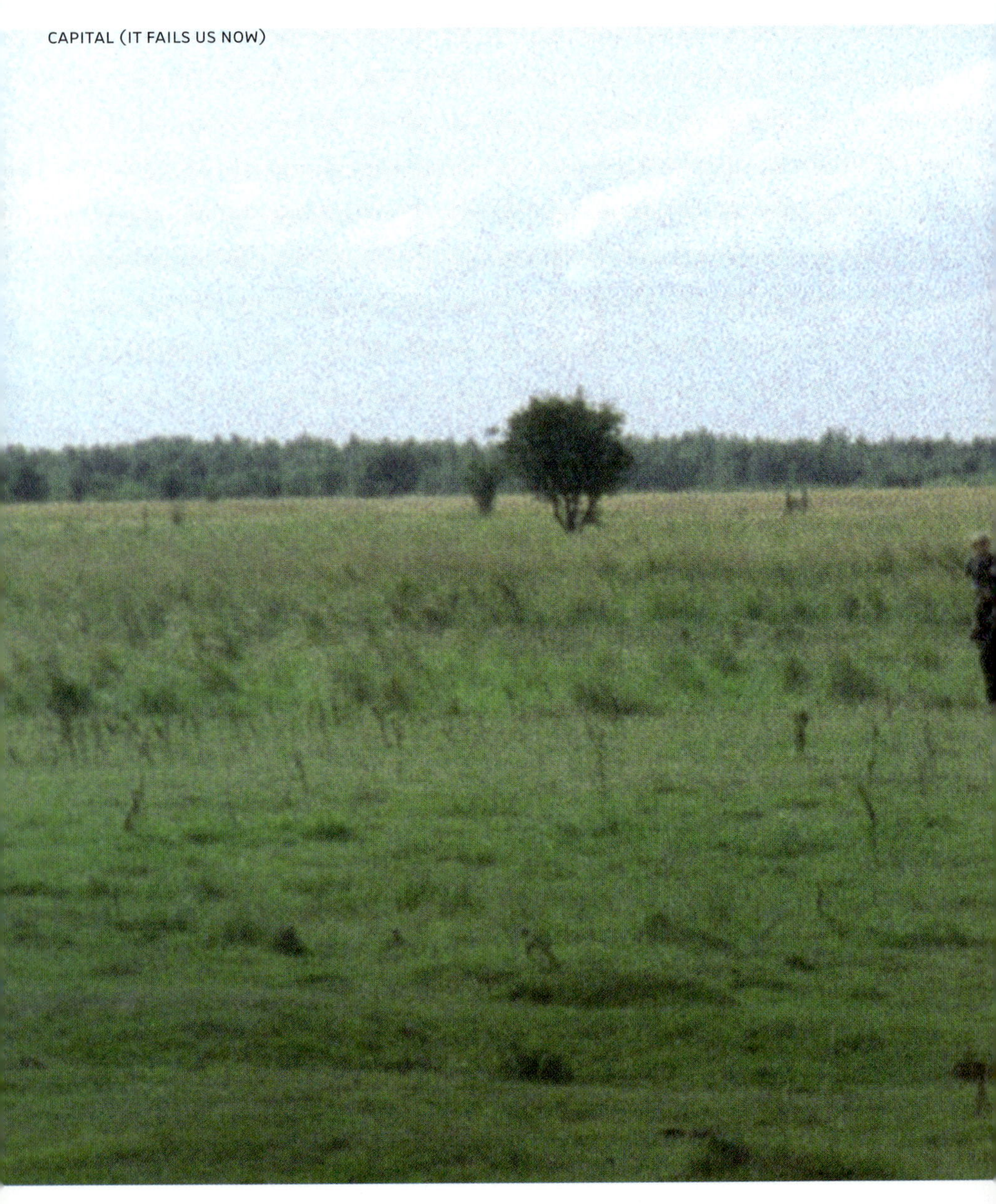

CAPITAL (IT FAILS US NOW)

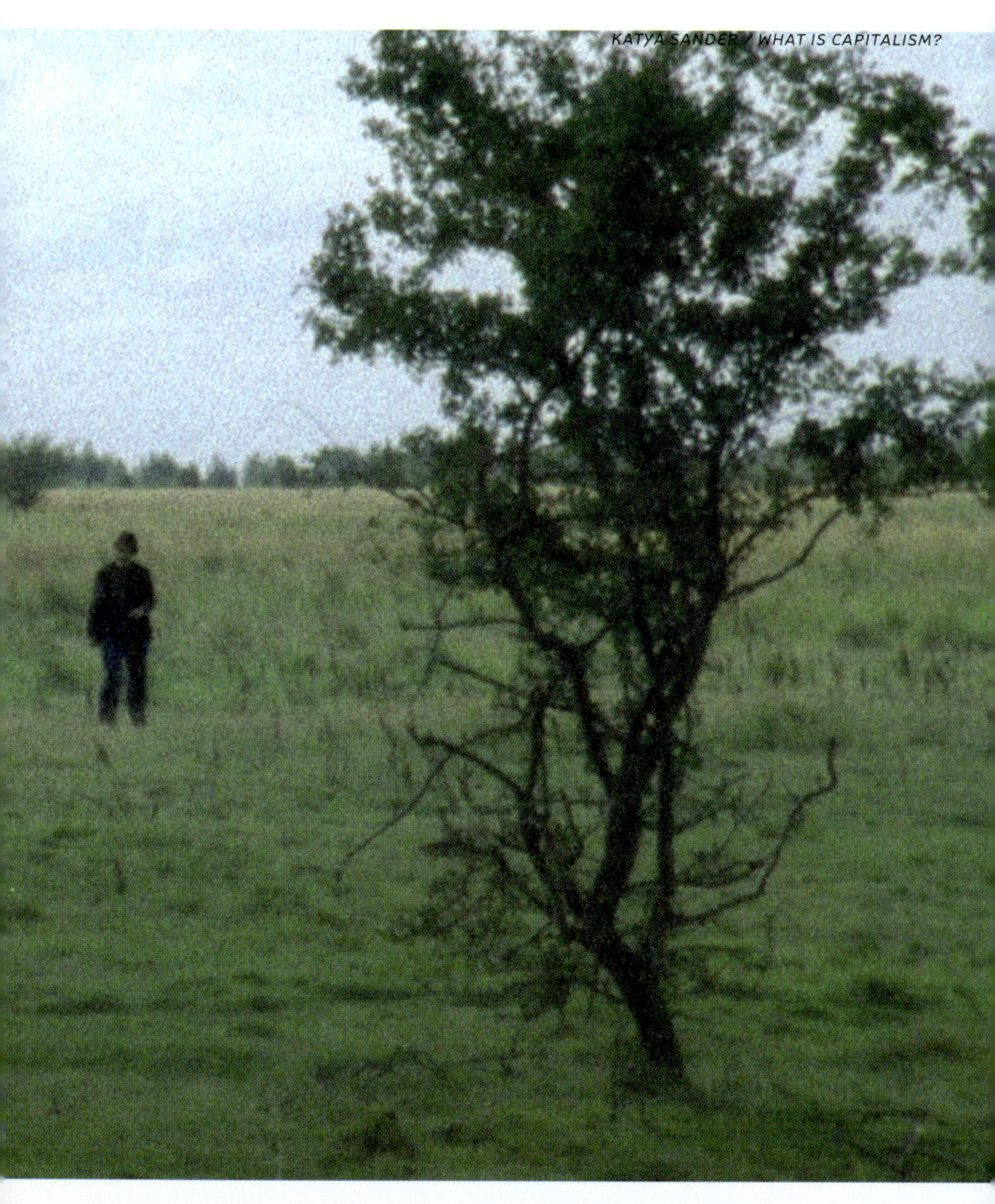
KATYA SANDER / WHAT IS CAPITALISM?

never be stopped by force...

Interviewer: Okay. Thanks.

Person 3: Sure.

[Person 3 exits]
[Person 4 enters]

Interviewer: Excuse me Miss, can I ask you a question? ... Ehm, what what... what is capitalism?

Person 4: Yeah well, I'm not sure, I guess that capitalism... well, it's a system of representation... like money represents value, or a contract represents ownership of land... representation, like images of something... an endless succession of images... or maybe more like an... an accumulation of images. It's when everything becomes the same, when everything becomes an image... like... ehm... image production... producing everything as image...

Interviewer: Thanks.

[Person 4 exits]
[small family enters: Mother, Father, Child]

Interviewer: Sorry, sorry, but can I just ask you a question?

Father: ...Yeah?

Interviewer: Eh, I would like to ask you what capitalism is.

Father: Hmm... capitalism... well... capitalism... I guess it's about value... about accumulation of value... through exchange, of course...

Interviewer: Okay...

Father: Yeah, it's a kind of economy... well, it is a kind of economy... that is also the exchange of labor... images... faces... words... languages... knowledge... power... travel... sex... There is nothing left but a little price tag... the index of changeability... it is nothing, but at the same time it is enormous... it is something else... everything is rational in capitalism, except capital itself.

Child: *Ehhh*.

Mother: *Moooo oooo*... Yeah, that's the cows.

Interviewer: Okay, okay, thanks...

[Child reaches out after microphone]

Interviewer: What? ...Would you also like to say something? Would you also like to say something? Do you know what capitalism is? Do you wanna try and hold it? Try and hold it.

Mother: Try and hold it. Can you say *mooo*? ...What do cows say?

Interviewer: What about you, do you wanna say something? About capitalism? No? Okay, thank you.

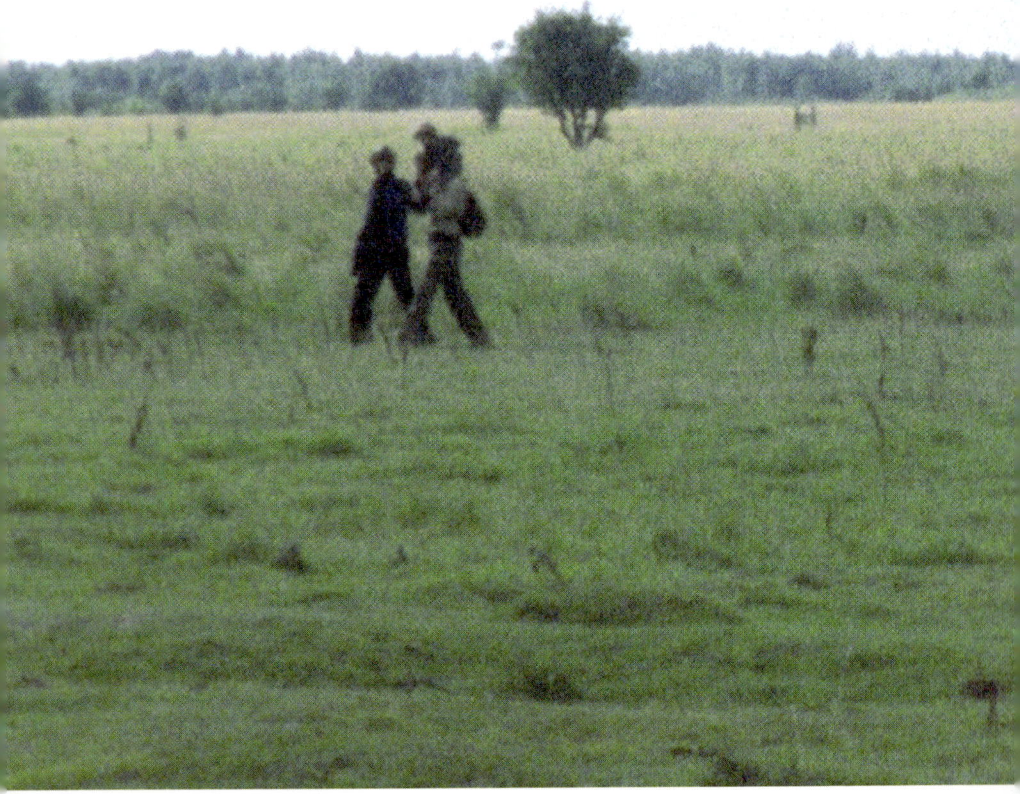

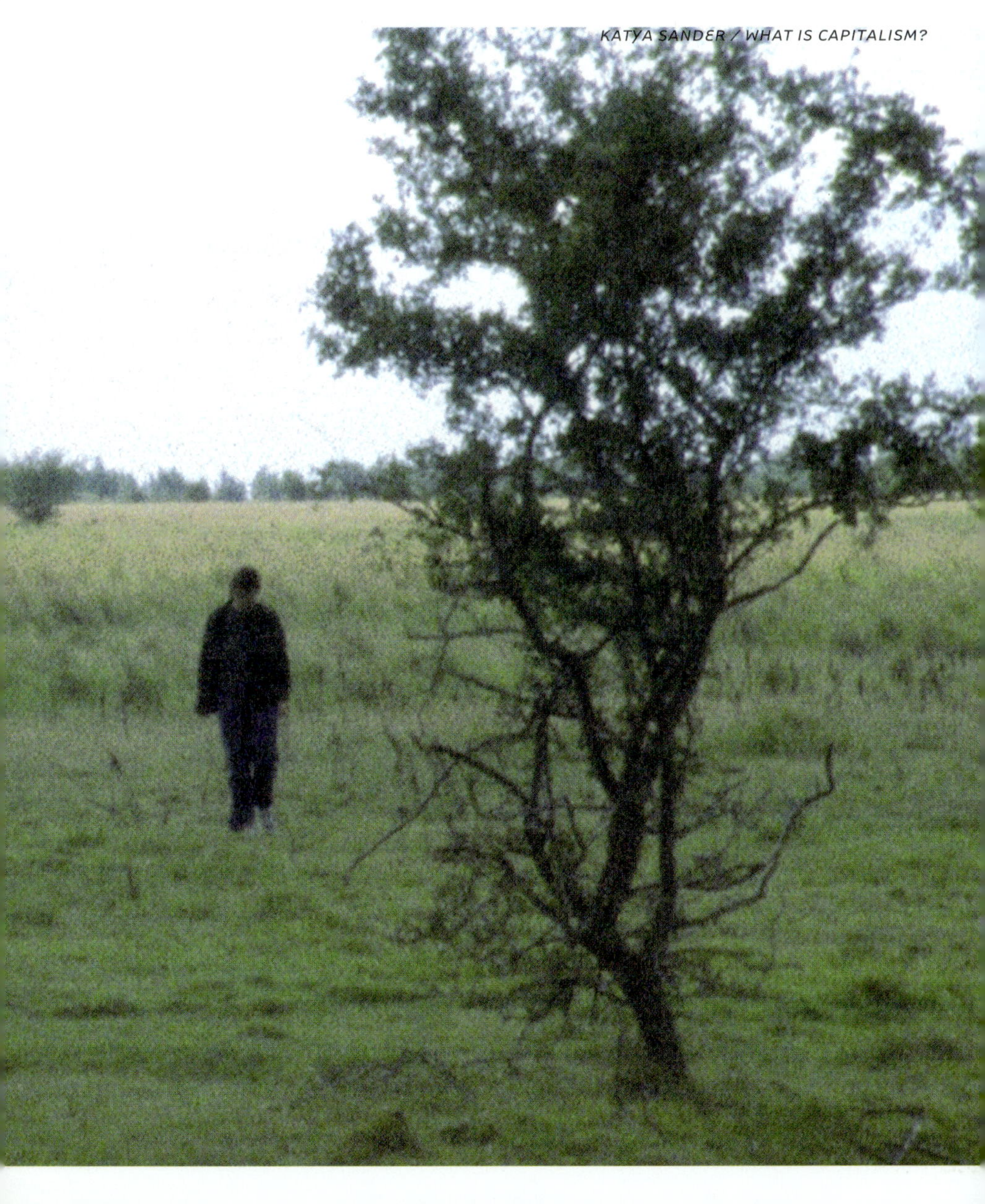

Father: You're welcome.

Child: Bye.

Mother: Bye.

Father: You wanna come to daddy again?

Mother: We should get going, no? Shall we look at the hens again before we go home?

Child: Yeah.

Mother: What does a hen say?

Child: *Eee meee. Cluck-cluck.*

Mother: Yes, that's what a hen says. Do you wanna ride in the car?

Child: *Yeaaah.*

Father: That was strange... that was a strange question.

Mother: Yeah, that was weird...

Child: Ice.

Mother: Do you want an ice cream?

Father: Where are we going?

Mother: I think we are going along this path. It's the only one I can see.

Father: Yeah. Let's go this way. I think I saw a kiosk or a Coke sign over there somewhere...

Child: *Aaeeiiii.*

Mother: Are you sleepy? Shall I find the pacifier?

Child: *Aaaauuuuoooooaaaauuuuoooo!*

Mother: Yeah, that's the microphone.

Child: *Ooooouuuuuuuaaa.*

Mother: Can you sing a little song into the mic?

Child: Yes.

[sound of airplane]

[Interviewer has meanwhile reached the camera again, but without the microphone.]

For video-credits, see page 357.

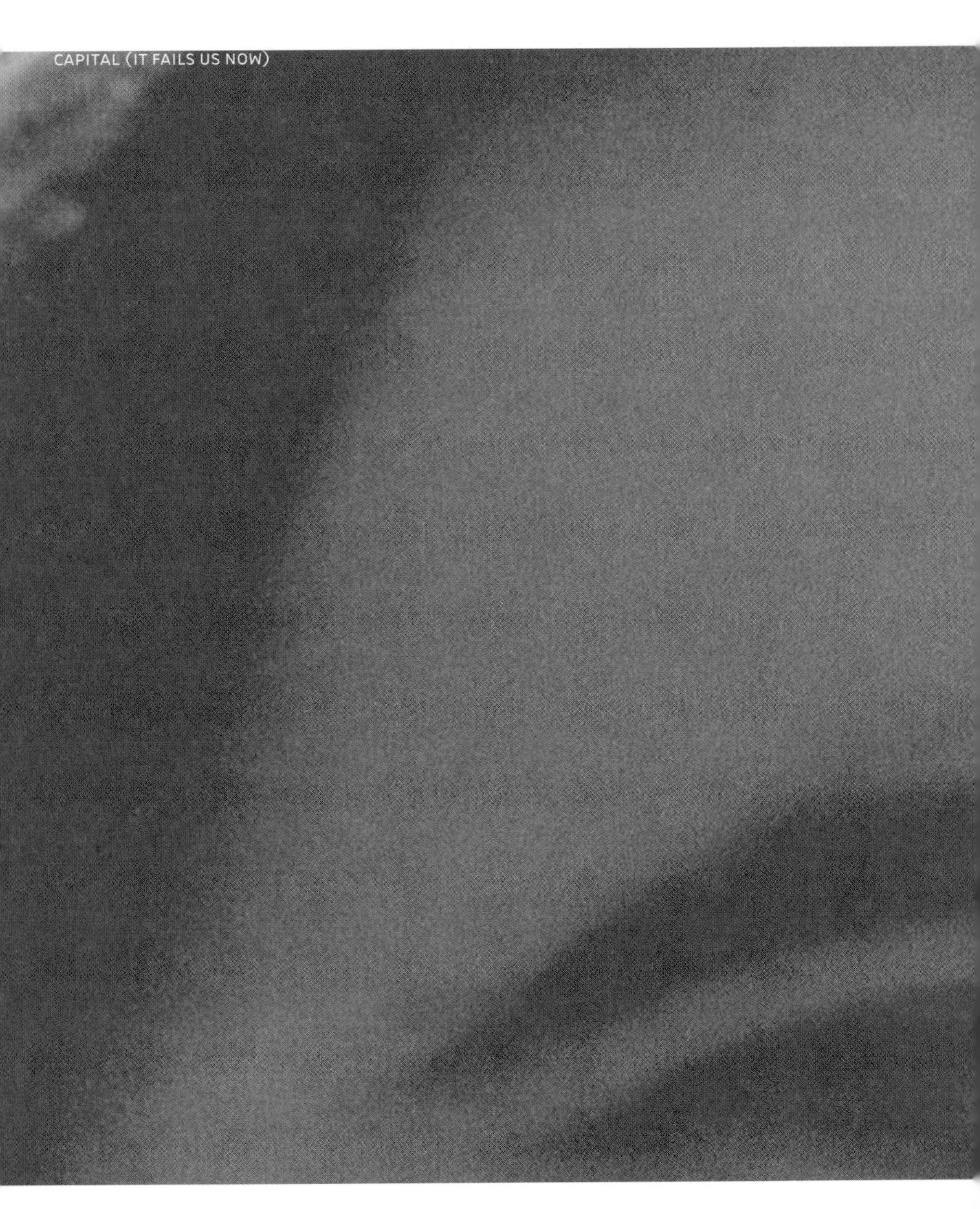

said the interpreter: "You are going to complain? You? And just who are you? ... You have no passport. In any civilized country he who has no passport is nobody. He does not exist for us or for anybody else. We can do whatever we want to. And that is exactly what we're going to do right now. If we want to, we can even hang you or shoot you or kill you like a louse. Just like that; chip, and off you are." He snipped his fingers and rubbed the nails of his thumbs one against the other. "Out with him," he commanded... "We have jails, we have camps for people without papers."

B. Travern, *Death Ship*

Glossary Definition #26: **SLAVERY**

We often define slavery as being just forced, unpaid labor, but perhaps it is much more complex than just that. Historically in slave societies, something else happens before forced labor can take place. This 'something else' is the establishing of a fundamental difference between the dominant group of a society and other individuals or minority groups. While this difference manifests itself in many ways, according to the specific society, it is always with regard to status, based upon perceived differences in levels of 'humanity' – this means that some people are perceived as more human, others as less human, or indeed, non-human altogether. This designation as less or non-human is then the basis for altering the 'other's' status in society, where even though they are located geographically within the society, they are not counted among its citizens, its agents, even its members; they are physically there and alive, but socially they are dead. Indeed, this process is the basis of establishing race, a process of race-making or racialization. Once placed in this outsider status, where society is not 'theirs', then it follows that they are the society's property, its belongings, who live there upon its graces, whose purpose is thus to reciprocate, to help build, serve and maintain that society. As property, they are either owned by the state itself, or they are distributed as private property among the society's official members.

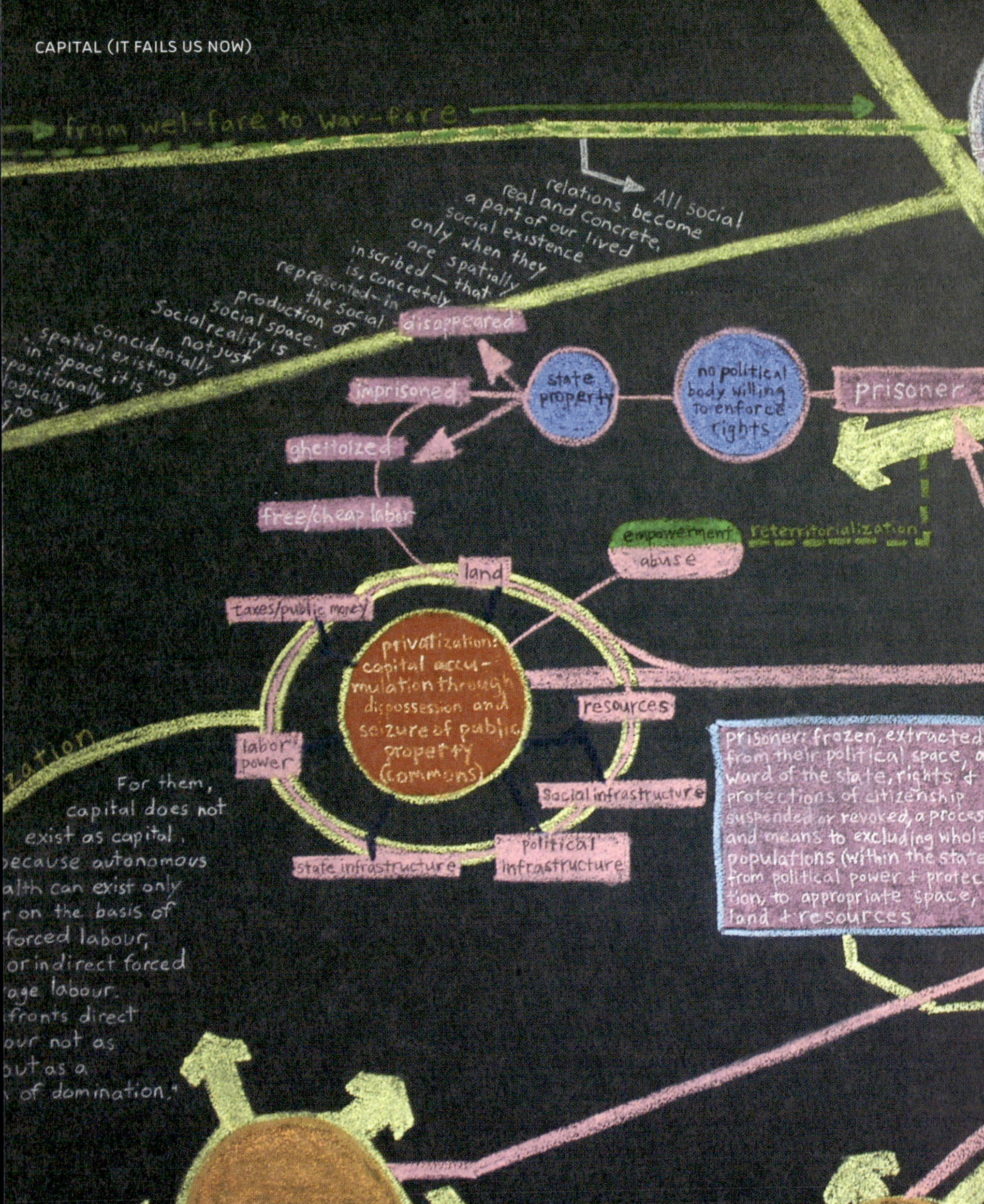

from wel-fare to war-fare
All social relations become real and concrete, a part of our lived social existence only when they are spatially inscribed — that is, concretely represented — in the social production of social space. Social reality is not just coincidentally spatial, existing "in" space, it is presuppositionally and ontologically spatial. There is no...
disappeared
imprisoned
ghettoized
free/cheap labor
state property
no political body willing to enforce rights
prisoner
empowerment
abuse
reterritorialization
land
taxes/public money
privatization: capital accumulation through dispossession and seizure of public property (commons)
resources
labor power
social infrastructure
state infrastructure
political infrastructure
prisoner: frozen, extracted from their political space, a ward of the state, rights & protections of citizenship suspended or revoked, a process and means to excluding whole populations (within the state) from political power + protection, to appropriate space, land + resources
...zation
For them, capital does not exist as capital because autonomous wealth can exist only on the basis of forced labour, or indirect forced wage labour. It confronts direct labour not as capital, but as a relation of domination."

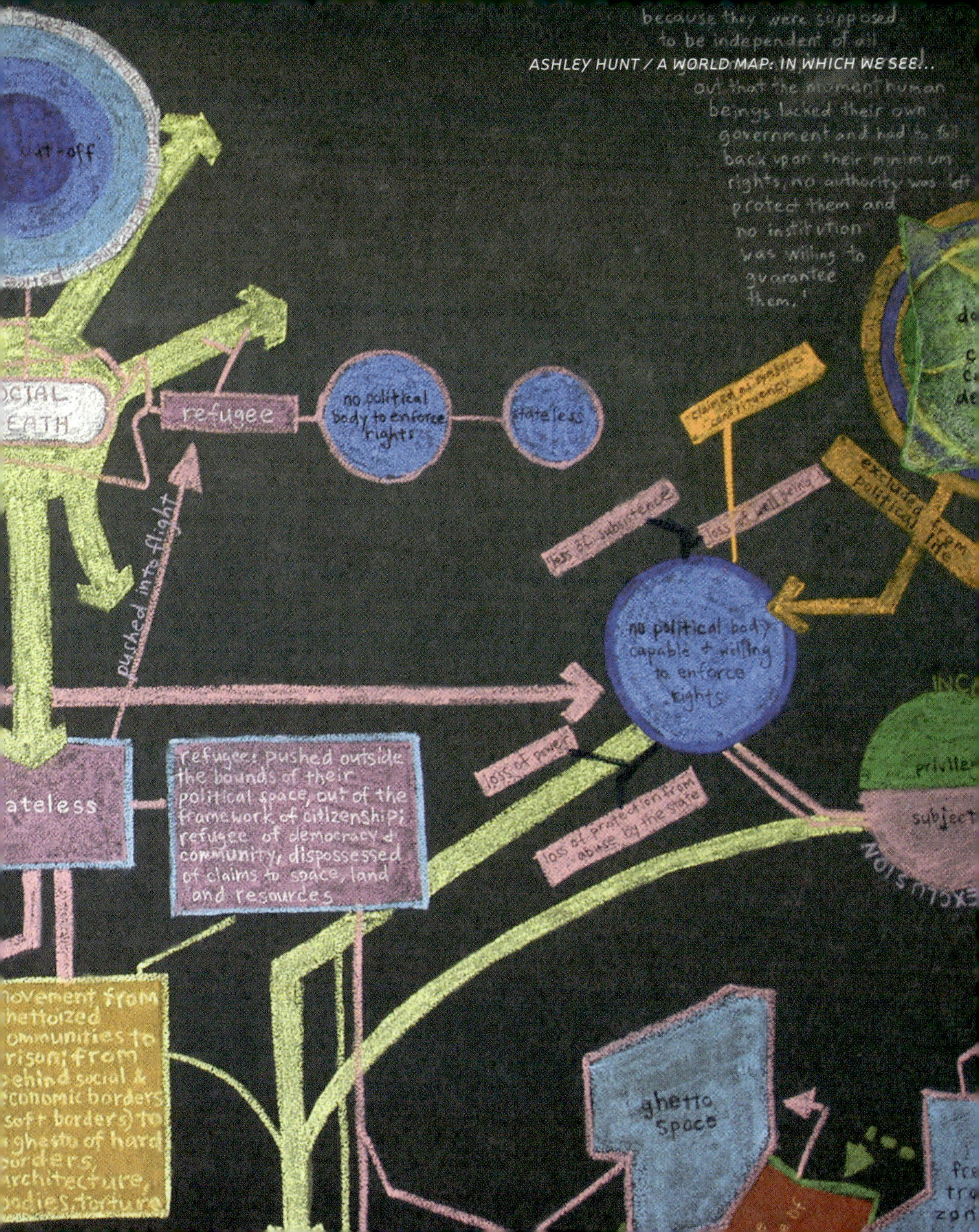
because they were supposed
to be independent of oil
ASHLEY HUNT / A WORLD MAP: IN WHICH WE SEE!..
out that the moment human
beings lacked their own
government and had to fall
back upon their minimum
rights, no authority was left
protect them and
no institution
was willing to
guarantee
them."
cut-off
SOCIAL
DEATH
refugee
no political
body to enforce
rights
stateless
claimed as symbolic
constituency
loss of subsistence
loss of well-being
excluded from
political life
pushed into flight
no political body
capable + willing
to enforce
rights
stateless
refugee: pushed outside
the bounds of their
political space, out of the
framework of citizenship:
refugee of democracy +
community, dispossessed
of claims to space, land
and resources
loss of power
loss of protection from
abuse by the state
INCA
privile
subject
EXCLUSION
movement from
ghettoized
communities to
prison; from
behind social &
economic borders
(soft borders) to
ghetto of hard
borders,
architecture,
bodies, torture,
ghetto
space
fr
tr
zo

A flight of the state (nation); flight of that form for the organization of people, territory, resources, the consolidation of economy and power, a political space founded upon some originary violence, instrument for dominance, yet not altogether so simple.

Thrust into crisis by larger forms emerging above it and below it (or through it?) and by the struggle between bodies within it (corporate bodies, human bodies) it takes flight: leaving so many bodies behind, forcing others into flight of their own.

Emptying itself of its historical content, it nonetheless fortifies its appearance so as to remain recognizable, respected, feared (real), barricading the imaginary borders that delimit it – those lines drawn between points where warring factions had finally come to rest.

The flux of bodies throughout it, across it; passing in and out without regard for these lines drawn in the sand (for who can afford to regard them?) except that they might be caught there, interned, 're-patriated', or killed. (Perhaps that is what makes a state 'real'?)

corporate state:
a political geography
absent of civil
structure, void of
individual rights and
popular citizenship,
constituency for
governance are
corporations, where
freedom is defined by
unregulated
accumulation,
without regard to
rights or health of
individual citizens

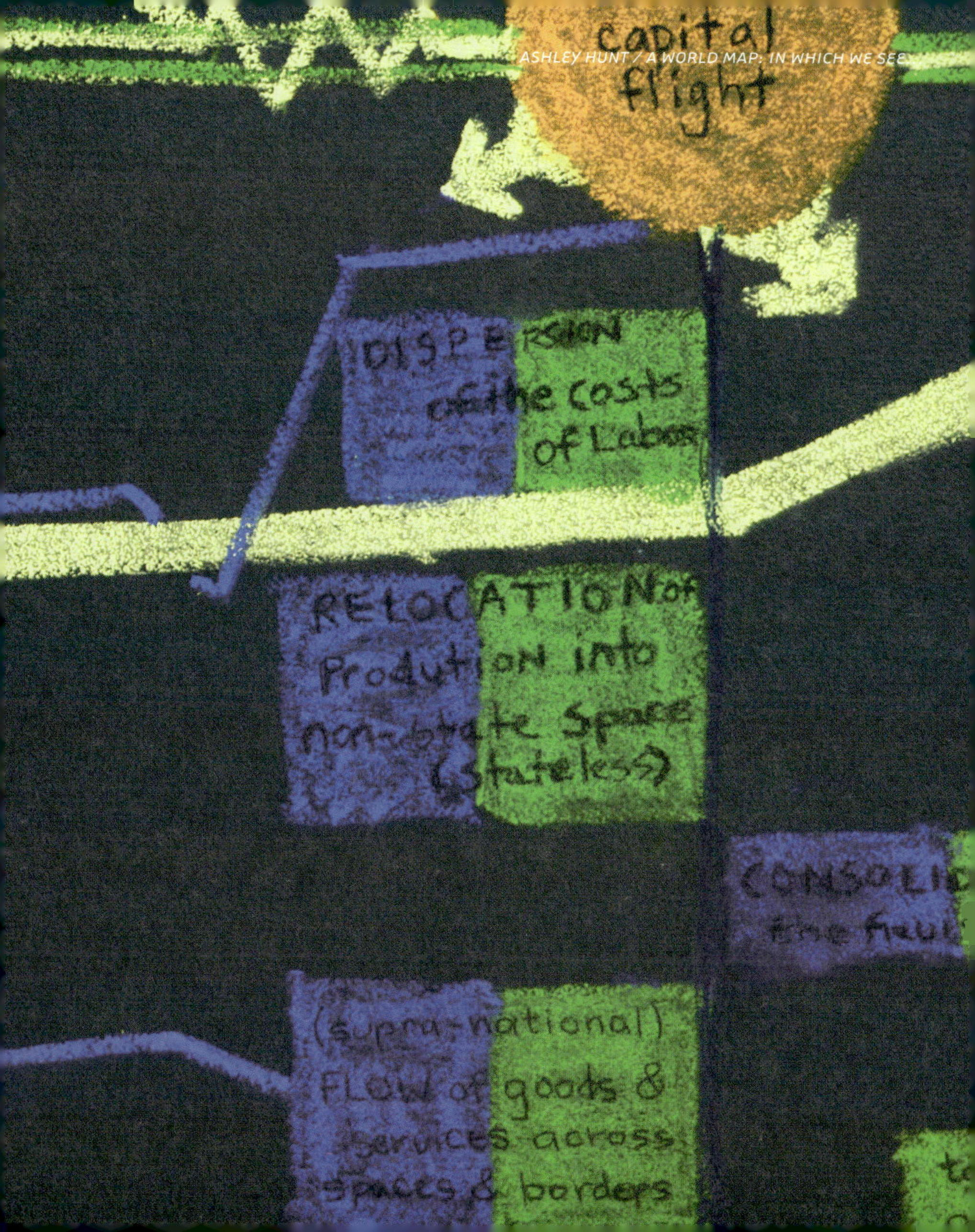

capital
flight

DISPERSION
of the costs
of Labor

RELOCATION of
Production into
non-state space
(stateless)

CONSOLID
the flow

(supra-national)
FLOW of goods &
services across
spaces & borders

Everywhere people forge spaces unknown to the state, which the state has yet to codify, yet to map, yet to police, so the state packs its borders and interior with an excess of violence.

Some states (any state), predicated on a logic of expansion (accumulation), cannot stop or slow for fear of collapse. Expanding into themselves and outward over others, their flight is motorized by an asymmetrical power, a technology which washes over lines not their own – borders, barricades, people and resources.

To bodies not flung into flight nor folded into armies for expansion (they too think the state to be an extension of themselves) such borders and the spaces imagined between them must become mythic: concretized, eternal, continuous, contours of an ideal; absent of myth, an identity fades quickly and subjects become wobbly and unstable – light as a feather; swept up by flows or fixed in place by frictions, people grasping for power grab furiously for something fundamental, immoveable to stop their sliding: ('a People'-ness), -isms to cling to, to claim (national, patriot, race, sex, moral, fundamental); a

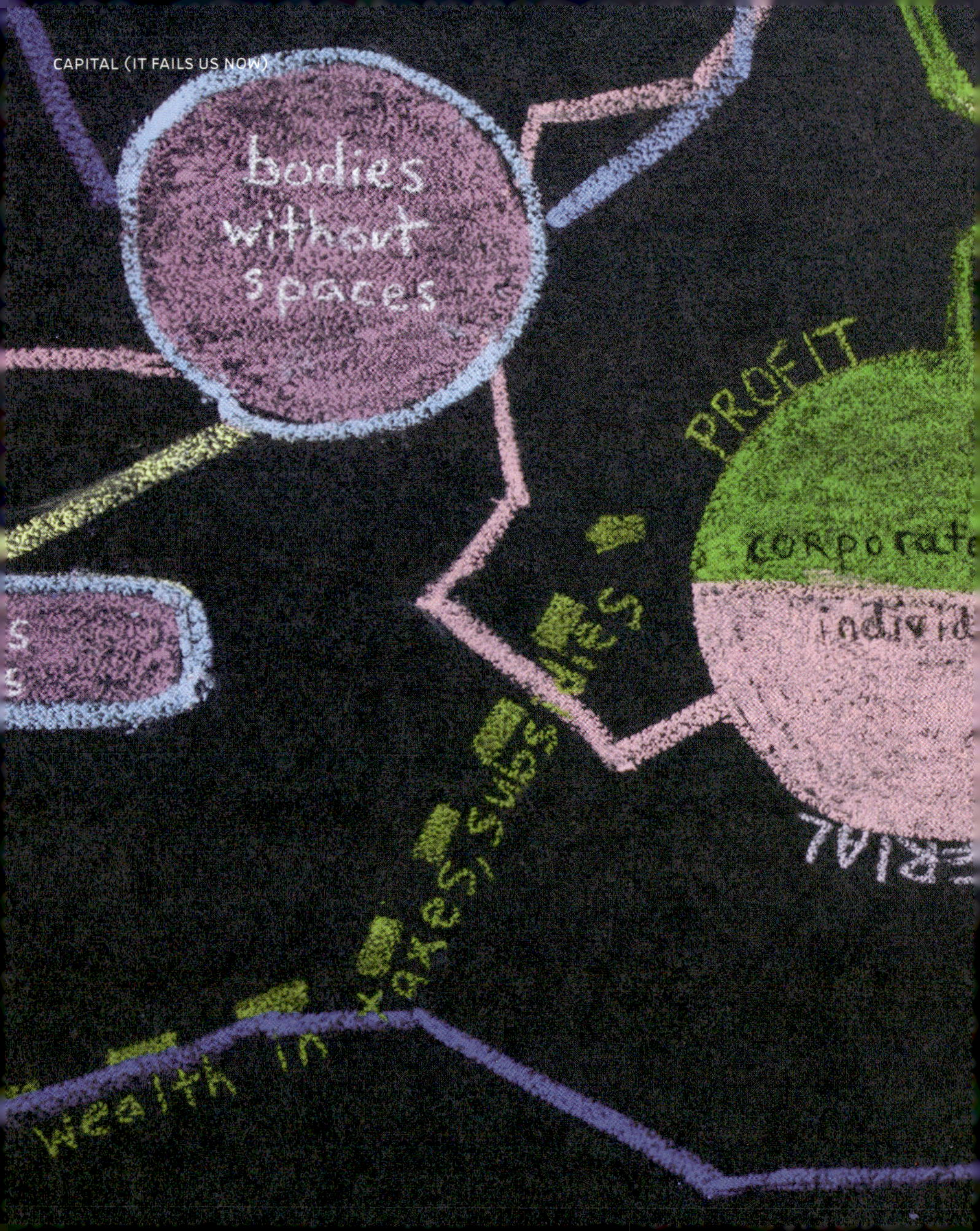

bodies
without
spaces

PROFIT

corporate

individ

wealth in taxes subs

S
S

...le to appropriate, to again be
under his sway all those things
that are kept at a distance by
difference, and find in
them what might be
called his abode. 8

dies

SOCIAL
DEATH

position to claim in distinction to others, to persecute from behind, to compose oneself within. A container of discontent and hope alike, nation mobilized as violence, segregations, war, elections.

Installation shots from Capital (It Fails Us Now), Kunstihoone, Tallinn and UKS, Oslo. A World Map: On Which We See... by Ashley Hunt. Photos: Ashley Hunt, Katya Sander and Halvar Haugerud.

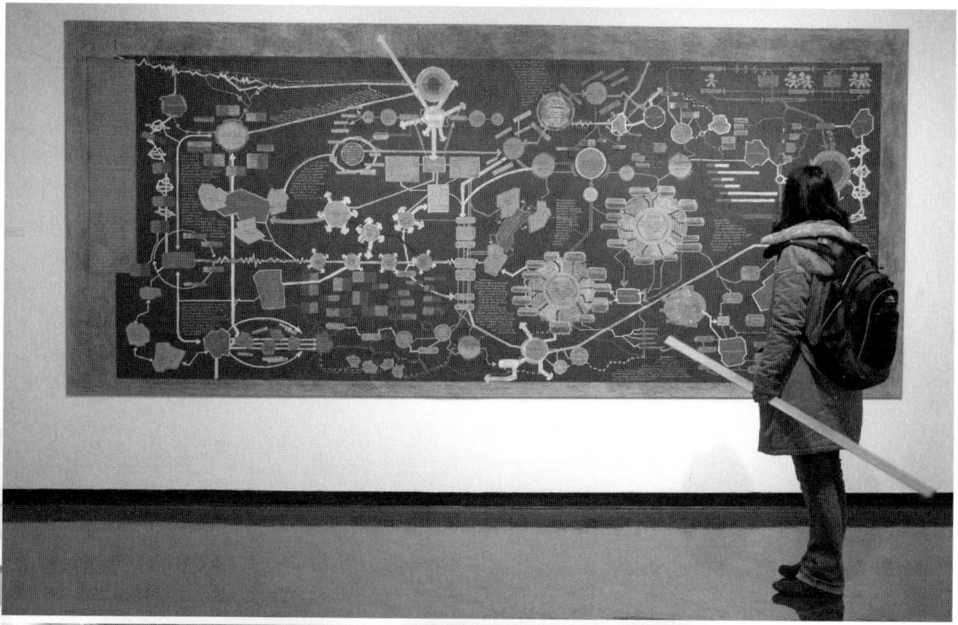

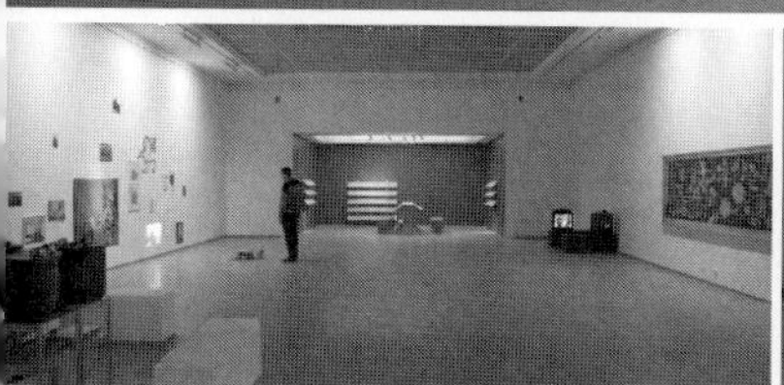

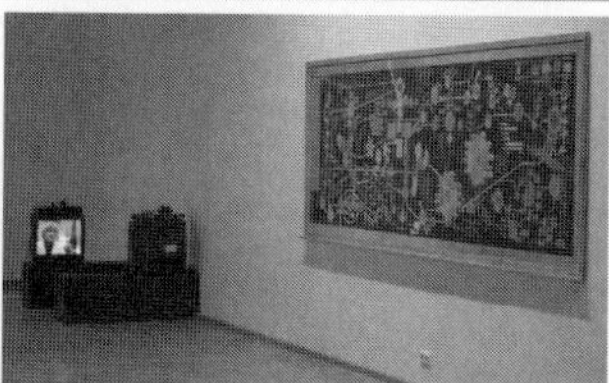

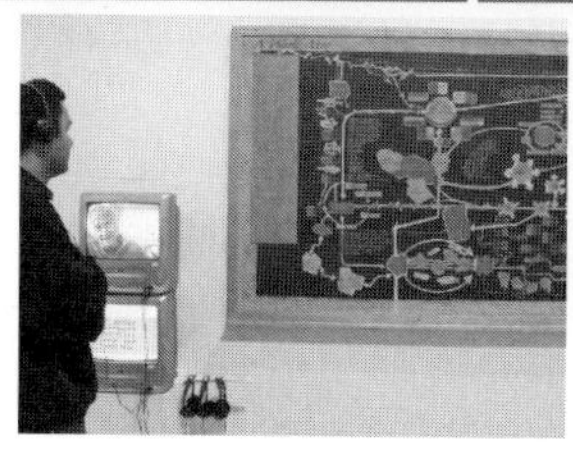

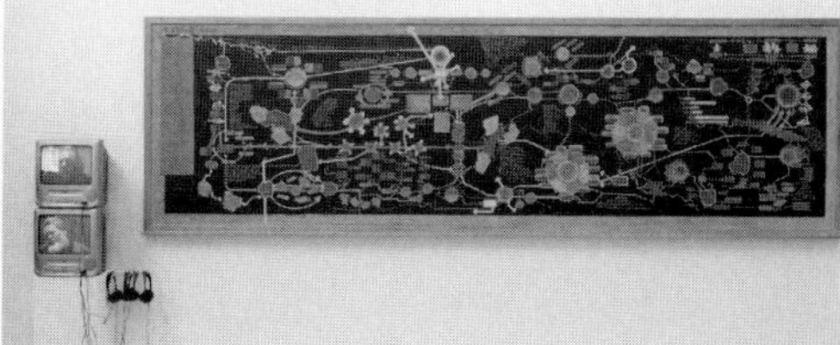

Free Cooperation, with Christoph Spehr, 32 min., 2003

There are three aspects that have to be taken into account if you want to build a free cooperation. The first is that all rules in this cooperation can be questioned by everybody... The second... is that people can question and change these rules by using this primary material force of refusing to cooperate... And the third aspect... is that the price of not cooperating should be similar for all participants in this cooperation.

Inclusive Democracy, with Takis Fotopoulos, 37 min., 2003

The overall aim of the inclusive democracy project is to create a society in which people determine themselves, in which, in other words, the 'demos', as it was the classical concept for the people, has overall control over the political sphere, the economic sphere and, the social sphere in general.

Workers' Self-Management in Yugoslavia, with Todor Kuljic, 23 min., 2003

But compared with the present state of Yugoslavia, for example, where a wild type of capitalism reigns, it was a relatively well-functioning democracy. The working class and the poor people had a type of sovereign right, which they do not have today. One cannot reject Yugoslavian self-management as a whole as totalitarianism.

Installation shots from Capital (It Fails Us Now), Kunstihoone, Tallinn.
Alternative Economics, Alternative Societies by Oliver Ressler.

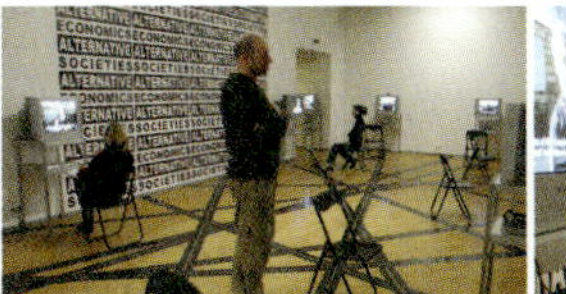
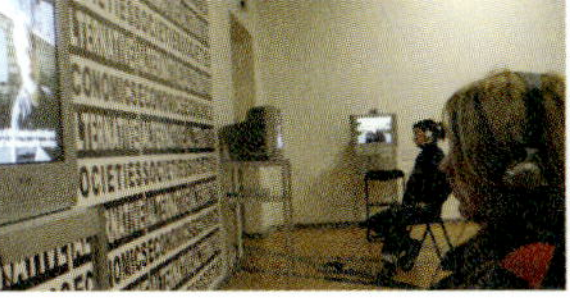
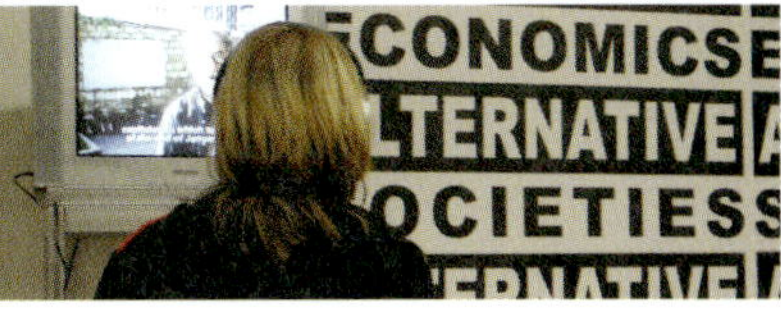

the revolutionary movement which was
very important since the first international

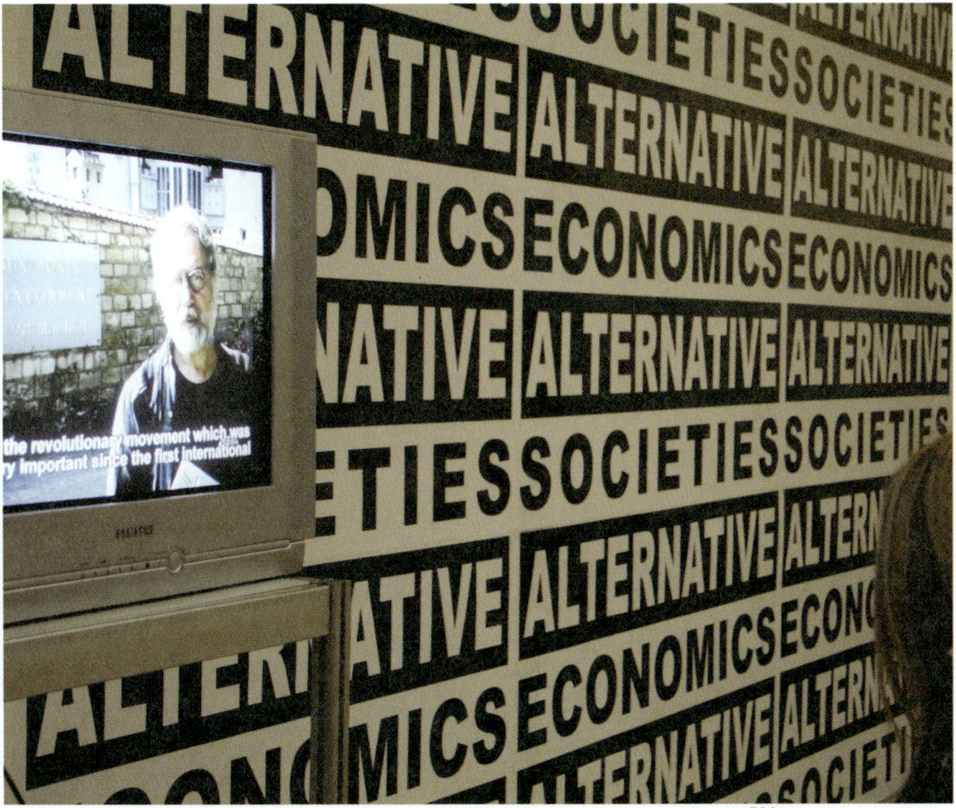

Caring Labor, with Nancy Folbre, 20 min., 2003

Caring Labor… whether we are coming from a corporate capitalist point of view or from a socialist point of view, we have to recognize that there is this kind of labor that is different than other kinds, that is not as reducible to the logic of exchange or to the logic of central planning or bureaucratic administration.

Participatory Economics, with Michael Albert, 37 min., 2003

The values of participatory economics are equity, solidarity, diversity and self-management. Equity refers to how much we get from our work. And the norm is that we should be remunerated for effort and sacrifice, not for property or power.

Workers' Collectives during the Spanish Revolution, with Salomé Moltó, 22 min., 2004

No one was forced to join the collectives but everyone was eager to do so because it signified a higher income, your needs were covered and apart from that, if a system of that kind is afoot it is not a small percentage of the population which supports it but 99 percent of the nation.

bolo'bolo, with p.m., in collaboration with Lia, 22 min., 2004

It would probably take longer to explain that the communism that I am talking about is not the one that I saw. It is easier to simply say I am for bolo'bolo, and then everyone starts to think of the things all over again, to re-think them.

Installation shots from Alternative Economics, Alternative Societies by Oliver Ressler.

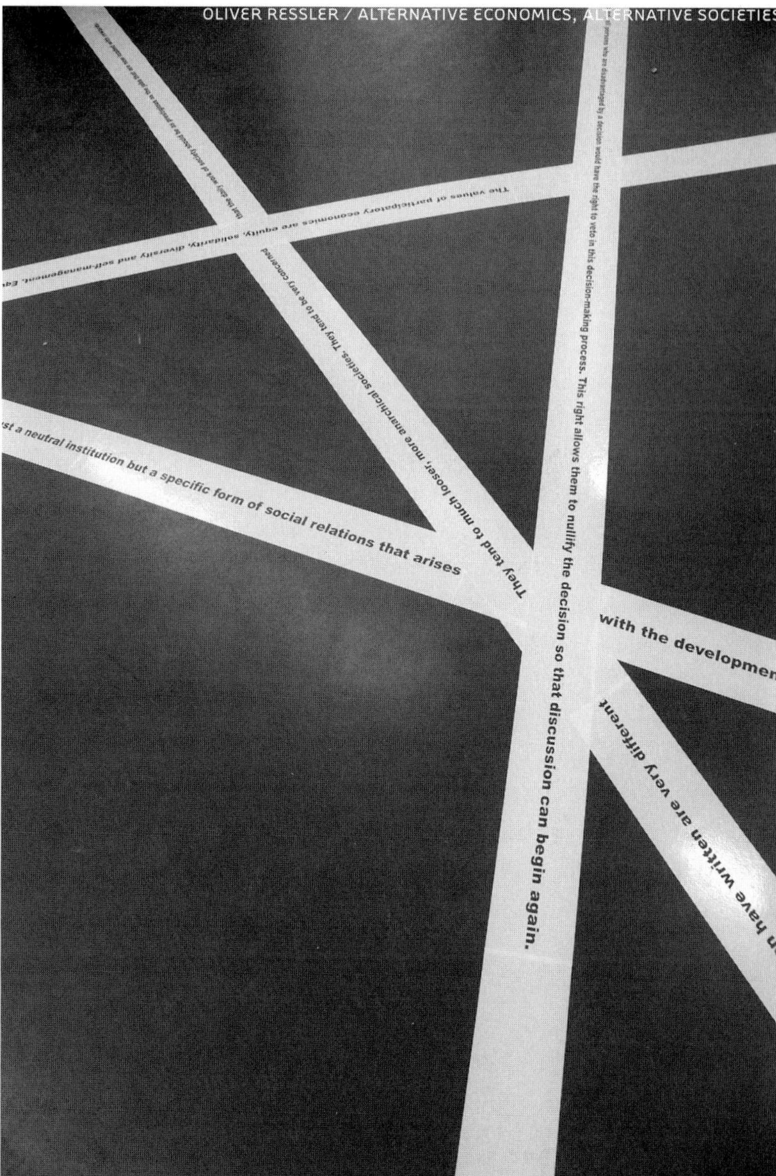
The values of participatory economies are equity, solidarity, diversity and self-management. Eq
st a neutral institution but a specific form of social relations that arises
They tend to much looser, more anarchical societies. They tend to be very concerned
the right to veto in this decision-making process. This right allows them to nullify the decision so that discussion can begin again.
with the development
n have written are very different.

Change the World Without Taking Power, with John Holloway, 23 min., 2004

There is simply something wrong with the whole idea of trying to transform society through the state. The failure to transform society through the state has to do with the nature of the state itself, that the state is not just a neutral institution but a specific form of social relations that arises with the development of capitalism.

The Paris Commune 1871, with Alain Dalotel, in collaboration with Rebond pour la Commune, 25 min., 2004

One thing that must really be stressed is that the Paris Commune of 1871 is a direct democracy. And this particular direct democracy has nothing to do with participatory democracy. The Commune is not about reforming the public services, it's about changing society, not adapting it. In 1871, people want revolution and think they have the capacity to make it happen with guns and cannons.

Anarchist Consensual Democracy, with Ralf Burnicki, 29 min., 2005

First, in an anarchist consensual democracy, affected persons would have the right to be consulted on decisions. Second, all persons who are disadvantaged by a decision would have the right to veto in this decision-making process. This right allows them to nullify the decision so that discussion can begin again.

The Subsistence Perspective, with Maria Mies, 26 min., 2005

All in economics is based on the assumption that at the center is individual use, individual interest. If instead, there were something there such as mutual aid, reciprocity, communality, collective work, and also collective enjoyment, then that would be another matter.

Installation shots from Capital (It Fails Us Now), Kunstihoone, Tallinn. Alternative Economics, Alternative Societies by Oliver Ressler.

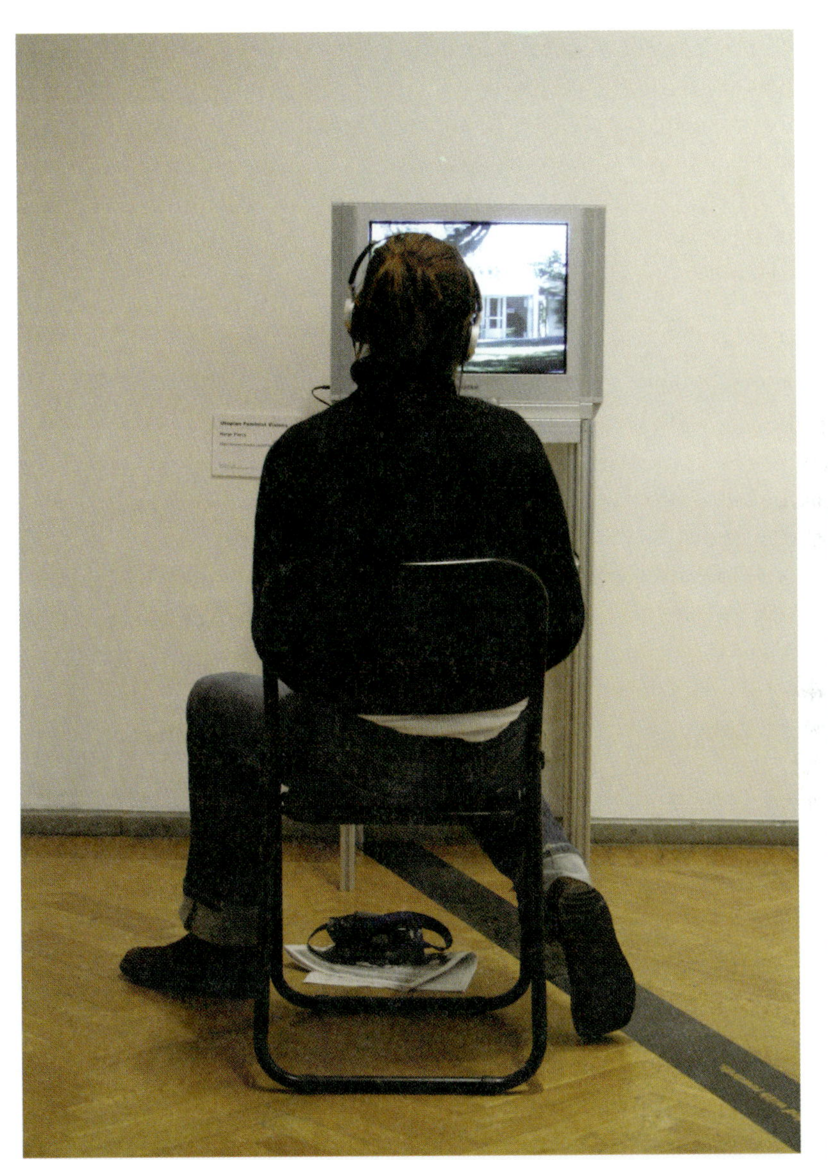

After the loss of a counter-model for capitalism – which socialism, in its real, existing form had presented until its collapse – alternative concepts for economic and social development face hard times at the beginning of the twenty-first century. In the industrial nations, broadly discussed are only those "alternatives" that do not question the existing power relations of the capitalist system and representative democracies. Other socio-economic approaches are labeled utopian, devalued, and excluded from serious discussion if even considered at all.

The thematic installation, *Alternative Economics, Alternative Societies*, focuses on diverse concepts and models for alternative economies and societies, which all share a rejection of the capitalist system of rule. An interview was carried out for each concept. Interview partners include economists, political scientists, authors and historians. From these interviews, a video in English was produced. In the exhibition, these single-channel 20- to 37-minute videos are each shown on a separate monitor, thus forming the central element of the artistic installation.

The project presents alternative social and economic models such as 'Inclusive Democracy' from Takis Fotopoulos (GB/GR), 'Participatory Economy' from Michael Albert (U.S.A.) and 'Anarchist Consensual Democracy' from Ralf Burnicki (D). Chaia Heller (U.S.A.) presents 'Libertarian Municipalism', Marge Piercy (U.S.A.), the feminist-anarchist utopias of her social fantasies, and the underground author p.m. (CH), the ideas of his concept 'bolo'bolo'.

Other videos focus on certain principles that might be of importance when discussing alternative economics and societies: Nancy Folbre (U.S.A.) speaks about 'Caring Labor', Christoph Spehr (D) about 'Free

Cooperation', Maria Mies (D) about the subsistence perspective and John Holloway (MEX/GB) about his ideas of how to 'Change the World Without Taking Power'.

As interesting historical models, Todor Kuljic (SCG) thematizes workers' self-management in Yugoslavia in the 1960s and 1970s, Salomé Moltó (E) talks about the workers' collectives during the Spanish Civil War (1936-1938), and Alain Dalotel (F) discusses the Paris Commune of 1871.

Chosen from each of these thirteen videos is one quotation significant for the alternative model that it presents. The quote is placed directly on the floor of the exhibition room as a several meter long text piece. This floor lettering, made from adhesive film, leads exhibition visitors directly to the corresponding videos and thereby provides a kind of orientation within this non-hierarchically arranged pool of videos. These videos offer stimulus and suggestions for contemplating social alternatives and possibilities for action.

The whole exhibition project started in Ljubljana in 2003 with five videos. Meanwhile, the installation has grown to include thirteen videos with a total length of almost six hours. The project is ongoing. Further economic and social concepts will be continually added in the coming years.

Alternative Economics, Alternative Societies received initial support as a grant from republicart (www.republicart.net) and the BKA section for the arts.

www.ressler.at

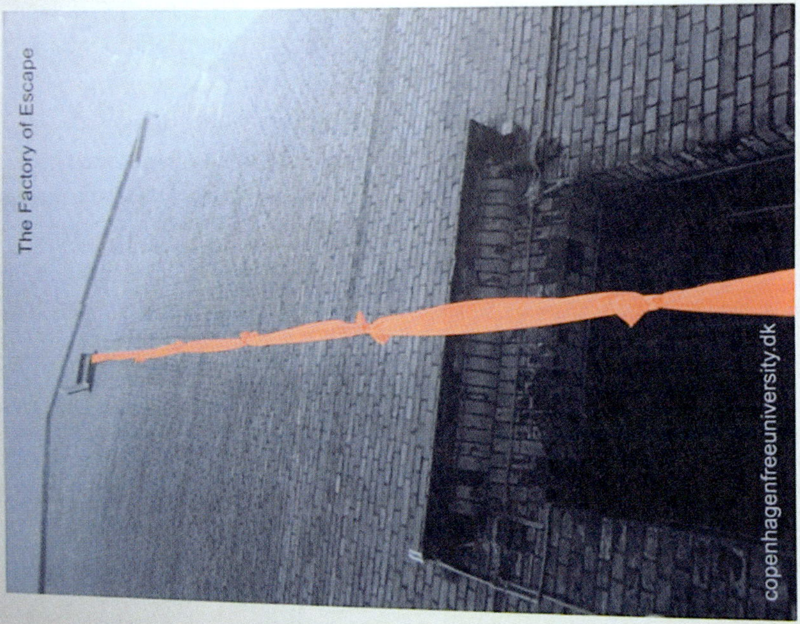

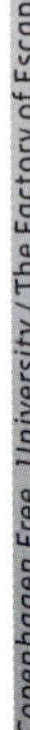

The Copenhagen Free University / The Factory of Escape

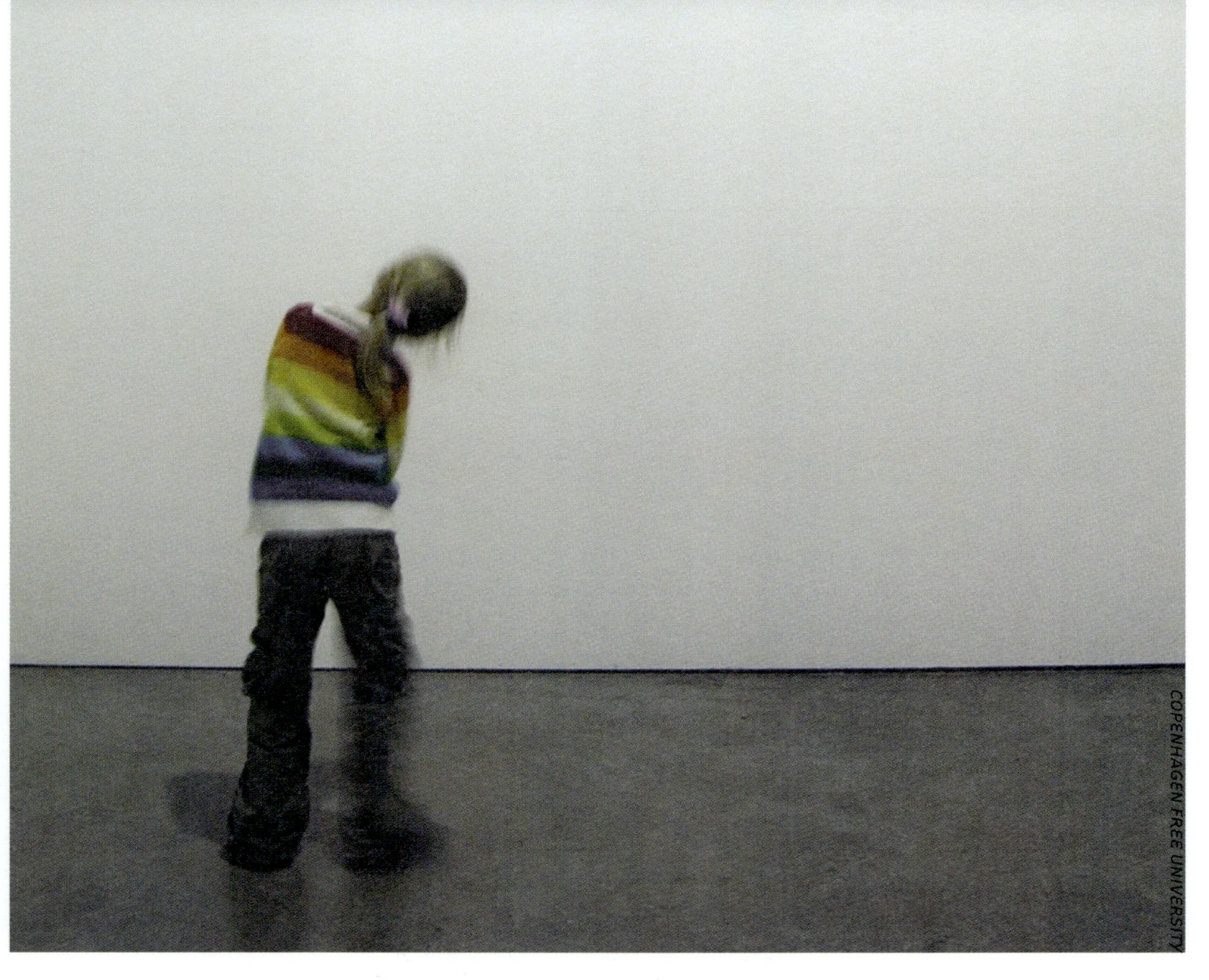
COPENHAGEN FREE UNIVERSITY

Taking Power, Refusing to become Government
17 Theses on Knowledge Production

We are concerned with how knowledge can be turned into life.

We are concerned with how knowledge can be turned into life.

We want to think knowledge in a social perspective and not in relation to capital.

The knowledge economy is about how knowledge can be turned into money.

We are concerned with how knowledge can be turned into life.

A university is a moulding of the body.

During industrial times knowledge was generally understood as mastery of a certain process of production; you needed to know how to operate a simple machine to get it to carry out its task.

Now knowledge is dealing with code, with communication, with interaction.

There is knowledge connected to all human activities.

Even the smashing up of a bus shelter demands certain skills.

We are concerned with how knowledge can be turned into life.

Research can also be research into how to be together with others, to be together with others, how to get closer, how to relate, communicate.

We work with forms of knowledge that are fleeting, fluid, schizophrenic, uncompromising subjective, uncompromising, subjective, uneconomic, acapitalist, produced in the kitchen, produced when asleep or arisen on a social excursion, collectively.

Waking up in the morning. The world is new;
it is appearing around me, it is becoming.
There it is.
There it is.

I start communicating, relate. Listen to the radio.
There is a text-message, the phone rings.
I start to cooperate, building the network that is us.
building the network that is us.

I make breakfast, eat. I communicate
I am at work, this is labor, living labor.
this is labor, living labor.

We are concerned with how knowledge can be turned into life.

A university works like a bank; both guarantee a system of value.
A university works like a bank; both guarantee a system of value.

Knowledge is between us, is alive and is not an interior. The mind is public.
The mind is public.
The mind is public.

There is a gap between what I say and what I feel – as always... I really don't know what to say.
I really don't know what to say.

I use every hour of the day and night to collect knowledge that informs me of my own death.
I listen to all the sounds that indicate death and shiver; the news, the ambulances in the street,
the yelling and crying of the neighbors.
the news, the ambulances in the street,
the yelling and crying of the neighbors.

I read about it in the papers. I notice it around me.
I read about it in the papers. I notice it around me.

We perform knowledge,
we present it to others, not as a mastery,
but as investigative beginnings,

We perform knowledge,
we present it to others, not as a mastery,
but as investigative beginnings,

as socialized research,
as socialized research,

The presence of others.
The presence of others.

The presence of others.
as an open space for mutation, proliferation, overspill of knowledge.

Our nervous systems want to be able to connect and reconnect the lines of exchange
connect and reconnect the lines of exchange
just for the sake of investigating them.
just for the sake of investigating them.

just for the sake of investigating them.

We are communicated,
I am communicated,
you are communicated,

you are communicated.

we are communicated,
I am communicated,
we are communicated.

we are communicated,
I am communicated,
we are communicated,
I am communicated,
you are communicated,
we are communicated.

We are concerned with how knowledge can be turned into life.

Knowledge is not one thing, even though the knowledge economy wants us to believe so.
Capital wants to make use of all aspects of our lives,
Capital wants to make use of all aspects of our lives,
and it wants to recode the flows of thought and affect into a code that it can decipher and transfer.

But there are many modes of knowledge constantly being re-evaluated and given new meanings;
But there are many modes of knowledge constantly being re-evaluated and given new meanings;
brought to new uses.

So I believe there is a slip there, a gap, where knowledge can be turned around
So I believe there is a slip there, a gap, where knowledge can be turned around
and used against the domination of capital,

a temporary pocket of free and dangerous knowledge.
a temporary pocket of free and dangerous knowledge.

What one learns at school or in the university is not essentially a content or data,
What one learns at school or in the university is not essentially a content or data, but a behavioral model.
What one learns at school or in the university is not essentially a content or data, but a behavioral model.

That is political.

They live within an institution,

They live within an institution,

They live within an institution, a university, without graduation, without assessment,
without graduation, without assessment,

without teachers.
without teachers.

The sound of knowledge.
How to turn sound into movement, rhythm.
How to turn sound into movement, rhythm.

How to turn knowledge into vibration; action.
How to turn knowledge into vibration; action.

How to turn sound into knowledge, vibration into rhythm.
How to turn sound into movement, rhythm.
Movement into action.
How to turn knowledge into vibration; action.

How to turn sound into knowledge, vibration into rhythm.
Movement into action

Movement into action.

How to turn knowledge into vibration; action.

Henriette Heise & Jakob Jakobsen
Copenhagen Free University 2005

MARIA EICHHORN PUBLIC LIMITED COMPANY

As my contribution to *Documenta11* a public limited company will be established that will continue to exist for an undetermined length of time. Within the structure of the public limited company, its functions will be adapted and its attributes rewritten, that is to say, the form and content will be developed and established in ways that differ from those usually practiced in joint stock companies. The assets assigned to the company when it was founded will remain unchanged. The assets should neither flow into the macro-economic conduits of the circulation of money and capital accumulation nor be used to create surplus value. All of the stock is possessed by the company. The company is thus the owner of all its own shares. The money that the company received in the form of investments at the time of its incorporation thus still belongs to the company. The company, however, no longer belongs to the shareholders, as they have transferred their shares to the company. The company belongs to itself, as it were. That is to say, in the end it belongs to no one. The company's assets – its money – no longer stand in any relation to the shareholders or to any other person. The concept of property loses its meaning here.

Maria Eichhorn, *Maria Eichhorn Public Limited Company,*
2002

Maria Eichhorn Public Limited Company

Incorporator, managing board: Maria Eichhorn
Supervisory board: Okwui Enwezor (chairperson), Tilman Bezzenberger (deputy chairperson), Dee Williams

Characteristics of *Maria Eichhorn Public Limited Company*

The company has two characteristics that mark it out from other companies. The concept of ownership is voided by transferring ownership of the company's shares to the company itself, and the company's capital is withdrawn from the wider economy's processes of monetary circulation and capital accumulation.

Transfer of Shares to the Company

Ownership of the shares was transferred free of charge to the company itself by means of the "Contract Between Maria Eichhorn Public Limited Company and Ms. Maria Eichhorn for the Transfer of All Shares in the Company to the Company Itself." In this way personal ownership of a thing (the money) was negated. The company is now the owner of its own shares. The shares represent the capital (the money) and its value. Consequently, nobody owns this capital any more, and it thus becomes common property of society as a whole.

Object of the Company

The object of the company is defined in clause 3 of its Articles of Incorporation: "The object of the company is to manage and preserve its own assets. The assets which the company has received by way of shareholder contributions upon its formation shall be preserved unchanged. These assets are not to become part of the macroeconomic circulation of money and accumulation of capital, nor shall they be used to create surplus value."

Presentation
The work's presentation was developed with *Documenta*'s broad international audience in mind. Consequently several levels of accessibility were worked into the exhibition setup: the documents, presented in back-lit displays; the money (€50,000 in bank notes) in a display case integrated in the row of documents; the furniture which played on the aesthetic of courtrooms and officialdom; and finally the publication, which contains reproductions of the founding documents.

Documents – Photographed reproductions of the joint stock company's documents were presented in specially backlit recesses formed by building a second wall in front of the actual wall of the exhibition room. The backlit displays were flush with the wall and appeared like frameless projections arranged in a row along the wall. Visitors followed the joint stock company's history in chronological order: from the Incorporation Deed *and the* Commercial Register Sheet *through to the* Contract for the Transfer of Shares.

Safe – The joint stock company's €50,000 share capital was presented as a stack of one hundred €500 bank notes in a transparent safe. Like the documents, the safe was also flush with the wall. It was placed at the chronologically correct position between the Minutes of the First Session of the Supervisory Board *and the* Report of the Incorporator on the Formation of the Company.

Publication – The publication documents the founding process of Maria Eichhorn Public Limited Company *and also contains an introductory text addressing the political, economic, legal and art theory issues involved. The introductory text provides a starting point for discussing and disseminating the work. The publication also provides an appropriate record of the work after the exhibition has closed.*

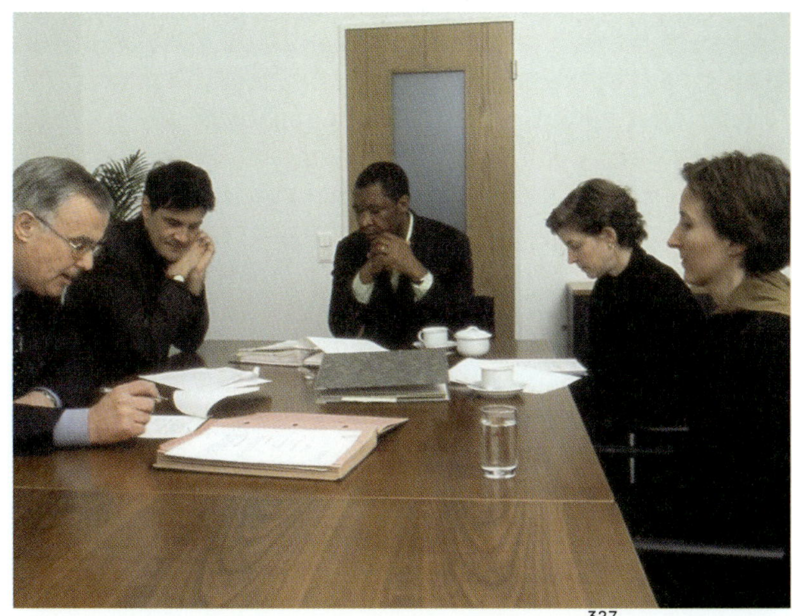

Furniture – The furniture was an integral part of the presentation of the work. Above and beyond its functionality (a bench allowing visitors to rest or to sit down to read the documents, the lectern for setting down the publication), it also makes its own institutional references. Such beechwood furniture with dark green linoleum inlays is found in courtrooms and government offices. In the context of the exhibition room it points to the real-life setting of the documents and the associated institutional, legislative, judicial and legal history aspects.

Publicity / Publication

The real depository of the documents shown in the exhibition is the Commercial Register, where the originals can be examined (even if the company has been dissolved). The legal structure of the joint stock company brings with it a requirement for a certain degree of openness. When a joint stock company is entered in the Commercial Register this is announced in daily newspapers and in the *Bundesanzeiger,* and every change to the articles of incorporation, share capital, managing board, supervisory board, etc. must also be published. The Commercial Register is a public place where the documents of all companies can be examined. This form of publicity represents a significant aspect of the work. Independently of its status as a work of art, *Maria Eichhorn Public Limited Company* is also part of another sphere of social relations. The original documents are available for viewing in the Local Court. This also throws up questions about which is the 'original' work of art and which

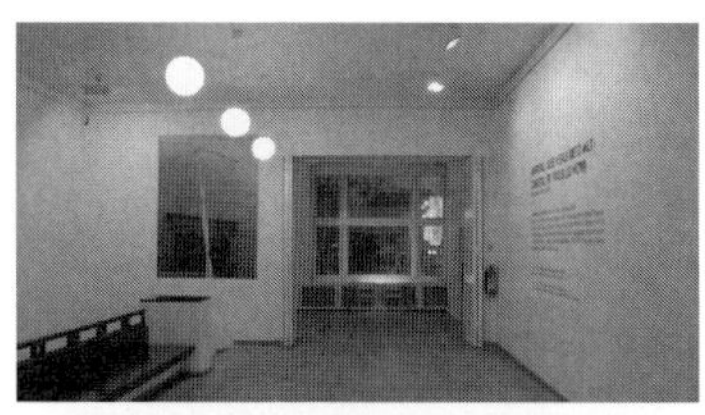

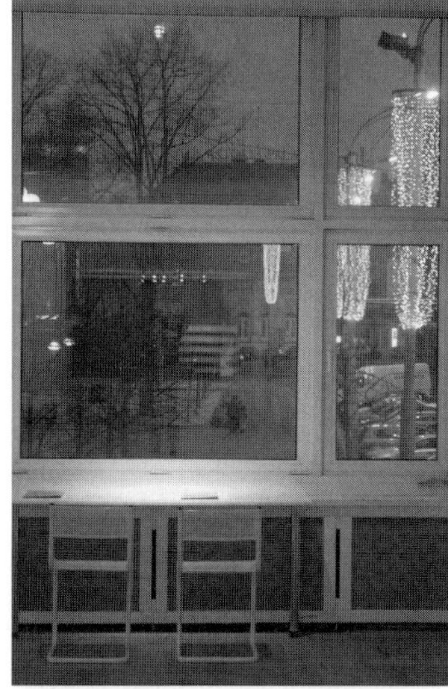

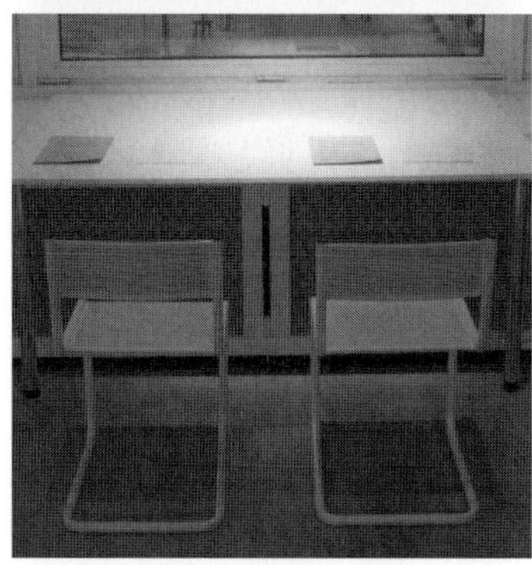

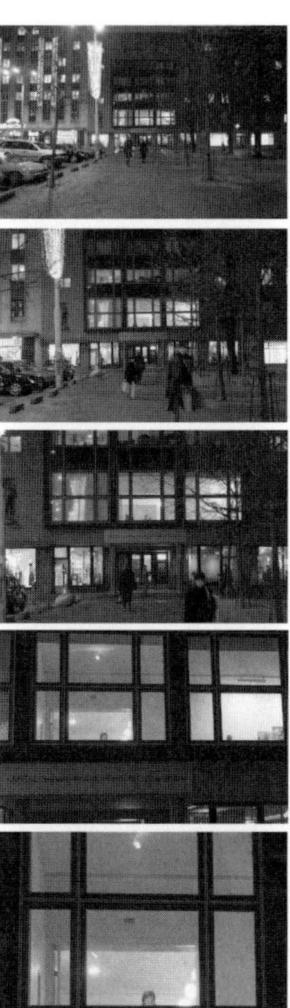

Installation shots of Maria Eichhorn Public Limited Company as installed in Capital (It Fails Us Now) at Kunstihoone, Tallinn. Reading material placed by window with a view to the central square in Tallinn.

is the 'reproduction'. Alongside its 'publication' in the Commercial Register, the work also exists within the context of art, raising questions as to the possibilities and potential of contemporary artistic practice in an ever-changing social context.

Detail: Maria Eichhorn Public Limited Company, safe, €50,000 deatail from installation, Documenta11, Kassel. Photo: Werner Maschmann.

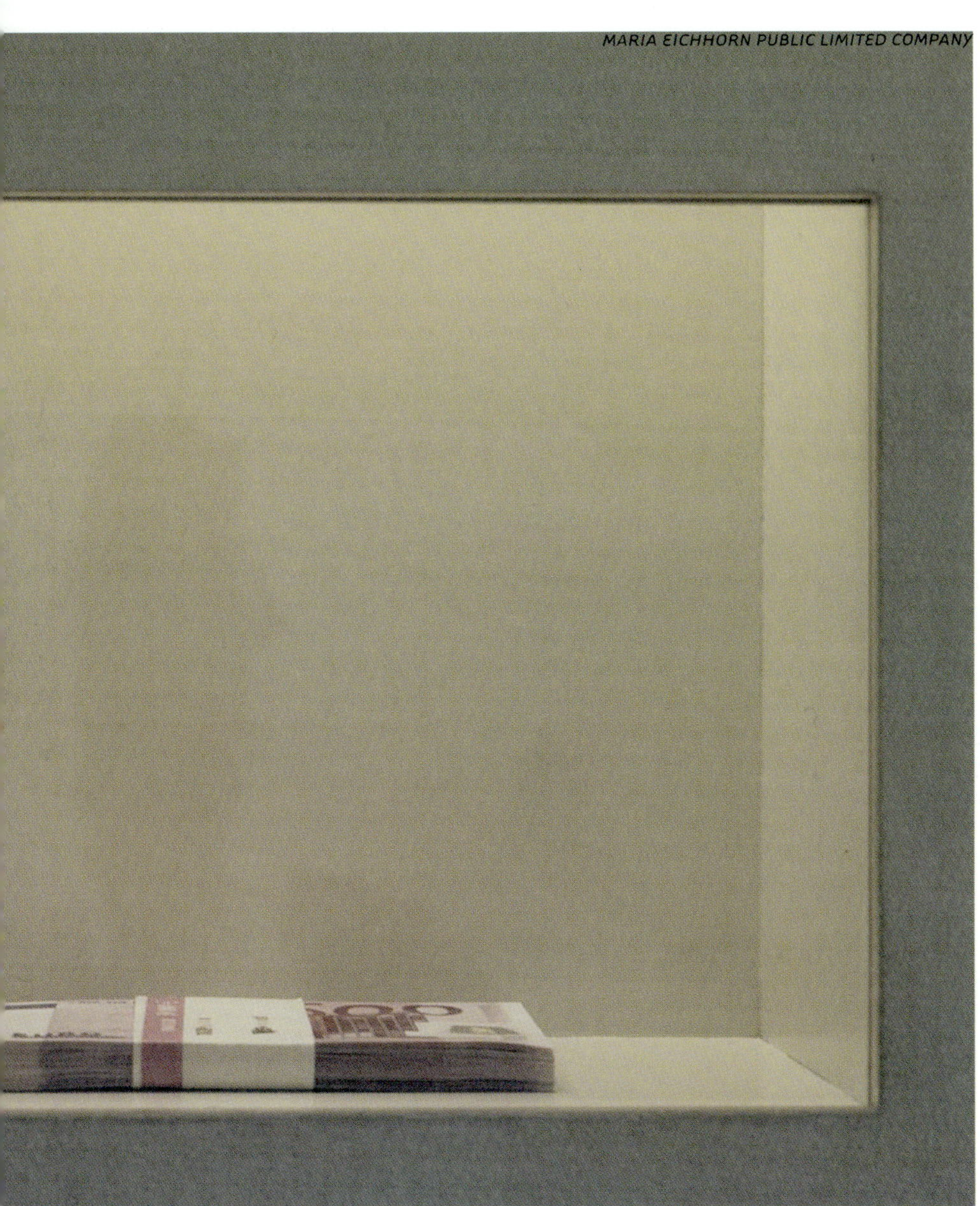

Maria Eichhorn Public Limited Company (2002)
at *Documenta11*, Kassel

Media/materials/events: notarized incorporation and inaugural meeting of the supervisory board; joint stock company; Incorporation Deed; Articles of Incorporation; Minutes of the First Session of the Supervisory Board; Report of the Incorporator on the Formation of the Company; Report of the Members of the Managing Board and of the Supervisory Board on their Audit of the Formation of the Company; Formation Audit Report; Application by the incorporator and the members of the managing board and the supervisory board for registration of the company in the Commercial Register; Commercial Register Sheet; public announcement of Commercial Register entry; Contract for the Transfer of All Shares to the Company; €50,000; safe-deposit box ; safe; bench; lectern; publication Maria Eichhorn Public Limited Company; corporation income tax returns; annual reports; management reports; supervisory board meetings; bank account; etc.

I. Financial Statement for the Year 2003

1. Balance Sheet as at December 31, 2003

Assets		Liabilities	
Fixed Assets		Equity	
Cash	50,000.00 €	Subscribed Capital	50,000.00 €
Current Assets	0.00 €	Debt and Provisions	0.00 €
	50,000.00 €		50,000.00 €

2. Profit and Loss Account for the Year 2003

1. Income	0.00 €
2. Expenses	0.00 €
3. Profit/Loss	0.00 €

Detail: Annual Financial Statement and Report of the Managing Board Maria Eichhorn Aktiengesellschaft for the Financial Year 2003 Photo: Jens Ziehe.

Annex 2

Translation

Annual Financial Statement and Report of the Managing Board
Maria Eichhorn Aktiengesellschaft
for the Finacial Year 2003

I. Financial Statement for the Year 2003

1. Balance Sheet as at December 31, 2003

Assets		Liabilities	
Fixed Assets		Equity	
Cash	50,000.00 €	Subscribed Capital	50,000.00 €
Current Assets	0.00 €	Debt and Provisions	0.00 €
	50,000.00 €		50,000.00 €

2. Profit and Loss Account for the Year 2003

1. Income	0.00 €
2. Expenses	0.00 €
3. Profit/Loss	0.00 €

3. Notes to the Accounts

According to § 3 of the company's articles of incorporation, "the object of the company is to manage and preserve its own assets. The assets which the company has received by way of shareholder contributions upon its formation shall be preserved unchanged. These assets are not to become part of the macroeconomic circulation of money and accumulation of capital, nor shall they be used to create surplus value." The company's managing board has complied with these standards. The total shareholder contribution of 50.000 € which the company has received upon its formation in March, 2002, are still held in cash in a safe-deposit box. For accounting purposes, these funds are treated as fixed assets and not as current assets. They correspond to the company's subscribed capital of 50.000 €. There are no further accounting positions.

II. Report of the Managing Board on the Year 2003

The condition of the company is stable. No changes are to be expected.

Berlin, March 4, 2004

(Maria Eichhorn)
Sole member of the managing board

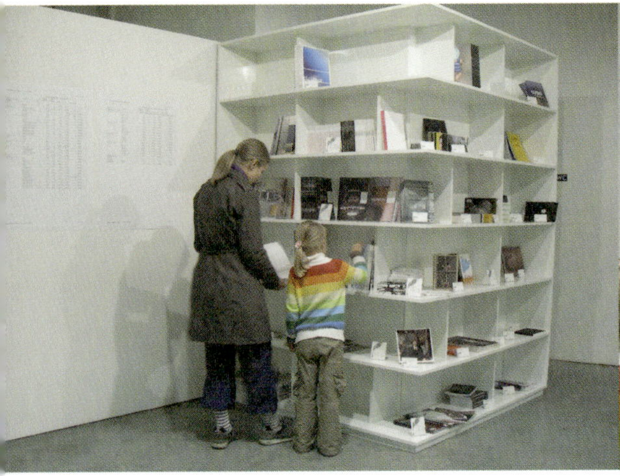

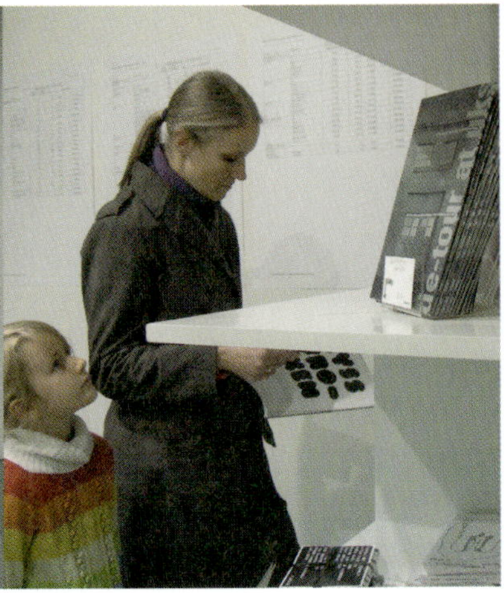

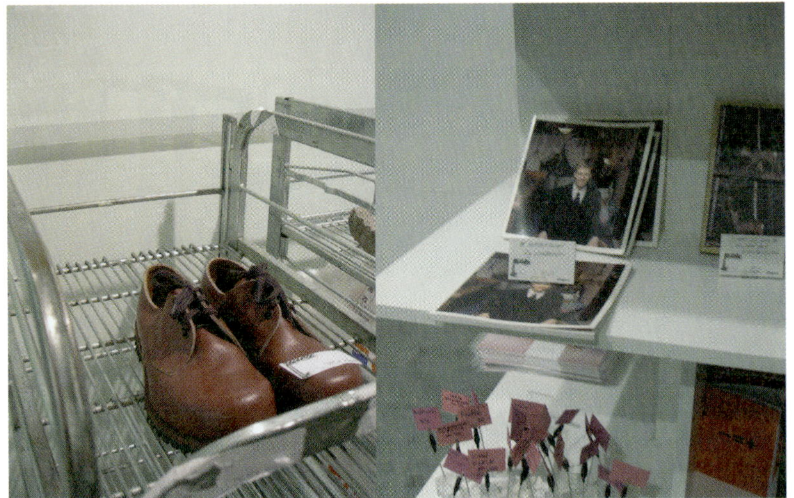

Details from installation of The 'Hidden' Flow in Capital (It Fails Us Now) in UKS, Oslo.

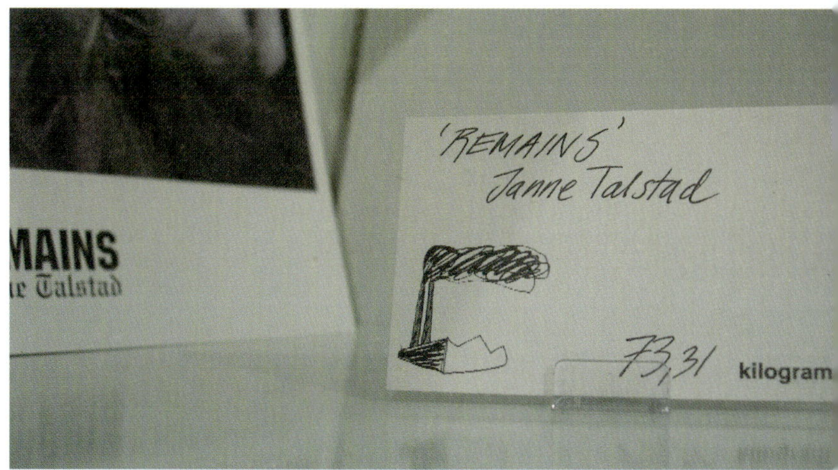

'REMAINS'
Janne Talstad
73,31
kilogram
Gilde

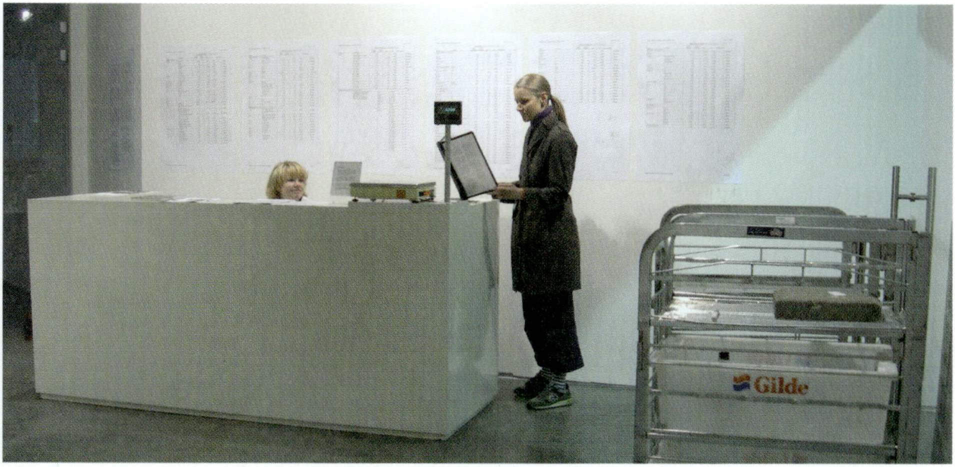

'Hidden' Flow Exchange at Capital (It Fails Us Now), UKS Oslo
Throughout the *Capital* show, the items – catalogues, books, magazines etc. – for sale at UKS could no longer be purchased with Norwegian crowns but only with *'Hidden' Flow Currency*. This was the only viable currency at UKS for the period of the *Capital* show. In order to purchase at the shop, one had to bring items which were exchanged for this currency. The exchanged items were then added to the stock of the shop.

The *'Hidden' Flow Currency*[1] is based on the notion of the *Ecological Rucksack*, a concept introduced by the Wuppertal Institute for Climate, Environment and Energy. The *Ecological Rucksack* signifies the collected Material Intensity; all the raw material, fuel and transport services that have been taken into use when the material or product was produced, minus the weight of the product.[2]

Why 'Hidden'?
Since the material intensity is not to be found in the final product, and is never introduced in the economic sphere, economists describe it as *hidden flows*. The *'Hidden' Flow Currency* appropriates this terminology so as to comment on this contradictory perspective (considering that for the population in the South, were the vast majority of the world's extraction and production is based, the process of material flows must be experienced as anything but hidden!). The production processes, on the contrary are commonly having a devastating – and most visible – impact on the environment, as well as grave health consequences for the people living in these areas.

The *'Hidden' Flow* Exchange project aims at functioning on a pedagogical as well as an operative level. The objective is to insert a different criteria for evaluation when ascribing value to an object, thus reflecting on different value systems. Furthermore, the project promotes recycling of goods, contributing towards the re-use of as well as enhancing the life-time of products. In so doing, it additionally aspires to raise awareness of environmental issues aiming at constructive forms of optimization.

Notes:

1. The currency was first introduced as a *Swop Network* project, a collaboration between Andrea Creutz & Lise Skou in 2004. *Swop Network* functioned as a platform for the production and dissemination of material and ideas surrounding contemporary political, economic and social debate. The project presented models for economic systems that exist as counterparts to the dominant monetary economy.

2. For information on the implementation of analysis according to the MI and MIPS concept (Material Input Per Service Unit, a measure developed at the Wuppertal Institute to estimate the environmental impacts caused by a product and serves as an indicator of precautionary environmental protection) see www.mips-online.info.

According to calculations by Michael Ritthoff and Jana Krahl from Wuppertal Institute for Climate, Environment, Energy Sustainable Production and Consumption Research Group the ecological rucksack of this book is 119,715 kg.

This book is calculated as 330 g:

abiotic material 3.9 kg
biotic material 1 kg
air 0.55 kg
water 113 kg

The activity of printing (including printer's ink) is relativly low:

abiotic material 0.157 kg
biotic material 0.002 kg
air 0.016 kg
water 1.09 kg

Calulated with the use of 1.2611 kg unbleached paper per 1 kg book.

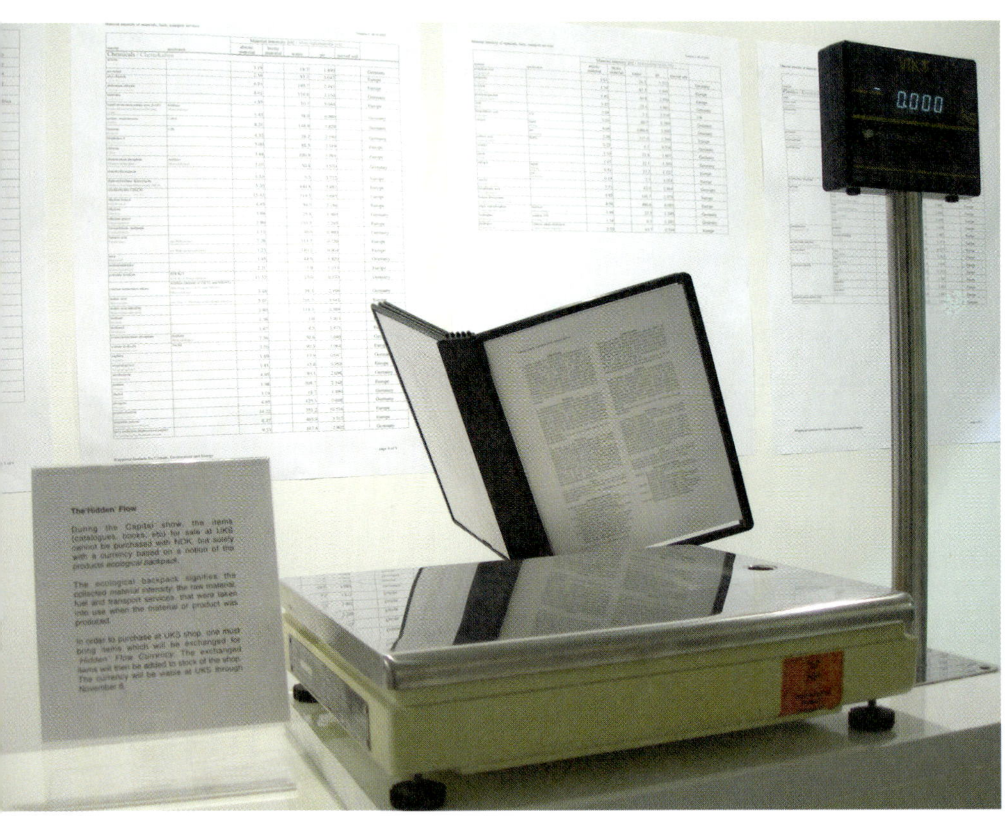
The 'Hidden' Flow

During the Capital show, the items (catalogues, books, etc) for sale at UKS cannot be purchased with NOK, but solely with a currency based on a notion of the products ecological backpack.

The ecological backpack signifies the collected material intensity, the raw material, fuel and transport services, that were taken into use when the material or product was produced.

In order to purchase at UKS shop, one must bring items which will be exchanged for 'Hidden' Flow Currency. The exchanged items will then be added to stock of the shop. The currency will be viable at UKS through November 8.

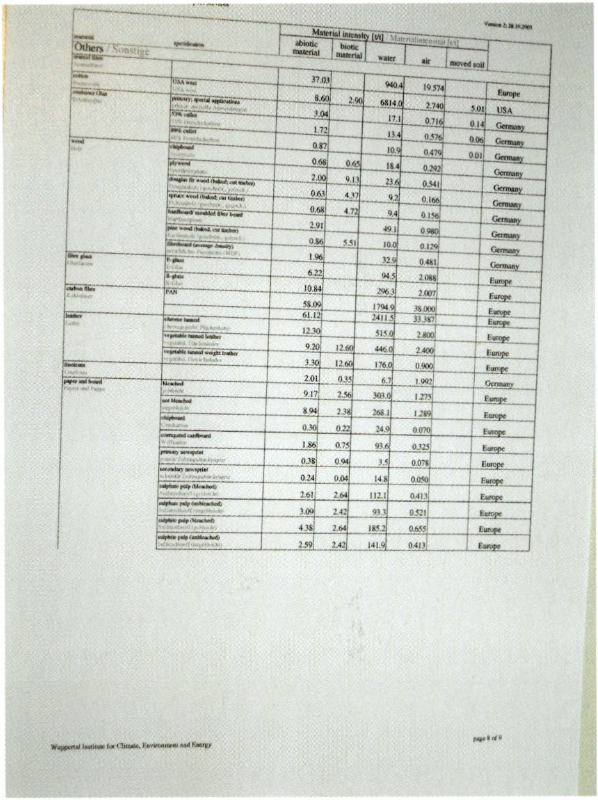

Tables etc. for calculation. Details from installation of The 'Hidden' Flow in Capital (It Fails Us Now) in UKS, Oslo, Oct. 2005.

Version 2; 28.10.2005

material	specification	Material intensity [t/t]					
Others / Sonstige		abiotic material	biotic material	water	air	moved soil	
natural fibre / Naturalfaser							
cotton / Baumwolle	USA wool / USA wool	37.03		940.4	19.574		Europe
consumer Glas / Verbundglas	primary, special applications / primär, spezielle Anwendungen	8.60	2.90	6814.0	2.740	5.01	USA
	53% cullet / 53% Fremdscharben	3.04		17.1	0.716	0.14	Germany
	89% cullet / 89% Fremdscharben	1.72		13.4	0.576	0.06	Germany
wood / Holz	chipboard / Spanplatte	0.87		10.9	0.479	0.01	Germany
	plywood / Sperrholzplatte	0.68	0.65	18.4	0.292		Germany
	douglas fir wood (baked; cut timber) / Douglasholz (geschnitten, getrocknet)	2.00	9.13	23.6	0.541		Germany
	spruce wood (baked; cut timber) / Fichtenholz (geschnitten, getrocknet)	0.63	4.37	9.2	0.166		Germany
	hardboard/ moulded fibre board / Hartfaserplatte	0.68	4.72	9.4	0.156		Germany
	pine wood (baked, cut timber) / Kiefernholz (geschnitten, getrocknet)	2.91		49.1	0.980		Germany
	fibreboard (average density) / mitteldichte Faserplatte (MDF)	0.86	5.51	10.0	0.129		Germany
fibre glass / Glasfasern	E-glass / E-Glas	1.96		32.9	0.481		Germany
	R-glass / R-Glas	6.22		94.5	2.088		Europe
carbon fibre / Kohlefasern	PAN	10.84		296.3	2.007		Europe
		58.09		1794.9	38.000		Europe
leather / Leder	chrome tanned / chromgegerbt, Flächenleder	61.12		2411.5	33.387		Europe
	vegetable tanned leather / vegetabil, Flächenleder	12.30		515.0	2.800		Europe
	vegetable tanned weight leather / vegetabil, Gewichtsleder	9.20	12.60	446.0	2.400		Europe
linoleum / Linoleum		3.30	12.60	176.0	0.900		Europe
paper and board / Papier und Pappe	bleached / gebleicht	2.01	0.35	6.7	1.992		Germany
	not bleached / ungebleicht	9.17	2.56	303.0	1.275		Europe
	chipboard / Graukarton	8.94	2.38	268.1	1.289		Europe
	corrugated cardboard / Wellkarton	0.30	0.22	24.9	0.070		Europe
	primary newsprint / primär Zeitungsdruckpapier	1.86	0.75	93.6	0.325		Europe
	secondary newsprint / sekundär Zeitungsdruckpapier	0.38	0.94	3.5	0.078		Europe
	sulphate pulp (bleached) / Sulfatzellstoff (gebleicht)	0.24	0.04	14.8	0.050		Europe
	sulphate pulp (unbleached) / Sulfatzellstoff (ungebleicht)	2.61	2.64	112.1	0.413		Europe
	sulphite pulp (bleached) / Sulfitzellstoff (gebleicht)	3.09	2.42	93.3	0.521		Europe
	sulphite pulp (unbleached) / Sulfitzellstoff (ungebleicht)	4.38	2.64	185.2	0.655		Europe
		2.59	2.42	141.9	0.413		Europe

What is to be done?
Questions for the 21st Century

Lenin's description of imperialism as the highest stage of capitalism now seems like a self-fulfilling prophecy. After the collapse of the Soviet bloc the total spread of unregulated global capitalism is seen as inevitable. With this spread, a third of the world's population lives on less than $2 a day and the poorest countries in the world owe a $422 billion debt that can never be paid. Yet events in Porto Alegre, Genoa and elsewhere show that global capitalism can be resisted. Do you think that Lenin's ideas are of any use today? What are the burning social and political questions of our time?

The Lenin Museum in Tampere where this archive began, was the site of Lenin and Stalin's first meeting. Lenin's ideas are often seen as leading inevitably to Stalinism and the terror of the Soviet Empire. This has been called the Leninist Tragedy. How can we prevent political change from turning into a situation where the same power structures are re-established only with different players at the top?

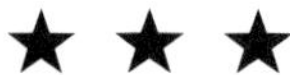

When Lenin wrote 'What is to be Done?' in 1902, he wanted to distinguish between radical revolutionary politics and the reformists who just wanted to patch things up. Lenin was intolerant of questions that failed to really challenge the dominant political order. How can we provoke significant change today and do you think any real shift can really happen under our present system?

In the early 20th century, the mobilization of workers' movements was the most effective way of achieving international solidarity. The phrase 'workers of the world unite' may now seem like an impossible ideal since late capitalism has crushed union power and pitted the workers of the world against one another. In Ireland alone almost half of the working population is employed by American multinational corporations. Despite this gloomy picture, from where you stand right now, what are the possibilities for international solidarity today?

In short, what is to be done?

Please e-mail a response to
whatistobedone@excite.com

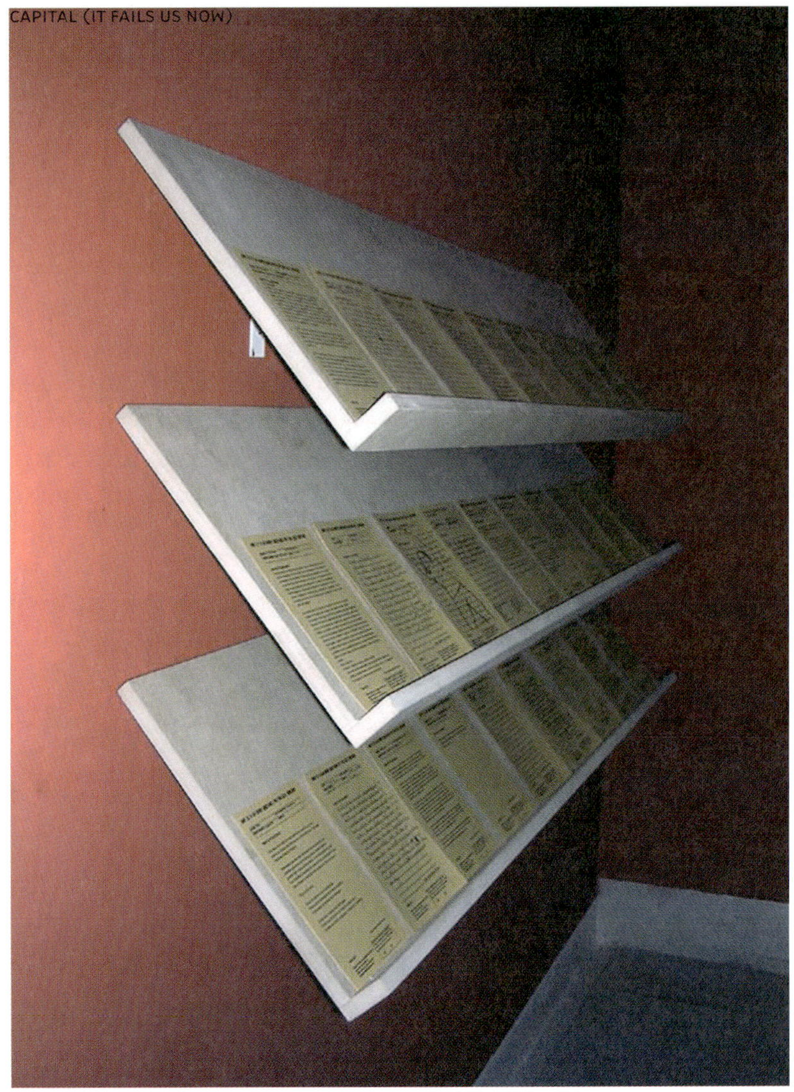

NAME: BADIOU	CITY/COUNTRY: PARIS
WEEK ENDING:	TIME IN:

WHAT IS TO BE DONE?

Dans "que faire ?", Lénine veut définir une nouvelle conception de la politique. Il s'agit d'avoir comme point de départ, non pas l'État ou le pouvoir, mais la conscience révolutionnaire. Le Parti doit résulter de l'organisation de cette conscience.

Nous devons refaire le chemin de Lénine. La forme-Parti est maintenant impraticable. Mais la nécessité d'organiser la subjectivité politique en dehors de toute soumission aux règles de l'État demeure. En particulier, nous devons critiquer complètement la "démocratie" électorale.

Il faut inventer une politique "sans-parti", soumise à la discipline des processus politiques concrets.

TIME OUT:

Please continue overleaf if necessary

Can we make copies of your response for Museum visitors to take away with them? (Please circle)

(YES)   NO

wh-at IS to be done ?
Grammars of organisation

by Susan Kelly

First the question should move from the passive to the positive – to 'What do we do?' even to 'What are we doing?' Lenin could use the passive form, he could assume an army of followers moving along the reasonably well mapped-out road of socialism. Having neither armies nor road nowadays, the passive question indicates nothing more than armchair theorizing. [...] We can't answer the question – 'what do we do?' – can't even deal with it in any meaningful way until we build axes of community and of solidarity from ourselves, through our lives, concomitant with our work. Building structures in which we can communicate and ask these questions – not just of myself or yourself, but to a society of others. For the moment, what we can do is to build these structures and structure ourselves within them. Build these relationships within our lives so that we'll be able to ask this question in a meaningful way – What is to be done?

David Landy, Tampere, Finland

WH- QUESTION. INTERROGATIVE. ALLOWS SPEAKER TO FIND OUT MORE INFORMATION ABOUT TOPIC.

WH- INTERROGATIVE CLAUSES OFTEN FOLLOWED BY TO-INFINITIVES WITH A COVERT SUBJECT.

IS – THIRD PERSON SINGULAR PRESENT 'TO BE'. - LINKING VERB, AUXILIARY VERB, HELPING VERB.

AS AUXILIARY CAN BE USED TO INDICATE SOMETHING THAT IS DUE TO HAPPEN.

TO: AS IN, IN ORDER TO.

BE: AN IRREGULAR AND DEFECTIVE VERB. PRIMARY AUXILIARY VERB. HAS PROGRESSIVE OR DURATIVE ASPECT.

What kind of question is 'What is to be done?' So often it marks the moment when thought is over and action must proceed: a question that punctuates and firmly separates the realm of thought from the realm of action. A question that, as Jean-Luc Nancy has noted, is often posed to philosophers who seemingly think too much and do little. It is a question that embodies so many knots of theory and practice, of thought and action and the ways in which those relationships are organized.

Solutions to questions of a scientific nature remove the need for the question. The problem is solved and so the question becomes redundant. By contrast, in philosophy and much cultural analysis, questioning operates as a particular procedure that builds a way not to a solution that would absolve the question, but to an altered, and perhaps critical relationship to the thing questioned. As Heidegger argues, such procedures of critical questioning are said to prepare a 'free relation' to the thing questioned. One might say then, that the scientific question is rather closed in comparison to this more open-ended form of philosophical questioning. The scientific question assumes a certain level of knowledge already and requires only clarification of a detail: a piece of information that will remove the question itself. Closed questions get answers that the questioner expects. The act of answering within those pre-defined terms could be seen therefore as a rather passive act.

And so, I ask again: what kind of question is 'What is to be done?' It may seem to be an incredibly open question, one that is almost too large to contemplate. Yet, if we consider the grammar of the question itself and the context of its public address, particularly in Lenin's utterance of it, the question begins to resemble something much more closed in its rhetorical force, perhaps almost an imperative, an attempt to have a public do something that the questioner wants done.

* * *

hang out the washing
clean the loo
read the paper
pick up the dog
watch *Desperate Housewives* tonight at 10pm

M. Kearney, Dublin, Ireland

TO BE: TO-INFINITIVE. PRESENT INFINITIVE. INFINITIVE IS BASE. UNMARKED BASE FORM OF VERB. TO-INFINITIVE CAN BE COMBINED WITH PASSIVE CONSTRUCTIONS. TO-INFINITIVES USUALLY HAVE NO SUBJECT, ALTHOUGH ITS SUBJECT IS IMPLIED BY THE CONTEXT. INFINITIVE IS NON-FINITE. FORM DOES NOT BIND VERB TO A SPECIFIC SUBJECT OR TENSE. TO BE ALSO USED TO INDICATE SOMETHING THAT IS DUE TO HAPPEN: BRIDE TO-BE. IT REMAINS TO BE SEEN.

Verbs describe states, events and actions. The tense of the main verb of a sentence establishes the time frame of an action. Infinitives however, are unmarked and unbound to any particular tense. Specifying the time frame in 'What is to be done?' is postponed or left open. As a result, the verb in this seemingly most active of active questions, in our question that contains an implicit critique of non-action, behaves in fact like a state and not an action.

Post Bolshevik revolution, the question originally formulated in Russian

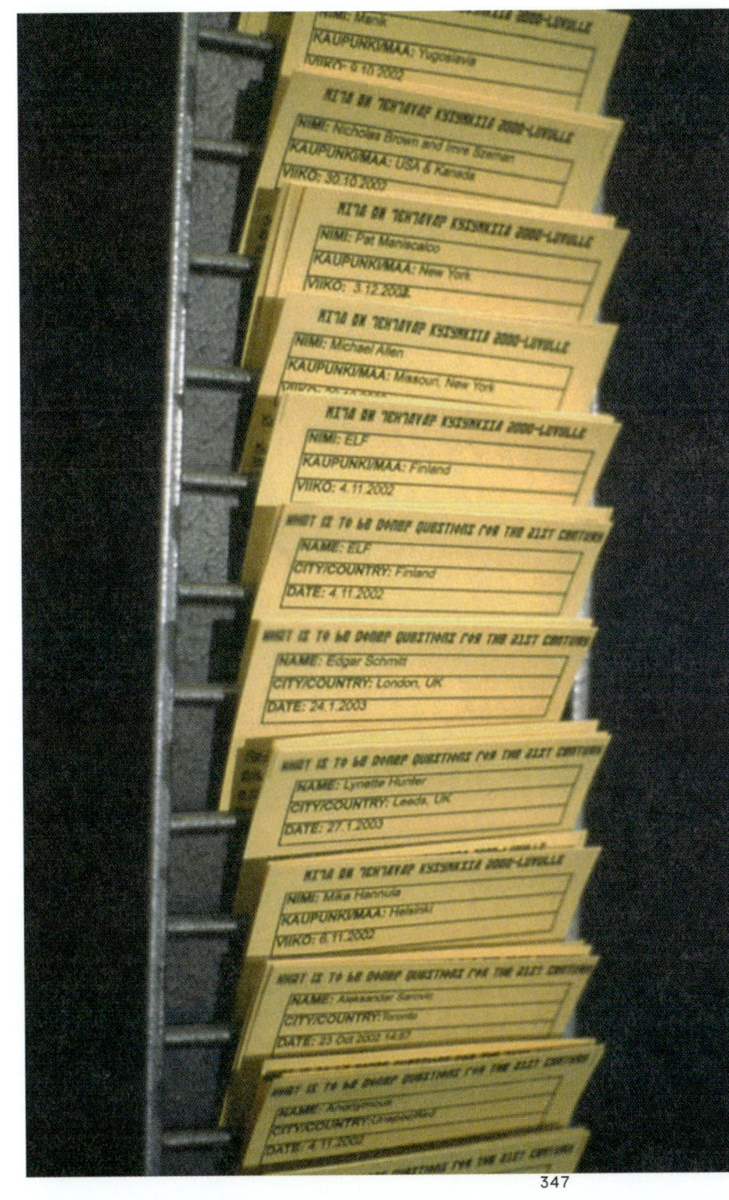

NIMI: Merik
KAUPUNKIMAA: Yugoslavia
VIIKO: 4.10.2002
NIMI: Nicholas Brown and Imre Szeman
KAUPUNKIMAA: USA & Kanada
VIIKO: 30.10.2002
NIMI: Pat Maniscalco
KAUPUNKIMAA: New York
VIIKO: 3.12.2002
NIMI: Michael Allen
KAUPUNKIMAA: Missouri, New York
NIMI: ELF
KAUPUNKIMAA: Finland
VIIKO: 4.11.2002
WHAT IS TO BE DONE? QUESTIONS FOR THE 21ST CENTURY
NAME: ELF
CITY/COUNTRY: Finland
DATE: 4.11.2002
NAME: Edgar Schmitt
CITY/COUNTRY: London, UK
DATE: 24.1.2003
NAME: Lynette Hunter
CITY/COUNTRY: Leeds, UK
DATE: 27.1.2003
NIMI: Mika Hannula
KAUPUNKIMAA: Helsinki
VIIKO: 6.11.2002
NAME: Aleksander Sacmiot
CITY/COUNTRY: Toronto
DATE: 23 Oct 2002 12:37

is translated into English not as 'What to do?' (which would be closer also to the French, German and Finnish translations), but as 'What is to be done?'. 'What to do?' bears similar problems to the more common English formulation, but the insertion of the 'done' edges what might be due or imminent (the 'to-be') into the realm of the already over, decided and done for. This fact that the slippage of translation from the Russian 'Chto Delat? (literally 'What to do?' in English) to the English phrase 'What is to be done?' happens in 1929, well after the October Revolution seems significant.

* * *

[...] The 21st Century Left need have no identity, no head office, leadership, or fixed territory. Participants need only agree on a manner of collective decision-making, which values breadth of participation and is biased toward operating by consent, minimizing coercion. Such a mode of collective decision making encourages self-defence, and tends to block the formation of conventional armies and policing. It disabuses the group of any aspiration to exercise power, whether over a territory, a people or an epoch. Zones of this kind are the way forward.

Kathy Kang, Sydney, Australia

DONE: PAST PERFECT, OVER, COMPLETED. CAN ALSO FUNCTION AS ADJECTIVE. GERUND.

TO BE DONE: INFLEXIONAL FORM OF VERB: TO DO. TO ÁCCOMPLISH, FINISH, BRING TO A CONCLUSION. EXPRESSES A STATE AND NOT AN ACTION. PRESENT INFINITIVE USING PAST PARTICIPLE.

[WH-] **IS TO BE DONE**: PASSIVE VOICE BECAUSE OF 'BE' BEFORE VERB PHRASE IN PAST PARTICIPLE. PASSIVE VOICE OMITS THE AGENT. AGENTLESS PASSIVES. USED TO FOCUS ATTENTION ON TARGET OF ACTION RATHER THAN PERFORMER. PASSIVE INFINITIVE.

Our agents are covert, oddly omitted in the seeming conferral of direct public address. The passive formulation can only assume a public already on board, as Landy points out above, or serve to obscure or naturalize a source of power. Subjectivity is separate from action here. Action is a task, a piece of work already defined, that must be done. Thinking, experiencing, making decisions, deciphering how to proceed with, or into a future, is rendered unnecessary to our question.

The grammar of any sentence organizes the relationship between subjects – verbs – objects (or agents – actions – telos). The time frame and passive voice established by the question 'What is to be done?' circumscribes a form or action that relates to the future only in the form of a volunteering to carry out a task in which the passive subject has had no part in formulating. The future, decided on yesterday, can be signed up for today. Action is bound to a rigid notion of consciousness that produces a will and a rational decision to serve. 'What is to be done?' emerges as a profoundly scientific question.

Arguably, the grammar of organization that this influential and oft-quoted question reveals (and indeed inaugurates) is passive, fixed and authoritarian. This statement is not necessarily an argument for making our questions less scientific and more philosophical, nor is it meant to re-capitulate old debates between Marx and Bakunin. Questions of power, organization and modes of interrupting the repetition of old structures in future societies have long since been addressed and radically developed through feminist discourse, indigenous and post-colonial struggles. The sense of urgency and pragmatism that often accompanies the utterance of the question 'What is to be done?' must be maintained, but we must remain wary of how such an appeal pre-determines the future and constitutes the subjects present as *a priori* Revolutionary agents. So when this question is re-stated in 2005, we must re-think the specific forms of organization, relationships with each other, and relationships with the future that were implicit in Lenin and Chernyshevky's original question. Such a re-thinking certainly involves a critical assessment of forms of organization such as the Party or the soviet, but as I have suggested it also necessitates a careful examination of the rhetoric of the question 'What is to be done?' itself.

> What is to be done? [...] perhaps the uncertainty of what is to be done today is so great, so fluctuating, so indeterminate, that we do not need even to do this: to raise the question. Especially if one already knows what it is right to think, and that the only issue is how one might then proceed to act. [...] 'What is to be done?' means for us: how to make a world for which all is not already done (played out, finished, enshrined in destiny) nor still entirely to do (in the future for always future tomorrows). What will become of our world is something we cannot know, and we can no longer believe in being able to predict or command it. But we can act in such a way that this world is a world able to open itself up to its own uncertainty as such. These are not vague generalities. [...] Where certainties come apart, there too gathers the strength that no certainty can match.

> *Jean-Luc Nancy, France*

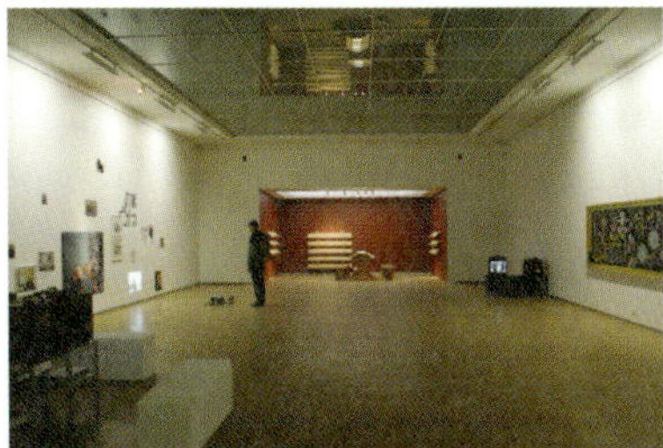

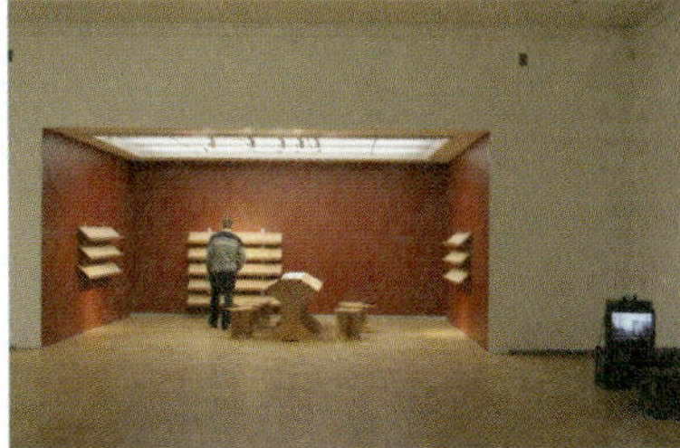

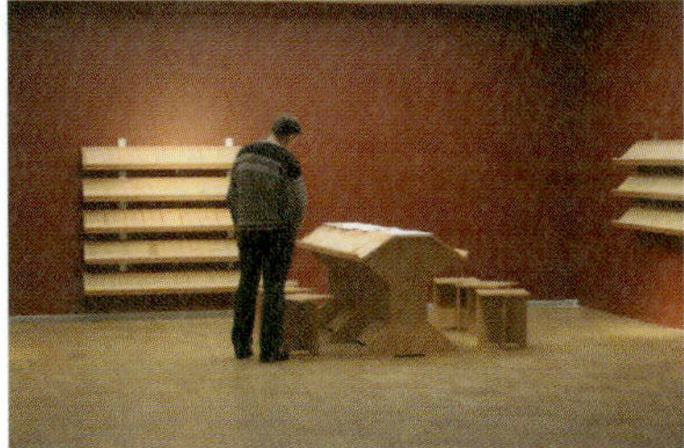

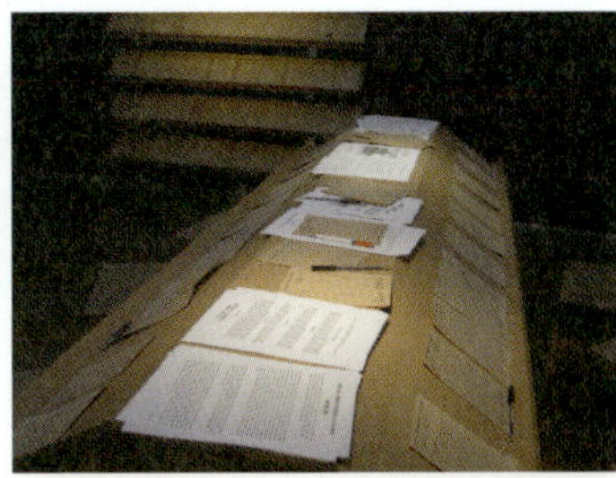

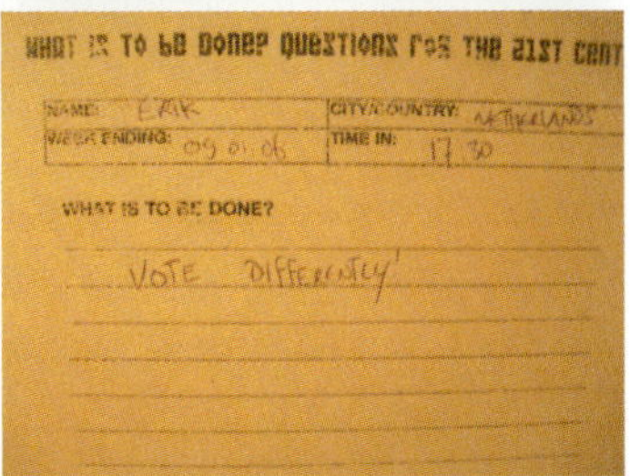

Details from installation of What is to be done? in Capital (It Fails Us Now), Kunstihoone, Tallinn.

Chto delat? /// What is to be done?
A Platform for Engaged Creativity

Founded in early 2003, 'Chto delat?/What is to be done?' brings together artists, philosophers, social scientists and writers from Moscow and Petersburg. This workgroup publishes an English-Russian newspaper on issues central to poetics and politics today, with a special focus on the Russian artistic-intellectual situation. The workgroup also engages in a variety of art projects, including video works, installations, public actions, radio programs, and artistic examinations of urban space. Its most recent exhibition and research project is 'Drift – Narvskaya Zastava', a community-examination of a constructivist-proletarian neighborhood in Petersburg.

Our newspaper – of which 10 issues have appeared so far – reflects the heterogeneity of our workgroup, for whom cross-disciplinary encounters are neither only articulations of personal similarities or differences, nor academic exercises but a non-alienated means of getting together and producing counter-knowledge adequate to the conditions under which contemporary Russian culture is evolving.

Each issue of the newspaper is an experiment that draws artists, critics, and philosophers into a heated editorial process, which results in theoretical essays, art projects, open-source translations, questionnaires, dialogues, and comic-strips. On the whole, its format could be described as something between a theoretical journal and a fanzine, although the key difference to a 'zine' is that reclaiming the voice of our micro-community or speaking to an intimate audience is not our only goal. This copyleft publication is usually made in connection with specific events and is distributed for free at congresses or exhibitions, where it reaches a broader cultural public. As a supplement to artworks or as an intervention, the newspaper is a tactical medium, a trigger that pushes the reader to perceive and partake of a space that is on the periphery of the dominant orders of exchange. This tactical trigger pursues a strategic goal, namely to extend this space as an experience-base for solidarity, both in a micro-political and an internationalist sense. Locally, we do not only want to engage in a confrontational re-reading of various theoretical and practical approaches from the critical Left, but to find new ways of bringing people together to rewrite their situation. Internationally, we want to contribute to the unfolding discussion on the changing relationship between art and politics at large by 'arranging meetings' between a variety of contributors, collectives, and communities from both Russia and abroad. The goal: to provide a platform for engaged creativity where they can think, argue (and hopefully act) together.

David Riff and Dmitry Vilensky, editors of the newspaper 'Chto delat?'

Internet version of all issues can be found on www.chtodelat.org.

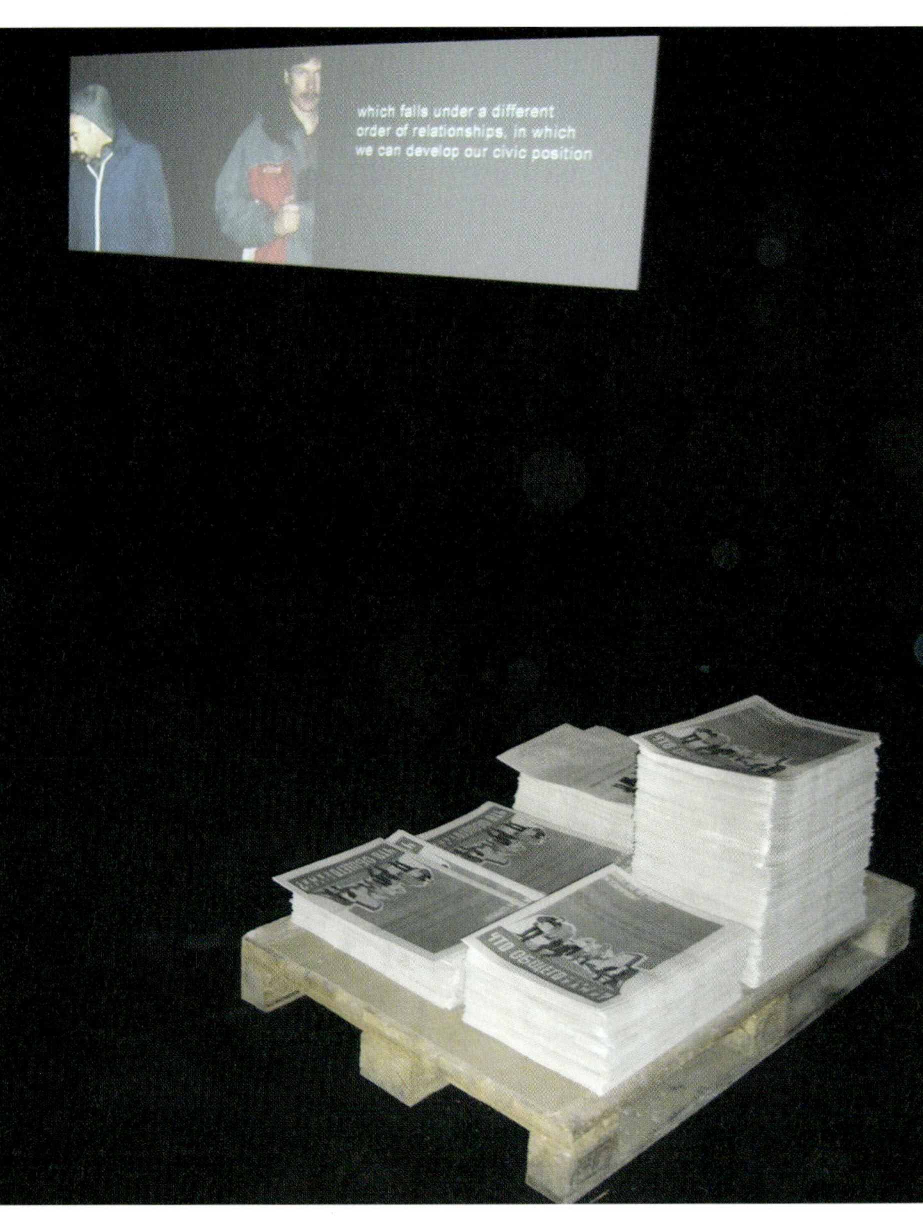

which falls under a different
order of relationships, in which
we can develop our civic position

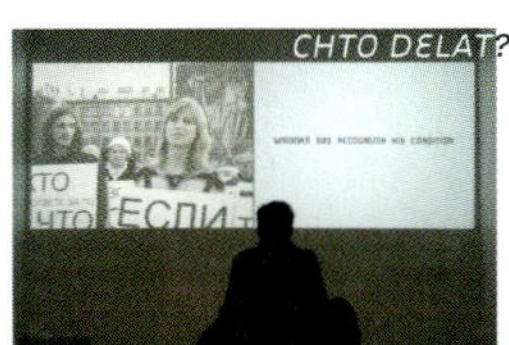

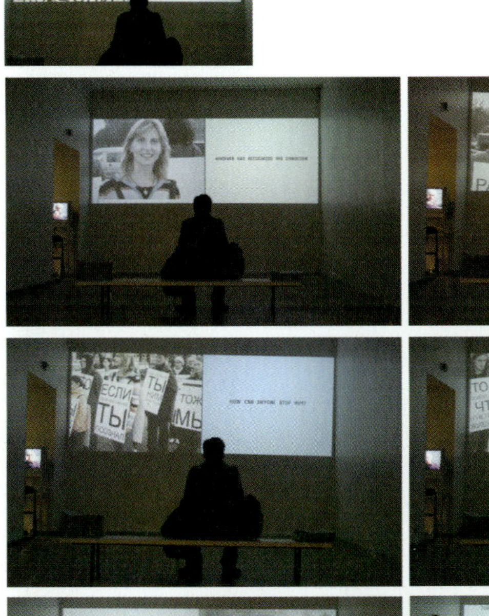

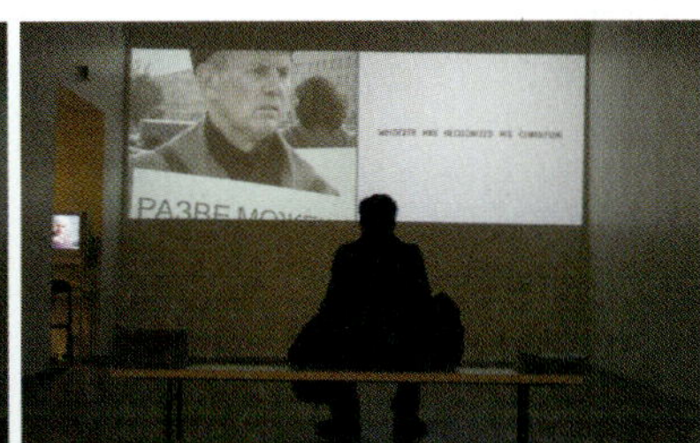

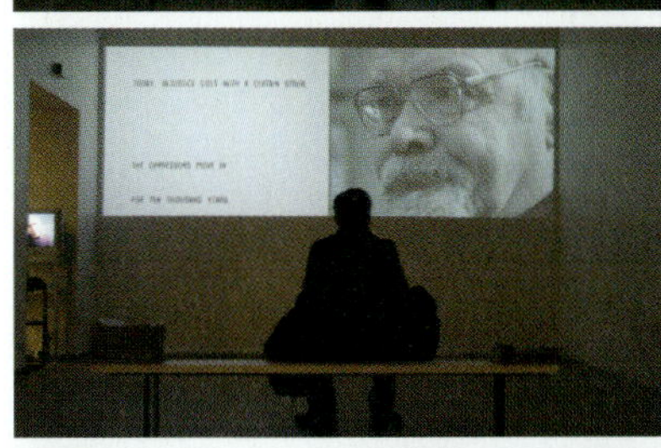

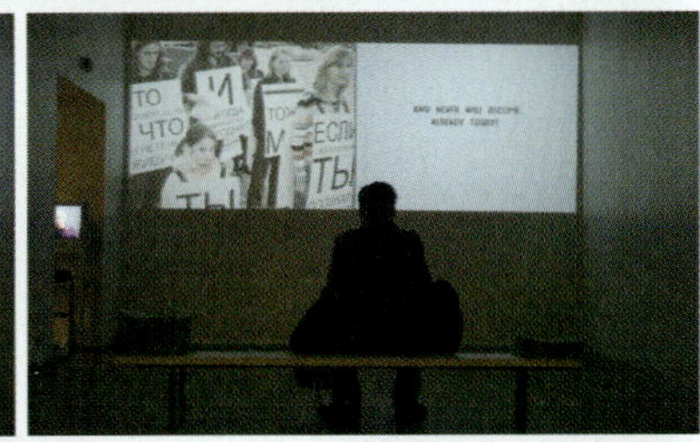

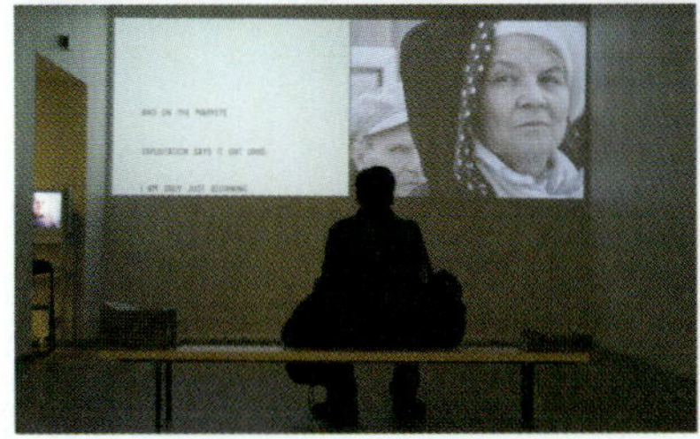

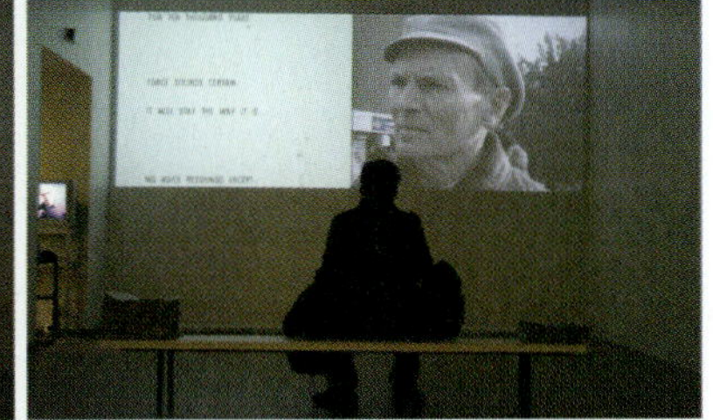

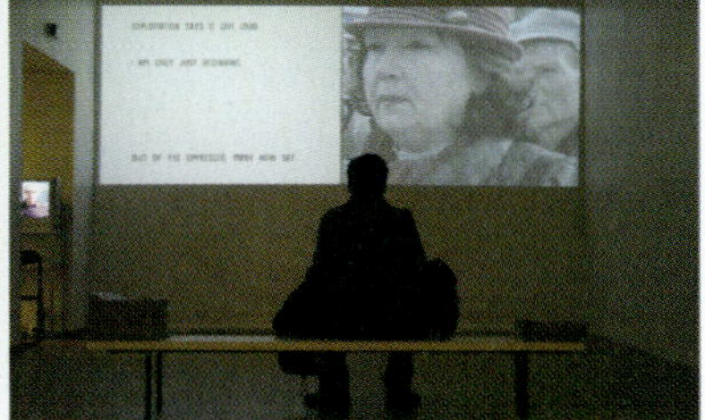

Installation shots from Capital (It Fails Us Now), Kunstihoone, Tallinn, Jan.-Feb. 2006.

Brecht: In Praise of Dialectics

Today, injustice goes with a certain stride,
The oppressors move in for ten thousand years.
Force sounds certain: it will stay the way it is.
No voice resounds except the voice of the rulers
And on the markets, exploitation says it out loud:
I am only just beginning.
But of the oppressed, many now say:
What we want will never happen
Whoever is still alive must never say 'never'!
Certainty is never certain.
It will not stay the way it is.
When the rulers have already spoken
Then the ruled will start to speak.
Who dares say 'never'?
Who's to blame if oppression remains? We are.
Who can break its thrall? We can.
Whoever has been beaten down must rise to his feet!
Whoever is lost must fight back!
Whoever has recognized their condition –
how can anyone stop them?
Because the vanquished of today
will be tomorrow's victors
And never will become: already today!

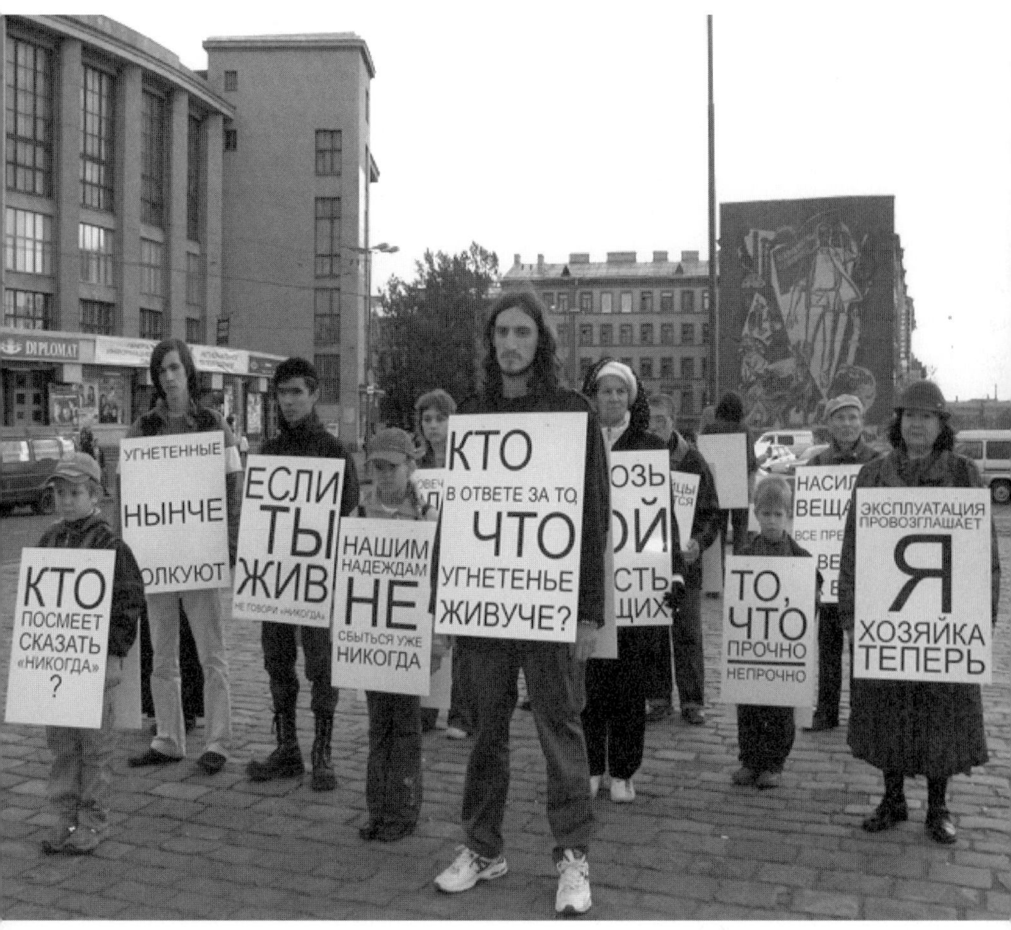
УГНЕТЕННЫЕ
НЫНЧЕ
ТОЛКУЮТ

КТО
ПОСМЕЕТ
СКАЗАТЬ
«НИКОГДА»
?

ЕСЛИ
ТЫ
ЖИВ
НЕ ГОВОРИ «НИКОГДА»

НАШИМ
НАДЕЖДАМ
НЕ
СБЫТЬСЯ УЖЕ
НИКОГДА

КТО
В ОТВЕТЕ ЗА ТО
ЧТО
УГНЕТЕНЬЕ
ЖИВУЧЕ?

ТО,
ЧТО
ПРОЧНО
НЕПРОЧНО

НАСИЛ
ВЕЩА

ЭКСПЛУАТАЦИЯ
ПРОВОЗГЛАШАЕТ
Я
ХОЗЯЙКА
ТЕПЕРЬ

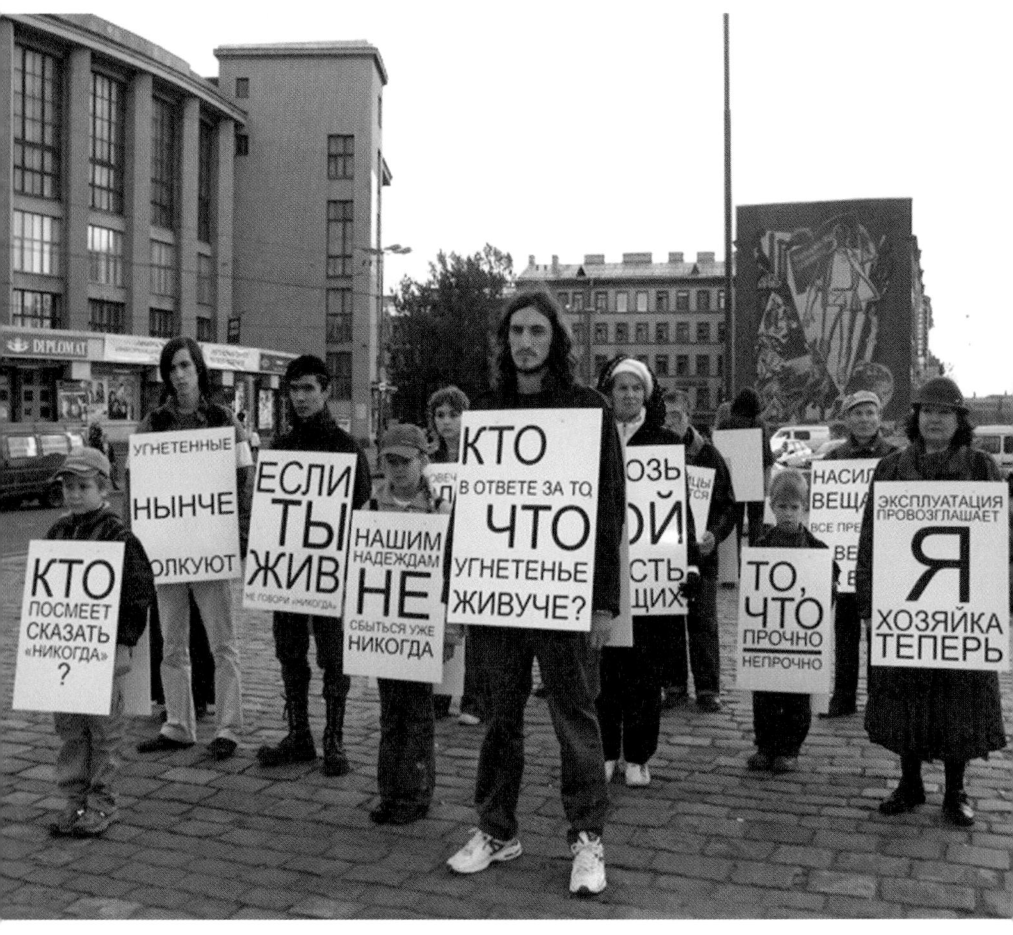
УГНЕТЕННЫЕ
НЫНЧЕ
ОЛКУЮТ
КТО
ПОСМЕЕТ
СКАЗАТЬ
«НИКОГДА»
?
ЕСЛИ
ТЫ
ЖИВ
НАШИМ
НАДЕЖДАМ
НЕ
СБЫТЬСЯ УЖЕ
НИКОГДА
НЕ ГОВОРИ «НИКОГДА»
КТО
В ОТВЕТЕ ЗА ТО,
ЧТО
УГНЕТЕНЬЕ
ЖИВУЧЕ?
ОЗЬ
ОЙ
СТЬ
ЩИХ
ТО,
ЧТО
ПРОЧНО
НЕПРОЧНО
НАСИЛ
ВЕЩА
ВСЕ ПРЕ
ВЕ
В
ЭКСПЛУАТАЦИЯ
ПРОВОЗГЛАШАЕТ
Я
ХОЗЯЙКА
ТЕПЕРЬ
DIPLOMAT

What is Capitalism?

video installation, 2003

(transferred from 16 mm) 10:14 min

Staged after script based on real interviews.

Projected as video in installation with two mirrors.

Appearances (either as voice, image or both):

Matthew Buckingham

Sharon Hayes

Laura Horelli

Maryam Jafri

Lars Mathisen

Steen Møller Rasmussen

Nina Sander

Katya Sander

Stephan Sander

Megan Sullivan

Simon Sheikh

Axel Wieder

Emilie Weiss

August Sander Weiss

Camera: Steen Møller Rasmussen

Sound: Jon Paludan, Katya Sander

...deeply___to the notion that the___world is___to the observer...
(commited) (real) (external)

video installation, 2004

www.possest.de/notaboutoil.html

Appearances:

Caroline Peters, Julika Jenkins

Camera: Minze Tummescheid

Sound: Rashad Becker

Sound Assistant: Jana Hickechier

Director Assistance and Advice:

Judith Hopf, Ines Schaber, Erik Wiegand

Image Research: Ines Schaber

Portable Sign Construction:

Marian Burchardt

Witness Accounts from 1973:

Thomas Schunke, Torsten Oetken, Birgit Behle

Thanks to:

Erik Wiegand, Kortwich Berlin, Herrn Zoschke, DEGES,

Otonom, visomat inc., meinebank. , Behrooz Abdolvand,

Maria Lind, Ulrike Uhlig, Ute Waldhausen

BIOS

Michael Blum is an artist based in Vienna. After studying history in Paris and photography at ENP Arles (France), he developed a body of work – videos, publications, installations… – that aims at critically and humourously re-reading the production of culture and history. Recent projects include *17 Aandbloem Street* (Very Real Time, Cape Town, 2003), *The Monument to the Birth of the 20th Century* (O.K Centrum, Linz, 2004 ; Revolver Verlag, 2005) and *A Tribute to Safiye Behar* (9th Istanbul Biennial, 2005).

The Copenhagen Free University is an artist-run institution dedicated to the production of critical consciousness and poetic language. We do not accept the so-called new knowledge economy as the framing for understanding knowledge. We work with forms of knowledge that are fleeting, fluid, schizophrenic, uncompromisingly subjective, uneconomic, acapitalist, produced in the kitchen, produced when asleep or arisen on a social excursion – collectively.
www.copenhagenfreeuniversity.dk

Andrea Creutz is a visual artist based in southern Sweden and in Copenhagen. She graduated from The Royal Danish Academy of Fine Arts in 2000, and participated in The Whitney Independent Study Program, 2002-2003. In her work she investigates how value systems and social conventions function. Together with Danish artist Lise Skou, she initiated *swop network* – a project examining and presenting economic systems that function as counterparts to monetary economy. She is a member of the feminist collective *Women down the Pub*. Additionally she was, in 2005, guest professor at Copenhagen University's Department of Sociology.

Katja Diefenbach is a writer living and working in Berlin.

Maria Eichhorn lives in Berlin. Studied at the Berlin University of the Arts. Solo exhibitions from 1986, including shows in Amsterdam, Berlin, Berne, Barcelona, Warsaw, Zurich and Tokyo. Participation in group exhibitions includes shows in London, Paris, Sydney, New York and Yokohama. Participated in the 'International Istanbul Biennial' in 2005 and in 1995, in 'Documenta11' in Kassel in 2002, in 'Sculpture: Projects in Münster 1997' and in the 'Venice Biennial' in 1993. Has, since 2003, taught at the School of Art and Design in Zurich. Recent books and catalogues: *Maria Eichhorn*, Campus, Verlag der Buchhandlung Walther König, Cologne 2005; *Maria Eichhorn, Restitutionspolitik / Politics of Restitution*, Verlag der Buchhandlung Walther König, Cologne 2004; *Maria Eichhorn, 1. Mai Film Medien Stadt / May Day Film Media City*, Portikus, Frankfurt am Main 2003; *Maria Eichhorn, Maria Eichhorn Aktiengesellschaft / Maria Eichhorn Public Limited Company*, Documenta11, Silke Schreiber Verlag, Munich 2002; *Maria Eichhorn, Das Geld der Kunsthalle Bern / Money at the Kunsthalle Bern*, 2 Volumes, Kunsthalle Bern, Berne 2001/2002.

Stephan Geene is a member of *minimal club* and *b_books*. He has published in *springerin, tageszeitung, jungle world, Texte zur Kunst* among others. Director of the full-length feature, *After Effects*, 2006. Author of *money aided ich-design, techno/logie subjektivität geld*, Berlin, 1998. Co-editor of A.N.Y.P. and *geld.beat.synthetik, abwerten von gentechnologie*, Berlin, 1996. Worked on the film-projects *tv sehen + wohnen* and *Le Ping Pong d'Amour*.

Olafur Gislason lives and works in Hamburg. Studied from 1980-1983 at the Icelandic College of Art and Craft, Reykjavík, from 1983-1988 at the *Hochschule für bildende Künste*, Hamburg. Solo Exhibitions include: 'Gemeinschaften' Krefelder Kunstmuseen, Krefeld in 2004; 'Interventionen 28', Sprengel Museum Hannover in 2002; 'Share and Exchange', Gallery I8, Reykjavík in 1998. Group Exhibitions include: 'A Whiter Shade Of Pale', Art from the Nordic Countries on the Lower Elbe, Germany in 2005; 'Migration' Kunstmuseum Liechtenstein in 2003; 'Park' Momentum – Nordic Festival of Contemporary Art 2000, Moss, Norway.

Natascha Sadr Haghighian is part of *possest group* (www.possest.de). Any part of possest group can change. That can include a change of name, coordinates and any other representational data.

Brian Holmes is an essayist and activist-researcher. He has a Ph.D. in Romance Languages and Literatures from the University of California at Berkeley, and now lives in Paris, collaborating with journals such as *Multitudes* (Paris), *springerin* (Vienna) and *Brumaria* (Barcelona). All his work can be found online at www.u-tangente.org, including the collective project *Continental Drift* as well as the books *Hieroglyphs of the Future* (Zagreb: WHW, 2002) and *Unleashing the Collective Phantoms* (New York: Autonomedia, forthcoming).

Ashley Hunt is an artist and activist based in Los Angeles who works with video, mapping and installation to interrogate modes of learning and to generate public discourse. Interested in the construction of power and powerlessness, political possibility and economies of wealth, his work of the past six years has dealt with the growth and commercialization of the U.S. prison system, expanding most recently into the field of contemporary globalization. Hunt's work has been exhibited at the Contemporary Museum in Baltimore, the Martin Luther King Jr. Center in Atlanta, Kunst-Werke Institute for Contemporary Art, the Museum of Modern Art, as well as at numerous grassroots and community based venues throughout the U.S.

Susan Kelly is an artist, writer and researcher based in London. Her work has been included in exhibitions at Mercer Union, Toronto; The Lenin Museum and Muu Ry, Finland; Art in General and LMCC, New York; Krasnoyarsk Museum Centre and the National Centre for Contemporary Art, St. Petersburg, Russia; Museum of City of Skopje, Macedonia; Project Arts Centre Dublin, and the Prague Biennial. She has also published articles in *Public Culture, Journal of Visual Cultures, Social and Cultural Geography, Chto Delat?* and *Kunstforum*. She is a graduate of the Whitney Independent Study Program,

New York, and is a lecturer in fine art at Goldsmiths College, London where she is also working toward a Ph.D.

Trude Iversen is a theorist and curator based in Oslo (Norway). Former director of UKS, currently writing a Ph.D. at the University of Oslo on aesthetics and politics.

Oleg Kireev is an artist and art and media critic, an editor of the project *ghetto* (http://www.getto.ru), dedicated to anarchist culture and politics. Producer of the collective books *Against all P's* (M., ghetto, 2001) and *Lifestyle* (M., ghetto, 2003), and of his personal *Media-activist cookbook* (M., Ultra.Culture, in print). He is a translator, political activist and participant in a number of civil disobedience actions & campaigns, including 'Against all parties' (1999-2003). Author of publications on arts, politics and new media in Russian and international press. Based in Moscow.

Isabell Lorey, political scientist, is assistant professor in gender and postcolonial studies at the University of Arts in Berlin and also teaches at Humboldt University Berlin. She is currently part of the group *Kleines postfordistisches Drama/kpD* and worked for many years as a freelance journalist at several public TV-stations in Germany, chiefly making news for kids.

Stephen Morton is a lecturer in Anglophone Literatures and Cultures at the University of Southampton, UK. After completing a doctoral dissertation at the University of Leeds in 2000, he worked as a research fellow at the Whitney Independent Study Program, New York, and subsequently as a lecturer in English Philology at the University of Tampere, Finland. He has published in *New Formations, ARIEL: A Review of International English Literature, Interventions: An International Journal of Postcolonial Studies, Public Culture, Circa: Irish and International Visual Culture* and *Atlantic Literary Review*. His book on the thought of Gayatri Chakravorty Spivak was published by Routledge in 2002. He is currently preparing a monograph on terrorism in postcolonial literature and culture.

Gerald Raunig is a philosopher and art theoretician living in Vienna. He is co-director of eipcp (European Institute for Progressive Cultural Policies), Vienna, coordinator of the transnational research projects *republicart* (2002-2005) and *TRANSFORM* (2005-2008) and editor of the journal *Kulturisse* (http://www.igkultur.at/igkultur/kulturrisse). Numerous lectures, essays and publications in the fields of contemporary philosophy, art theory, political aesthetics and cultural politics. Recent books: *Kunst und Revolution. Künstlerischer Aktivismus im langen 20. Jahrhundert*, Wien: Turia+Kant 2005 and as editor with Ulf Wuggenig: *PUBLICUM. Theorien der Öffentlichkeit*, Wien: Turia+Kant 2005.

Oliver Ressler lives and works in Vienna. Ressler is an artist who is doing projects on various socio-political themes. Since 1994 he has been concerned with theme specific exhibitions, projects in public space and videos on issues of racism, migration, genetic engineering, economics, forms of resistance and social alternatives.
http://www.ressler.at

Katya Sander lives and works in Berlin. In her work, she questions issues of space, narration, desire and structures of power through video, film, photography, text and architectural interventions. Sander recently had a solo exhibition, 'The Most Complicated Machines are Made of Words', at MuMoK in Vienna, and her most recent project, *Exterior City* was also produced with and shown in 'Whatever Happened to Social Democracy?' at Rooseum in Malmö (Sweden). She produced *Was ist Öffentlichkeit?* for a solo exhibition at Munich Kunstverein, and in collaboration with Andrea Geyer, produced *Meaning is What Hides the Instability of One's Position* at Esbjerg Kunstmuseum, Denmark. She is a member of a research collective with Andrea Geyer, Ashley Hunt, Sharon Hayes and David Thorne, and series editor of OE–Critical Readers in Visual Cultures (with Simon Sheikh).

Fia-Stina Sandlund is an artist based in Stockholm (Sweden). She graduated from Konstfack in 2003. Her works often analyze various forms of social oppression and inequality, sometimes developing into direct actions, sometimes written or spoken word, radio, video or installations. Some of her better known works are *He came, he saw, he conquered*, a project where she was getting a place in her home town named after her mentally handicapped brother, and *The Artists Club*, a sound piece/radio documentary where she examines a 150 year old society for male artists only.

Jason Simon is a media artist whose work combines documentary and conceptual art interests. Some of his subjects include advertising, fine art restoration and shopping and his films and videos are distributed by The Video Data Bank and First Run/Icarus Films. His installations and photographs have been shown in solo exhibitions at Pat Hearn Gallery and American Fine Arts Co. and he is currently a member of the cooperative gallery Orchard. His work has appeared at The Whitney Museum Biennial, National Museum of Osaka, Neue Gallerie, Graz, The Jersey City Museum Biennial, The New Museum and The Kitchen. His writing has appeared in the art journals *Frieze*, *Parkett*, *Purple* and *Afterimage* and he has curated programs for Exit Art (*Man Trouble*), Artists Space (*The Talking Cure*) and a traveling show of American videos entitled *Downsizing the Image Factory*. He worked to establish The Art and Technology Department at the Wexner Center for the Arts from 1989 to 1991. He is associate professor of cinema at the City University of New York, College of Staten Island.

Chto delat? /// What is to be done? (www.chtodelat.org) is A Platform for Engaged Creativity. Founded in early 2003, *Chto delat?/What is to be done?* brings together artists (Tsaplya and Glucklya, Nikolai Oleinikov, Kirill Shuvalov, and Dmitry Vilensky), philosophers (Artem Magun, Oxana Timofeeva, Alexei Penzin), social scientists and writers (David Riff, Alexander Skidan) based in Petersburg, Moscow, Nizhny Novgorod and Berlin. This workgroup publishes an English/Russian newspaper on issues central to poetics and politics today, with a special focus on the Russian artistic-intellectual situation. The workgroup also engages in a variety of art projects, including video works, installations, public actions, radio programs, and artistic examinations of urban space. Its most recent exhibition and research project is *Drift – Narvskaya Zastava*, a community-examination of a constructivist-proletarian neighborhood in Petersburg.

Elin Wikström, artist and professor at the Fine Arts Academy, Umeå University, Sweden, encourages investigations of social and economic values and norms such as *Too Much Organisation, Too Little Organisation or the Wrong Kind of Organisation*, ADAM, Smart Project Space, 2005 and *Thanks to Elisabet, Sören, Morten, Bente, You don't live here anymore*, Center for Curatorial Studies, Bard College, 2006.

Knut Åsdam is based in Oslo. He studied at the University of Oslo; Goldsmiths College, London; Jan van Eyck Academie, Masstricht; and at the The Whitney Independent Study Program, New York. Knut works mainly in film, video, photo and installation. His work is engaged with manners and psychology of language, and narrations of sexuality and economy within an urban architectural context. Knut Åsdam is a Senior Research Fellow at the Birmingham Institute of Art and Design, University of Central England.

oe — organizational excess

oe is a series of critical readers into contemporary visual cultures; their emergences, contingencies and possibilities. The series is edited by Katya Sander and Simon Sheikh, artist and theorist. We are committed to theory, but not to discipline, and every reader thus revolves around a specific notion or event, seen and discussed from various vantage points or positions. Through an analysis of visual cultures – art, film, tv, the net, the street and so on – different regimes of visuality can be located. The circulation, production, reproduction and interpretation of images is seen as crucial to an understanding of contemporary politics, not just of representation, but also of the imaginary. Analysis is therefore not only to be understood as reflective, but also as active or activating. It is proposition(s).

#1: The Meaning of Site

Notions of space analyzed through practices of site-specificity

Edited by Katya Sander, Simon Sheikh and Cecilie Høgsbro Østergaard. Texts by Katya Sander, Marion von Osten, Jochen Becker, Simon Sheikh, Poyin Auyoung and Cecilie Høgsbro Østergaard.

#2: Death Drive

Art and Film Beyond the Pleasure Principle

Edited by Gertrud Sandqvist. Texts by Gertrud Sandqvist, Laura Mulvey, Friederich Meschede, Matts Leiderstam / Peggy Phelan and Denise Robinson.

#3: Rent

About the temporary relation many people have to things around them

Edited by Stuart Koop. Texts by Rex Butler, Edward Colless, Stuart Koop, Gary Foley, Philip Brophy, Elizabeth Grosz and John Leigh.

#4: I said I love. That is the Promise.

The tvideo politics of Jean-Luc Godard

Edited by Gareth James and Florian Zeyfang. Texts by Dave Beech, Elisabeth Büttner, Manthia Diawara, Simon Sheikh, Jason Simon, Stephan Geene, Kaja Silverman and Michael Eng.

#5: In the Place of the Public Sphere?

On the establishment of publics and counter-publics

Edited by Simon Sheikh. Texts by Miwon Kwon, Nils Norman, Valerie Tevere, Bojana Pejic, Frans Jacobi, Stephan Dillemuth, Charles Esche, Marion von Osten, Gunnar Krantz, Copenhagen Free University, Stephan Geene, Ultra Red and Pauline van der Mourik Broekman.

Forthcoming:

#6: Here and Elsewhere

Routings, Relationalities and Imaginings between places

Reader & DVD. Edited by Katya Sander and Simon Sheikh. Texts & videos by An Architektur, François Bucher, Zach Formwalt, Andrea Geyer, Sharon Hayes, Brian Holmes, Janna Holmstedt, Ashley Hunt, Anders Michelsen, Yates McKee, Gerald Raunig, Georg Schöllhammer, Hito Steyerl, Alex Villar, Ulf Wuggening, among others.

#8: Work the Room

A handbook of performance strategies in contemporary art

Investigating critical actions and the forms they take, this collection of documents criss-crosses the field of performance work tying together threads of political investment. How can politics be performed when the public consists of those present and sharing a room? How can the space between performer and audience be activated? What if emotional states are more of a common denominator than shared views and opinions? With contributions by Christa Benzer, Linda Bilda, Gregg Bordowitz, Stephan Dillemuth, Discoteca Flaming Star, Marie-Thérèse Escribano, Achim Hochdörfer, Andrea Fraser, Sharon Hayes, Judith Hopf, Christof Kurzmann, Xavier Le Roi, Matthew Lyons, Sabine Marte, Mattin, Katrin Pesch, Yvonne Rainer, and Britta Scholze. Edited and with an introduction by Ulrike Müller.

Titles available through b_books